ALSO BY ANDREW K. DIEMER

The Politics of Black Citizenship:
Free African Americans in the Mid-Atlantic Borderland,
1817–1863

VIGILANCE

VIGILANCE •• THE LIFE OF WILLIAM STILL, FATHER OF

THE UNDERGROUND RAILROAD •• ANDREW K. DIEMER

ALFRED A. KNOPF NEW YORK 2022

THIS IS A BORZOI BOOK
PUBLISHED BY ALFRED A. KNOPF

www.aaknopf.com

Library of Congress Cataloging-in-Publication Data
Names: Diemer, Andrew K., author.
Title: Vigilance : the life of William Still, Father of the
Underground Railroad / Andrew K. Diemer.
Other titles: Life of William Still, Father of the Underground Railroad
Description: First edition. | New York : Alfred A. Knopf, 2022. | "This is
a Borzoi book published by Alfred A. Knopf." | Includes bibliographical
references and index.
Identifiers: LCCN 2022001897 (print) | LCCN 2022001898 (ebook) |
ISBN 9780593534380 (hardcover) | ISBN 9780593534397 (ebook)
Subjects: LCSH: Still, William, 1821–1902. | African American
abolitionists—Pennsylvania—Philadelphia—Biography. |
Abolitionists—Pennsylvania—Philadelphia—Biography. | Underground
Railroad—Pennsylvania—Philadelphia. | Antislavery movements—United
States—History—19th century. | Fugitive slaves—United
States—Biography | Philadelphia (Pa.)—Biography.
Classification: LCC E450.S85 D54 2022 (print) | LCC E450.S85 (ebook) |
DDC 973.7/114092 [B]—dc23/eng/20220126
LC record available at https://lccn.loc.gov/2022001897
LC ebook record available at https://lccn.loc.gov/2022001898

Jacket images: (upper right and spine) William Still. FLHC25 / Alamy;
(lower right and back) Underground railroad map. Pictorial Press Ltd. /
Alamy; (center) Front and Walnut streets, Philadelphia, c. 1855.
Library Company of Philadelphia
Jacket design by Jenny Carrow

Manufactured in the United States of America
1st Printing

For Marcus

CONTENTS

VIGILANCE

INTRODUCTION

Peter Freedman saw danger in the unfamiliar faces around him. He had come to Philadelphia looking for parents he had not seen in decades, not since he was a small child. The journey from Alabama had been long and arduous, but now that he was here, he was unsure if he should have come. He remembered an old house on a hill above the Delaware River, but though that river flowed past the city of Philadelphia nothing here looked like it did in his memory. Would he even recognize his parents if he saw them? It had been more than forty years, after all. He remembered his brother's face, and he looked on each dark face he passed, hoping to see some resemblance.[1]

Peter had good reason to be wary. Though he was now legally free, having purchased his own freedom after decades of bondage, he had heard stories of kidnappers who were always on the lookout for unsuspecting Black men like him. He had been told that some of them even posed as abolitionists. Upon arriving in the city, Peter had gone to the boardinghouse of a Black man, Dr. James Bias, a man he was told he could trust, but he was not sure he could. Bias was out of town, but his wife, "a bright mulatto woman, with a kind smile and a pleasant voice," welcomed Peter and arranged for a guide who would help him look for his parents.

The two walked the city, inquiring among various Black men and women they met if any had known a man named Levin and his wife, Sidney (sometimes spelled Cidney), who had lost two children forty years before.

They spent two days in this search with no success. No one was surprised by Peter's story. The kidnapping of Black Philadelphians, especially children, was common, but no one knew Levin or Sidney. It was at this point that Mrs. Bias suggested Peter go to the Anti-Slavery Society office, to a man named William Still who worked there and who kept records of fugitive slaves passing through the city. Perhaps, she thought, there might be some records of his parents there.

Mrs. Bias arranged for the same guide to show Peter the way; it was about six in the evening when they set out. Peter got the sense that this guide did not believe his story, and this only accentuated his anxiety. As they walked through the streets in the late summer heat, the guide stopped occasionally and talked to those he seemed to know. He did so in a low voice that Peter could not make out.

When they finally reached the Anti-Slavery Society office, Peter peered through the window and saw a young Black man, neatly dressed, writing at a desk. They entered the office and the young man they had seen through the window rose to greet them. Peter's guide and the young clerk, William Still, seemed to know each other. Still was dark-skinned and fairly tall, with short-cropped hair and strong features.[2]

"Good evening, sir," said the guide. "Here is a man from the South that says he is hunting for his people; and he wants to make me believe he was born in Philadelphia. Mrs. Bias sent me here with him—she thought possibly you might find the names of his parents on some of your books."

"What were you parents' names?" asked Still.

"I was stolen away from the Delaware river," said Peter, "with my brother Levin, when I was about six years old. My father's name was Levin, and my mother's name was Sidney; and we had two sisters—one named 'Merica and the other Charity; though my brother always said that 'Merica was our cousin . . . We used to talk a heap about our mother, but nineteen years ago my brother died in Alabama; and now I've bought my liberty, and come back to hunt for my relations."

Peter felt a subtle change come over the clerk. Still had been courteous at first, but now as Peter told his story Still seemed to become intensely interested. He asked Peter to repeat the names of his parents and older brother. He did so. Still asked if there were any other names, other than those he had already mentioned, that he could remember from his time with his parents. Peter thought for a moment. He remembered a white man, named S.G., who lived near his parents. Peter recalled playing with this man's children.

Still asked Peter if the two might wait for a bit while he finished preparing the mail to be sent. Peter was uneasy, but what could he do? He and the guide sat quietly for a while, waiting for Still to finish his work, all the while keeping watch over the door, half convinced that these two men were conspiring against him.

Eventually, after nearly an hour had passed, Still returned to the two visitors.

"It will take some time," he said, "to look over those old papers, and this man may as well go home. I will show you the way back to Mrs. Bias'."

The guide rose to leave. Peter, relieved at the chance to escape this situation, rose as well. "I'll go, too," he said.

"No, no—stay," said Still. "I will do my best to find your friends."

"Yes, stay—by all means," added the guide. "If he will look for them, it isn't worth while to go away now."

Once the guide was gone, Still sat down next to Peter and looked him directly in the face.

"Suppose I should tell you that I am your brother?"

"Supposin' you should?" responded an incredulous Peter.

"Well," continued Still, his voice trembling, "from all you have told me, I believe that you are a brother of mine. My father's name was Levin, and my mother's name is Sidney, and they lost two boys named Levin and Peter, about the time you speak of. I have often heard my mother mourn about those two children, and I am sure you must be one of them."

.   .   .

William Still lived a remarkable life. Born free in 1821 to parents who had been enslaved, he lived until 1902, witnessing the
dawn of the twentieth century. He would rise to prominence as a
leader of the Underground Railroad, the effort to aid and protect
those fleeing from bondage, an enterprise that had already taken
on a legendary aura even as it continued to shuttle thousands of
slaves to safety. In the decade before the Civil War, Still would
have a hand in some of the most dramatic events in the growing struggle over slavery, establishing himself as a major figure in
the abolitionist movement. He would continue his work on behalf
of Black rights in the decades following the abolition of slavery,
and when he died, Still was one of the most famous and respected
Black men in America. There was, however, no moment in his life
more remarkable than this unlikely reunion with a brother he had
never met.

It was, of course, a moment of deep personal importance, but it
was also something more than that. Still was born in an ostensibly
free state, New Jersey, but it was a state that did not pass a gradual
abolition law until 1804, a law that applied only to those born after
July 4 of that year. Even then, the children of slaves would be freed
after serving a lengthy apprenticeship, a type of pseudo-slavery.
Men were bound until their twenty-fifth birthday, women until
their twenty-first. In these same years, Lower North states like
New Jersey and Pennsylvania (the state where Still would live most
of his adult life) became a refuge for those fleeing the upper South.
Some of these refugees had been legally emancipated like Still's
father; and others, like Still's mother, fled from bondage, hoping
to evade their masters' clutches. Many of Still's free Black friends
and neighbors, therefore, were themselves fugitives from slavery.
Others had stories, like Still's, of long-lost family members, sold
South, never to be seen again. Some even had tales of sons, daughters, brothers, and sisters, stolen from the streets of their Northern communities, seized by legally sanctioned slave catchers or by
outlaw kidnappers—often the two were indistinguishable. Free
Black people, in other words, had personal, familial connections
to bondage; they lived in the shadow of slavery.[3]

Still had always known about his family's connection to slavery, and from an early age he was drawn to the antislavery struggle. His work in that struggle has, however, been often overlooked. Here, too, his meeting with his brother is instructive. As remarkable as Peter's appearance in William's office seemed to both men, it was no coincidence. William Still had placed himself at the center of a vast network of men and women who were committed to aiding fugitives from slavery in their dangerous flight north. This network was built on word of mouth, on carefully compiled records, on letters and telegraph wires, on steamship lines, railroad tracks, and country roads, all converging on Still and the Anti-Slavery Office in Philadelphia. While Still's work would sometimes bring him face-to-face with the enemy—an arrogant slaveholder on the Delaware docks or a villainous slave catcher in a Philadelphia back alley—most often his work found him, as he was that night when Peter walked in, seated at his desk, writing.

Still was a seemingly ordinary man who did extraordinary things. This helps explain why we know far less about him than we do about some of his better-known contemporaries. Frederick Douglass, for example, born just a few years before Still in the same region of Maryland's Eastern Shore where Still's parents had been enslaved, is a useful comparison. Douglass was extraordinary by any standard. His vivid prose and searing oratorical style made him an international star of the abolitionist movement. In his quieter moments, though, Douglass helped ferry fugitives across the border to Canada, fugitives who often had been sent on from Philadelphia by Still. Many of these fugitives would never have made it to Douglass had it not been for Still's work in Philadelphia. Similarly, Harriet Tubman, also born enslaved in the same region of Maryland, has become one of the most famous figures of the Underground Railroad, her almost superhuman physical courage enabling her to travel into the lion's den to rescue friends and family, all the time facing re-enslavement and worse, winning her the admiration and fascination of generations since. Yet Tubman was but one of innumerable "conductors" with whom Still worked, shepherding fugitives to safety. Still's work, ordinary as it might sometimes seem, linked together these two and countless more like them, in a vast abolitionist web, aiding hundreds of desperate fugitives from slavery.[4]

Beyond this, what Still's work accomplished, and one of the reasons that work speaks to us today, is that it organized and empowered the everyday work of fugitive slaves, their struggles for freedom, their flight from bondage. In 1872, Still published his monumental account of this work, *The Underground Railroad*, almost 800 pages recounting the stories of hundreds of fugitives he helped on their way north. For those looking to recover Still's actions this book has sometimes proven frustrating; Still is by no means the center of attention. In fact, for pages at a time it can be difficult to find Still's hand at all. This absence is by design. Still understood, and wanted his readers to understand, that fugitive slaves themselves were the engine of the Underground Railroad. Here too the contrast with his ally Tubman is useful. Tubman's story can sometimes leave the impression that enslaved people were in need of a savior, someone to rescue them from bondage. Still's work, on the other hand, shows us that enslaved people were prepared to save themselves—they simply needed a hand.[5]

That hand would come primarily from the grassroots effort of African American families who opened their arms, and homes, to fugitive slaves. Still's work connected fugitives with those who stood ready to help them. To be sure, there were white allies who helped in this work as well, but it was the willingness of Black communities across the North to harbor fugitive slaves upon which Still most relied. He had grown up in a family and in a Black community where this willingness to aid fugitives was unquestioned. Later, when he moved to Philadelphia, he would join a much larger, more dynamic Black community, but here too he would find the same commitment to aiding fugitive slaves. Still's work would eventually tie together hundreds of communities, stretching all the way across the border to Canada. Still's life, then, is not a story of the triumph of the heroic, lone individual; it is, rather, a story of community struggle, and of one man's critical part in that struggle.

Still's life also helps us to see the longer story of the fight for Black freedom and Black citizenship rights. As central as this Underground Railroad work would be to Still's life, it would prove to be but a part of his longer fight for the rights of Black people. The end of slavery in the North would leave free African Americans as second-class citizens: generally denied the right to vote, excluded from most of the best-paying work, segregated in public accommodations and schools. Abolitionism was the beginning, not the end, of the struggle for Black freedom. Even as he was engaged in the everyday work of assisting fugitive slaves in their flight from the South, Still also committed himself to the fight for full Black citizenship, and indeed he rightly understood that these struggles were inextricably bound together.

Throughout all this, Still was also a son, a father, and a husband, and yet for a Black man in nineteenth-century America, each of these roles was necessarily weighted with ideological and political significance. Free Black people daily confronted a white majority that assumed them to be lazy, undisciplined, intemperate, and generally a threat to their community. Black leaders disagreed about the exact origins of this overwhelming prejudice, but most understood that it was the responsibility of each individual to live a life that disproved these pernicious lies. For Still, this meant hard work, prudence, and a life-long pursuit of the "respectability" that came with material success. Eventually he would prosper, becoming one of the wealthiest Black men in Philadelphia, mostly due to his success as a coal dealer. Economic success would enable Still and his wife, Letitia, to live in increasing comfort, to provide their children with opportunities they had been denied, and to share their wealth with the Black community. In a sense Still's story is a classic nineteenth-century rags-to-riches story. At times, he would depict himself as a self-made man, but he was always keenly aware that his prosperity was not simply a tribute to his own resourcefulness and hard work. Still never lost sight of those who had made his success possible, and he sought to turn his success into an argument for the inherent value of Black people, who, Still reminds us, continued to struggle against great odds in their efforts to secure for themselves and their families that which white Americans took for granted.

And yet, Still's success, both his economic prosperity and his rising prominence as a Black leader, helped to make him some enemies and to reveal tensions within the Black community. Still could be warm-hearted and generous, but he could also be stubborn and sanctimonious. He had little tolerance for those who were less committed to the cause than he, and he was openly dismissive of Black leaders who squandered their gifts. As he grew older, he was increasingly confident in his own judgment, and this confidence looked like arrogance to his rivals. His advocacy for Black "respectability" struck some as puritanical. While he often sought to deflect attention from his own work, at other times he seemed embarrassingly intent on receiving what he viewed as appropriate credit for his contributions. He was, in other words, a human, full of contradiction and idiosyncrasy.[6]

"It is safe to say," wrote the Black abolitionist and author William Wells Brown of his friend William Still, "that no man has been truer to the fleeing slave than he."[7] Still's contemporaries understood him to be one of the most important figures in the abolitionist movement and one of the leading Black men of the nineteenth century. Upon his death, newspapers across the country remembered him as "the father of the Underground Railroad."[8] If we think of a father simply as someone who gives life to something, then Still was most certainly not its father; the Underground Railroad had existed long before he became involved with it. But if we think of a father as one who nurtures, one who protects, one who guides and shapes, then Still, as much as anyone, deserves to be called a father of the Underground Railroad. In the more than hundred years since his death, though, Still has been marginalized, sometimes even forgotten, by histories of the movements to which he contributed so much, in part due to his own tendency to emphasize the work and stories of others, in part due to the seemingly mundane nature of his work on the Underground Railroad. This book seeks to remedy that erasure, to return Still to his rightful place at the center of the struggle against slavery.

CHAPTER ONE

A BOY IN THE PINES

William Still was born October 7, 1821, in a remote corner of the southern New Jersey pinelands, the youngest of eighteen children of Levin and Charity Steel. Their home was, as William's older brother recalled, "a log house, with one door and no glass windows in it," on the southern edge of Burlington County in what is now Shamong Township, but which was then part of Washington Township, a few miles east of the small town of Medford. The soil was sandy, and the Stills' property was one of the small farms that had been carved out of the pine forest that to this day stretches over the gently undulating ground of southern New Jersey. Black residents, the vast majority of them free, made up less than 5 percent of the population in Burlington County, and while robust Black communities could be found in parts of the county, the Stills settled in an area where they were one of few Black families.[1]

What had brought the Still family to this place? Neither Levin nor Charity had been born in New Jersey. Both had been born into slavery, a hundred miles to the south on the Eastern Shore of Maryland, in Caroline County. In contrast to Dorchester County, to its immediate south, bordering the Chesapeake, Caroline County, inland and abutting the state of Delaware along its eastern border, contained somewhat fewer slaves, about 20 percent of the population in 1800. As young children, both had

been enslaved to one William Banning, but when Banning died in
1780, Levin, who was then about ten, became the property of his
widow, Margaret, while Charity, then about eight and known as
Sidney, passed to Banning's daughter, Lydia Morton, who later
sold her to Alexander Griffith (a man William Still would later
remember as Saunders Griffin). Margaret Banning died soon
after her husband, and Levin became the property of her grandson, William Wood, who was about the same age as Levin.[2]

Slavery had been the foundation of the economy in this part of
Maryland for more than a century, but that economy was changing. The turbulence of the American Revolution helped catalyze a
significant shift. Planters who had once almost exclusively focused
on a single crop, tobacco, now increasingly grew grains, fruits, and
vegetables, and raised livestock. Wheat in particular found a ready
market across the Atlantic as the French Revolution and its aftermath disrupted agriculture across Europe. With this diversified
agricultural economy came a corresponding demand for different
kinds of labor and a transformation in the seasonal rhythms of
production. Wheat, for example, required two intense periods of
labor during its cultivation: planting and harvest. At these times,
farmers sought all the work they could get. The rest of the year,
however, there was far less to be done in order to tend to the crop.
This posed a problem for planters, who saw that their enslaved
labor force continued to grow over these years. Ever creative in
their exploitation of slave labor, masters turned this problem into
an opportunity. In the decades which followed the American Revolution, slave laborers were put to work grinding grain, tending
livestock, and transporting crops to market. They worked as coo-
pers, smiths, millers, and tanners.[3]

While slave masters did their best to get the most value out
of their enslaved property, there was a growing sense among the
planters of the Chesapeake region that they had more slave labor
than they needed. Some responded by selling slaves south and west
to the burgeoning cotton frontier where the lust for slave labor
was almost insatiable. The division of enslaved families became the
hallmark of this "generation" of Chesapeake slavery. Other masters hired out underused slaves for a period of time. Many of these
hired-out slaves were put to work in towns, large and small, across

the region. There was also the escalating fear among masters that their property in slaves was endangered by the possibility of flight. Slaves had always run away, of course, but the gradual abolition of slavery in the states just north of Maryland, along with the growth of free Black populations closer to home, especially in Baltimore, where fugitives might find refuge, meant that fugitives were ever more likely to be successful in evading recapture.[4]

Enslaved Marylanders were quick to take advantage of these conditions. Masters were desperate to find some way to control enslaved property that seemed increasingly beyond their control, and as a result more and more were willing to negotiate with their slaves in order to secure them as long as possible; for some this would provide a path to freedom. Levin Steel was one of these who made his desires clear. "I'd sooner die than stay a slave," he told his master. Rather than risk losing his slave for nothing, Levin Steel's young master agreed to allow him to purchase his own freedom. They settled on a price and then it fell to Levin to find ways to meet that price. The complex economy of the Chesapeake presented opportunities for a man like Levin to make extra money, but this was, of course, for work done above what was already demanded of him by his master. He would have had to work late into the night, and on the Sundays that slaves were typically given off. Often enslaved families pooled their labor to pay for the manumission of a single member; perhaps this was the case for the Steel family. Levin was resolute, and on November 22, 1798, his efforts were rewarded: his master, William Wood, signed his manumission. Levin was twenty-four years old, and it had taken him years, and sacrifices at which we can only guess, to buy his own freedom.[5]

Levin had a problem, however. His wife, Sidney, was still enslaved, as were their four children, two boys and two girls. They had a different owner, so perhaps Sidney's owner was unwilling to negotiate with her as Levin's master had with him. Even if their master was willing to sell, perhaps the prospect of paying the price for five manumissions was not feasible. Levin and Sidney knew that every year it took to pay the price of manumission increased the risk that a master would sell his property to the highest bidder, potentially separating the family forever. Whatever the case, Levin decided to leave his family behind, heading north to New Jersey.

It is possible that Levin hoped he would be able to make more money in this new home and that he planned to return to purchase his wife and children. Perhaps he and Sidney had planned for her to run away when the opportunity arose. In any case, likely sometime in 1807, Sidney and the four children fled from their master and joined Levin in New Jersey.[6]

The family was reunited in the small town of Greenwich, New Jersey, located along the water where the Delaware River broadens into the Delaware Bay. They likely made their home in the Black community known as Springtown, in the northeastern portion of town. Across southern New Jersey, such Black settlements provided community and protection to Black residents. Communities like Springtown also relied on close relationships with sympathetic white Quakers who were prominent in the region; Friends had been among the earliest settlers of Greenwich. Fugitives from slavery like Sidney were particularly aware of their vulnerability. New Jersey had passed a gradual abolition law in 1804, stipulating that all enslaved people born after July 4, 1804, would become free, upon their twenty-first birthday for women, and upon their twenty-fifth birthday for men, but that meant that there were thousands of people still legally enslaved in the state. Even more pressing, the fugitive slave law of 1793 permitted slave catchers to travel into the state in search of those who, like Sidney and her family, had fled from bondage in another state. The family changed their last name from Steel to Still. Of course, the names sound quite similar, but there were already many Stills in the area, and the new family likely felt that in adopting this name they would be less likely to stand out.[7]

Unfortunately, Sidney's reunion with her husband did not last long. Within months, a gang of slave catchers had found her and the children. They seized the five of them and dragged them back to bondage on the Eastern Shore of Maryland. Her owner, Alexander Griffith, eager to prevent the expense of another flight, decided that Sidney would be locked in the garret every night until he could be sure that she was "cured of the desire to do so again." According to the census of 1800, Griffith owned nine slaves, so Sidney and her children constituted a significant portion of his wealth. Sidney, however, had already resolved that as soon as she could, she would run off again, but she knew she needed to convince her master that she had given up on her hopes for freedom. She did her best to project the appearance of tranquility. She consoled herself through the singing of "good old Methodist tunes." Griffith continued to confine her at night for several months, but eventually he became convinced that Sidney "seemed better contented than ever," and he let down his guard, concluding that she was no longer to be locked up at night. Within weeks, Sidney would once again flee north to freedom.[8]

This time, however, she made the heartbreaking decision to leave her two sons behind. The first journey to New Jersey had been difficult; she could be sure that the second would be even worse. There would be no doubt as to where she was headed, and as soon as she was missed, Griffith would have slave catchers on her trail. The girls, Mahalah and Kitturah, were quite young, just infants. She felt she could not leave them. The boys were a bit older; Levin was eight and Peter was six. Sidney's mother was still enslaved nearby, perhaps even on Griffith's property, and Sidney hoped that she would be able to look out for the boys. When the night came for her to leave, Sidney crept quietly to the places where the children slept on a little straw bed. Without waking the boys, she kissed them goodbye, lifted the still sleepy girls in her arms, and set out.[9]

When Griffith discovered that Sidney had once again fled, he was furious. He sold both boys, perhaps out of anger, or perhaps out of fear that Sidney might return for them one day. Levin and Peter, still unaware of what had become of their mother, were shipped off to Lexington, Kentucky. As Sidney made the dangerous journey back to New Jersey, her thoughts surely turned again and again to the boys she had left behind. Perhaps there were moments when she felt she had made the wrong choice, when the pain of leaving her boys behind was too much to bear. Perhaps she focused on the two little girls she had with her, reminding herself of the better life she hoped to provide them.[10]

With the girls in tow, Sidney once again successfully navigated the treacherous path north, but once she reunited with Levin, the two realized they could not remain in Greenwich. Griffith would certainly have agents there looking for them. They decided instead to settle in a more remote section of southern New Jersey, in Burlington County, up the Delaware River from Greenwich and further into the pinelands that spread across South Jersey. There were fewer Black families here, which may have concerned the young couple, but the area had been largely settled by white Quakers, which provided some reassurance that their neighbors might welcome them and, if necessary, might shelter Sidney if slave catchers came looking for her and the girls. There was also a small Indian reservation nearby, home to a settlement of Delaware people, who had been granted this land by the colonial legislature in 1758, though most had moved on by the time the Stills arrived. Sidney and Levin hoped that in this isolated corner of New Jersey they could find refuge and make a new life for themselves. Sidney took a new name, as fugitive slaves so often did. Hereafter she would be known as Charity Still.[11]

Western Burlington County, the part that abuts the Delaware River, was a land of rich farmland and relatively dense population, but the Stills made their home toward the east, where this farmland turns into the pinelands. Even today, this area is where suburban Philadelphia gives way to the eerie stillness of the Pine Barrens. The sandy soil of the region gives it a distinctive character. Pine trees flourish, as do wild (and cultivated) blueberries and cranberries. Small streams flow gently but steadily, twisting through the forest, their tea-colored "cedar water" often so dark that the riverbeds are obscured. The pines had long been a place of refuge. Rumor had it that during the Revolution, Hessian soldiers had deserted from the British army and found shelter in the Pine Barrens.[12]

Levin Still, newly arrived in this place and without land of his own, had to take whatever work he could find. In this, though, he was not alone. While the fertile lands to the west were home to prosperous farmers, the pinelands where the Stills resided were home to a different sort: poor, mostly white. William Still would later recall these neighbors as "if not favored with much wealth and education . . . yet a sturdy independent people." They survived by farming whatever small plots of land they could come by, chopping wood, charcoal burning, marl digging, and cranberry picking. This is likely the sort of work that Levin Still did at first to support his family. Eventually he found work at a sawmill that had been built years earlier by Delaware Indians and which was still called the Indian Mill.[13]

Levin's ambition, however, was not to work for others but to own land of his own. In the years since the Stills settled in New Jersey, their family had steadily grown; Samuel was born in 1807, shortly after Charity's flight from bondage, and was followed by Mary, Hannah, James, and Isaac. Around 1814, the rapidly growing Still family moved in with Cato, an elderly Black man. "It was an old log house, one story high and an attic, with one door, large fireplace," recalled James Still. "I think there were two rooms on the first floor and one on the second." While living with Cato for a year or two, Levin saved up enough money to buy from Cato some land of his own. On this land Levin built a small house that would be William Still's first home. Levin eventually acquired a horse and oxen, and on their small plot of land he and his family raised corn, rye, potatoes, and other vegetables. Even so, Levin struggled at times to provide for his rapidly growing family. Three more children would precede William: John, Charles, and Joseph. Food and clothing were sometimes scarce.[14]

From an early age, therefore, the Still children were put to work. In part this meant, as with any farming family, work on their own land. Despite Levin's assiduous labor, however, the Still lands were not enough to provide for the entire family. When they were old enough, some of the children were hired out to other families in the area. The girls who had come north with Charity Still, Mahalah and Kitturah, being the oldest, were the first to be "put out." When they were old enough, the boys were also put to work, often, as William Still recalled, in the fields of the "thrifty Quakers" who owned farms to the west, around the town of Medford. The children also found less formal ways of contributing to the family economy. William became quite adept at chopping wood, even at a young age, and he and his brothers traveled the pine forests surrounding their home in order to provide firewood for neighbors who paid handsomely. Sometimes they made charcoal from the wood they gathered. In other seasons the children would travel miles in order to pick and sell wild cranberries, blueberries, and huckleberries.[15]

The children worked in the good weather, but when rain prevented them from earning money for their family, the boys sometimes attended the local school. With such infrequent attendance, William and his brothers learned very little, but even had they been able to attend regularly, the quality of instruction seems to have been meager. Even worse, the Still boys were often harassed by their white peers, and white teachers had little love for these Black students. William Still in particular recalled a series of cruel and humiliating punishments that his teacher inflicted upon him. On one occasion Levin Still was present to witness this humiliation and was so infuriated that he confronted the sadistic teacher. Levin was not a gentle father. As James Still recalled, his father's whole religious mind seems to have been represented by "the thirteenth chapter of Proverbs, which reads, 'He that spareth his rod hateth his son; but he that loveth him chastiseth him betimes.'" And yet, he refused to allow his sons to be demeaned by this white teacher: he pulled his sons from the school and prohibited them from returning until the teacher was replaced. As a result, William Still did not attend school with any regularity until years later.[16]

Eventually, once the school had acquired a more agreeable teacher, William Still did return to school for a short period: a full quarter at the age of seventeen and four weeks the following winter. He was able to put aside other work and focus on school for these brief intervals. This was hardly enough to make him an educated man, even by the standards of his time and place, but it seems to at least have given him the rudiments of literacy and to have opened the door for a lifetime of self-education. Still would read whatever he could get his hands on. He was especially drawn to *The Young Man's Own Book*, a classic text of nineteenth-century self-improvement, filled with advice about the "formation of habits," "means of improving the memory," "letter-writing," and the "importance of early rising." Still was so enamored of the book that he purchased a copy of his own, which he read while "paring apples, shelling corn, and performing such tasks as were set the children during the long winter evenings." In this way he attempted to fill in the gaps in his formal education.[17]

Still's recollections of his early life, coming as they do from much later, may better reflect the way that he wished to think of himself: as a self-made man. Nevertheless, this vision of Still as a serious-minded young man, disciplined and intent on self-improvement, fits with what we know about him. It also seems likely that *The Young Man's Own Book* resonated differently with Still that it did with the book's typical white reader. The gospel of self-improvement preached by the book, while certainly appealing to white readers, was particularly meaningful for Black strivers like Still, who saw self-improvement not simply as a means of improving one's own lot in life but also as a confirmation of Black capability in the face of entrenched white denial of the very possibility of Black progress.

Still had been born at a time when the nation was riven by conflict over slavery. This conflict could be found in nearly every corner of America, but it was most evident in the confrontation over the expansion of slavery into the territory west of the Mississippi River. In 1819, just two years before Still was born, a portion of this territory had petitioned to become the state of Missouri. Much of this territory had been settled by slaveholders and so the new state, it was assumed, would guarantee the right to own slaves. Missouri would not be the first slave state to be added to the union, but a few factors made the potential addition of Missouri as a slave state an explosive proposition in 1819. First, the gradual abolition laws of the Revolutionary era had helped to solidify the notion that there were free states and slave states, creating a self-conscious regional identity in both sections. Second, the expansion of the cotton frontier, the intensifying growth of slavery into the Southwest, had put to rest any idealistic notion that slavery was gradually withering away on its own. Lastly, due to the fact that the U.S. Senate granted representation equally to each state, the addition of Missouri as a slave state would have upset the equilibrium that had emerged in the Senate between free and slave states. Long-simmering tensions over slavery bubbled to the surface of American politics. Northern politicians warned of Southern domination, while Southern politicians warned that attempts to limit slavery's expansion threatened to tear the nation apart and even suggested that Northerners were inciting slave rebellions. Eventually the Missouri crisis was resolved by the introduction of the free state of Maine as a balance to the slave state of Missouri, and by the extension of Missouri's southern border into the west as a boundary between future slave and free states, but while the immediate crisis may have been resolved, the Missouri debates revealed tensions in American society.[18]

One of these tensions, of course, was the demand of slaveholders that Northern states cooperate in the return of fugitive slaves. As the years wore on, Charity likely felt more and more secure in her freedom, and in the freedom of her two girls, but even though they lived in an ostensibly free state, slavery was never far away. In contrast to the situation in states further north, or even across the Delaware in Pennsylvania, New Jersey slaveholders remained committed to extending their right to enslaved labor well into the middle of the nineteenth century, and they often found that political leaders were willing to support them in this effort. This was especially true in the northeastern portion of the state, nearer to New York City, but even in southwest New Jersey, where Quaker influence was strongest and where slavery was less common, the abolitionist movement was weak and disorganized. In 1821, sixteen years after the state passed its gradual abolition statute, and the year William Still was born, New Jersey courts established the presumption that all Black residents were slaves unless proven free. Though this decision would be overturned a few years later, it was clear that even legally free Black people faced a legal and political system that was skeptical, often hostile, to their claims of freedom.[19]

This situation was even more perilous for those, like Charity Still, who were fugitive slaves. In 1826, New Jersey had passed a "Personal Liberty Law," similar to the one passed the same year in Pennsylvania, which sought to protect legally free Black people from being claimed as fugitive slaves. The law, however, was often circumvented by judges who were skeptical of the testimony of those who insisted that accused fugitives were in fact legally free. Charity Still was, of course, not legally free, but even if she had been able to secure testimony to the contrary, as fugitives were sometimes able to do, there was no guarantee that the courts would accept this evidence. Slave catchers were able to operate in New Jersey, if not with impunity, at least with less open hostility from white residents than they would frequently find elsewhere in the North. What this meant was that fugitive slaves in New Jersey had little legal protection from slave catchers; they needed to find other means to protect themselves.[20]

As a boy, William Still witnessed firsthand the risks that fugitive slaves faced. According to Still's later recollections, Thomas Wilkins, whom Still remembered as "an old bachelor," employed in his household "a great, powerful colored man who had run away from bondage." According to the 1830 census, Wilkins resided in Evesham, a short distance from where the Still family lived. Unfortunately for this unnamed fugitive slave, men in the employ of his former master tracked him to his new home and fell upon him "with the bludgeon and fist to disable him." Having subdued their quarry, this slave-catching gang was about to drag him off in chains when his employer, Wilkins, and his two elderly sisters, intervened. If Still's recollections are to be believed, one of Wilkins's sisters seized a shovelful of burning coals from the fire and threw them into the middle of the gang, creating a confusion that enabled the fugitive slave to fight off his assailants and escape from the scene. The man knew that he could not remain in the area or his former master would surely find him again. He reached out to friends for help. Perhaps he was friends with the Still family, or perhaps Wilkins had some dealings with the Stills. Whatever the case, that same night, William and his brother-in-law, Gabriel Thompson (he had married Mahalah in 1826), escorted the fugitive, still bloodied from the assault, through the rainy night, traveling the dark back roads through the pines, to Egg Harbor, near the Atlantic shore.[21]

This recollection from Still's childhood takes on a larger significance due to the role that aiding fugitive slaves would play in his later life, but it also tells us quite a bit about how what was not yet called the Underground Railroad functioned. There is no evidence that the Still family was connected to any broader network of safe houses or hiding places for fugitive slaves. This seems simply to have been a matter of a friend in need of help. Fugitives relied on Black communities for such help, and it was common for

free Black families like the Stills to open their homes to those in
need. This is not to say that all Black people were to be trusted;
in fact, in this particular case the slave-catching gang had used a
Black accomplice to put their prey at ease and the white Wilkins
family had put themselves at risk to aid their employee. However,
Still's youthful involvement with this particular fugitive slave helps
to show that the Underground Railroad had always been grounded
in Black communities. It also shows that Still was raised in a family
in which helping fugitive slaves was expected, despite the legal risk
of doing so. Certainly the fact that his mother was a fugitive slave
herself helped solidify the family's commitment to aiding those in
flight from bondage.

If the responsibility to aid fugitive slaves was something that
Still learned from his family, he also showed an early interest in the
wider abolitionist movement that was entering a new, more radical
phase as William Still came of age. While recent scholarship has
revived the reputation of the Revolution-era abolitionist movement, emphasizing its interracial character and celebrating its significant achievements, it is clear that the public face of abolitionism
had changed in the late 1820s and early 1830s. Epitomized by the
North Carolina–born Black activist and printer David Walker and
by the fiery white publisher and reformer William Lloyd Garrison, these abolitionists built on the work of the "first wave" of
abolition, but did so in a newly aggressive and confrontational
manner. "Now, Americans!" asked Walker in his inflammatory
1829 pamphlet, *Appeal to the Coloured Citizens of the World*, "I ask
you candidly, was your sufferings under Great Britain, one hun-
dredth part as cruel and tyrannical [*sic*] as you have rendered ours
under you?" This new wave of abolitionism was publicly confrontational and unambiguously interracial; Black abolitionists played
a prominent role, fighting alongside white allies, which provoked
a correspondingly intense backlash. Anti-abolitionist mobs terrorized Northern cities and towns. Southern politicians censored the
mail to prevent the infiltration of abolitionist mailings, and they
instituted an infamous "gag rule," to prevent even the discussion
of slavery in the halls of Congress.[22]

Still's interest in the movement led him to subscribe to the
Colored American, a Black-owned and -published newspaper, edited

by the Black abolitionist pastor Samuel Cornish. Founded in 1837 as the *Weekly Advocate* and quickly renamed to reflect both its publishers' race consciousness and their commitment to full American citizenship for African Americans, the *Colored American* became, according to historian Manisha Sinha, "the national voice of black abolitionism." It is notable that Still chose to subscribe to the *Colored American* rather than to Garrison's more established, Boston-based *Liberator*, or to the Philadelphia-based *National Enquirer* (later renamed the *Pennsylvania Freeman*). Black subscribers across the Northeast supported the newspaper as a distinctively Black voice of abolitionism.[23]

Still willingly paid the $1.50 annual subscription for the weekly paper, but he soon discovered that not everyone was as eager to support a Black newspaper as was he. Since the *Colored American* was published in New York City, Still was to receive his copies via the mail, but the white postmaster, who "did not consider it altogether proper to dispense this kind of literature through the mail," decided to withhold Still's copies for several weeks. When Still went himself to the post office in order to claim the papers that were being withheld, the postman handed him a bundle of newspapers. Assuming these were his undelivered copies of the *Colored American*, Still paid the postage and took them home. When he got home and unwrapped the bundle, however, Still discovered to his dismay that the postman had given him other newspapers, not those to which he had subscribed. Still realized he had little recourse and accepted his fate, but fortunately the postman was merely malicious and not a committed anti-abolitionist. After this initial disappointment, Still was able to get his regular issues of the *Colored American*.[24]

In the *Colored American*, Still would have found not only fuel for his growing abolitionist consciousness, but guidance for a young man of ambition. The newspaper confirmed and reinforced the young Still's commitment to the idea that free Black people had a responsibility to better themselves as a means of promoting the progress of the Black race. "Should we as a people," insisted an article from the March 1837 issue, "become more religious and moral, more industrious and prudent, than other classes of community, it will become impossible to keep us down." This progress, in turn, would strike a blow against the idea that slavery was the only fitting status for Black people. The paper saw a clear connection between such self-improvement and the struggle against slavery. This was a lesson Still would not forget.[25]

In the fall of 1841, as Still neared his twentieth birthday, he decided to strike out on his own. That fall he found little work, and continued to do the odd labor to which he had grown accustomed, but the following spring he signed a year-long contract with Joshua Borton, a Quaker who resided in Evesham, a few miles from the Still home. Borton owned a hundred-acre farm but had little experience as a farmer. He hired Still, then, not simply as a laborer but as an experienced hand who could help him manage the enterprise. Over the course of the year, Still had a hand in nearly every aspect of the farm's operation. He directed the hired hands in laying out the crops, preparing the grounds, and sowing and harvesting. When the time came, he also took the crops to market to ensure that they brought the best possible prices. Much of this was the sort of work that he had been doing for years, on his family's farm and as a hired hand, but the responsibility entrusted to Still was gratifying to the young man, and years later he would reflect on this experience as the moment where his confidence in his own abilities was awakened. He also finished the year with earnings of sixty or seventy dollars, a substantial sum for one in Still's position.[26]

In the midst of his year under contract to Borton, though, Still suffered the greatest tragedy of his young life. His father died on the day before Christmas 1842. While his older brothers James and Samuel served as executors of their father's estate, William Still experienced a religious crisis as a result of his father's death. Charity Still was a committed Methodist, but Levin seems not to have been particularly religious. Young William seems to have followed in his father's spiritual path, but now that Levin was gone, William feared that he "had rejected the proffered salvation of Christ, preferring to follow the voice of the stranger who was seducing me from God and Heaven." One morning, brooding on his father's death, Still found himself driving a team of horses amidst the snow-covered pines when all of a sudden he felt God's presence. The light of the sun shone and the snow seemed to melt.

"Streams of joy," he later recalled, "peace and gratitude overflowed my heart. I felt that the wonderful Providence that had wrought in me such a radical change was entitled to my thanksgiving and praise while I lived."[27]

This spiritual awakening inaugurated a period of religious searching in Still's life. In 1843, like thousands of other Americans, Still fell under the sway of the millennial religious teachings of William Miller. "Father Miller," as Still called him, had served as a captain during the War of 1812 and had become convinced that his country's salvation during that war could only have been a result of divine intervention. After the war, Miller returned to his farm in New York, along the Vermont border, where he devoted much of his time to reading the Bible. Miller became convinced by his intense Bible study that he had uncovered a message indicating that the world would end sometime between March 1843 and April 1844. For years he kept his theories to himself, but beginning in 1831, Miller began to spread his message, ultimately via a sophisticated print network, including the daily newspaper the *Midnight Cry*, which reprinted Miller's lectures and popularized and explained his Biblical methods of prediction. It is likely that Still became aware of Miller from one of these publications.[28]

Miller's teachings, and more broadly the belief in Christ's imminent return, were surprisingly popular in antebellum America, even among some of the best educated and influential theologians. Miller drew his support from the rural and small-town middle class of the United States. In a way, his radical vision of the millennium was the flip side of the postmillennial, reformist culture of the period, which saw economic, cultural, and spiritual progress as the necessary predecessor of Christ's second coming. It is clear, though, that there was not a stark divide between pre- and postmillennial belief. Surely some of Miller's followers, those who had sold their businesses, quit their jobs, and left fields untended in anticipation of the predicted day of judgment, were shaken by the failure of his predictions. Others, including Still, were untroubled by Miller's mistake. For Still, Miller's fallibility in no way undermined his faith in the Bible and in Christ's ultimate return. "So when 1843–4 passed," he would later recall, "my faith and hope remained unchanged in the All-Supreme." Rather than simply waiting in anticipation of the final days, Still channeled his religious zeal into his desire to change the world around him.[29]

The abolitionist movement to which Still was increasingly drawn was suffused with this sort of millennialism. Black and white abolitionists issued warnings of wrathful destruction if a sinful America persisted in its commitment to human bondage. David Walker had famously warned that slave rebellion would be the tool of divine justice. "Remember Americans," wrote Walker in his 1829 jeremiad, *Appeal to the Colored Citizens of the World*, "that we must and shall be free and enlightened as you are, will you wait until we shall, under God, obtain our liberty by the crushing arm of power? Will it not be dreadful for you?" Other abolitionists embraced the idea of Christian "perfectionism," which they saw as the route to perfecting human society. Doing so, wrote John Humphrey Noyes, would allow humankind to "abandon human government and nominate Jesus Christ for the Presidency, not only of the United States but of the world." For Still, the struggle against slavery would ever after be tinged with religious passion.[30]

Still's childhood in the pines had been formative. He was free. He had always been free, but slavery loomed over the Still family. The Stills might have been isolated in the pines of Burlington County, one of the few Black families in the area, but the sprawling Still family was a community unto itself. The family closely guarded the secret of Charity's past; her story was one they told only among themselves, never trusting outsiders with the truth. They kept alive the memory of the boys, Levin and Peter, who had been left behind in bondage, whom they expected never to see again. Hatred of slavery was a given. The family also supported itself in other ways. Young William had always had to work, whether for his father or hired out to others. Such work had been a necessity, but it also became a source of pride. Still could look back on his early life and see this difficult childhood as a vital school of character and as a training ground for what was to come.

CHAPTER TWO

A YOUNG MAN IN THE CITY

In the spring of 1844, William Still moved to Philadelphia. Later in his life he would recall that he arrived with no more than three dollars and only his "meagre" wardrobe. "Of city friends and counsellors," Still recalled having "none." If he were to succeed, if he were to rise in the world, it would not be due to any connections but rather to his own "steady, well-grounded habits, a good stout heart, and a desire to succeed on the only sure basis of perseverance, economy and integrity." Whether or not he correctly recalled his financial status, it is unlikely that he was as alone in this new city as his memories suggested. His sister Mary almost certainly was already living in Philadelphia when William arrived, and a few years earlier at least another of his sisters, Kitturah, was as well.[1] From the very start, Still had family nearby in the city. Nevertheless, if Still overstated the extent to which he was on his own, in moving to the city he had, as a part of his self-making, like so many young people before him, torn himself free from the familiar community in which he had been nurtured.

Despite the presence of at least some family members, the city of Philadelphia, "its throng of people, its street mazes, its business hurly-burly," must have been overwhelming and disorienting for a young man who had grown up in rural south Jersey. William Penn had famously laid Philadelphia out as a model of

Quaker orderliness, its tree-named streets, Walnut, Pine, Spruce, running straight and wide from the Delaware waterfront to the Schuylkill, numbered streets intersecting them at right angles. "All is square built," remarked a correspondent for the abolitionist newspaper the *Liberator*, "those stately, beautiful blocks of buildings, with marble door-steps, and marble fronts, and marble porticoes." Those stately houses remained, but by the 1840s, decades of migration and growth had led the city to overflow this grid. Some ambitious developers turned this growth inward, seeking to wring every bit of space out of the city's once-spacious layout, building cheap dwellings on back lots and alleys. Others turned outward from the original city grid; north and south of the city, clustered along its borders, independent municipalities like Northern Liberties, Spring Garden, Moyamensing, and Kensington provided cheap housing, much of it wood frame. By 1840, each of these cities ranked on its own as one of the twenty most populous in the nation. Each maintained its own government, laws, and police force, and yet for a newcomer like Still walking the streets of this burgeoning metropolis it would have been unclear where one ended and the next began.[2]

Philadelphia had long served as a refuge for African Americans, and wherever Still went, he likely saw dark faces mingling with light ones. Pennsylvania had begun its own process of gradual abolition in 1780. This process was essentially complete by the time of Still's arrival; the census of 1840 recorded more than 10,000 Black residents of the city of Philadelphia, all of them free, roughly 10 percent of the city's population. While almost all Black Philadelphians were legally free (some of those counted in the census were surely fugitive slaves), this did not mean that they were treated as full and equal citizens. With few exceptions, Black workers were closed out of all but the lowest-paying work, and as a result Black Philadelphians were far more likely to be impoverished than their white neighbors. African Americans frequently faced violent white mobs who policed the city's public spaces, and in 1838, Pennsylvanians ratified a new constitution formally disfranchising Black voters, though even before this legal disfranchisement, Black Philadelphians had been kept from the polls through violence and intimidation.[3]

In contrast to what would become common in later years, there was no "Black" neighborhood, one where African Americans predominated. Instead, Black Philadelphians could be found across the city and county. Most often, African Americans found homes in the crowded alleys and back lots of the city and its adjacent municipalities, generally alongside (or above or below) poor whites and just steps from the homes of more affluent whites that lined the main streets of the city. While neighborhoods were not segregated, African Americans were not evenly distributed either. In some cases, specific blocks were disproportionately Black. In other cases, Black homes clustered within a few blocks of major Black institutions, churches especially, but also schools, beneficial societies, and fraternal organizations. The largest such concentration in mid-nineteenth-century Philadelphia spanned the southern border of the city, crossing over into Moyamensing; at the center of this community along a two-block stretch of Lombard Street were Mother Bethel African Methodist Episcopal (AME) Church, Wesley AME Church, Little Wesley AME Church, and Second African Presbyterian Church.[4]

This was not, however, the neighborhood where William Still chose to settle, at least not at first. Instead, he found a home in Northern Liberties, just north of the city proper. He had come to Philadelphia to seek work and so perhaps it is unsurprising that he sought out one of the city's burgeoning industrial suburbs. Early manufacturers had established themselves in the southern portion of the neighborhood along Pegg's Run, which they had, by the early nineteenth century, turned into a fetid sewer that was subsequently overlaid by a street and then later by a railroad. Mid-nineteenth-century maps show tanners, brewers, and lumberyards side by side with houses, many of them cheaply built for the masses of workers who flocked to the neighborhood. Some of these hopeful workers were Black, though they only made up about 3 percent of the population in 1840. There were pockets within the neighborhood, however, where significant numbers of African Americans lived close together. A Black enclave on Paschall's Alley, for example, was only a few blocks from where Still first settled.[5]

Still's home was on Fifth Street, north of Poplar, in the northern edge of Northern Liberties, where densely packed houses and factories gave way to more open space. Lumberyards and potato patches were interspersed with modest homes. Still described his own first house as an "old frame shanty of rickety construction and slim proportion." Perhaps for one who had spent all his life in the country, the relative space afforded him here appealed more than the cramped confines of the city proper. Perhaps he simply sought to be near the sorts of low-wage work he hoped to find. In either case, the rickety dwelling on the edge of urban Philadelphia was about all he could afford.[6]

Still arrived in Philadelphia at an inauspicious time. He had barely settled into his new abode when the city erupted in one of the most destructive riots in the city's history. African Americans were not the only migrants who swelled the population of Philadelphia in the early decades of the nineteenth century. Large numbers of white immigrants, many of them Irish and most of them Catholic, also looked to the workshops and factories of Philadelphia for opportunities denied them by desperate poverty in their homelands. In Philadelphia, many of them settled in the same sorts of back alleys and peripheral neighborhoods as the city's Black residents. This at times led to conflict between immigrant whites and their Black neighbors, but in 1844, white immigrants found themselves a target of virulent nativism at the hands of native-born whites. The immediate cause of the riots was a backlash to the efforts of some Catholic leaders to assert control over the use of the Bible in the public schools. The state legislature required that public schools use the Bible as a text in school, reasoning that it was "the best extant code of morality." Protestant control over the administration of public schools meant that it was the King James Bible that was read by students; this provoked objection from Catholics who demanded that their children be permitted to read instead the Douay Bible, approved by the Catholic Church. Native-born Protestants, already concerned by the dramatic increase in the Catholic immigrant population of the city and its surrounding areas, seized upon this issue to stoke fears of Catholic takeover. Across Philadelphia, membership in nativist "American Republican Associations" swelled in the early months of 1844, and amidst this growing confidence nativist leaders organized a mass meeting in Kensington, just north of Still's new home in Northern Liberties and home to a large immigrant population. This provocative demonstration produced the (perhaps hoped-for) violent reaction.

What began as street fighting between groups of immigrant and native toughs gave way to roving bands of native arsonists. Catholic churches were a special target. William Still recalled that a church "within almost a stone's throw" of his home was targeted by a mob and had to be saved by heroic firefighters. Once again it seems that Still's memory may have failed him. Contemporary accounts of the riots indicate that the mob ignored this specific church, St. Peter the Apostle, because it served a German Catholic congregation rather than an Irish Catholic one, suggesting something about the true motivations of the anti-Catholic mobs. In any case, other Catholic churches were not so lucky. In response to this violence and destruction the Common and Select Councils of the city of Philadelphia appropriated money to pay troops to guard every Catholic church in the city, and the mayor of Philadelphia city and sheriff of Philadelphia County placed their powers in the hands of the commander of the state militia, General Robert Patterson, who ruled by martial law for a week. Still, afraid to leave his house, could only hope that the militia, encamped on the common in front of his home, would prevent further destruction.[7]

Still was right to be afraid. Fire, of course, was something to be feared by all Philadelphians, especially those who lived in rickety wood homes. Beyond this, though, Still surely knew that while white mobs might have been fighting each other in the spring of 1844, such mobs could very easily turn against their Black neighbors. Black Philadelphians faced the near-constant threat of white violence. The city's small Black middle class was a particular target, as white mobs sought to terrorize those who rose above what they deemed their proper station. Less than two years before Still's arrival in the city, white mobs had burned down the Second African Presbyterian Church and Smith's Beneficial Hall, built and owned by Black businessman Stephen Smith, both symbols of Black progress, in response to a Black temperance parade held in the Moyamensing district on the southern edge of the city. Many Black Philadelphians fled the city for a time, camping out in New Jersey to wait out the fury of the white mob.[8]

Once peace had been restored to the city and county of Philadelphia, William Still set out to do the thing that had drawn him to the city in the first place: he went looking for work. In this regard as well, he had chosen an inauspicious time. The same years that witnessed rising levels of white violence directed at black Philadelphians also saw decreasing economic opportunities, especially for African Americans. Even though the city's Black elite had established itself and fought to maintain this status, beyond this relatively small group, the city saw fewer Black artisans and factory workers. This sort of work had the potential to provide a stable living for ambitious young men like William Still, but fewer and fewer white craftsmen were willing to take on Black apprentices, and factories increasingly looked to white immigrants as workers. Even in lower-wage work, Black laborers found themselves competing, often unsuccessfully, with white immigrants.[9]

One form of work that remained open to Black Philadelphians, but which William Still was reluctant to embrace, was household service. Even here, white immigrants had begun to compete with Black workers, but a sizable percentage of the Black labor force of Philadelphia continued to work as servants in white households. This sort of work, the young Still believed, "was a life of dependence, with no future in it." It is unsurprising that he would feel this way. Many reform-minded African Americans expressed their concern that discrimination was pushing free Blacks into such servile occupations, which in turn reinforced among whites the belief that African Americans were naturally servile. "Until we become farmers, and mechanics, and artisans, and help to constitute the bone and sinew of the land," warned the *Colored American*, "we must ever expect to remain as we now are, a despised and persecuted people . . . Our youth must be properly trained up, educated, and at a suitable age, instead of being made *servants* and *waiters*."[10] As a devoted reader of the *Colored American*, Still might have read this very article; he was surely familiar with the sentiment.

Before his search for work was interrupted, Still had decided to look to the city's brickyards for employment. Such work was not typical for Black Philadelphians, but there were sixty-seven Black brickmakers recorded in the Quaker census of 1847. Philadelphia builders showed an almost insatiable demand for bricks, and it so happened that a rich layer of clay lay just below the surface of the ground throughout much of the region. Given the difficulty of transporting bricks, builders sought a source as close to their construction sites as possible. The work of brickmaking was labor-intensive; nearly two thousand Philadelphians were employed in the trade in 1849, beginning with the digging of pits to expose the clay, and ending with the molding, drying, burning, and sorting of the finished bricks. At least some of the work was seasonal, as brickmakers believed that leaving the exposed clay open to the elements during the winter months would make for better bricks in the spring. Philadelphians had been making bricks since the early days of the city, but as the city itself filled up, brickyards spread to the outlying areas of the city and its surrounding districts as brickmakers exhausted the superficial deposits available in more centrally located lots. The relatively low cost to set up a brickyard, and the fact that large enterprises did not have much if any competitive advantage over small ones, meant that there was an abundance of brickyards in the city and the county.[11]

This meant that when Still went looking for work in brickyards, he did not have to look far from his home in Northern Liberties. Initially, though, he was unsuccessful. It was spring, which meant that the work that needed to be done took greater skill than the digging of the winter season. The proprietors of brickyards preferred men who had some experience in this sort of work. Fortunately for Still, it seems that one of the brickyards where he applied for work was built on a steep grade, and so he found work as a wheeler. After the clay was mixed with sand and water, the wheeler transported it to the molding table. Experienced wheelers were unwilling to take on this task in such difficult circumstances, so Still was given his chance. He worked at this job for the rest of the season, but eventually it proved too much for him as well, and he left the job "with a little extra cash on hand" and looked for other employment.[12]

Like many workers in the city of the early republic, especially Black workers, William Still found employment on an irregular, informal basis. Though attaining more predictable, long-term jobs remained the goal for most workers, employers often preferred the flexibility of casual labor that was contracted as needed and for as long as it was needed. Such economic relationships, often established orally and leaving little in the way of evidence, remain elusive for historians seeking to document them. Some employers placed advertisements in the day's penny press, but more often workers simply congregated in places where they knew work might be found.[13]

Still likely looked for such work within the general vicinity of his home. The "transportation revolution" had only just begun to permit some Philadelphians to separate home from work; most in this walking city needed to live close to their place of employment. This was especially true of casual, short-term workers like Still. He briefly worked for a man "whose garb bespoke him a Quaker," threshing oyster shells into powder, for what purpose Still did not know. Perhaps it was to be used as lime in the making of plaster, but the work proved so arduous and so unlikely to provide him subsistence that Still quit after a few days.[14]

After this failure, Still found work along the wharves of the city with a man named Shanklin. Still did not mention the man's first name, but there was a Black man by the name of Edward Shanklin, a carter, who lived not far from Still.[15] After unsuccessful stints working for white employers, perhaps Still was pleased to be working alongside another Black man and a neighbor. Together they hauled wood and other items along the wharves of the city. Some days there was a great deal of work but other days there was little, and Still found that this work barely paid his expenses. After a few weeks with Shanklin, he moved on, looking for work that would be more stable and lucrative. He found nothing of the sort but settled for a few different temporary jobs that enabled him to survive the winter. He worked briefly at a stove store, one of many lining Second Street, one of the main commercial corridors in Northern Liberties. Such establishments helped ensure that Philadelphians could keep warm during the cold winter months, but for those like Still struggling for steady work, it was never certain that one's stove (assuming one had a stove) would be supplied with the fuel to keep it running. One observer, reporting on some of the poorest

Black neighborhoods in the city, found dozens of African Americans who had died from the cold that year.[16]

Still, though, survived his first winter in Philadelphia, and in the spring returned to the brickyard, working there through the fall. Once again, the work was difficult, but he made enough to cover his expenses and to put a little away. He was surviving, but he longed for more stability, and he looked for work that would permit him, as he would later put it, "the opportunity for mental improvement." This sentiment was by no means unique to Still. In general, nineteenth-century Americans prized economic independence, but African Americans in particular, closed out of much of the most lucrative wage work, looked to own their own businesses as a means of securing financial security. If a Black Philadelphian hoped, as Still did, to become something more than the "hewer of wood and drawer of water" for others, owning one's own business seemed the likeliest path to success.[17]

One of Still's jobs during his first winter in Philadelphia had been running errands for the owner of an oyster cellar, and he decided to set up one of his own. African Americans had pioneered the selling of oysters in Philadelphia, first out of carts and then later in shops known as oyster cellars.[18] Some of these, especially the ones in the city of Philadelphia, were elaborate establishments, catering to a wealthy clientele. The writer George Lippard opened his urban gothic novel, *The Quaker City*, in just such an oyster cellar, "all light and glitter, and show . . . ornamented at its extreme end, by a tremendous mirror, in which a toper might look, time after time, in order to note the various degrees of drunkenness through which he passed."[19] Most Philadelphia oyster houses, however, were far humbler establishments, though the drunkenness of Lippard's scene was more or less typical.

Still's oyster house, established along the Northern Liberties commercial corridor of Second Street, was doubtless of the humbler variety. He had, by his own admission, "little capital," which made it impossible to emulate the more opulent cellars of the city. Perhaps this is one reason the hoped-for customers did not show up, but a more likely reason was Still's reluctance to serve alcohol. Northern Liberties had a reputation for debauchery and drunkenness, in part because it stood outside the legal authority of the city.

To compete with other oyster houses it was necessary to provide "something a little stronger than oyster broth" to go with the oysters. This Still, who had sworn off alcohol when he was just a boy, was unwilling to do, and before long he was forced to abandon the business.[20]

William Still's first forays into entrepreneurship show the extent to which such businesses drew on the help of friends and neighbors. Still had gotten his start in the oyster business by working for "an old colored man who was quiet noted for his excellent stews and unrivalled pepper-pot." This help could cut both ways, however. Shortly before abandoning his oyster cellar, Still was swindled out of what remained of his capital by a white man who he believed to be "a friend of the colored people."[21]

Not deterred from his ambitions, Still then partnered with "a colored friend." This friend had promised that if Still could provide a place to sell them, he could secure a supply of second-hand clothing. This trade, like oyster-selling, was one that was dominated by Black Philadelphians; the Quaker census of 1847 listed forty-one Black residents engaged in this business. Still does not specify the exact source of this supply of used clothes, leaving us to wonder just how this friend came upon them. It is possible that they were stolen, but just as likely they had been cast off as unwanted. Already having secured the basement space for his oyster house, Still then turned it to this new use. Once again, though, his trust was misplaced. This business failed in less time than the previous one, lasting just a week before Still gave up. If his first venture had brought him close to bankruptcy, "this was a plunge directly into it." The little money he had been able to save up was now gone.[22] Still continued to see business ownership as the path to financial independence, but thus far his hard work had only brought him failure.

Winter was approaching, Still's second in Philadelphia, and he was desperate for work. He spent the early part of the winter digging wells and grading yards for a builder who was constructing homes near where Still lived, but once that work was complete, he had trouble finding any more. Construction slowed considerably in the winter. The sort of out-of-doors work that Still had been doing was particularly difficult when the ground was frozen.

Builders might take advantage of a warm day here or there, but there was little promise of sustained work.[23]

Still had lived in Philadelphia for a year and a half and he had little to show for it. Work had been sporadic, and his business ventures had squandered what little he had been able to put aside. In desperation, he decided to look for a sort of work he had thus far avoided: waiting, which in the nineteenth century typically meant household service. When he looked to the penny newspaper of the day, the *Public Ledger*, he found no shortage of offers. Generally, such advertisements directed the job seeker not directly to the employer, but instead to an "intelligence agency" hired by the employer. The job seeker paid a fee to the agency, and only then would he be given directions to the employer who sought his services. Still contacted this agency as directed in the advertisement, paid his dollar, but when he arrived at the appointed place there was no work for him.[24]

Once again, Still felt swindled by those who claimed to be his allies, but at this point he was resolved to find work as a waiter. He continued to scan the pages of the *Ledger*, and his search eventually bore fruit. The proprietor of a hotel, the Broad Street House, was looking for a waiter, at the pay of five dollars a month. This hotel was on Broad Street near Vine, on the northern edge of the city, amid extensive coal yards. There were many grand and elegant hotels in the city of Philadelphia, but this was not one of them. The hotel, owned by Joseph Hogentobler, seems to have had some connection to the Reading Railroad, which had a depot adjacent to it, and Still recalled that most of the clientele were from the Reading. This road primarily brought anthracite from the Schuylkill coal fields into Philadelphia. Conditions were, Still tells us, "disgusting." His bed was a straw pallet under the stairs, into which he crawled each night as "a dog enters its kennel." He decided, reluctantly, that this was his best option and that he would put up with these conditions at least until the spring brought better opportunities.[25]

He was relieved, however, when a better option emerged just three weeks into this job. A wealthy widow, Elizabeth Langdon Elwyn, needed domestic help. She was a daughter of a former governor of New Hampshire and had moved to Philadelphia after the death of her husband. In his almost two years in Philadelphia, Still had spent his time in the poor and working-class sections of the city. It was with some trepidation, then, that he arrived at her home on Chestnut Street to interview for the position. This high society home, around the corner from the elegant, neoclassical façade of the First Bank of the United States, was surely a dramatic change from the Broad Street House where he had been working. Mrs. Elwyn also had a reputation for severity, which was confirmed by her intense questioning of her prospective employee. Still was forced to admit that he had no experience in the sort of domestic work that she needed done, but to his surprise, this did not end his interview. She laid out for him her expectations and she asked him for references, which he provided. Evidently, she was satisfied with what Still had to say and the way he conducted himself. In the spring of 1846, he left the Broad Street House and went to work for Mrs. Elwyn for the salary of fourteen dollars a month.[26]

Mrs. Elwyn proved to be a strict employer, but a fair and kind one as well. Still proved himself a reliable and prudent worker and was given more and more responsibility in the household. He was charged with the maintenance of the house and grounds, carried messages for Mrs. Elwyn, and in general was entrusted with the household finances. Even with these broader responsibilities, Still found that he had ample free time, time he planned to use for his own self-improvement. Mrs. Elwyn was pleased with her young employee's ambition and she encouraged his education. Still would remember this time as "by far the most profitable school he had ever attended." She selected books from her extensive library for Still to read, and she "often entertained him for hours by her eloquent disquisitions on men and measures, and her lucid descriptions of scenes and manners in the old world and the new." Still had not forgotten his initial misgivings about domestic service, but he was eager to take advantage of the opportunities that service for a family such as this afforded him.[27]

At some point prior to his employment by Mrs. Elwyn, William Still had begun to volunteer his services at an institution known as the Moral Reform Retreat. Managed by a Black woman, Hester "Hetty" Reckless, the Retreat was housed in a modest two-story wood-frame building on Lombard Street. Reckless herself, noted one contemporary, was "one in whom, after a half hour's talk, you would scarcely fail to be interested." The prime mission of the Retreat was to "raise their race from the degradation into which their vicious habits, and the influence of parents and associates have sunk them." Reckless would visit "some of the lowest haunts of the miserable and destitute," in search of "colored girls and women of the most destitute class." These women were offered a place in the Retreat, where they would live for a few weeks while learning how to escape the "evil habits" of their former lives: chiefly drunkenness and prostitution. The Retreat ensured that its charges restrained from all intoxicating beverages and taught them the virtues of cleanliness and hard work. Reckless then sought appropriate positions for these women, generally looking to place them in service to respectable families, especially families outside the city.[28]

Still was pleased, if somewhat surprised, that his new employer allowed him the time to continue his work at the Moral Reform Retreat. The operators of the Retreat were exclusively African American, mostly women, and their conduct suggests the role of such Black-run institutions in Philadelphia's Black communities. It might have received financial support from the white and Black elite of the city, but the day-to-day work of the Retreat was done by those, like Still, not far removed physically or economically from the people whom they sought to aid. Chronically underfunded, it needed to appeal to white supporters, but while the financial patrons of the Retreat might have viewed it as a form of philanthropy, for its workers it was more a means of expressing their commitment to serving the community in which they lived. In addition to housing and training the women who resided there, the Retreat also hosted a "school for infants," further suggesting that this institution was committed to helping provide Black women with the tools to survive in a brutal urban economy, not simply a means of cultivating "respectability" among Black Philadelphians. It is unclear exactly what sort of work Still did at the Retreat. He would later speak of teaching at a "Sunday-School at the Moral Reform Retreat." In any case, even as Still struggled for economic subsistence, and even as he sought his own improvement, he also believed that he had a responsibility to serve.[29]

There was, perhaps, another reason why Still was so eager to continue his attachment to the Moral Reform Retreat. While working there, he met a young woman, Letitia George, and they fell in love. We have little evidence illuminating her life before she met Still, but what we have presents some tantalizing clues as to who this woman, who would become so important to Still, was. In 1841, she appears as a depositor in the Philadelphia Saving Fund Society (PSFS).[30] This organization was founded with the object of encouraging saving among the poor and working classes. In fact, its first depositor was the African American servant of one of the organization's founders.[31] The record lists Letitia George's occupation as "service." We do not know how she felt about this work, whether she shared William Still's ambivalence about household service. The fact that she was depositing her income in the PSFS, however, suggests that she shared Still's frugal nature and that she had ambitions to use her wages as a stepping-stone to a more independent life.

We know even less about Letitia's family. The United States Census of 1900 records that she was born in 1819 in Pennsylvania, and that both her father and mother were also born in Pennsylvania (though not necessarily in Philadelphia).[32] The Quaker census of 1847 lists six households with the last name "George." It is impossible to know for sure which one (if any) of these was Letitia's family, so we are left to speculate. Letitia and William Still would name one of their sons "Robert George Still," and it so happens that there was a man named "Robert George" who lived in Philadelphia in 1847 and who may well have been Letitia's father. He and his wife lived not more than a block away from where Letitia and William Still lived in the same year. Robert George and his wife operated a small school (recently established in 1847) out of their home. They also taught a night school for adults.[33] Here too, if we can assume for a moment that these were, in fact, Letitia's parents, we can see that her family background suggests values that she shared with William Still: a belief in education, self-improvement, and service.

William and Letitia also had another experience in common; they had both served in white households that ranked among the elite of the city. The records of the PSFS list Letitia George's residence as 145 Walnut Street, the home of William Short.[34] Short had retired to Philadelphia after a brief but distinguished career in diplomatic service, followed by a successful business career. He had, in fact, served as the personal secretary to Thomas Jefferson, who would later refer to Short as his "adoptive son." Though he had been born in Virginia, he grew to oppose slavery and even expressed his belief in the "perfectibility of the black race." Around the time that Letitia George worked for him, Short served as vice president of both the American and the Pennsylvania Colonization Societies, organizations that sought to promote gradual emancipation by encouraging the emigration of free Blacks to the West African colony of Liberia. Black Philadelphians were nearly unanimous in their denunciation of such schemes, but many whites, Short among them, saw colonization as a moderate form of antislavery, as a necessary prelude to a broader program of abolition.[35] It is unclear how long Letitia continued to work in the Short household, but given Short's sympathies it would be unsurprising if he, like Still's employer, Mrs. Elwyn, approved of her desire to work at the Moral Reform Retreat. Both families were a part of a broadly philanthropic class of white Philadelphians, not necessarily abolitionists, but committed to reform and at least sympathetic to the city's African Americans.

Work at the Moral Reform Retreat also brought both Still and George into contact with some of the city's most committed Black abolitionists. The Moral Reform Society, which had founded the Retreat, comprised many of Philadelphia's most prominent Black leaders. The women who were most responsible for the day-to-day operation of the Moral Reform Retreat, Hetty Reckless and Hetty Burr, were also involved in the effort to aid fugitive slaves and to protect free Black Philadelphians from the kidnappers who roamed the streets and wharves of the city. Some historians speculate that from time to time Reckless housed fugitive slaves in the Retreat itself.[36]

There is a certain logic behind the seeming connection between the work of moral reform and the work of aiding fugitive slaves. Slavery remained legal in Delaware, a little more than ten miles from the city's southern border, and at least quasi-legal across the river in New Jersey. Even prior to the infamous Fugi-

tive Slave Law of 1850, federal law empowered slave catchers to
seize accused fugitives and return them to their alleged masters.
Often legal slave-catching and illegal kidnapping were indistinguishable. State laws designed to protect Black Pennsylvanians
from such kidnapping might make this somewhat more difficult,
but this trade in human flesh continued. While all Black Philadelphians lived under the shadow of slavery, the population that
the Moral Reform Retreat sought to serve was particularly vulnerable. Young people were especially at risk of kidnapping, as
were the most impoverished Black Philadelphians who, desperate
for work, were liable to find themselves the victims of kidnappers
who promised jobs. We have already seen that William Still was
robbed of his savings by unscrupulous partners; other Black Philadelphians were robbed of their freedom.[37] Of course, Still, son of a
mother who had been seized by slave catchers and who remained,
legally, a fugitive from slavery, felt this threat acutely. Among the
other benefits that he derived from the patronage of his wealthy
white employer was security; kidnappers were unlikely to target
the servant of such a prominent family, and if they had, the Elwyn
family would have been able to provide access to legal defense that
many Black Philadelphians lacked.

Still appreciated the security his work brought him, and he continued to win the confidence of his employer. The summer after
he had begun working for her, Mrs. Elwyn departed for extended
travels and left Still in charge of her household. Not long after she
returned, she took up residence in somewhat smaller quarters, and
Still went with her. When, finally, she left the city, to go live with
her daughter in New York City, she helped secure for Still employment in the household of another prominent Philadelphian, William Wurts.[38]

In Wurts, Still found yet another powerful, reform-minded
patron. By the time Still went to work for him, Wurts had retired,
but in earlier years he and his brothers had been instrumental
in developing the anthracite fields of northeast Pennsylvania.[39]
Wurts seems to have been at least somewhat sympathetic to anti-
slavery of the moderate, gradual sort. He named his son William
Wilberforce Wurts (after the renowned British abolitionist), he
was an elder in the church of antislavery pastor Albert Barnes, and

he was on the board of managers of the Pennsylvania Colonization Society (while William Short was a vice president). Perhaps
due to these sympathies, Wurts, like Elwyn, allowed Still to continue his work at the Moral Reform Retreat.[40] Still tells us little
about his work in the Wurts household. Wurts's correspondence
reveals nothing about Still's work, though it does indicate that
during the time that Still worked for him, Wurts was dealing with
the personal trauma of his wife's death and with his own failing
health.[41]

Still had only been working for Wurts a short time, though, when
he began to look for other opportunities. He clearly appreciated
the stability that household service had afforded him, but he longed
for the independence that such work made impossible. This was
particularly pressing for Still because he and Letitia had decided to
get married, which they did "without any ostentatious ceremony."
Certainly, it was possible for married couples to live apart. Many
Black Philadelphians did just this out of necessity. Still, however,
longed to find some way to establish an independent household
with his new wife.[42]

     Just such an opportunity soon arose, an opportunity that would
prove to be a turning point in William Still's life: he received word
that the Anti-Slavery Society was looking for a clerk. How Still
received news of this position is unclear. J. Miller McKim, who
both managed the society's office and edited its newspaper, the
weekly *Pennsylvania Freeman*, was also one of the men responsible
for visiting the Moral Reform Retreat and reporting back to the
Anti-Slavery Society. Perhaps he spoke to Still directly, or perhaps
he shared word of this opening with someone else at the Retreat.[43]

     The Pennsylvania Anti-Slavery Society (PASS), which should
not be confused with the older, more moderate Pennsylvania Abolition Society (PAS), was an organization of radical abolitionists.
It was founded in 1837 and operated out of its offices on Fifth
Street, just north of Arch Street (across from where the National
Constitution Center now stands). The PASS, aligning itself with
the national leadership of Boston abolitionist William Lloyd Garrison, called for immediate abolition and supported the granting

of full, legal equality to African Americans. Out of its Fifth Street office, the PASS operated a bookstore and reading room and published the *Pennsylvania Freeman*.[44]

This office was also the unofficial headquarters of Philadelphia's Underground Railroad. Some Philadelphians, especially Black Philadelphians, had long committed themselves to aiding fugitive slaves. In 1837, a group of men and women, many of whom were associated with the PASS, met to form the Vigilant Association, which would focus and support these efforts. The Vigilant Association, in turn, elected the smaller acting committee (often simply called the Vigilance Committee), which would take primary responsibility for this work. While many white abolitionists supported this work, the acting committee was largely made up of Black Philadelphians. The first president of this committee was Black dentist James McCrummell, and the records of the organization show that its meetings were largely attended by African Americans, though McKim was notable among the white participants; he later served as the organization's secretary.[45]

Still first contacted Peter Lester, a Black shoemaker and member of the Vigilance Committee, about the position in the Anti-Slavery Society office. Lester sent him along to McKim, who received Still cordially and urged him to write a formal letter of application for the job. This was surely an unnerving task for Still, who had spent years preparing for just such an opportunity but who understood better than anyone his own lack of formal education. The opening of the letter suggests an awkward desire to impress with the formality of his writing, even if it lacks the polish that his prose would show in later years. "Dear Sir," he began. "I have duly considered your proposal to me, and I have come to the conclusion of availing myself of the privilege, esteeming it no small honor, to be placed in a position where I shall be considered an intelligent being, notwithstanding the salary may be small." There is very little in the letter to suggest that his desire to accept the job was based on a commitment to the antislavery cause; his emphasis instead is on the opportunity for advancement that the position will grant him. Only in his closing, "I go for liberty and improvement," does he hint at the deep commitment to the cause that he would ultimately bring to this position.[46]

The executive committee of the Anti-Slavery Society was satisfied with Still's application and offered him the job at a salary of $3.75 per week. This was only slightly more than he had made as a waiter, but to Still, this position offered possibilities for advancement that were not available in his previous line of work. Even his letter of application had hinted at this possibility of advancement. "If I am not directly rewarded," he noted, "perhaps it may be the means of more than rewarding me in some future days." Notably, in the Quaker census of 1847, William Still is one of only two Black Philadelphians identified as a clerk.[47]

Historians have identified the clerk as a quintessential figure of the nineteenth-century city. A sort of catch-all term, encompassing an army of men (almost all were men) who worked in the banks, stores, import houses, insurance brokers, law offices, and warehouses of the city, clerks were an essential part of what made urban commerce function. The actual work they did varied, but what set them apart from the laborers of the city was the fact that their main work was done with paper and pen, often at a desk. In fact, historian Michael Zakim notes that one astute observer of the urban scene termed the rise of such clerks "deskism." Beyond this, clerks of the nineteenth century typically saw their position as a training ground, perhaps as a stepping-stone, on their way to greater things. Clerks were "strivers," who ultimately hoped to be their own bosses, to own their own businesses, even if the reality was that few would succeed in this ambition.[48]

This is clearly how Still saw his position. It was his opportunity to make something of himself. Even more, it was an opportunity to do so while contributing to the fight against slavery. Still had come to Philadelphia with great ambition, but he had struggled to find the opportunity that matched that ambition and his talents. At last, he had found that match. He would later recall that his responsibilities as a clerk at the Anti-Slavery Society did not initially include any dealings with fugitive slaves. He cleaned the office. He managed the office's substantial mail. He assisted McKim in the distribution of the *Pennsylvania Freeman*. It seems preordained, however, that Still would ultimately become involved in the cases of fugitives who passed through the office. He had aided fugitive slaves as a young man in New Jersey. There is no definitive evidence that he aided fugitives in his first few years in Philadelphia, though at least one historian suggests that Still had "probably" had some association with the Vigilance Committee prior to his hiring. Certainly, he had connections with those who did.[49]

Whatever his responsibilities, Still was pleased that his new position allowed him to settle his family into a new home. He and Letitia moved into a "humble" two-room apartment in a small house on Washington Street, a small side street stretching from Eleventh to Twelfth Streets, between Lombard and South Streets. This was the heart of "Black Philadelphia," the part of the city in which the highest concentration of African Americans lived, the location of the most prominent cultural institutions of Black life. While the area itself was racially mixed, the block on which they lived (typical of such back streets) was heavily populated by African Americans, most of them porters, waiters, and laborers. Still's sister Mary lived on the opposite side of the street. The houses on the block were packed together and many were divided up among multiple families. At least one other Black family also occupied an apartment in the Stills' house, and the house itself was tucked into the back lot of another small house, also occupied by African Americans.[50]

However happy Still was to have secured steady employment and to have established an independent household, he continued to have ambitions for something greater. Still's regular hours at the Anti-Slavery Society permitted him some opportunity to pursue additional, outside work to supplement his income. He briefly started a night school. Still already had some experience teaching at the Moral Reform Retreat's Sunday school, and if in fact Robert George was Letitia's father, then he had the additional model of his father-in-law, who ran his own night school. Still's sister Mary was also, according to the census of 1847, a schoolteacher. Still, however, abandoned this plan after quickly realizing that it paid little relative to the work that such teaching demanded. After this, he learned that the Apprentices Library, an institution that encouraged self-improvement and reading among the city's young apprentices, was looking for "a trusty person thoroughly to clean the books and shelves of the library." The library was less than a block from the offices of the Anti-Slavery Society, so Still was able to do this work before the office opened or after it closed, earning an additional six dollars a month. He held this job for two years, until the Anti-Slavery Society had raised his salary enough for him to afford to devote his full energies to that work. Letitia earned extra money for the family as a dressmaker, work she may have shared with her sister-in-law and neighbor, Mary, who supplemented her own teacher's wages by making dresses.[51]

Still's work on the side seems not to have interfered with his performance at the Anti-Slavery Society, where he continued to win the confidence of his employers. They, in turn, continued to expand his responsibilities. Later he would recall that in these years he "became acquainted, even intimate" with the mostly white, Quaker executive committee of the Anti-Slavery Society, men and women like James and Lucretia Mott, Mary Grew, Benjamin Bacon, and Sarah Pugh. Still had known white people who were sympathetic to the antislavery cause, but these men and women showed a passion for abolition that approached his own. This was an important lesson in the sorts of allies he might find in his abolitionist struggle.[52]

As important as these white allies were, the member of the executive committee who would prove most important to Still, as an ally and as a model, was Robert Purvis. Born in South Carolina, son of a white father and mixed-race mother, the light-skinned Purvis was a driving force behind the creation of the Philadelphia Vigilance Committee, and by 1839 he had assumed its presidency. In many ways Purvis was strikingly different from William Still. Purvis had inherited a substantial estate from his cotton merchant father and had been educated at a private New England school; he married Harriet Forten, daughter of James Forten, the wealthy Black sailmaker and abolitionist. By the time Still met him, Purvis had moved his family to a rural estate outside the city in order to protect them from the white mobs that tormented Black Philadelphians. What Purvis and Still had in common, though, was a fierce devotion to abolition, in particular the "practical abolition" of the Vigilance Committee.[53]

By the time Still accepted the job with the Anti-Slavery Society, the Vigilance Committee seems to have become somewhat less active than it had been. Some historians have suggested that the lull in the formal work of the committee was spurred by the particularly nasty and destructive riot in 1842, before Still moved to the city; the Vigilance Committee, which had become increasingly brazen in its work, was forced to back off, at least publicly.[54] We certainly have less evidence of the committee's work in the mid to late 1840s than we do from the preceding years. This is not to say that the work of aiding fugitives from slavery had ended. This work, largely through the labor of Black individuals and Black-led institutions, continued whether or not the Vigilance Committee met to coordinate it.[55]

The work of aiding fugitive slaves, then, the work of the so-called Underground Railroad, fell to Black households, like the one Letitia and William Still had established on a back lot of Washington Street. This informal work was already, as early as 1842, being referred to as the "Underground Railroad," though labeling it as such suggested a more systematic enterprise than was generally the case. We do not know for sure when the Stills first began to harbor fugitive slaves in their home, but for William and Letitia, as for many Black Philadelphians, there was no clear line between the work that they did to make ends meet and the work they did to protect fugitives from slavery. The work of raising their own child, Caroline, born early in 1849, was not separate from their work to aid and uplift their friends and neighbors. In the words of historian Erica Ball, the Stills sought "to live an antislavery life."[56] This is not to say that Still was bereft of personal ambition. He hoped to rise in this world. He hoped to provide for his family. But he always understood that his own success and failure was linked to the Black community in which he had made his home.

CHAPTER THREE

THE ANTI-SLAVERY OFFICE

The office at 107 North Fifth Street[1] was a busy place. It was in this office that the executive committee of the Pennsylvania Anti-Slavery Society put together the *Pennsylvania Freeman*, the society's official newspaper and the voice of abolition in the city. The newspaper was printed a few blocks away in Carter's Alley, but it was from the office on Fifth Street that it was edited and later distributed to the paper's subscribers. Beyond this, the office, which also contained a bookstore and reading room, was a sort of clearinghouse for the antislavery cause. If you needed to get in contact with the abolitionist movement in Philadelphia, this was the place to which you went.

Miller McKim ran the office. Born James Miller McKim on a farm in Carlisle, Pennsylvania in 1810, he was educated at Dickinson College. Following a religious conversion, he studied for the ministry at both Princeton Theological Seminary and Andover before returning to Carlisle to finish his training. Even before completing this preparation, though, he had turned to what would ultimately be his life's work: abolition. As was often the case, McKim had been radicalized by a connection with free African Americans. In his case, the connection was John Peck, a Black barber in Carlisle. It was through Peck that McKim was exposed to William Lloyd Garrison's *Liberator*. In 1833, McKim traveled to

Philadelphia to join with abolitionists from around the country in establishing the American Anti-Slavery Society (AASS).[2]

In 1836 he would give up his pastorate in order to serve as a traveling agent for the AASS. This was a difficult life. McKim went from town to town spreading the abolitionist message, never staying in any place long and often facing hostile crowds. Generally, this meant jeering or throwing rotten vegetables, but the threat of serious violence always loomed. These were some of the most perilous years of the struggle against slavery. Garrison himself was nearly tarred and feathered by a Boston mob in 1835. The abolitionist editor Elijah Lovejoy was murdered by a proslavery mob in Illinois in 1837, and in 1838 a Philadelphia mob set fire to the abolitionist Pennsylvania Hall (just a block from where McKim's Fifth Street office would be). Abolitionists faced violent mobs almost wherever they went.[3]

In 1840, McKim was hired as a publishing agent in Philadelphia, a job that suited him and allowed him to settle down. Years later, William Still would recall McKim as a man of "peculiar fitness" for his antislavery work. He was prudent, hardworking, and judicious. The abolitionist movement was full of fiery, charismatic, even eccentric figures. In McKim, the movement found a man of rare "practical sense." Still would write of McKim, "his influence upon men and the times has been less as a speaker than as a writer, and perhaps still less as a writer than as an organizer, a contriver of ways and means."[4] As one historian put it, "he applied a fundamentally conservative temperament to the prosecution of a radical cause."[5]

William Still was hired to assist McKim in this work. Officially, this meant that he cleaned the office and bookstore, aided in the mailing of the *Freeman*, helped selling antislavery literature, and assisted with the society's voluminous correspondence. In reality his work involved him in all sorts of business that passed through the office or centered on it. For example, a "free labor" (that is, not produced by slaves) marketplace had emerged in cities like Philadelphia; the Free Labor Dry Goods Store itself was a few doors down from the Anti-Slavery Society office, but inquiries were directed to 107 North Fifth Street. Other businesses, many of them located within blocks of the office, marketed themselves to an abolitionist clientele, including the bootmaker Peter Lester, who had introduced Still to McKim and who advertised in the back of the *Freeman*, noting that "Anti-Slavery men are requested to call." Other business that passed through the office seemed to have little or no relation to the abolitionist cause. Still was, for example, listed as the contact for those who wished to purchase "green corn," that is sweet corn, suitable for eating, as opposed to field corn, which would be used to feed livestock or ground into cornmeal.[6]

Still's employer at the Pennsylvania Anti-Slavery Society, J. Miller McKim

For Still, these early years in the Anti-Slavery Society office were a crash course in the business of abolition. On days when the *Freeman* was mailed out, work went far into the night, but at other times Still's work was light. While McKim was no longer a traveling agent, his position still required him to be out of the office quite often. Still managed the place in his absence but would later recall that in these times "the office was quite a propitious place for study." Still dedicated his free time to self-improvement. Not only did he have an abundance of reading material from the antislavery bookstore, but the nature of newspaper publication in the nineteenth century meant that this was supplemented by antislavery writing from across the country. Like its contemporaries, the *Pennsylvania Freeman* did not have a stable of reporters covering the news of the day. Instead, it mostly relied on letters from correspondents across the country and on articles reprinted from other papers. McKim pieced together each issue of the *Freeman* from these sources. From this office in Philadelphia, then, Still was able to immerse himself in the burgeoning abolitionist print culture of his day.[7]

Those who worked in the Anti-Slavery Society office took special note of a particular sort of content that only occasionally made it into the newspaper: fugitive slave advertisements from Southern newspapers. Typically, the *Freeman* made use of material from Southern newspapers to illustrate the cruelties of slavery or it brought to its readers' attention the proslavery words and actions of Southern politicians.[8] Fugitive slave advertisements, however, a common feature in Southern newspapers, also provided intelligence for Philadelphia abolitionists looking to stay one step ahead of the slave catchers. Still later noted that the Anti-Slavery Society subscribed to the *Baltimore Sun* and the *Richmond Dispatch* for just this purpose; he and others scoured their pages daily for information on fugitives who might have found their way to Philadelphia. Sometimes this information was passed along to abolitionists in other cities as well.[9] Examples of these advertisements can be found pasted into the record book that Still kept during his time in the Anti-Slavery Society office.[10] Still and McKim made it their business to know about fugitive slaves who might need their help, even before those individuals came asking for it.

Still's work in the Anti-Slavery Society office also tied him into a national network of abolitionists, and necessarily involved him in the controversies of that broader movement. During the decade or so between the commencement of McKim's antislavery work and Still's start at the PASS, schisms had splintered the abolitionist movement and the AASS. Many abolitionists had become critical of Garrison and his followers on a number of fronts. Some objected to his renunciation of voting, which Garrison saw as a compromise with a political system corrupted by slavery. Others bristled at his venomous criticism of American churches and his call to "come out" of what he deemed the proslavery denominations of American Christianity. Even more criticized his willingness to embrace women as full participants in the abolitionist movement. In general, many of these critics felt that Garrison's radicalism and his willingness to combine supposedly extraneous issues with abolition was detrimental to the cause. When they failed to push Garrison out of the AASS, some of these critics left to found new abolitionist organizations, such as the somewhat more moderate American and Foreign Antislavery Society and the antislavery Liberty Party.[11]

The PASS had aligned itself with the Garrisonian faction. Many Philadelphia abolitionists held a deep respect and admiration for Garrison himself, but the leadership of the PASS also found common ground with Garrison for ideological reasons. Women like Lucretia Mott, Sarah Pugh, and Mary Grew had long played important leadership roles in the abolitionist movement in Philadelphia, so Garrison's feminism was appealing rather than alienating for many Philadelphia abolitionists. Mott and others among the city's largely Quaker white leadership of the PASS embraced Garrison's radical "nonresistance." In general, Black abolitionists were among Garrison's earliest supporters and they remained his fiercest defenders. This was especially true in Philadelphia, where Robert Purvis maintained his devotion to Garrison. There was some dispute among leaders of the PASS in regard to the morality of voting, but by 1845, the year Purvis was elected the first Black president of the society, the PASS had embraced a strict non-voting policy, denouncing the Constitution in very Garrisonian terms as "an unholy league with oppression."[12]

These arguments only went so far, though. Abolitionists fiercely disagreed about many issues, but all were outraged by the role that their cities and states played in the capture and rendition of accused fugitive slaves. This was a particularly pressing issue in Pennsylvania, due to the state's border with multiple slave states. In 1846, not coincidentally with Purvis as president, the PASS began agitating the state legislature for greater protection of the state's Black citizens. The society's petitions were well received and a delegation was invited to the state capital of Harrisburg to plead their case.[13] In February of 1847, the state legislature (controlled by Whigs) passed a new anti-kidnapping bill and the Democratic governor, Frances Shunk, signed it into law. This law protected Black Pennsylvanians in a number of ways. First, it imposed harsh penalties on those who would seek to claim legally free African Americans as fugitive slaves. Second, it banned state officials from participating in the recovery of fugitive slaves and prohibited the use of the state's jails for the holding of accused fugitives. Lastly, it repealed portions of an earlier law that permitted slaveholders to legally bring slaves into the state for six months and that banned slaves from testifying in court.[14]

None of these provisions explicitly denied the constitutional obligation of Pennsylvania to return fugitive slaves, but collectively they made it significantly more difficult, and even dangerous, for slaveholders to recover fugitives who had made it to Pennsylvania. It essentially functioned as a legal complement to the extralegal work of Still and others who assisted fugitives in transit through Philadelphia. This multifaceted effort helped ensure that Pennsylvania was "Free Soil," that it was territory hospitable to fugitives and hostile to slavery. It is sometimes easy to imagine the borders between freedom and slavery as fixed, set in stone, but those engaged in the everyday work of aiding fugitive slaves knew better. The borderlands of slavery were always a place of struggle.

These efforts by Pennsylvanians to protect fugitive slaves can more broadly be seen as a part of the escalating sectional tensions of the late 1840s. An expansionist war with Mexico reopened political conflict over slavery that many had thought resolved by the Missouri Compromise. In the midst of the war, a war that many Northerners denounced as a slave-state land grab, the Wilmot Proviso, which would have outlawed slavery in any territory purchased from Mexico, split the nation; partisan differences that had so recently driven American political behavior paled in comparison to the new, sectional divide. Northern Whigs and Democrats made common cause in their effort to prevent the expansion of slavery; Southerners, whatever their party, closed ranks in opposition to the Proviso, which they denounced as rank abolitionism.[15]

In border slave states, like Maryland, slaveholders felt targeted from all directions. Not only was the political power of slave states under attack in the debate over westward expansion, but a new generation of border-state abolitionists, men like Cassius Clay, the boisterous antislavery Kentuckian, and Joseph Snodgrass, publisher of the moderately (by Northern standards) antislavery newspaper, the *Baltimore Saturday Visiter*, led to fears that non-slaveholding whites were becoming a Southern abolitionist fifth column. Some particularly bold Northern abolitionists even began to venture into the South itself in order to assist fugitive slaves. Add to this the passage by Northern states of so-called "Personal Liberty Laws," like the one Pennsylvania passed in 1847, and the slaveholding class of border states felt increasingly vulnerable.[16]

Whatever the legal barriers that Pennsylvania placed before them, though, border-state slaveholders were intent on pressing their right to recover fugitives. On May 1, 1847, officials seized a man named Isaac Brown, who had been living in Philadelphia. Brown was a fugitive from slavery, but he was not seized as such. His pursuers, fearful of falling afoul of Pennsylvania's anti-kidnapping law, engaged in a bit of subterfuge. Brown was instead arrested for the attempted murder of one Alexander Somerville. Two years earlier, Brown, then enslaved to Somerville, had been accused of the same crime by authorities in Calvert County, Maryland. Brown maintained his innocence, but was given two hundred lashes as punishment. He was later sold to a plantation in Louisiana. It was only after he was sold that he made his escape and settled in Philadelphia, making a new life as a free man. Somerville, his former master, somehow became aware of where he was, and Maryland authorities sought to circumvent the strict new anti-kidnapping law by claiming Brown as an attempted murderer, not as a fugitive slave.[17]

Philadelphia abolitionists were outraged that the law they believed to be a sure defense for men like Brown was being thwarted. Black Philadelphians were especially incensed, and a large contingent of Black observers filled the court when Brown had his hearing.[18] Brown was defended by two able attorneys with distinguished histories in the abolitionist cause: Thomas Earle, a member of the Pennsylvania Anti-Slavery Society, and Charles Gibbons, a prominent Whig politician. They sought to make clear to the court that what was being portrayed as a criminal trial was truly a fugitive slave case. When the prosecution called its first witness, in order to establish Brown's identity, the defense questioned him not on the particulars of his testimony, but on his profession.

"What business are you engaged in?" asked Gibbons, the defense attorney.

"I am an agent" came the witness's reply.

"What kind of agent?"

"I am a general agent—I follow a general agency."

"Whose agent are you?"

"I have been agent for Hope H. Slatter of Baltimore for several years."

"What is Hope H. Slatter's business?"

"It is to buy and sell negroes and send them to the South."

Gibbons went on to argue that the attempted murder charge "was a mere trick to evade the late act of the Pennsylvania Legislature for the punishment of kidnapping."[19] If he could convince the court that the case was about recovering a fugitive slave and not about the alleged crime, Gibbons was sure that Brown would be safe.

The prosecution objected to Gibbons's grandstanding pronouncement, and the judge sustained this objection, but he was concerned enough about these allegations to adjourn for a few days while he conferred with the governor and attorney general of the state. In the meantime, however, Gibbons went to the state supreme court and requested, and received, a writ *de homine replegiando*, which secured Brown's release from jail on the promise that he would return to answer the charges against him. When the court reconvened a few days later and the judge sent for Isaac Brown, he was nowhere to be found. What's more, Brown's legal counsel brought a suit for attempted kidnapping against the various parties who had sought to claim Brown as a fugitive from justice. At this point, according to one abolitionist publication, "the defendants . . . *prudently returned to Maryland in the first public conveyance.*"[20] They knew that they had been beaten.

Despite the fact that the case had not ostensibly been about fugitive slave recovery at all, the legal difficulties presented to Brown's would-be captors demonstrated the perils of fugitive slave recovery in Pennsylvania. A few months later, Maryland's governor, Thomas Pratt, devoted a significant portion of his annual address to the Brown case, lamenting that "the constitutional right of the citizen of a slave state to demand and receive his slaves when they escape to a non-slaveholding state, if not disregarded by the authorities, is successfully resisted with impunity by the citizens of that state." He warned that if this was allowed to continue, it might lead to the "dissolution of the Union."[21]

Philadelphia abolitionists seemed pleased by the legal and political conditions in their state that protected fugitives and free Blacks alike. "To the close discerner of the signs of the times," wrote Lucretia Mott, "the constant agitation of the Abolitionists, has shaken all these strong holds, and has made the oppressor tremble." As evidence, she noted, among other signs, "Legislators hear and answer the prayers of the advocates for freedom—as in our own state last session—abolishing the '6 months law' & removing the facilities for the recovery of fugitives."[22] A piece in the *Pennsylvania Freeman*, likely authored by Miller McKim, bragged that "there is one railroad in our country upon which we cannot reckon the business by the amount of receipts per month or quarter; yet we have good proof that it is increasingly prosperous. We were reminded of this the other day by noticing in a single copy of the Baltimore Sun, advertisements of eleven fugitive slaves, who had escaped in the course of ten or twelve days."[23] Such public pronouncements on the success of the Underground Railroad helped buoy abolitionist optimism and helped create a climate in which protecting fugitives was commonplace and accepted. It also showed that the activists of the Underground Railroad were increasingly willing to flaunt their blatantly illegal aid to fugitive slaves.

While abolitionists celebrated the escape of fugitive slaves, they were not always in agreement as to what role their organizations should take in that escape. The executive committee of the PASS, for example, frequently noted that the work of the Vigilance Committee did not fall "within our province as a Society," and while many of the members of the committee welcomed fugitives into their own homes, the 1844 annual report offered backhanded praise for the Vigilance Committee, noting that it receives support "from those who will do nothing towards the deliverance of the less fortunate victims of tyranny still toiling in hopeless bondage, cheered by no prospect of a resting place beyond the spoiler's reach. We rejoice that they who will do no more will do this much for freedom, and we heartily wish prosperity to the Vigilance Committee so long as there is need for its benevolent work."[24] These committed abolitionists lamented the fact that fugitive slaves, who represented only a tiny fraction of the enslaved population of the United States, received so much more sympathy than the vast majority who had little opportunity to escape from bondage.

Notable among these abolitionist critics of the Vigilance Committee was Lucretia Mott, who was personally supportive of fugitive slaves but who doubted the efficacy of the work that Still and his allies did. Still would later recall that "of all the women who served the Anti-slavery cause in its darkest days, there is not one whose labors were more effective, whose character nobler, and who is more universally respected and beloved."[25] Mott was born in Nantucket in 1793 to a family of Quakers. She moved to Phila-delphia with her family in 1809 and at the age of eighteen mar-ried James Mott. She was a Quaker minister, a feminist, and an abolitionist. Mott helped to found the Pennsylvania Female Anti-Slavery Society, and in 1844 she was a member of the executive committee of the PASS. The words of the annual report in regard to the work of the Vigilance Committee might very well be hers; they echo her position as stated elsewhere. Mott warned her fellow abolitionists that they must not be distracted by peripheral work, as important as it might be, from the central work of attacking and destroying slavery itself, root and branch.[26]

If William Still shared these concerns, he never gave any indi-cation. He certainly respected Mott, and he shared her desire to strike at the root of slavery, but at the moment he was fully com-mitted to the work of aiding whatever fugitives found their way to Philadelphia. The kidnapping bill of 1847 had made life some-what more secure for those fugitives who managed to get to Phila-delphia, but the road to freedom was still perilous for those who would flee from bondage, and there were many slave catchers who were willing to risk prosecution under Pennsylvania law, since the profits available for recovering fugitive slaves were substantial.

The path was difficult enough for the vast majority of fugitives who escaped from border slave states like Maryland, Virginia, and Delaware, but on occasion slaves were able to escape from much farther south. Such was the case for a couple who were among the most famous American fugitive slaves and who escaped to Philadelphia in these years. William and Ellen Craft were born into slavery in Georgia. Though enslaved to different masters, the two were married and shortly thereafter began to develop a plan to escape from slavery. They knew that the path to a free state would be long and dangerous. Suspicious authorities carefully monitored trains and steamships, which were their likeliest means of traveling the great distance to the North. Black passengers, at least those not enslaved and traveling with their masters, were sure to be confronted; those without proof demonstrating their free status would be seized and turned over to slave catchers. Without such proof any flight seemed likely to end in failure, but in December 1848, the Crafts concocted a plan. "Notwithstanding my wife being of African extraction on her mother's side," William Craft would later write, "she is almost white—in fact, she is so nearly so that the tyrannical old lady to whom she first belonged became so annoyed, at finding her frequently mistaken for a child of the family, that she gave her when eleven years of age to a daughter, as a wedding present." The Crafts would take advantage of Ellen's light skin.[27]

Ellen's complexion might have let her travel north without arousing suspicion, but William was a different story. Ellen would have to pose as his master; there would be nothing strange about a slave traveling with his owner. Yet even this situation, they feared, would arouse suspicion. A woman traveling with a male slave might prompt questions that Ellen could not answer. Better if she disguised herself as a man. She wrapped her face as if she had a bad toothache in order to conceal her lack of a beard, and since their trip would take many days, she placed her right arm in a sling as an excuse for why she would not be able to write her name in the registration book at the hotels where they would need to stay. Ellen carried a cane in her other hand and claimed to be hard of hearing as a further excuse to avoid any conversation, and the disguise was complete. Ellen was to be an ailing planter, traveling to Philadelphia to seek medical care. The two took a train to Charleston, and then a steamer to Wilmington, North Carolina, where they took a train to Richmond and from there on to Washington, Baltimore, and ultimately Philadelphia. At a number of points Ellen was challenged to prove that she was, in fact, William's master, since train and steamship companies were wary of the liability of aiding fugitive slaves. Ironically, as the two got closer to Philadelphia a guard on the train took William into his confidence. "Let me give you some friendly advice," he said. "When you get to Philadelphia, run away and leave that cripple, and have your liberty." Later on, he received similar advice from a free Black man traveling on the same train, along with a suggestion for a boardinghouse where he would be safe if he did so.[28]

Shortly after their arrival at the boardinghouse that had been suggested to them by the free Black traveler, the Crafts revealed their true identities. At first the landlord was incredulous. "Where is your master?" he asked William, who pointed to Ellen. Once the truth of the situation became clear, the landlord warned the Crafts that they would not be safe in Philadelphia, and he turned to "several of the leading abolitionists of the city," who came to the boardinghouse to offer their advice and support. Still may have been among these initial contacts, and he certainly met with the Crafts while they were in Philadelphia. "Never can the writer forget the impression made by their arrival," Still later wrote. "Even now, after the lapse of nearly a quarter of a century it is easy to picture them in a private room, surrounded by a few friends." These Philadelphia abolitionists advised the brave couple to continue moving, to Massachusetts, where they would be safer than in Philadelphia; the Crafts took this advice and settled in Boston.[29]

A year later, Still took part in an even more dramatic escape from slavery. Henry Brown was born in 1815, enslaved to a Virginia planter. When Brown was fifteen, his master died, and when his property was divided up, Brown was separated from his family and sent to Richmond to work in tobacco manufacturing. In Richmond, Brown met and fell in love with a woman named Nancy. She was enslaved to a different man, but Brown received the permission of her master and the two were married. Brown struggled mightily to build a household in such circumstances, but for a time he was able to do so; Henry and Nancy had three children, and with a friend as an intermediary Brown was able to rent a house (which Brown, as a slave, was not legally able to do on his own). One morning in August of 1848, however, while at work in the tobacco factory Brown received word that his wife and children had been taken from their home and were to be sold south, to North Carolina. Brown begged his master to purchase his wife and children in order to keep the family together, but to no avail. He could only watch, helpless, as his family was marched out of the city on their way south, "with ropes about their necks and staples on their arms." His eldest child called out to him from a passing wagon, "Father! Father!" His wife, loaded with chains, reached out to grasp his hand. "While my mind felt unutterable things," Brown would later recall, "my tongue was only able to say, we shall meet in heaven!" He walked along with her, holding her hand, for perhaps four miles, and then she was gone.[30]

In the months after this brutal, sudden separation from his family Brown began to conceive of a plan to flee from bondage. He approached a shopkeeper with whom he had done some business, Samuel Smith, who was originally from Massachusetts, and asked for advice about how he might run away. This was certainly a bold step. "The man asked me if I was not afraid to speak that way to him," Brown later recalled. "I said no, for I imagined he believed that every man had a right to liberty. He said I was quite right, and asked me how much money I would give him if he would assist me to get away." Perhaps Brown knew that Smith had fallen on hard times and would be receptive to offers of cash in return for help, or perhaps he had some reason to suspect antislavery sympathies from the shopkeeper. In any case, he offered Smith half of the $166 he had managed to save and the two began to consider how Brown might escape to the North.

Smith suggested some of the means that he knew slaves had used to escape, but none appealed to Brown. Only later did Brown have the revelation that would change his life. "One day, while I was at work," he later recalled, "the idea suddenly flashed across my mind of shutting myself up in a box, and getting myself conveyed as dry goods to a free state." Just a few years earlier such a plan would have been far less feasible, but advances in transportation had dramatically cut the time that it took to get from Richmond to Philadelphia. By 1849 the trip took less than a day. Even so, this would be quite a long time for Brown to stay sealed in a box. At first Smith was opposed to the plan, but Brown insisted that this was the means by which he would get to the North.

If Brown was to be mailed north, then he would need an address. Smith traveled to Philadelphia in the beginning of March 1849 in order to investigate their options. Unsurprisingly, he found his way to William Still and the Anti-Slavery Society office on North Fifth Street.[31] Still's boss, Miller McKim, was skeptical but Smith insisted that Brown was adamant in his plans to escape in this manner. They agreed that Brown would be mailed on the following Tuesday, March 13, 1849.

Shortly thereafter, McKim received word that the plan would have to be postponed. Ice on the Susquehanna River meant that the trip might take even longer than the twenty-four hours for which they had already planned. McKim was relieved. Since Smith's visit he had grown increasingly concerned about the danger of this plan. Would Brown survive the trip? What would they do if he did not and they opened the box to find a suffocated Henry Brown? McKim decided that he could no longer be a part of this

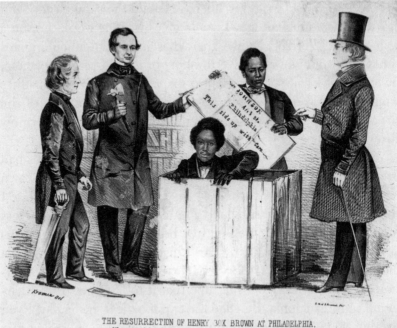

THE RESURRECTION OF HENRY BOX BROWN AT PHILADELPHIA.
Who escaped from Richmond Va. in a Box 3 feet long 2½ ft. deep and 2 ft. wide.

Henry Box Brown's arrival in Philadelphia—Still is directly behind the box scheme and he wrote to Smith in Richmond informing him of his change of heart. Nevertheless, Smith and Brown decided to proceed as planned, and informed McKim that the package would depart Richmond on March 20. On the morning when Brown was to arrive, McKim went himself to the depot in order to ensure the safe transport of the box. It was, Still would later write, "one of the most serious walks he ever took." When all the freight had been unloaded, however, at the appointed time of 3:00 a.m., there was no box that fit the description. Later that day McKim received a final message from Richmond informing him that Brown would arrive the following day. By now McKim worried that his presence at the depot would begin to arouse suspicion and so he and an ally, Edward Davis, arranged for a trustworthy porter named Dan, "an Irishman," to meet the box at the depot and bring it directly to the antislavery office.[32]

The next morning, Dan secured the box and brought it to the Anti-Slavery Society office, where a small group nervously awaited it: McKim, now "perfectly composed" after days of anxious antici-pation; Professor Charles D. Cleveland, a regular ally of the Vigi-lance Committee but on this occasion overpowered with emotion; Lewis Thompson, a longtime abolitionist printer; and William Still. "All was quiet," Still would later write. "The door had been safely locked. The proceedings commenced. Mr. McKim rapped quietly on the lid of the box and called out, 'All right!' Instantly came the answer from within, 'All right, sir!'" The men went to work with saw and hatchet and the hickory hoops were cut and the lid of the box was off. Brown rose from the box but in his weakened condition almost immediately fainted. He soon recov-ered and sang a psalm that he had prepared. "I waited patiently, I waited patiently for the Lord," he began. Brown spent the next few days recovering in the home of James and Lucretia Mott, fol-lowed by two days in the Still household, after which he departed for Boston where he would go on to publish his story, which made him famous as Henry "Box" Brown.[33]

Most fugitives who came into Still's hands, however, did not come from as far as the Crafts nor in as dramatic fashion as Henry "Box"

Brown. The Anti-Slavery Society office lay at the center of a complex and informal web that fugitives traveled. Those fleeing from bondage often traveled by whatever means they could manage, seeking shelter and aid where they could find it, but once they got closer to Philadelphia there was a somewhat more established path, or rather set of paths, that brought them to Still's door. Fugitives who found their way to Harrisburg would often seek the aid of Joseph Bustill, a mixed-race teacher, abolitionist, and longtime ally of Still's, who would frequently forward them on to Philadelphia via train, arranging for Still or one of his co-workers to meet them at the station.[34] In Phoenixville, west of Philadelphia, they might seek out Elijah Pennypacker, a former state legislator who sheltered fugitives in his home; he also maintained a connection with Still and frequently sent groups of fugitives to Philadelphia.[35]

Perhaps Still's most important such ally was Thomas Garrett, a white Quaker merchant who lived in Wilmington, Delaware. Garrett, stocky and powerfully built, was a fearless defender of fugitive slaves. He had become a committed abolitionist at an early age; growing up he had witnessed his parents sheltering fugitive slaves in their Upper Darby, Pennsylvania, home. When he moved out on his own, though, and settled in the slave state of Delaware, his abolitionism became more dangerous. The 1847 anti-kidnapping law and an increasingly antislavery political climate had made protecting fugitive slaves somewhat less risky for Pennsylvanians, but Delaware was a different story. In 1848, not long after William Still had begun working at the Anti-Slavery Society, Thomas Garrett was sued for his role in aiding a family of fugitives escape to Philadelphia. The trial, presided over by Supreme Court Chief Justice Roger Taney (presiding over the U.S. Circuit Court), found Garrett guilty and assessed him $5,400 in fines as compensation to the alleged owners of the family he had aided. Garrett delivered a defiant address at the end of the trial. "I now pledge myself," he assured the court, "to use all lawful and honorable means to lessen the burdens of this oppressed people, and endeavor according to ability furnished to burst their chains asunder." Garrett was unrepentant.[36]

While many fugitives made use of this network of Underground Railroad "conductors" and "station masters," perhaps just as many found their own way to Philadelphia, and while many fugitives came to the Anti-Slavery Society office looking for aid, others simply arrived and sought to blend in. Interestingly, the most famous fugitive to arrive in Philadelphia, Harriet Tubman, did so outside of the underground network that was coalescing around the office. Tubman had been born Araminta Ross in Dorchester County on the Eastern Shore of Mary-

Still ally Thomas Garrett

land. She took the name Tubman in 1844 when she married a free Black man named John Tubman. Around the same time, she also changed her first name to Harriet in honor of her mother. In September 1849, frightened by rumors that she was to be sold, Tubman ran away, accompanied by her two brothers, Ben and Henry. Within a few weeks, the brothers had grown fearful of the dangers that stood in the way of their flight, and they convinced their sister to join them in returning.

A few weeks later, Tubman fled again. This time she was alone, and she was determined not to return to slavery. She traveled mostly at night, with the North Star as her guide. By the time Harriet fled there was already an informal network of safe houses dotting the landscape of the Eastern Shore; at each house along the way, Harriet would receive instructions for finding the next one. She made her way, carefully, never quite sure who she could trust. "When I had crossed that line," she would later recall, "there was no one to welcome me to the land of freedom. I was a stranger in a strange land." She might have gone to the Anti-Slavery Society office for aid, but instead she just sought to blend into the Black community of Philadelphia, working in hotels and private homes and saving her wages.[37] It would only be later, when she resolved to return to her former home in an effort to rescue family members, that Harriet Tubman would seek the assistance of William Still and his network.

The anti-kidnapping law of 1847 had made Pennsylvania somewhat safer for fugitive slaves, but Black Philadelphians like Still and Tubman, whatever their legal status, faced discrimination and violence on the streets of their city. It is unclear where Tubman lived during these years, but sometime during 1849 William and Letitia Still moved from the cramped apartment on the back lot in Washington Street and settled in a small newly constructed row house a few blocks away on Ronaldson Street.[38] The Stills' small block was mostly populated by African Americans, but the neighborhood in general was racially mixed, with a significant population of recently arrived Irish immigrants. This sometimes proved a volatile mix.

This volatility was demonstrated in October of 1849 when white street toughs, members of a gang known as the Killers, attacked a tavern frequented by Black patrons and known as the California House. The California House, located just blocks from the Stills' home, was owned by a Black man who was rumored to be married to a white woman. For much of the day on October 9, 1849, a white mob gathered around the tavern, brandishing knives and guns and occasionally scuffling with Black passersby. Later in the evening, at the direction of the leader of the Killers, the Moyamensing Hose Company rammed the California House with a wagon of flaming tar. As the building burst into flames, the Black men and women who had been inside fled into the streets, where the awaiting mob fired upon them and pelted them with bricks. When other fire companies arrived to put out the blaze, the mob attacked them as well. It was only the arrival of several companies of the state militia that finally dispersed the mob in the early morning hours. By that time the California House had burned to its foundations. "There is not a city in the Union," commented the antislavery newspaper the *National Era*, "more shamefully mob-ridden than Philadelphia."[39]

The Stills were not the sort to frequent a place like the California House; they aspired to be a part of the better class of the city's Black community, but class pretensions mattered little to white mobs. Often, in fact, middle-class African Americans were the specific focus of such mobs, even if that was not so in this case. Even as William Still struggled to make a more comfortable life for his wife and small daughter, even as he conducted himself in a way that asserted his respectability, he knew that such actions might only make him a target.[40]

Still always saw the fight against slavery and the fight for Black equality in the United States as two parts of the same struggle. Even as his role with the Anti-Slavery Society grew, so too did he take on a public role as a part of the struggle to secure the American citizenship rights of free Black people. In April 1850, Still served as president of a "large and respectable meeting of Colored Citizens" that met at the Philadelphia Institute to condemn the "Colonization Scheme." While some white reformers (William and Letitia Still's former employers, for example) believed that such efforts were an essential part of a gradual path to abolition, Still and the meeting spoke for most Black Philadelphians in rejecting the colonization position, which insisted that African Americans could never become full citizens in the United States, the country of their birth.

A small number of free African Americans had embraced this opportunity to escape the land of their former bondage, but most vehemently opposed colonization and the national organization that championed it, the American Colonization Society (ACS). For many free African Americans, their resistance to this organization was not driven by their opposition to emigration per se. It was, rather, that the ACS was a white-dominated organization whose interest in removing free Black people from the United States seemed driven by a sense that free Black people were a threat to the country and could never be welcome there. "We are not going to leave our native land," announced Still's meeting, "at the suggestion of any who are no more Americans than we are."[41]

His work at the Anti-Slavery Society office positioned him ideally for this struggle. While many critics of slavery, especially but not exclusively those who were drifting toward electoral politics as a means of advancing the cause, insisted that their hatred of chattel slavery was not necessarily an endorsement of racial equality, the PASS was committed to both the fight against slavery and the fight for Black equality. The organization insisted that immediate abolition must be accompanied by full equality for the emancipated. The work that Still did for the PASS, whether assisting in the publication of the *Pennsylvania Freeman*, selling abolitionist literature, or aiding fugitive slaves, was a part of this broader, radical abolitionist struggle.

The mission of the PASS was to aid African Americans, free and enslaved, in any number of ways, and so while William Still was shocked on that August 1850 day when his brother Peter walked into his office, it was not at all surprising that a person like Peter would come to Still looking for help finding lost family. Unsurprisingly, Still's reunion with Peter was a pivotal moment in his life. He had already committed himself to the abolitionist movement and to the Underground Railroad, but Still would later recall that his reunion with his brother was a primary reason why he began to keep records on the fugitives who passed through his office (though it seems to have been a few years before he actually did so). Keeping such records was certainly risky, but Still felt that if they might provide to fugitives some possibility of "restoration of lost identities, and the reunion of severed relationships" then it would be worth the risk. Still, whose family had long ago been torn apart by slavery and flight from it, understood that freedom was more than not being a slave. Freedom also meant the freedom to be with those you love.

When this stranger first mentioned his parents' names, when Still first began to realize that the man sitting in front of him was his brother, it was difficult for him to believe. At first, he was suspicious. Still had generally kept his family's history secret; even his employers did not know about it. Could this man have somehow learned his secret? It would not be the first time that a stranger showed up in the office with a clever story looking for some quick cash. He peppered Peter with questions, hoping to catch him in some inconsistency, but eventually he was convinced.[42]

When he finally composed himself enough to reveal his knowledge to his brother, Peter was understandably suspicious himself. William did his best to convince Peter that he was genuine. He shared as much as he could remember of what his mother had told him about the brother he had never met. Peter remained incredulous. Their mother lived across the river, in New Jersey, William told his brother, but their sister Mary lived close by. He pleaded with Peter to come with him to visit her. Peter relented.

Mary Still lived on Bonsell Street, not far from William and Letitia.[43] She was in her early forties and single. She taught some school, she made dresses, and she sometimes took in boarders at her small home. William asked Peter to tell her what he had told him earlier. As soon as she heard Peter's story she cried out, "O Lord! it is one of our lost brothers! I should know him by his likeness to our mother. Thank God! one of our brothers has come!" Peter remained skeptical. This was quite a shock. But he agreed to stay with his brother William for the night and to return to Mary's the following day so that he might meet some of the rest of the family.[44]

At noon on the next day, he and Mary visited another sister, Kitty (Kitturah), a few years older than Mary, who lived in another part of the city. After that the two sisters took Peter on a steamship across the Delaware. Once in New Jersey they took a coach to the home of James Still. Peter would later recall that if he had any doubts at this point they were dissipated by the appearance of James, who so resembled Peter's beloved brother, Levin. They stayed at their brother James's home for the night and then in the morning traveled the eight miles to their mother's home.

Charity Still was nearly eighty. When her daughters first told her the news she, too, seems to have not believed it. "Who are you?" she asked as she approached the stranger. "My name," he said, "is Peter, and I had a brother Levin. My father's name was Levin, and my mother's name was Sidney—."

"O, Lord," she cried, "how long have I prayed to see my two

sons! Can it be that they have come? Oh! if you are my child, tell me how d'y' once more!" It had been more than forty years since Charity had seen her son. She had never forgotten the two boys she left behind, but for all her prayers she surely knew that there was little chance she would ever see either of them again, yet here he was. Mother and son embraced, tears running down both their cheeks.[45]

Henry Brown had not lingered very long in Philadelphia. He stayed for a while among his new friends, including a few nights with the Stills, but they all warned him he was not safe. Even with the protection of the anti-kidnapping law of 1847 in place, it was better for Brown to move on. He went first to New York. Perhaps Still guided him to the station and sent word ahead. In New York he met with abolitionists who helped forward him on to Boston and ultimately to New Bedford, a well-known haven for fugitive slaves.[1]

It was not long, though, before Brown's dramatic exploits became widely known. Brown's former owner seems not to have placed a runaway advertisement for him, but clearly word had gotten around about Brown's means of escape. The company in Philadelphia, Adams Express, that had unwittingly accepted the box containing Brown had learned of the incident and sent word to their office in Richmond warning them to be on guard for further such attempts. Within a month of Brown's escape, newspapers were reprinting accounts of it. Less than two months after Brown's flight, his accomplice, Samuel Smith, was apprehended while trying to mail two more fugitive slaves north to Philadelphia.[2]

Southern newspapers gleefully reported on the capture of Smith, but while it was clear that the force of state law was gen-

erally adequate to deal with such incidents, it was also evident
that once fugitives escaped to the North the law ceased to be an
effective ally. This was made obvious by the increasing publicity granted to Henry Brown. In May of 1849, just two months
after his escape, Brown was introduced on the stage of the New
England Anti-Slavery Convention, and by the end of the convention he had become known as Henry "Box" Brown. Before long he
was an abolitionist celebrity. Song sheets featuring an image of a
box and lyrics celebrating his escape soon appeared at antislavery
meetings across New England.[3]

For years Southern slave holders had complained about the
refusal of Northern states to abide by the constitutional mandate
to return fugitive slaves. States across the North had passed "personal liberty" laws. Such laws, like the one in Pennsylvania, were
often specifically designed to protect free Blacks from kidnapping,
to ensure that those claimed as fugitive slaves were, in fact, fugitive
slaves, but in general they also made it difficult for slave catchers to
recover their prey. Beyond this, slave catchers often and increasingly faced hostile Northern crowds and unfriendly judges. For
border slave states, like Maryland, Virginia, and Kentucky, the
losses due to slave flight had become intolerable. For slaveholders from further south, in places where fugitives were less likely
to escape to the North, the audacity of fugitives like Henry "Box"
Brown and their Northern supporters furthered their conviction
that the North was irredeemably hostile to slavery.[4]

In January 1850, Senator James Mason of Virginia introduced
a new fugitive slave law that would replace the law of 1796, which
most Southerners believed was no longer effective. Mason specifically cited Pennsylvania's anti-kidnapping law of 1847 as one of the
main reasons why new federal legislation was needed. Mason and
his allies in the Senate scoffed at supposed Northern fears of kidnapping, the ostensible justification for such laws. It was, instead,
slaveholders, argued Senator Jefferson Davis of Mississippi, who
had to fear the kidnapping of their "servants" while traveling in
the states of the North.[5]

Mason's proposed law was ultimately supplemented with a
series of amendments, but the final law was intended to circumvent Northern opposition to the recovery of fugitive slaves. It

did so in a number of ways. First of all, it established a system of commissioners, appointed by the U.S. Circuit Courts, who would be responsible for issuing a warrant in fugitive slave cases. These commissioners would be empowered to determine the legitimacy of fugitive slave claims. If they determined that an accused fugitive was, in fact, a fugitive slave, the commissioner would be paid a fee of ten dollars; if he decided that the claim was false (i.e., that the accused individual should go free), he would be paid five dollars. There would be no jury trial and accused fugitives were denied the right to testify on their own behalf. Those convicted of aiding or concealing fugitive slaves were to be fined up to $1,000 or subject to up to six months in prison. Marshals who refused to comply with a warrant for a fugitive slave were also subject to a $1,000 fine, and they were liable for the full value of any slave who escaped while in their custody.[6]

The fugitive slave bill provoked fierce opposition across the North. The strongest congressional voices of the antislavery movement particularly opposed the bill's denial of jury trials to accused fugitives, reasoning that without this protection the law was likely to condemn legally free Black Northerners to bondage. Nevertheless, this opposition was not enough. Slaveholders and their allies in Congress had stoked fears that without a significantly strengthened fugitive slave law it was only a matter of time before the Union collapsed. When the time for the vote came, enough reluctant Northern congressmen were conveniently absent that the fugitive slave bill passed, as a part of a larger Compromise of 1850. President Millard Fillmore signed it into law on September 18, 1850.[7]

Black Philadelphians did not need to wait long to see the bitter fruit of this new law. On the afternoon of October 17, at the request of Thomas Jones of Maryland, a deputy marshal arrested Henry Garnett. Jones claimed that Garnett, who worked in Philadelphia as a hod carrier (a manual laborer working in construction), was his slave. The following morning, he was brought before Judge Robert Grier, an associate justice of the U.S. Supreme Court, who was in Philadelphia serving his duties on the circuit court. Overnight, the Pennsylvania Abolition Society (PAS) had assembled a team of experienced attorneys, including David Paul Brown and

Charles Gibbons, men with years of experience defending accused fugitives.[8]

The PAS, it should be remembered, was not the organization that employed William Still. Often referred to as the "old" abolition society in order to distinguish it from the more recently founded, and more radical, Pennsylvania Anti-Slavery Society (PASS), the PAS eschewed the confrontational tactics of the PASS and instead emphasized legal means of assaulting slavery. And yet the distinctions between the radical PASS and the moderate PAS were always blurry. There were men and women who were members of both organizations, and in certain ways, whatever their differences, the two organizations were complementary.

In the Garnett case, the moderate PAS seems to have worked hand in hand with more radical elements in the abolitionist movement. While the court met in its rooms in the Old State House, which would only later come to be called Independence Hall, outside a crowd of African Americans gathered, waiting to hear news. Garnett's lawyers assured the judge that they had "already held meetings for the purpose of allaying the excitement among the colored population, growing out of the passage of the fugitive slave law." At the same time, they called into question the legitimacy of the documents that Jones's lawyer had presented as proof of his ownership of Garnett. In fact, Judge Grier had privately met with Jones and warned him not to proceed until his evidence was conclusive. Despite this warning, Jones proceeded with his case.

Grier was acutely aware of the politically contentious nature of the situation. He had no sympathy for radical abolitionists and yet he wanted to be sure that this case, one of the first to be prosecuted under the Fugitive Slave Law, was beyond reproach. Any irregularity on the part of the court might be disastrous. He knew that just days earlier a mob of African Americans had attacked a courtroom in Harrisburg, Pennsylvania, in order to liberate condemned fugitives. He wondered what the crowd of Black Philadelphians gathered outside his courtroom was planning to do. Ultimately, Grier decided that Jones's lawyer had not sufficiently proved his case; he released Garnett to a cheering crowd outside, which carried him "away amidst the most extravagant shouts of exultation."[9]

. . .

The Garnett case provided concrete evidence for the dangers that the Fugitive Slave Law posed even to legally free African Americans, but it also showed the power of Black resistance. Free Blacks and their white allies sprang into action across the North in response.[10] In Philadelphia, leading Black abolitionists organized a meeting at Brick Wesley Church, a "large and commodious building"[11] on Lombard Street, not far from where the Stills lived. William Still, in fact, was chosen as secretary for the meeting. Many of the men who joined him in the leadership of this meeting were far more experienced and had deeper roots in the Black community of Philadelphia, but clearly Still's work as a clerk at the Anti-Slavery Society placed him in the forefront of the fight for fugitive slaves.[12]

The Black community of Philadelphia was up in arms at the newly passed law, and the meeting church was "densely crowded" and enthusiastic. The leadership committee introduced a series of resolutions that were unanimously approved by the attendees. They appealed both to the "inalienable rights" of the Declaration of Independence and to the protections of the Constitution against illegal imprisonment. This Fugitive Slave Law, insisted the meeting, was "in clear, palpable violation" of these founding principles. Beyond this, the "colored citizens of Philadelphia" appealed to God's justice. "We deem the laws of God at all times paramount to any human laws," they insisted. "We shall never refuse aid, and shelter, and succor to any brother or sister who has escaped from the prison-house of Southern bondage." They would do so, even if it cost them their lives. To strike home the Revolutionary resonance of this commitment, to show that their resolution to fight the Fugitive Slave Law was not a repudiation of their American citizenship but its fulfillment, they quoted Patrick Henry: "Give me Liberty, or give me Death."[13]

Nor was this sentiment purely rhetorical. Black abolitionists had long championed the use of force in defense of their freedom. In a letter published in the *Pennsylvania Freeman*, Still recounted an incident in January 1851. A group led by a deputy marshal named Halzell had arrived at a house where they believed they would find a fugitive slave they had been engaged to claim. Instead, when they got to the house they found "a Committee of colored men ready to receive them."[14] Not only were free Blacks mobilizing to prevent the enforcement of the Fugitive Slave Law, Still also made sure that such efforts were publicized, as a warning. He wanted slave catchers to know that even with this new law on their side they would not have an easy task if they wanted to claim fugitive slaves.

Two additional incidents, in late 1850 and early 1851, would reinforce the sense of all Black Philadelphians, whether they were legally free or not, that they were vulnerable to the new Fugitive Slave Law. On December 21, 1850, Adam Gibson was standing on the corner of Second and Lombard Streets when he was seized by three men, including the notorious slave catcher, George Alberti, dragged into a carriage, and driven to the statehouse, where counsel for William Knight of Cecil County, Maryland, claimed that Gibson was in fact a slave named Emery Rice. After a brief hearing, in which several Black witnesses claimed that Gibson was who he said he was, U.S. commissioner Edward Ingraham decided that Gibson was actually Rice and remanded him to the counsel for the claimant. They were escorted by a marshal and twenty-five officers to make sure that they made it safely to the ferry, where they would begin their journey back to Maryland. According to witnesses, "a large crowd of all colors followed, but made no attempt to rescue him." When Gibson arrived in Maryland, however, his supposed owner, William Knight, took one look at him and said, "That is not my slave; I know this man, Adam—he was formerly a slave in this neighborhood; how he obtained his liberty, I do not know; he is not mine." Gibson was returned to Philadelphia, but the reliance on the honesty of slaveholders to confirm the identity of legally free Blacks was hardly reassuring.[15]

On February 6, 1851, Euphemia Williams, who lived with her husband and six children in Kensington, then a municipality to the north and east of the city of Philadelphia, was arrested as a fugitive slave. Her claimant insisted that her name was Mahala Purnell and that she was a slave who had fled from Worcester County, Maryland, in 1829. As in the Gibson case, Williams and her counsel, in this case veteran abolitionist lawyer David Paul Brown, produced compelling witnesses who testified that Williams was who she said she was. The claimant, on the other hand, could produce only witnesses who had not seen the supposedly enslaved woman in more than twenty years. Their descriptions were, unsurprisingly, vague. Given the imbalance in the evidence, Judge John Kane of the Eastern District Court was forced to dismiss the case, despite his admitted sympathies for the Fugitive Slave Law. When he announced his decision, the courtroom erupted with applause and the newly freed Williams was paraded through the streets and back to her home by a crowd of Black women.[16]

Despite this happy result, there were grim lessons to be learned from the Williams case as well. Certainly, it was possible for accused fugitive slaves to win cases, but to do so would require expert legal support, and even then, only in the most clearcut cases could legally free Black citizens of Philadelphia hope to defend their hard-won liberties. Of course, those who were actually fugitives from slavery could take little comfort in the Williams case. For Still and his allies, the lesson was that it was best to keep fugitive slaves out of the courtroom altogether.

In the meantime, Still found himself once again embroiled in his brother's affairs. Shortly after reuniting with his family, Peter Still had returned to Alabama to see his wife, Vina, and his children. Upon reaching them, he told them of the plan he had developed: he would return to the North, where he could earn enough money to buy his family and bring them north to live with him. Peter spent two months in Alabama, earning enough for his trip back north. He then returned to Philadelphia, to William's house, at the end of November.[17]

While he was absent from Philadelphia, Peter Still had become an abolitionist cause célèbre. Just a week after reuniting with his brother, William Still had written a letter detailing the incident that was published in the *Pennsylvania Freeman*.[18] In the time that Peter was gone, supporters had contributed one hundred dollars to help pay for the purchase of his family. When he returned to his brother in Philadelphia, however, many of his new supporters began to urge him not to purchase his family, but to help them escape. It is unclear what William thought of this new plan, but evidently "many of [William's] friends were earnest advocates of such a plan." First, the cost of purchasing Peter's whole family would be substantial. Peter, for example, had purchased his own freedom for $500. It would take some time to raise such a sum for each family member. Who knew what would happen to Peter's family in the meantime? Additionally, many abolitionists in William's circle were philosophically opposed to paying slaveholders to emancipate their slaves. Doing so, they argued, "would in some sense recognize the right of the slaveholder to claim property in human flesh."[19]

Peter was uncertain about the new plan, but he felt somewhat intimidated by his brother's associates. He knew better than they did the risks that such a plan entailed. The greatest barrier, as Peter saw it, was the need for an individual who would actually go south to Alabama in order to pull this scheme off. This barrier was managed, however, by the appearance of a white man named Seth Conklin (sometimes spelled Concklin). Conklin was a bit of a mystery. He was in his late forties, and he had been born in New York. He lived, it appears, in a South Philadelphia boardinghouse with his two sisters. He had not been a member of any abolitionist society, though he seems to have long been a supporter of the movement and in particular a defender of fugitive slaves. Conklin had been so moved upon reading Peter's story that he resolved to do anything he could to rescue his family. He was, according to one observer, "plainly dressed, and slightly built, but evidently active and vigorous, with a face expressive of great decision." Conklin set out for Alabama in January 1851.[20]

His plan was to first explore the route that they would use to escape. Peter's family was enslaved on a plantation in the northwest corner of Alabama, so an escape route was bound to take them hundreds of miles through slave states, and of course even once they had gotten to the North they would continue to be in danger. After he made contact with Peter's family, they would all make their way north by any means they could discover.[21]

Conklin periodically updated William Still as to his progress. His letters show an increasing sense of the difficulty of the path set before them. He had hoped to identify white allies in the counties just across the Ohio River, but found doing so more difficult than expected. Describing the area opposite Paducah, Kentucky, "the whole country, fifty miles round," he wrote to Still, "is inhabited only by Christian wolves." He could rely on little aid in these areas. He made contact with Peter's family, but he was acutely aware of the danger he faced. "I am evidently watched," he wrote to Still.[22] Two weeks later he again wrote Still, this time informing him of a change of plans. Rather than bring Peter's family directly to Philadelphia, Conklin, now calling himself "Miller," would head north, through Indiana, and take them to Canada via Detroit. This would get them off the Ohio River and away from slave territory sooner.[23] In March, Still received word that Peter's family had made their escape and were in southern Indiana.[24]

Just as quickly as their hopes were raised, though, they were dashed. Only a few days after this last message, Still spotted a short paragraph in a Philadelphia newspaper. "At Vincennes, Indiana, on Saturday last, a white man and four negroes were arrested. The negroes belong to B. McKiernon of South Florence, Alabama and the man who has running them off calls himself John H. Miller." Not long after, Still received letters from abolitionists N. R. Johnson and Levi Coffin, confirming this story. Peter's family had been captured and were being taken back to Alabama. Conklin was seized as well and it was presumed that he would go south to face slaveholder justice, but he never made it. His body, still shackled, his skull fractured, was found on a riverbank.[25]

Not long after this, Still reached out to McKiernon, on Peter's behalf, in order to inquire about purchasing Peter's family. They knew, of course, that McKiernon had never been interested in selling, and that the attempted escape would only make him less interested, but they could only hope that he might somehow change his mind. On August 8, 1851, Still received a letter from McKiernon, setting the price for Peter's family—his wife, Vina, and his three children—at $5,000.[26] This was an exorbitant sum, but Still responded to this letter on Peter's behalf, offering $2,500, which he was nearly certain that they would not be able to raise. He appealed to McKiernon's "humanity," to his "heart," his "conscience." He never received a response.[27]

· · ·

Even as Still sought to negotiate for the purchase of his brother's family, he continued to be vigilant for slave catchers prowling the alleys and wharves of Philadelphia. "We have not had any more fugitive cases in Philadelphia since I last wrote you," he informed Henry Bibb in May 1851, "but we are at this moment watching the kidnappers, with whom it is reported we are to have a combat; indeed we are now all the while on the lookout for them."[28] Still and his allies were well aware which of the policemen and constables of their city were willing to work as slave catchers, and they kept careful watch on these disreputable characters.

The Anti-Slavery Society office was the center of a network that brought fugitives into Philadelphia in order to forward them on to places up north, but for similar reasons it was also a center for collecting information to be distributed along that same network. This was especially the case in the years after the passage of the Fugitive Slave Law. This information often proved vital to the cause. In September 1851, Still received word of an impending attempt to seize four men in Christiana, Pennsylvania, some forty miles west of Philadelphia, near Lancaster. Edward Gorsuch, the Maryland slaveholder who claimed these men as his property, had traveled to Philadelphia in order to appeal to Judge Kane of the Eastern District Court for warrants under the Fugitive Slave Law. Still and his abolitionist allies had informants throughout the city, but in this case the information likely came from Judge Kane's own son, Thomas, who had become a committed abolitionist. The younger Kane passed along word that within a few days a party would be leaving Philadelphia with the warrants.[29]

Swift action was needed if the claimed fugitives were to be alerted to the threat. Still knew one Samuel Williams, a Black man who was reliable and who had lived near Christiana. He enlisted Williams as an agent, paying his expenses so that he might bring this news to the Black community of Christiana. Williams actually traveled along with the slave-catching posse, gathering information as they traveled and then departing from them as they neared their destination.[30]

Christiana and the surrounding countryside were home to a

close-knit Black community that had good cause to be vigilant against threats like the one they now faced. On one hand, a fair number of the members of this community were in fact fugitive slaves; they were well aware that the new Fugitive Slave Law made their liberty tenuous. Beyond this, though, the region had witnessed an epidemic of kidnappings in recent years, many of them carried out by the infamous "Gap Gang," a notorious group of villains involved in horse-stealing, counterfeiting, and burglary on top of their robust business as kidnappers. Black residents of this region, therefore, were well prepared to defend themselves.[31]

Gorsuch's party, led by Henry Kline, a man Still termed "a notorious slave-catching constable from Philadelphia," approached the house of William Parker before daylight on September 11, 1851. They had been told that two men claimed by Gorsuch had taken refuge in the house. Parker himself was a fugitive slave. A man named Joshua Kite had just left Parker's house when he spotted the group. Kite, who was in fact one of the men Gorsuch sought, raised the alarm and retreated to Parker's house. They followed him into the house, attempting to seize Kite, but Parker intervened. Kline identified himself and called for Parker to surrender the two men. He refused, and a tense exchange between the two groups continued for some time. Parker's wife, Eliza, crept up to the garret of the house, lifted a horn they kept there, and used it to sound an alarm. This spurred Gorsuch to fire his pistol at Parker, who was then leaning out the window. Parker and his allies returned fire.[32]

Before long, in answer to the horn, neighboring supporters, most but not all of them Black, began to arrive at the Parker home. Within an hour and a half there were between thirty and fifty, "most of them armed in some way." One of these arrivals, Castner Hanway, a white miller and Quaker, tried to convince Kline to leave; shortly afterward, he was joined by another white Quaker, Elijah Lewis. They could not possibly prevail, the two warned the slave catchers, and by continuing to press the issue they were placing their lives in jeopardy. Kline, frustrated but clearly afraid, decided to withdraw to safer ground, but Gorsuch remained. Finally, one of the group, Samuel Thompson, one of the fugitives, came to the door and warned Gorsuch, "Old man, you had better go home to Maryland." Infuriated, Gorsuch told Thompson to "give up and come home with me," whereupon Thompson stuck his former master in the side of the head with a pistol, dropping him to his knees. When Gorsuch attempted to rise, Thompson knocked him back to the ground and then shot him. Others fell upon Gorsuch with guns, blades, and clubs. Gunfire blazed on all sides. When Gorsuch's son attempted to come to his father's aid, one of Parker's allies blasted him at short range with a shotgun, though he would live. His father, however, was dead. The rest of the group fled in the face of armed Black resistance.[33]

Unsurprisingly, it was not long before such bold action brought an equally forceful response. Within two days of the successful defense of the fugitives at Parker's house, a U.S. marshal, accompanied by a U.S. district attorney, forty-five U.S. marines, and about forty members of the city marshal's police force had all arrived from Philadelphia. They, along with a large number of local constables, attempted to round up all who had been involved. To a significant extent this meant indiscriminate seizure of any Black man they could find along with the two white men who had attempted to intervene. Parker and the two men whom Gorsuch had attempted to claim had already fled the scene, ultimately heading for Canada.[34]

While the men at the center of the resistance at Christiana were gone, there was tremendous pressure on the government to make an example of all who remained. Southern defenders of slavery howled and pointed to Christiana as evidence that the North could never be trusted to honor the Compromise of 1850.[35] After a brief hearing in Lancaster (mostly relying on the testimony of white authorities and coerced Black witnesses), and at the urging of the president of the United States, the accused were remanded to authorities in Philadelphia where they were to be tried by the federal courts for treason.[36]

While the prisoners were held in Moyamensing Prison in South Philadelphia, abolitionists, and in particular Black Philadelphians, rallied to their cause. On October 10, Still and several allies from the Vigilance Committee called for a County Convention of Colored People that would raise funds for "our brethren now in prison, falsely charged with treason."[37] Such was the interest in supporting the Christiana prisoners that there were competing groups raising money. A group calling itself the "Special Vigilance Committee," made up of Black abolitionists (not including Still), issued its own appeals for support, while the PASS recommended that funds be entrusted to a committee headed by Passmore Williamson, a white abolitionist who was both secretary of the PAS, the old Abolition Society, and a staunch defender of fugitive slaves and a close ally of Still in this work.[38] In a move that alienated some of his Black allies in the movement, it seems that Still expressed his support for Williamson and the PAS- and PASS-sponsored committee, believing that the Special Vigilance Committee was inefficient and wasteful with its funds. Years later Still would point to this disagreement as the genesis of a long-running feud with some members of the Special Vigilance Committee.[39]

Nor was the support for the prisoners limited to fundraising. The man whom Still had enlisted to bring word to Christiana in the first place, Samuel Williams, was empowered by the PAS

The Christiana Rebellion, as depicted in Still's *Underground Railroad*
(Library Company of Philadelphia)

to visit the prisoners and see to their needs. A sympathetic U.S. marshal made it possible for Williams and others to visit the prisoners.[40] The same marshal, whom Still would years later reveal to have been "a friend of the Underground Rail Road," helped two of the prisoners escape when it was discovered that they were fugitive slaves.[41] A group of abolitionist women paid for barbers to visit the prisoners and provided identical clothes for them, so that when the Black defendants arrived in court they were clean-shaven and identically clothed with matching red, white, and blue scarves, a bit of theater that demonstrated the respectability of the defendants even as it made it difficult for witnesses to differentiate them; the scarves reminded the jury that these men were American citizens.[42]

Ultimately, these efforts paid off. The prosecution decided to try each defendant separately, and when the jury took only fifteen minutes to acquit the first defendant, Hanway, on all charges, the prosecution realized its odds were hopeless and decided not to press charges against the others. In the view of Maryland attorney general Robert Brent, the jury's decision, and the ultimate failure to convict any of the defendants, was a result of conditions in the courtroom, especially the presence of large numbers of Black spectators. "Free negroes," Brent alleged, "were admitted through the Marshal's office into the courtroom, while crowds of white citizens were kept outside the door." Black Philadelphians, it seems, had used their physical presence to influence the court. White Southerners were outraged, and even "moderate" whites feared that the Christiana violence and the acquittal of its perpetrators would only lead to more violence.[43]

Abolitionists, on the other hand, were ecstatic. In the aftermath of the trial, Still was one of many abolitionists who sought to take advantage of the favorable verdict in order to advance the antislavery cause. In a letter to Henry Bibb's *Voice of the Fugitive*, published in Canada among a community of Black refugees from the United States, Still celebrated what he hoped would be the renewed attention to the illegal kidnapping that took place under the cover of the Fugitive Slave Law. "There is one feature about this trial which affords us very gratifying intelligence," writes Still, "the utter exposure of Kline and his villainous gang, who, under shelter of the Fugitive Slave Law, manage to acquire the title of 'Marshall,' whereby they have felt that they were authorized to commit all manner of outrage upon colored people with impunity."[44] In a letter to *Frederick Douglass' Paper*, Still taunted the governor of Maryland, Enoch Lowe, comparing him to an "Austrian Boar" he had recently seen in a painting exhibited in Philadelphia. Lowe's rage at the release of the Christiana prisoners, Still observed, resembled the boar, "black with madness, because his tyrannical savagery was defeated." The Christiana rebels had sent a message to slave catchers, that catching slaves was a dangerous business and that those they hunted were prepared to fight back. Still tried to ensure they got that message.[45]

Whatever sense of triumph that the defenders of fugitive slaves felt at the Christiana verdict, they also knew that the backlash to this dramatic act of self-defense was destined to be severe. Even after the passage of the Fugitive Slave Law, Pennsylvania continued to offer accused fugitives the defense of the state's 1847 anti-kidnapping law. Opponents claimed that this law violated the Compromise of 1850, and therefore threatened the Union itself, and both houses of the state legislature passed amendments that repealed some elements of the law that were most offensive to border-state slaveholders. The Whig governor of the state, William Johnston, though, vetoed these amendments, insisting that the 1847 law was an essential protection for the state's free Black citizens. The Christiana riot had made the law an issue in the gubernatorial election of 1851. Johnston's Democratic opponent, William Bigler, insisted that one of his first acts in office would be to repeal the offending portions of the 1847 anti-kidnapping law. When Bigler defeated Johnston, at least in part due to the broad revulsion that white voters across the state felt at the violence in Christiana, he made good on his promise.[46] Fugitive slaves escaping into Pennsylvania now knew that they could no longer rely on the protection of state law.

The denial of state protection only led Black Philadelphians to other means to protect themselves and their neighbors. On November 2, 1852, George Bordley was seized in South Philadelphia by local authorities under the leadership of George Alberti. He was brought before Commissioner Ingraham and found by the court to be a fugitive slave. Bordley was remanded to his alleged owner in Cecil County, Maryland. On the evening that Bordley was apprehended, a group of Black Philadelphians assaulted a Black man named Daniel Dempsey, who they believed had betrayed Bordley to the slave catcher Alberti. Newspapers reporting on the incident contended that Dempsey would have been killed had it not been for the intervention of "two white gentlemen" and then the police, who arrested "six or eight" of the assailants. Unscrupulous Black agents were often enlisted as allies by slave catchers and kidnappers. It is unclear what sort of evidence led Dempsey's assailants to believe that he had aided slave catchers, or even if he was truly guilty. Nevertheless, this group of Black Philadelphians sought to make sure that such allies would think twice before casting their lot with the enemy. If the law would not protect fugitive slaves, violence and intimidation would have to suffice.[47]

This conflict over the recovery of fugitive slaves, of course, meant that Still's work was increasingly dangerous, but closer to home he also continued to work with his brother Peter in order to rescue his family from bondage. Peter and William realized that if they were to have any hope of raising the money necessary to purchase Peter's wife and children, they could not simply rely on local abolitionists. In the fall of 1852, Peter set off to raise the money. He started for New York, where he stayed with his brother John, who had settled there, and proceeded to New England and then eventually to the abolitionist hotbed of the "Burned-Over District" of western New York. William wrote to Peter periodically, as his brother traveled from one abolitionist community to another. Wherever he went, Peter's story received a sympathetic hearing, and over the course of the journey, some of the most famous leaders of the abolitionist movement, Samuel May, Harriet Beecher Stowe, Horace Greeley, and Gerrit Smith among them, lent their name to Peter's effort. Black churches were particularly supportive, and thankfully, by the end of Peter's travels he had raised enough to purchase his family. They engaged an agent who facilitated the transaction, and the family was finally, and joyfully, reunited in Cincinnati, on the last day of 1854.[48]

William Still had contributed $50 of his own to his brother's effort to recover his family, which suggests something of the economic progress he had made in his time working for the Anti-Slavery Society. By no means was Still rich. The family continued to live in the small house on Ronaldson Street, adjacent to the cemetery, but several years of a steady salary, combined with William Still's frugality, seems to have enabled the family to put some money away. William and Letitia did their best to provide their small family with a safe and comfortable home.[49]

That home, of course, also welcomed increasing numbers of fugitive slaves. For Still and his allies, these were somewhat chaotic times. A great many fugitives passed through Philadelphia in these early years of the Fugitive Slave Law, and many fugitives from slavery who had settled in Philadelphia now no longer felt it was safe to remain. Newspapers frequently commented on the number of Black residents who were departing for settlements in Canada.[50] Many of those who aided fugitive slaves in Philadelphia felt that the time had come to reorganize the moribund Vigilance Committee. Its driving force, Robert Purvis, had moved his family out of the city. Accusations of the misappropriation of funds plagued the organization, and while the Vigilance Committee continued to occasionally aid those in need, by Still's account, most of the aid rendered to fugitives in these years came from those operating outside the formal structure of the Vigilance Committee. As a result, this work was "performed in a very loose and unsystematic manner."[51] In many cases, individual fugitives went directly to Black churches or wealthy abolitionists in order to beg for money that would enable them to move on from the dangerous ground of Philadelphia.[52]

In order to address these conditions, Still and a group of like-minded men met on December 2, 1852, to reorganize the Vigilance Committee. The stated goal of the meeting was to establish an organization that would be made up of trustworthy individuals, "who could be relied upon to act systematically and promptly, and with the least possible expenditure of money in all cases that might require their attention." This last part was essential. In the

Members of the Philadelphia Vigilance Committee—Still is in the
lower right-hand corner

years immediately prior to the establishment of this new Vigilance
Committee, many fugitives had been turned away due to lack of
sufficient funds. If the new committee was to aid as many people
as possible, it would need to be efficient.[53]

In order to achieve this efficiency, the men agreed, the association needed to be organized as simply as possible. There would

be a general committee, with a chairman to call meetings, raise funds, and supervise the acting committee. This acting committee would serve as the heart of the abolitionist community's work aiding fugitives from slavery. Still was named secretary of the larger general committee and chairman of the acting committee. The work that Still had been doing informally as an employee of the Anti-Slavery Society was now his official responsibility as head of the acting committee. While the general committee, chaired by Robert Purvis, was a mix of white and Black abolitionists, three of the four members of the acting committee were Black. Along with Still, this included veteran Underground Railroad activists Jacob C. White and Nathaniel W. Depee; the only white member of the acting committee was Passmore Williamson.[54]

One of the chief instructions that the organizing committee had given to the acting committee was that the chairman should keep records of all their actions and expenditures. Presumably they wished to avoid any dispute about such expenditures that might undermine the committee's work. It fell to Still, then, to keep these records, what would ultimately become the most valuable source historians have in uncovering the operations of the Underground Railroad. On Christmas Day, just weeks after the establishment of this new committee, Still entered the following in the committee's journal:

> Arrived—Hannah Jane Thompson; left Susex last Jan'y— first stopped with Jacob Paxson—went from his house to his Cousin's at Upper Dublin where she stayed 7 mos— Expenses + forwarding to J.R.G. $3.20[55]

Thompson had been staying for some time in settlements just outside of Philadelphia, sheltered by veteran activists with long-standing commitments to protecting fugitive slaves.[56] What spurred her to want to leave the area we cannot know for sure. Perhaps the rising number of fugitives remanded to the South under the Fugitive Slave Law convinced her that it was only a matter of time before her former master came looking for her. Perhaps there was something more personal, perhaps word that slave catchers were on her trail. In any case, she came to Still, who paid for her to move on to someplace safer. She would be the first of hundreds of fugitive slaves chronicled in Still's records who would make their way to freedom with the help of Still and the newly reconstituted Vigilance Committee.

CHAPTER FIVE

THE BUSINESS OF
THE UNDERGROUND RAILROAD

Henry Levison's road to Philadelphia was long and difficult. He had been enslaved to a Mrs. Peters, in Norfolk, Virginia, who died sometime in late 1852 or early 1853. Her estate was to be settled a year after her death, which meant that he was likely to be sold; the man who was to have taken possession of him had already told Levison as much. "I can get fifteen hundred dollars for you easily," he told him, "and I will do it." Levison swore that this would never happen, and he began to look for a way out of bondage. As the first of January, the day when this new owner would take possession of him, approached, however, Levison grew worried. It had been harder than he expected to find someone who could connect him to the Underground Railroad. Finally, though, Levinson found a man who would help him in return for thirty dollars. This was no small sum for Levison, but he was somehow able to put it together. Perhaps he had been saving up small sums here and there. Perhaps he borrowed it from a friend. However he managed it, it was all for nothing. The man in whom he had placed his trust betrayed him, taking his money and leaving him back where he started.[1]

When January 1 came, Levison had still found no connection to the Underground Railroad, so he hid. It is unclear where, exactly, but Levison hid out for ten months, waiting for some opportunity to get out of Norfolk. The port city was home to a substantial free Black population, so it is likely that he received aid from that quarter.[2] Finally, he received word that John Minkins, free Black steward on the steamship *City of Richmond*, would help him. Minkins agreed to hide Levison aboard the vessel for the two-day journey to Philadelphia. The six-foot-three, powerfully built Levison would need to conceal himself in a tight space, directly over the boiler, with barely enough room to sit up, but he deemed this a small price to pay for his freedom. Unfortunately, two days turned into eight, as stormy seas slowed the passage of the ship. When he arrived in Philadelphia, though, after the long, excruciating voyage, he told William Still that "he had resolved to die rather than give up to be taken into slavery." His triumph had come at a cost, however: he had left behind a wife and three children.[3]

Levison's story is typical of the accounts given to Still and the Vigilance Committee in the early years of its reconstituted existence. Over and over fugitives cited the fear of being sold as a prime catalyst for running away, even if that meant leaving behind loved ones. For many, family had been the thing holding them in place all along, and they were ready to risk flight if their masters intended to tear them from their families anyway. While fugitives sometimes ran away with family members, often this was not possible. Additionally, Levison's case shows that it was not a simple thing to make contact with the Underground Railroad; frequently those claiming to have some connection with it were simply looking to take advantage of desperate men like Levison. In addition, once an individual ran away, it often took some time before he or she found a way to travel very far. If they were lucky, would-be fugitives found someone like Minkins, a man they could trust, who could help them and who had connections in the North—a man who could get him in touch with William Still.[4]

Levison's escape is but one illustration of the ways that Still's Underground Railroad network capitalized on the explosion of transportation networks. The expansion of coastal steamship service, a major part of what historians have termed the "transportation revolution," in the 1840s and 1850s opened tremendous opportunities for fugitive slaves. Regularly scheduled packet lines made travel between Philadelphia and bustling slave-state ports like Norfolk, Wilmington, and Charleston more reliable, and these journeys took far less time than they had just a few years earlier.[5] Of course, local authorities were also keenly aware of the possibilities these ships posed for fugitive slaves and did their best to make sure that ships leaving their waters were not carrying fugitives.[6]

As Levison's escape shows, however, there were quite a few men and women who were ideally positioned to help fugitives elude these authorities. Still and the Vigilance Committee had long-standing connections to some of them. Men like John Minkins, who aided Levison in his escape, are sometimes referred to as agents or conductors. Such language risks overstating the formality and organization of the vast, decentralized enterprise that sought to aid fugitives. Often those who aided fugitives did so without much connection to a broader network. In this case, though, it is clear that Still did have some sort of ongoing relationship with Minkins, and with others like him. Local networks like the one in Norfolk, where Minkins operated, needed to get word to Still and his allies so that they were ready to assist fugitives once they reached Philadelphia.

During 1853, in the year after the reformation of the Vigilance Committee of Philadelphia, Minkins became one of Still's most reliable allies and the ship on which he served, the *City of Richmond*, became one of the most frequent means by which fugitives came to Philadelphia. On September 23, Still recorded that $1.25 was spent in order to secure John Henry Hill passage aboard the *City of Richmond*.[7] A month later, another fugitive, Nelson Harris, also secured passage aboard the same ship. He too told Still that he had been induced to run away out of fear of being sold; the Vigilance Committee provided him with one and half days' board, paid $2 for his fare to New York, and sent him on his way with an additional dollar in cash.[8] Then, on December 13, three more fugitives arrived in Philadelphia, all three hidden aboard the *City of Richmond*. Once again, these men were clearly aided by Minkins and Willam Bagnell, a white accomplice. In a letter sent from Toronto two months after their escape, one of these men, Isaac Forman, asked Still to "give my love to Mr. Bagnel [*sic*] and Mr. Minkins."

He also asked if Minkins had found any way to send Forman's wife along to Canada.[9] A little less than a year later, the Vigilance Committee paid the substantial sum of $30 to William Bagnell.[10] The committee's records do not specify the particular purpose of this expenditure, but certainly it was compensation for money Bagnell had spent in aiding fugitives.

White Virginians took notice of these exploits. Following the escape of James Mercer, William Gilliam, and John Clayton, who hid aboard the *City of Richmond* in a small space near the boiler "where the heat and coal dust were almost intolerable," their former mistress, a widow, enlisted the slave-trading agency Toler & Cook to find them. An editorial in the *Richmond Dispatch* (which Still clipped and kept in his files) reported that "these negroes . . . have been raised with the greatest indulgence" and that "their flight has left her penniless." Sometime later, the widow discovered that Gilliam had settled in Canada, where she sent him a letter scolding him for "acting most dishonorably" and complained that she was "badly situated" and "miserably poor." Perhaps Gilliam and Still had a good laugh at the laments of this "kind-hearted widow," but somewhat more serious was the fact that suspicion for the escape had fallen on John Minkins. He was arrested and placed in jail, though ultimately there was not enough evidence found against him and he was released. In his correspondence with Still, Gilliam, writing from St. Catharines in Canada, insisted that he be kept informed of the legal troubles that his "friend Mr. Meakins [*sic*]" faced.[11]

It was of course imperative that Still and his allies do much of this work in the shadows, but nevertheless the Vigilance Committee had taken on increasingly public responsibilities in the years after its reestablishment. The leaders of the effort to aid fugitive slaves realized that the only way to raise enough money to support their clandestine labor was, ironically, to do so in public. American abolitionists had long found allies across the Atlantic, and British abolitionists became an important source of financial support. American abolitionists corresponded with their British brethren, and many made the journey across the Atlantic in order to personally ask for support from the British public. In April of 1853, Still's employer, Miller McKim, was sent by the PASS on a public tour to raise funds among the abolitionists of Great Britain.[12]

In such cases it was common for prominent abolitionists to provide letters of introduction to encourage the trust of abolitionists across the Atlantic. The Vigilance Committee provided McKim with just such a document, a resolution authorizing him to represent and promote the work of the committee while on his journey; the committee presented him with a beautifully hand-scripted copy of this resolution, bearing Purvis's and Still's signatures, to take with him, assuring all readers that McKim was "an uncompromising advocate of universal Freedom."[13]

While McKim was gone, much of the work that he did in the Anti-Slavery Society office would fall on Still's shoulders, even more than it already did. The fact that the PASS largely trusted him to run the office on his own in McKim's absence suggests just how much confidence the leadership of the society had developed in Still over the years that he had been working there. In recognition of the increased work that they were handing over to Still, the executive committee agreed to raise Still's salary to thirty dollars per month. During McKim's absence, Still took over greater responsibility for the publication of the *Pennsylvania Freeman* and for other assorted publication work related to the business of the PASS. The everyday functioning of the organization was increasingly the responsibility of William Still.[14]

Despite the enormous demands that this additional responsibility placed on Still's time, he was also taking a greater, more public leadership role within Philadelphia's Black community. This public role included continuing participation in the periodic demonstrations of Black opposition to the American Colonization Society (ACS). As before, Still's opposition to the ACS and to its local and state auxiliaries was not driven by any abstract opposition to emigration. After all, he was increasingly involved in sending fugitive slaves outside the United States in order to evade the Fugitive Slave Law. What Still and his allies objected to was colonization's explicit insistence that free Black people could never be citizens in the land of their birth. Any support for African colonization, then, was a tacit admission that Black people could not be

American citizens. In Still's mind, the flight of fugitives to Canada was a purely practical measure and made no such admission.

On August 30, 1853, Black Philadelphians hosted a meeting to express their opposition to colonization, to issue a "strong expression of detestation." Still was named the secretary of the meeting, which was held at Brick Wesley AME Church. A number of prominent speakers, some local and some who had traveled a great distance, laid out the case against the ACS, an organization that they believed was "striving to increase the prejudices of the whites against the free colored people." The ACS could not be trusted, insisted Robert Purvis in his speech to the meeting, "seeing that slaveholders and their apologists are among its most active supporters." Mary Ann Shadd, a Canada-based abolitionist and writer, denounced colonizationists for playing to the "lowest prejudices of the whites." Frances Ellen Watkins, a free Black woman from Baltimore, niece to prominent Black leader William Watkins, read two of her abolitionist poems. The keynote address was delivered by Charles Lenox Remond, a prominent Black abolitionist from Massachusetts.[15]

The meeting is notable for a few reasons. First of all, it shows that while Still was devoting the bulk of his time to a very specific form of abolition, the aid of fugitive slaves, he was also taking a greater role in other parts of the movement. His appointment as secretary of this meeting suggests the increasingly prominent position he held in the Black abolitionist community of Philadelphia. Second, public meetings like this brought together like-minded Black leaders from across the nation and therefore helped expand Still's network, helped him build relationships with abolitionists from across the country, perhaps especially with those who shared Still's commitment to aiding fugitive slaves.[16] Purvis, of course, was already a Still ally, but in the coming years Still would build close working relationships with both Mary Ann Shadd and Frances Ellen Watkins.

Once Shadd returned to her home in Windsor, Ontario, she and Still maintained a steady correspondence. Born in Wilmington, Delaware, Shadd was the daughter of Abraham Shadd, a prosperous shoemaker and prominent abolitionist, and had moved to Canada with her family following the passage of the Fugitive Slave Law of 1850. She became a staunch advocate for Canadian emigration, publishing *A Plea for Emigration or Notes of Canada West*, in 1852, making her case for the virtues of Canada for refugees from American slavery. By 1853, however, she had ambitions to publish a newspaper of her own; in March she published the inaugural issue of the *Provincial Freeman* but then suspended publication while she traveled through the United States building support for the fledgling newspaper. By the following year, the paper had begun to appear regularly, and it became a vehicle for Shadd's brand of abolitionism: supportive of Canadian emigration, but also deeply committed to racial assimilation.[17]

Still strongly supported Shadd's work, and Shadd, in turn, frequently published Still's correspondence in the *Provincial Freeman*, providing her readers with a running account of the abolitionist scene in Philadelphia, but their private correspondence shows that the two had developed a warm friendship that went beyond their professional obligations. A January 1854 letter from Still to Shadd shows a bit of his playful humor. After complaining about how many letters he had recently written he apologized that his letter to her would be brief and uninteresting. "I hope your liberality will pardon me," he continued. "You know you are one of the 'weaker vessels.' Therefor you are in duty bound to take what you can get."[18] In February of 1854 he sent her a "musty" volume of Shakespeare "as a New Year's present."[19]

Still also became a staunch supporter of the talented poet and abolitionist Frances Ellen Watkins. Watkins had been born in Baltimore to a prominent free Black family. At twenty-one she published her first collection of poems, *Forest Leaves, Autumn Leaves*. When she was twenty-six she moved to Ohio to take a teaching position, and eventually she settled in Philadelphia, where she published her renowned collection, *Poems on Miscellaneous Subjects*, in 1854. Still became a friend and ally and assiduously promoted her writing.[20] He wrote to Shadd asking her to print some of Watkins's poems and praising the work of the "gifted Miss Frances E Watkins." He assured Shadd that Watkins's work would "accord to the authoress high intellectual culture," and he predicted that her writing "will rank as high, if not higher, than any production of the kind ever published in this country by a colored person." Shadd evidently agreed with Still's assessment of Watkins's talent; she published a poem of hers in the September 2, 1854, issue of the *Provincial Freeman*, preceding it with Still's letter of testimonial.[21]

On one hand, Still's close working relationship with these women should be unsurprising. Women were the foundation of the abolitionist movement. While there were some abolitionists who felt that women should play an auxiliary role, that men should lead, Still was most closely aligned with the Garrisonian branch of the movement, which advocated for full equality of the sexes. From the time Still went to work at the PASS, the organization's executive committee had featured the work of dynamic women like Lucretia Mott, Sarah Pugh, and Mary Grew.[22] Even before that, his work at the Moral Reform Retreat had led Still to work side by side with Black women like Hetty Reckless and Hetty Burr.[23] On the other hand, Still's own marriage seems to have adhered to more traditional gender roles. Letitia Still was an important part of her husband's antislavery work, but for the most part the role she played was a domestic one. When Still opened their home to fugitive slaves, Letitia helped to ensure that they were welcome and comfortable. Perhaps this reflected the Stills', or at least William Still's, aspirations to middle-class status. In any case, his relationships with ambitious Black women like Watkins and Shadd showed his belief that women were capable of playing a vital role in the movement in any number of ways.

Closer to home, though, the Still household relied on Letitia's labor in addition to William's, as the couple struggled to establish themselves within Philadelphia's sizable Black middle class. She worked out of their home on Ronaldson Street, making dresses "in the best manner," and advertising these services in the *Pennsylvania Freeman*.[24] William also sought to supplement his regular but still meager salary at the Anti-Slavery Society with a series of side businesses. From his earliest days at the PASS, on the advice of his boss, Miller McKim, Still had put aside some of his salary in order to invest in real estate, beginning with a West Philadelphia lot he purchased for $33 in 1850. He would continue this practice throughout his life.[25] He had other small businesses as well. In

1853 he was listed as the contact for those looking to purchase "good Schuylkill coal," available at $5 a ton.[26] Whatever Still was able to make from these projects was a welcome addition to his growing family; he and Letitia had added a second child, a son, in February 1854. They named him William Wilberforce Still, in honor of the great British abolitionist, or perhaps in honor of the free Black Canadian settlement that had been named for Wilberforce, suggesting in either case that Still, like many American abolitionists, saw the fight against slavery as a global struggle. That same year, Still also began renting a pew at the First African Presbyterian Church, just three blocks from their home.[27]

Of course, the Stills often shared their home with other guests as well. Still estimated that 95 percent of the fugitives who sought the assistance of the Vigilance Committee stayed in his home. Undoubtedly this meant that the work of maintaining the Still household, which largely fell on Letitia's shoulders, was substantial. In this way, the Stills were similar to other Black families who opened their homes to fugitives. Women's work on the Underground Railroad was vital, but it is often difficult for historians to see since it tended to leave less evidence than the more public-facing work of men. Fugitives might arrive at any time of the day or night, and it was Letitia who found them temporary beds, washed and mended their clothes, nursed the sick, fed the hungry, and generally sought to make these desperate souls as comfortable as possible. At times, if her husband was away, she needed to determine if a fugitive needed to be hidden or not. All of this had to be handled while she managed her own two small children. The Vigilance Committee compensated them for some of their expenses, but nevertheless, the labor and expense involved were substantial.[28]

It was especially meaningful that the Stills opened their home to fugitives and made them welcome because for so many the act of running away had torn them from their own families. American slavery had from its very beginnings splintered families, ripped husbands from wives, parents from children. This violent separation of families had only accelerated in the antebellum era as the

insatiable demand for slave labor on the cotton and sugar plantations of the Southwest fueled the interstate slave trade. Nevertheless, enslaved people fought to maintain the families they had, and
when necessary they built new families. These relationships were
an essential means of surviving the brutality of slavery. Leaving
behind such families was never easy. It is unsurprising that many
of the fugitives who found their way to Still had run away because
the sale of a loved one had broken up a family, or threatened to do
so. William Davis, who ran away from Portsmouth, Virginia, in
December 1853 is an example. Davis was married to an enslaved
woman named Catherine and the two had a two-year-old daughter
and a seven-month-old son. He "loved them tenderly," but when
his master threatened to sell him, Davis ran off. As much as he
loved his wife and children, he knew that if his master sold him,
he would likely never see them again, so he decided that it was
worth the risk to head north for freedom. "Before escaping," he
told Still, he "dared not" say goodbye to his family and so he left
them behind without a word.[29]

Many of the fugitives who passed through the Still household clearly appreciated the welcome they had been given, and
later when they wrote to Still they made sure he understood this.
"Give my respects to Mrs Still, tell her i want to see her very bad
and you also," wrote one former lodger who was now living in
New Bedford. "I would come but i am afraid yet to venture."[30]
Another wrote, "Give my love to Mrs. Still and also your dear
little children . . . I have not met any person who has treated me
any kinder than she did since I left."[31] Yet another asked Still to
"please give my love and Charlotte's to Mrs. Still and thank her for
her kindness to us while at your house."[32] The Stills had, if only
for a short time, offered them the warmth of family that they had
left behind when they ran.

For many fugitives, though, the pain of having left behind
loved ones only became worse as time passed. Fear drove them
as they fled from masters and slave hunters, but once they found
a safe place to settle, their hearts turned once again to wives, husbands, children. "My soul is vexed," wrote one such fugitive, Isaac
Forman, "my troubles are inexpressible. I often feel as if I were

willing to die. I must see my wife in short, if not, I will die." Forman had fled from Norfolk, Virginia, in December 1853, and had hidden aboard the *City of Richmond* with the help of John Minkins and William Bagnell. After passing through Philadelphia, Forman had gone to Canada, but he longed to be reunited with his wife. It was too dangerous to contact her directly or to contact the men who had helped him to escape, but he hoped that Still would be able to do so for him. "I hope you will do all you can for me, and inquire from your friends if nothing can be done for me."[33] Still received many such requests. He would later recall that his original reason for beginning his meticulous record keeping was his own miraculous reunion with his brother Peter, which inspired his hope that he might be able to bring other shattered families back together. Sometimes Still was able to reunite lost lovers, children, and siblings; sometimes he was not. There is no record of whether or not Isaac Forman ever saw his wife again.[34]

Before such men could have any hope of reuniting with loved ones, though, there was the practical concern of making sure they themselves stayed a step ahead of slave catchers. At times this meant concealing a fugitive in Philadelphia until the danger had passed. More often the Vigilance Committee tried to move at-risk fugitives out of Philadelphia as quickly and unobtrusively as possible. The problem is that men and women who had made the journey to Philadelphia, on foot, concealed in a steamship, or on the back of a horse, often looked like fugitive slaves. Sometimes fugitive slave advertisements specifically mentioned the clothes that fugitives had been wearing when they fled, but even if they did not, fugitive slaves often stood out. This was especially problematic if these fugitives were sent along their way by train or ship, where disheveled Black travelers would stand out even more than well-dressed ones. One of the first tasks, therefore, of Still and his allies was to make fugitives look respectable. The three men who arrived in Philadelphia on April 12, 1854, "appeared travel-worn, garments dirty, and forlorn," Still later recalled, "but the Committee had them cleanly washed, hair cut and shaved, change of clothing furnished &c., which at once made them look like very different men." Still dutifully recorded in his accounts the 44 cents he paid to have their hair cut and faces shaved, as well as the 37 cents he paid to have their shirts laundered.[35]

Sometimes fugitives had fled in such haste that they were forced to leave behind their belongings. It was no small thing to start over from scratch in a new city, and from time to time Still was able to make arrangements to recover some of the things that fugitives had left behind. In February 1854, Solomon Brown wrote Still from St. Catharines, Canada, to inform him that he had "arrived safe in the land of freedom," but he also asked for help. He asked Still to arrange for one of the men who worked on the ship that Brown had used to escape from Virginia to recover clothes Brown had abandoned when he fled. He asked that Still send these clothes on to a Rev. Hiram Wilson in St. Catharines, who would be able to get them to Brown. It is unclear if Still was able to arrange the recovery of Brown's possessions, but fugitive slaves continued to write to Still in hopes that he could help them regain some small part of what they had left behind.[36]

A remarkable number of fugitives who came through Still's door would plainly admit that their former master had not been particularly cruel; for most fugitives it was not the cruelty of a particular master that led them to flee, it was the systemic cruelty of slavery. As historian Walter Johnson has argued, the constant threat of sale inculcated a sort of "perpetual dread" in enslaved people, whether or not their particular master treated them cruelly. On occasion, though, it was the cruelty of a specific master that drove a fugitive to the road. This was the case for Wesley Kinnard, who arrived in Philadelphia in August 1854. Kinnard, formerly known as Samuel Green, had been enslaved to a man he considered "the worst man in Maryland." Kinnard was twenty-four years old, dark-skinned, and below medium height. Still remarked that the former slave was "smart, active—reads & writes and seems quite intelligent." Kinnard had fled Dorchester and a master who had whipped him and "inflicted all manner of cruelty upon his servants." Once Kinnard ran away, he seems to have had an uneventful journey, arriving in Philadelphia a week after he left his home in Maryland. Still and the Vigilance Committee provided him with letters of introduction and a small amount of cash, and after putting him up for four days, they sent him on his way. He eventually settled in Canada.[37]

Aside from having "the worst man in Maryland" for a master, Kinnard's story was relatively unremarkable, except for the fact that his flight had been inspired and assisted by Harriet Tubman. It is unclear when Tubman first met William Still. As with many fugitives from slavery, especially in the years before the passage of the Fugitive Slave Law of 1850, it is likely that Tubman just hoped to blend in, to start a new life in a city where she was just another free Black woman. It is possible that she met Still soon after her arrival in Philadelphia, though she makes no mention of it, and she does not appear in Still's records until 1854.

Whether or not she was in contact with Still, she soon found herself in the business of aiding fugitives. In December 1850, Tubman received word from friends and relatives that her niece, Kessiah, was to be auctioned off. Again, it is possible that Still and the Vigilance Committee had served as a conduit for this information; certainly Still had such connections. In any case, Tubman headed south, staying with her brother-in-law, Tom Tubman, in Baltimore. She and John Bowley, Kessiah's husband, concocted a plan to spirit her away from under the nose of her owner. Bowley shuttled her by boat to Baltimore, and Harriet guided her the rest of the way to Philadelphia. She returned to Baltimore a few months later to help her brother Moses and two other men escape. In the fall of 1851, she even dared to return to her native Dorchester County in hopes of reuniting with her husband. When she found him, though, she discovered that John had moved on and taken a new wife. Harriet was devastated, but nevertheless led another group of fugitives back to Philadelphia, leaving her former husband behind. By this time, though, Philadelphia was no longer safe, due to the passage of the Fugitive Slave Law, so Tubman guided this group on their way to the safety of Canada via New York, perhaps relying on Still's connections, perhaps not. After staying with this group for a while in St. Catharines, Tubman returned to Philadelphia in the spring of 1852. That summer she worked as a cook in Cape May, New Jersey, earning enough money to fund yet another trip into Maryland, where she helped liberate another eleven fugitives.[38]

In the spring of 1854, Tubman had once again traveled to her former home in Maryland; by this point she was clearly making use of the Philadelphia Vigilance Committee in her work. Still recorded a Winnibar (also known as William) Johnson who had been brought to Philadelphia by Tubman; before moving on from Philadelphia, Johnson stayed with Vigilance Committee ally Luke Goines, a Black hairdresser who lived on Lombard Street, not far from the Still home.[39] Evidently, while Tubman was rescuing Johnson, she had also left instructions for fleeing north with Wesley Kinnard, who did so at the earliest opportunity, happily finding his way to Still and the Vigilance Committee and leaving behind "the worst man in Maryland."[40]

In December 1854, Tubman once again journeyed into Maryland in order to rescue members of her family from bondage. This time as the group, which included her brothers Benjamin, Henry, and Robert Ross, came north they sought refuge in Wilmington with Still's ally Thomas Garrett. Tubman entrusted the group to Garrett's care and returned south without accompanying them to Philadelphia, though not before Garrett provided her with a pair of shoes to replace the ones that had "worn off [her] feet." He then arranged for "one of our trusty colored men" to guide them the rest of the way to the Anti-Slavery Society office, where they were received by William Still, who recorded their arrival on December 29. Two days later he noted $4 to be sent to Harriet Tubman.[41]

It had been a busy fall for the Vigilance Committee. Still received a veritable parade of fugitives, from Norfolk, from Baltimore, from Richmond, from Easton, Maryland. Some had been spurred to flight by "fear of sale," others by "severe flogging." They came by foot and they came "stowed away on the boat, in a sitting posture with barely enough room to Sit." Still paid for and dutifully recorded the purchase of shoes, socks, shirts, portage, carriage rides, postage on letters to Canada, and, of course, the costs of housing all of them.[42]

All of this cost money. The Vigilance Committee operated out of the office of the PASS, but to a significant extent it functioned independently. Miller McKim's sojourn to Great Britain had been somewhat successful in bringing in donations, but in order to compensate for the increasing number of fugitives it was aiding, the Vigilance Committee stepped up its fundraising efforts. In the fall of 1854, Still organized two meetings with an eye on bringing in money to support the committee's work. Still knew that Philadelphians were frequently asked for donations and so made sure that these meetings would draw a crowd. In addition to local leaders, the program for each meeting included a pair of stars in the abolitionist movement. The first was the fugitive slave, abolitionist, and author William Wells Brown, recently returned from a tour of Great Britain. Brown and Still had met a few years earlier and struck up a friendship. The second speaker, though, was the most prominent abolitionist of them all, William Lloyd Garrison. Many of the most influential abolitionists, including Frederick Douglass, had drifted away from Garrison, especially critical of his rejection of electoral politics. Some of these men would become supporters of the antislavery Liberty Party, but the leaders of the abolitionist movement in Philadelphia remained loyal Garrisonians. The first meeting, at the First African Presbyterian Church (the Stills' church), was well attended and brought in a significant sum for the cause. Much to Still's dismay, though, a second meeting, held at Franklin Hall the following evening, was less well attended; after accounting for the costs of arranging it, the meeting brought less than $25 for the Vigilance Committee.[43]

As the Vigilance Committee sought to aid more and more fugitives, Still came under greater pressure to use his funds efficiently and to be transparent in doing so. Some supporters of the Underground Railroad began to use the language of capitalism, perhaps jokingly but with a touch of seriousness, to refer to their work. "No man who wishes to invest capital in railroad stock," noted the Canada-based, Black-edited Voice of the Fugitive, "can do better than take stock in this prosperous business this fall."[44] Still frequently reported in the abolitionist press on the "business" of the Vigilance Committee, including the donations he and the committee had received. By ensuring readers that the committee operated in an efficient manner, Still helped reassure donors that their contributions would be put to good use by the business-like Underground Railroad.[45]

A part of this work was ensuring that the significant sums of money that were being distributed to fugitives were not misspent on charlatans and con men. Given the limited economic opportunities available to free African Americans, deep-pocketed philanthropists must have posed a tempting mark for the unscrupulous. An article in the September 22, 1853, issue of the *Pennsylvania Freeman* warned of an "imposter" who was claiming to be collecting money to aid a fugitive slave who had settled in Canada. In part, the Vigilance Committee was a check on such fraud. Its leaders warned generous would-be patrons of fugitives not to give directly to those who claimed to need their assistance. When Still or some other member of the acting committee interviewed a fugitive, they were, among other things, evaluating his story, making sure that it seemed genuine. From time to time they doubted the truthfulness of someone who claimed to be a fugitive. Generally, the committee would simply spread the word about such a person, privately or in the press, but occasionally they turned to the police to help rein in such fraud.[46]

This financial pressure led to some conflict within Philadelphia's community of Black abolitionists. This conflict came to a head in a meeting held at the Philadelphia Institute in late 1853, during which Still critics William Forten and James Bias (a former ally who had worked with Still assisting fugitive slaves) enlisted the support of others, including Charles Reason, the principal of the Institute for Colored Youth, in order to call into question Still's management of the Vigilance Committee. All of these men had been intimately involved in the committee's work, and all had worked with Still at some point. The exact nature of the criticism is unclear, though, based on a letter from Still to Mary Ann Shadd describing the meeting, it seems to have been related to the policy to channel all claimed fugitives through the Vigilance Committee (as opposed to allowing private individuals to extend charity). There also seems to have been some deeper tension between Still and his old ally Dr. Bias, though again the specifics of this conflict are unclear. Whatever the particulars, Still vehemently defended himself, especially against Reason, who Still felt had betrayed him. "I concluded my remarks by denouncing him quite as severely as my non Resistant principle would allow," Still wrote. "I have not said such harsh things to anybody for the last 12 years."[47]

This conflict shows a side of Still that had not previously been evident. Still had won respect and admiration within the abolitionist community, both locally and beyond. He was hardworking, compassionate, and meticulous. He was also proud. He could be thin-skinned and defensive when challenged. Over time, as his confidence in his own abilities grew, Still could be impatient with those who did not meet his exacting standards or who disagreed with his methods. He could be especially dismissive of those like Forten, the son of the revered abolitionist and businessman James Forten, who in Still's eyes had been handed privileges and opportunities for which Still had struggled all his life. Still, whose own personal conduct bordered on the austere, could also be critical of what he deemed the frivolity of others. He had little patience for those who seemed less committed than he to the abolitionist cause or to the uplift of the Black community.

Not only did Still voice these criticisms in private correspondence, but he increasingly felt comfortable doing so in public as well. In a letter to Mary Ann Shadd, which she subsequently published in the *Provincial Freeman*, Still lamented the unwillingness of free Blacks in the United States to support Black abolitionist newspapers like the *Freeman*. It was not, he insisted, that the Black population of the United States could not afford to support such papers. Rather, Still contended, the free Black population spent its money on frivolity. "We want to adorn ourselves to be seen in a parade of some sort; or to go on an excursion; to a picknick; fancy ball, sumptuous supper &c." Not only did spending in this way divert money from the abolitionist movement and from the cause of Black elevation, but, Still warned, this wastefulness "adds largely to the capital of our oppressors—the whites."[48] Still likely hoped that his words would guilt some of his less committed brethren into a greater commitment to the cause, but his harsh words surely created some enmity as well.

Whether or not he cared about such detractors, Still took his antislavery work seriously, and he knew that in his line of business any wrong step could have dire consequences. In May 1854, a man named Stephen Pembroke arrived in Still's office with his sons, Jacob and Robert. They had fled from slavery in Sharpsburg, Maryland, walking fifty miles to Chambersburg, Pennsylvania, before they dared to ride the train the rest of the way to Philadelphia. Much to Still's delight he learned that Stephen was brother to Dr. James Pennington, a Presbyterian pastor and abolitionist in New York City. Pennington had long been a part of the city's Underground Railroad network and Still promptly contacted him to share the good news of his family's escape from bondage. A grateful and relieved Pennington responded to Still's message. "My burden has been great about these brethren," he wrote Still. "I hope they have started on to me. Many thanks, my good friend." Still provided the three men with tickets for New York and they departed that very day in the company of several other fugitives as well as an experienced guide. The group arrived safely in New York and were reunited with Pennington, but at three o'clock the following morning a band of slave catchers burst in upon them "hyena-like" at the home where they were staying and arrested them. They were promptly brought before the commissioner and then placed, in chains, on a train back to Baltimore. Later their master would contact Pennington and offered to sell him his brother for $1,000. The abolitionist community of New York was able to scramble to raise this sum, but when the two brothers were reunited a second time their meeting was bittersweet: Pennington's nephews had been auctioned and sold to the Deep South.[49]

Still felt there were at least two causes for this tragic failure of the Underground Railroad, what he referred to as "the first accident that had ever taken place on the road after passengers had reached the Philadelphia Committee." First, he felt that Pennington had been incautious in allowing his brother and nephews to remain in New York even for a few hours, rather than immediately sending them on. Still admitted that Pennington had powerful reason to want his long-lost kin to remain a bit longer with him, but he felt that the danger was too great to have done so and that the men should have been immediately sent north to safety in Canada. He also believed that an informant had compromised the route between Philadelphia and New York. Evidently the slave catchers had been alerted to the presence of the three fugitives, perhaps by means of passenger pigeons, and they had actually boarded the very train on which the fugitives had been riding. Still was so convinced that this leg of the Underground Railroad had become unsound that for some time after, whenever possible, he avoided routing fugitives via New York City, sending them instead directly to Elmira in western New York.[50]

Perhaps sensitive to the fact that his management of the Vigilance Committee had recently been criticized, Still took to the press in order to portray his version of events, in order to defend his own conduct and the conduct of his organization. "The Committee, into whose hands they fell, before reaching New York," he assured the readers of the *Provincial Freeman,* "spared no pains to render their success sure; which resulted in their landing safely in that city." On one hand, we might view Still's public criticism of his New York allies as an act of defensiveness, as a deflection from the possibility that it had been Still's fault the Pembroke family fell into the hands of slave catchers. On the other hand, Still had practical reasons to defend the Philadelphia Vigilance Committee, reasons that had nothing to do with his pride. If fugitives began to mistrust the committee, they would be less likely to ask for its help. The success of Still's vigilance work relied not only on his efficiency and diligence but upon the trust that others placed in him. Once that trust was gone it would be difficult to recover. Only the most desperate fugitive slaves would be willing to ask for his help. "But sad and unfortunate as this affair has been," he reassured his readers, "it will not stop the Underground. It will increase its success. It will doubtless make many friends for the slave and the fugitives."[51]

Still was increasingly confident in his own abilities and judgment, and his confidence in his work on the Underground Railroad translated into other avenues. His letters to Shadd, which were published more and more frequently in late 1854, show a man who was comfortable weighing in on the broader issues of the day, not just those related to his specific work on the Underground Railroad. In the same letter in which Still had defended the Vigilance Committee's role in the Pembroke affair, he also commented upon the passage of the "Nebraska Bill." In the spring of 1854, Senator Stephen A. Douglas, Democrat of Illinois, had pushed through Congress a bill to split the Nebraska Territory into two parts, opening up the southern part, Kansas, as possible slave territory. Under the principle of popular sovereignty, the territory was to decide on its own whether to permit slavery, but in order to make this possible the bill had repealed the long-standing Missouri Compromise of 1820, which had designated the entire territory as "free." Many Northerners were outraged by this betrayal and by the violation of a compromise that after more than thirty years had seemed inviolable. Black Philadelphians organized a public meeting in March 1854, protesting the Kansas-Nebraska bill. Still shared this outrage, but he also saw the possibility that some good would come of it. "Really," he opined, "the signs of the times do seem to indicate, at last, that the North begins to see and feel the folly of her past conduct, in the innumerable concessions made to the South, and that she will not take a defensive position." Already, he insisted, Northern public opinion had started to turn, and the backlash against the Kansas-Nebraska bill had made white Northerners less likely to honor the Compromise of 1850 and its hated Fugitive Slave Law. Still injected a sense of optimism in the midst of what for many abolitionists was a moment of despair.[52]

Perhaps it was no coincidence, then, that around this time Still began to make use of the extensive records he was keeping on the Vigilance Committee's work in order to combat the creeping pessimism that he worried was undermining the fight against slavery. While he was of course sympathetic to those fugitive slaves who fled to Canada as a defense against slave catchers, he also wanted to be sure that those who remained behind continued the struggle, that they refused to surrender to the fatalism that held the United States to be irredeemably corrupted by slavery. The success of fugitives in evading their masters had long been held up by abolitionists as evidence of the progress of the antislavery spirit of the North. Now those who aided fugitive slaves sought to use these stories to buoy the sagging confidence of many supporters. An anonymous letter writer—who may very well have been William Still—captured this sentiment in the *National Anti-Slavery Standard*. "These beautiful Providences, these hair-breadth escapes and terrible dangers, will yet become the themes of the popular literature of this nation," wrote the correspondent, "and will excite the admiration, the reverence and the indignation of the generations yet to come who will award slavery to its just doom."[53]

Increasingly in his signed and published correspondence to the *Provincial Freeman*, Still included details about his Underground Railroad work. He closed his April 17, 1855, letter with the postscript: "Just had, this evening, a fine arrival per underground."[54] He began his letter of June 9, 1855, by noting that "Slave Catchers, referred to in my last, have not been seen or heard in this quarter since." Still needed to strike a careful balance between secrecy and publicity, dropping carefully chosen details into letters that he knew would be published, but making sure that those details did not put the operation of the Vigilance Committee at risk. These stories tended to speak in generalities, of hiding in caves and of fleeing through swamps chased by bloodhounds. They certainly did not reveal details of the more common and ongoing routes that fugitives took to get to Philadelphia. More and more, though, Still was using his public platform to tell the story of the Underground Railroad.[55]

Even as fugitives continued to pass through the Anti-Slavery Society office and the entries in his ledger multiplied, Still increasingly understood the connection between his own work in Philadelphia and the escalating national political crisis over slavery and its expansion. While some white abolitionists might see the work of the Vigilance Committee as distinct from the larger antislavery struggle, as an admirable endeavor but not ultimately an effective assault on slavery itself, Still understood that the Underground Railroad was an essential element of the conflict between slavery and freedom. The increasing efficiency that Still's management of the Vigilance Committee brought to the Underground Railroad meant that more and more fugitives passed safely through Philadelphia. The success of such an enterprise, not just in Philadelphia but across the free states, and the boldness and audacity with which it was accomplished, drove slaveholders to increasingly desperate measures. Still, then, was unsurprised by the bloody work of Missouri "border ruffians." By the mid-1850s he was already a veteran of what historian Stanley Harrold has termed the "Border War," which unfolded in the decades before the Civil War.

"Perhaps none or but very few have ever supposed that Missouri slaveholders would quietly submit to see northern men establish free institutions in Kansas," he wrote to the *Provincial Freeman*. "[T]he master well knows that the temptation, on their part, to take a trip on the underground railroad, would in most cases be irresistible."[56]

CHAPTER SIX

••

THE JANE JOHNSON AFFAIR

July 18, 1855, was a sweltering Philadelphia summer day.[1] William Still was at the Anti-Slavery Society office when a boy he had never seen before came in and handed him a note. He noted the time: half past four. The note was hastily scrawled and barely legible: "Sir. Will you come down to Bloodgood's Hotel as soon as possible—as there are three fugitive slaves here and they want liberty. Their master is here with them, on his way to New York."[2]

Whatever work Still had at hand, he put aside; he knew that he had little time to act. If the master mentioned in the note was indeed headed for New York, he would likely take the ferry that left at five, taking travelers across the Delaware River to New Jersey, where they would then connect with a train for New York. Bloodgood's Hotel was not far from the Walnut Street Pier, about eight blocks from the office. He would have to hurry.

Rather than going directly to the hotel, though, Still first headed to the office of Passmore Williamson, his colleague on the Vigilance Committee. Most of the day-to-day work of the committee was done by African Americans, but there was a single white member of the acting committee: Williamson. It would be useful to have a white man with him if there was trouble, and the office Williamson shared with his father was just a few blocks from the Anti-Slavery Society office.[3]

Still strode into Williamson's office and placed the letter on his desk. Thomas Williamson, Passmore's father, picked up the letter and looked at it. He handed it to his son, who also read it. Before either could say anything, Still proposed that they ask a judge for a writ of habeas corpus. The Anti-Slavery Society often made use of such tactics in cases like this; doing so would buy them time to devise some means, legal or otherwise, of securing the freedom of the fugitives in question. Passmore Williamson objected that there was not enough time to find

Still's Vigilance Committee ally, Passmore Williamson

a judge to issue the writ, even if a willing judge could be found. He urged Still to go to the hotel himself to aid the slaves. Williamson regretted that he would not be able to accompany Still, since he had pressing business that would require him to leave the city that evening. He suggested that if Still were not able to help the slaves he might telegraph ahead to New York, where with some more time to prepare they might be more successful.

Still started for the door, but before he stepped out into the street he turned back to Williamson. Was there anything to prevent the slaves from leaving their master, he asked, if they decided to do so on their own? No, replied Williamson. "They have a perfect right to go where they please, and they can do so unless forcibly restrained by their master." With this information, Still stepped out the door and headed for Bloodgood's. Williamson returned to his work, but a few minutes later he threw down his pen, got up from his desk, put on his coat, and without a word to his father fled the office.

The detour to Williamson's office had taken Still two blocks in the wrong direction, so he needed to hurry if he was to be of any help. The note had been vague so he was unsure of what to expect when he arrived at Bloodgood's Hotel. Would the slaves mentioned in the note be looking for him? How would the master respond? To Still's surprise, Williamson had hurried as well and arrived on the scene first. Still surveyed the scene looking for familiar faces but the only person he recognized was the boy who had first alerted him to the situation. Likely the boy was able to point Still to those who had originally written the note. In any case, the two abolitionists soon had the information they needed: the person they were looking for was "a tall, dark woman, with two little boys." Now that they knew who they would be looking for, Still and Williamson headed for the wharf, hoping that they would not be too late.[4]

By the time they arrived, many of the passengers had already boarded the ferry. The two abolitionists stepped aboard. Still looked around the crowded first deck but could see no one meeting the description he had been given. Had he been given bad information? "They are up on the second deck," someone whispered. Still did not bother to look for the source of this voice. He and Williamson headed for the stairs and ascended to the second deck, the so-called promenade deck, the top deck of the ferry.[5]

Immediately they saw them, "the anxious-looking slave-mother with her two boys on her left hand." To her right, close by, was an "ill-favored" white man. In his hand he held a cane; Still thought the cane might have concealed a sword, though he was not sure. He and Williamson approached the woman. She was, Still later recalled, "tall and well formed, high and large forehead, of genteel manners, chestnut color."[6]

"Are you travelling?" asked Williamson.

"Yes," she responded.

"With whom?" The woman nodded at the white man next to her, who muttered something indistinct. Still turned to him. At first glance the man who Still took to be the woman's master looked to be "a little old man." Now that he got a better look at him, he was not so sure. The man was little for sure, slight of frame and below average height. But he was perhaps not as old as he looked. He seemed sickly.[7]

"Do they belong to you, Sir?" he asked.

"Yes, they are in my charge," he replied. With this, Williamson and Still turned to the woman.

"You are entitled to your freedom according to the laws of Pennsylvania, having been brought into the State by your owner," Williamson told her. "If you prefer freedom, as we suppose everybody does, you have the chance to accept it now. Act calmly—don't be frightened by your master—you are as much entitled to your freedom as we are or as he is—be determined and you need have no fears but that you will be protected by the law."

The white man repeatedly attempted to interrupt, insisting that the woman knew all about the law and that she wished to remain with him, but Williamson persisted.

"Judges have time and again decided cases in this city and State similar to yours in favor of freedom! Of course, if you want to remain a slave to your master, we cannot force you to leave; we only want to make you sensible to your rights. *Remember, if you lose this chance you may never get such another.*"

Again the man insisted that she wished to remain with him, that she wished to come with him to New York, but she denied this. "I am not free, but I want my freedom—ALWAYS wanted to be free!! But he holds me."

By this time a crowd had gathered around them. Some began to threaten the slave master. "Knock him down; knock him down!" they shouted. The bell rang. Williamson told her that if she wished to be free, she must act at once. The woman took one of her children by the hand and began to rise to her feet. The white man next to her, her master, placed his hands on her shoulders to hold her in place. Williamson reached out to her, offering her a hand to help her to her feet. Perhaps he pulled her arm, helping her escape her master's grip, though he would later deny this. When the white man tried to restrain her, Williamson took the smaller man by the collar, holding him so that she might get past.[8]

Another white man, also traveling on the ship, cried out, "Leave them alone; they are his property," but a group of Black men who had gathered around the scene surged forward and carried the group, the woman, her two children, Still, and Williamson, down the stairs to the first deck. The youngest boy, who looked to be about seven, began to cry. Still took hold of him and carried him, staying close to his mother.[9]

As the crowd bore the group away, two Black men took ahold

Jane Johnson's escape, as depicted in Still's *Underground Railroad*
(Library Company of Philadelphia)

of the master. One of them warned him that if he attempted to
draw a weapon or to reclaim the woman and her children then he
would "cut his throat from ear to ear." Another white man objected
and commanded that they release him, which they did.[10]

The master followed the crowd as closely as he could, down to
the first deck and then on to the wharf. The group moved south
along Delaware Avenue to where Dock Street met the waterfront.
Dock Street was wider than most of the narrow streets in this oldest section of Philadelphia, and in contrast to the rest of the city's
tidy grid, it snaked its way for a few blocks down to the water,
where it opened up to a wide plaza. There was a carriage waiting. Still, the woman, and her children climbed into it. One of the
Black men who had assisted her on the boat, a porter named William Custis, rode with them.[11]

Finally the master caught up with Williamson. He once again
confronted him and demanded to know what was to be done with
his servants. Williamson coolly responded that he would be personally responsible for any claims that might be made on these
servants. He identified himself and handed the master a business

card. Furious, the master strode up to a police officer who had been watching the whole affair and demanded that he do something. Williamson approached the officer and whispered something to him, whereupon the officer announced "that he would have nothing to do with catching slaves." The now furious master could do nothing but watch as the carriage rode off, away from the water and toward the center of town.[12]

Still and Williamson could not have known what trouble they had started. For years abolitionists had spoken of the "Slave Power," the sinister force wielded by Southern slave masters and their political representatives in government. Many Northerners had begun to fear that slave owners were no longer content to merely protect slavery where it existed but were actively engaged in expanding the reach of slavery, even into the free states. Slave owners, wielding the power of the extra representation given them by the Constitution's "three-fifths clause," had seized control of the federal government.[13] Now, unbeknownst to Still and Williamson, the Slave Power had come to the docks of the Delaware River. The man that they had confronted that day was John Wheeler. Born in Hertford County, North Carolina, to a prominent slave-owning family, Wheeler had been educated at Columbian College (now George Washington University) in Washington, D.C., and at the University of North Carolina. He studied law under the state's chief justice and was elected to the North Carolina legislature in 1827 at the ripe age of twenty-seven. Over the next decade and a half, he would serve in a number of elected and appointed positions in North Carolina government, before retiring from public life to a plantation where he pursued his literary interests. This work was supported by the twenty-five slaves he owned.[14]

Wheeler returned to the state legislature in 1852, and shortly thereafter moved to Washington, where he served for a time as personal assistant to President Franklin Pierce. In August of 1854, Pierce appointed Wheeler minister to Nicaragua. Though Pierce himself was a Northerner, he owed his presidency to the support of the powerful Southern wing of the Democratic Party and his administration reflected this debt; his cabinet was stacked with powerful Southern politicians.

Wheeler's appointment to Nicaragua was a critical one. By the 1850s, many Southern leaders, not content to merely spread slavery into the American West, had begun to cast greedy eyes upon Latin America. The most radical and reckless of these leaders, so called "filibusters," organized private paramilitary expeditions to establish slaveholding colonies. One such filibuster, William Walker, would later seize control of Nicaragua, installing himself as president and almost immediately reinstituting slavery (which Nicaragua had abolished following its independence). Many Southern politicians were wary of such adventurism, but even the cautious among them were united in their commitment to promoting slavery among America's southern neighbors and fighting against the "abolitionist" influence of Great Britain.[15]

It was Wheeler's task to press this case for the Pierce administration, to ensure that American slaveholders and not British abolitionists held sway in Nicaragua. As he recounted in his diary, Wheeler arrived in San Juan del Norte to the sight of the "frowning floating batteries of John Bull [a slang term for the British] which view us with distrust." He spent the next six months in negotiations with the Nicaraguan and British authorities, pushing for American interests, before he was finally able to return to the United States with a signed treaty in his possession, which he delivered to the secretary of state on July 11, 1855. Five days later, Wheeler was invited to dine with the president at the White House; he was seated in the place of honor next to the first lady. The following morning, he set off on the first leg of his return journey to his post in Nicaragua. This time, however, he took with him three slaves: Jane Johnson and her two sons, Isaiah and Daniel.[16]

Jane Johnson tried to calm her son Isaiah. Once they left the scene at Dock Street behind, the carriage proceeded slowly; the horses were tired due to the summer heat. Still instructed the carriage driver to take them to Tenth and Pine Streets. As they rode, Still tried to ease Johnson's fears, explaining to her what had happened to lead them to this point. Once they arrived at their destination, the entire group got out. Still paid the carriage driver $1.50 and tipped the two Black men 25 cents each; these two then accompanied Johnson and her sons to a safe house on Barley Street, a small alley that ran parallel to Pine. Later that evening, when it was dark and things had calmed down, Still would move the Johnson family to his own home, just a few blocks away, for the night.[17]

Once the family was safe at the Still home on Ronaldson Street, Jane finally had a chance to tell Still her story. Like many enslaved people, she was unsure of where she had been born or even how old she was. She had lived in Washington, D.C., as well as in Caroline County, Virginia, north of Richmond. On New Year's Day 1844, Jane and two of her sons, the two who were with her in Philadelphia, were sold by their master, Richmond businessman Cornelius Crew. Crew had not sold Jane's third son, and so when her new master, John Wheeler, took her with him to Washington, D.C., she had to leave this son behind.

She was not to remain in Washington for long, though. Wheeler had purchased Jane to serve as the personal maid to his wife. When Wheeler was appointed to his post in Nicaragua, his wife accompanied him. Initially, they had left Jane and her sons behind; with no mistress to serve, she was loaned out to relatives of her owners who worked her in the fields of their plantation. After nine months of this work, Wheeler returned to the United States and Jane learned that she was to accompany him on his return to Nicaragua. At first, he intended to leave Jane's two boys behind, but eventually, at Jane's insistence, he relented and all four of them set off for the long journey.[18]

This journey would take them through Philadelphia, which Wheeler knew would pose some legal risk. When Pennsylvania passed its gradual abolition law in 1780, the legislature included a provision allowing visiting slave owners to bring slaves with them into the state. Since at the time Philadelphia was the capital of the United States, the law permitted congressmen and "Ministers and Consuls" the right to bring slaves with them and retain possession of such slaves indefinitely. The law also made provision for other slave masters who might travel through the state. Such visiting slave owners were, however, only allowed to keep these slaves in Pennsylvania for six months. After that the slaves would be granted their immediate freedom. This law would have granted Wheeler ample protection, but in 1847, as part of the state's Personal Liberty Law, protecting free Black Pennsylvanians and making it difficult for masters to recapture fugitive slaves, the state also repealed the six-month clause and the clause that had protected the slaveholding rights of government ministers.[19]

Wheeler knew that in taking Jane and her sons through Philadelphia he was running a risk, but it was a risk he was willing to take. Perhaps this was the confidence of a slave master who was unused to having his authority challenged. Perhaps he assumed that as an important official on government business his power would protect his right to slave property. In any case, he planned to be careful. While they were still in Washington, Wheeler told Jane "to have nothing to say to colored persons, and if any of them spoke to me, to say I was a free woman travelling with a minister." He also planned to keep a close watch on her.[20]

Jane had made up her own mind, though, to try for freedom. She made her decision before she even left the South, and while they traveled north, she looked for her chance. Wheeler indeed kept a close eye on her, hardly letting her out of his sight, but when they missed the two o'clock ferry that would have taken them across the Delaware in Philadelphia, he let his guard down. While they waited for the next ferry, he decided to eat a quick meal at Bloodgood's Hotel, leaving Jane alone in his room. Even then he remained suspicious, returning to check on her just a few minutes after he left. With her master gone, Jane did what he had warned her not to do: She spoke to two different Black workers in the hotel. She told her story first to a woman, who replied to her "Poor thing, I pity you." Then she spoke to a man who promised to telegraph ahead to New York, where men would be prepared to help her. It was likely this second man who decided to get word to Still.[21]

Still listened to her story with interest. He was by this time accustomed to hearing such stories, but even so he was struck by Johnson's courage and resourcefulness. He knew, however, that she could not remain in Philadelphia. She could stay the night with the Stills but in the morning she and her sons would need to move on. The first step would be to get her to reliable allies in New York, though he was not sure that she would be safe there. After all, fugitive slaves were often recaptured in New York. While Johnson was not legally a fugitive slave, at least not in Still's estimation, that might not protect her from slave catchers who plied the docks and back alleys of New York City. Nevertheless, he was sure that his friends in New York would know what to do, and where she should go from there.[22]

After giving his card to Wheeler, Passmore Williamson departed the scene at Dock Street and returned to his office. His father, who had remained there the whole time, recalled that his son had only been gone a half hour. The younger Williamson immediately returned to the work that he had put aside earlier; he knew that later that evening he would need to take a train for Harrisburg and he had much to do to prepare for this business trip. He finally left the office at 10:30 p.m., and soon afterward the elder Williamson retired to his residence, which was in the same building, upstairs from the office. Not long after going to bed, he was roused from sleep by the ring of his doorbell. Thomas Williamson recognized one of the men on his door step as Deputy Marshal William Miller. He did not recognize either of the other two. One of them was John Wheeler.[23]

These men demanded to see his son in order to serve him with a writ of habeas corpus. When he informed them that Passmore had left for Harrisburg and would not return for two days, they seemed not to believe him and hinted that they would search the house and office for him. Thomas Williamson was insulted by this threat, and he sent the party away from his door without further discussion. He returned to bed, but was awakened again the following morning by Deputy Marshal Miller, who handed him the original writ, demanding that Passmore Williamson produce the bodies of Jane Johnson and her two sons. The elder Williamson accepted the writ this time, and took it to William Still at the Anti-Slavery Society office. Still and the elder Williamson then took it to an abolitionist lawyer, Edward Hopper, to handle the matter.

Hopper in turn went before the court to inform it that his client would be unable to answer the writ until he returned to Philadelphia (even though, technically, it had not yet been served to him), and the judge postponed action until the following day.[24]

When Passmore Williamson finally returned to Philadelphia, in the early hours of the morning on July 20, he learned from his wife what had transpired in his absence. Shortly before nine in the morning, he arrived at the office he shared with his father and the two went together to see Hopper at his office, where they drafted a response to the writ. At some point before the two went to the court, Williamson also stopped in at the Anti-Slavery Society office to see Still. Given the circumstances, Williamson did not want to know too much. He simply asked "Are they safe?" to which Still responded, with a smile, "Yes."[25]

When Williamson arrived at court at ten, on the second floor of the Old State House, he faced a hostile judge. Judge John Kintzing Kane had been appointed to his seat on the United States District Court for the Eastern District of Pennsylvania by President James Polk in 1846. By that time, Kane had established himself as a loyal Democrat. He had also made clear his feelings on the long-running conflict in his state over the recovery of fugitive slaves. He had specifically criticized Pennsylvania's Personal Liberty Law of 1847, arguing that "its consequences have apparently been most unhappy," and that it was a "menace" to the "harmony between the States of the Union." He applauded the Fugitive Slave Law of 1850 as an effective means of dealing with abolitionists, whom he termed "fanatics of civil discord." Kane, who had presided over many of the earliest cases brought under the law in Philadelphia, had, in fact, already had multiple confrontations with Passmore Williamson, and certainly knew what sort of work he and Still did in the Vigilance Committee. While Kane saw himself as an impartial and fair jurist, he clearly had little sympathy for fugitive slaves or for the abolitionists who helped protect them.[26]

Immediately after his confrontation with Williamson on Dock Street, Wheeler had consulted with Judge Kane. The judge was sympathetic to Wheeler's plight, and he was also likely eager to be of assistance to a man so intimately connected to the Democratic president of the United States, but Kane also knew that the

Fugitive Slave Law would not apply in this circumstance. Johnson had not fled to Pennsylvania as a fugitive; her master had willingly brought her there. Later he would disingenuously claim that "I know of no statute of Pennsylvania which affects to divest the rights of property of a citizen of North Carolina . . . because he has found it needful or convenient to pass through the territory of Pennsylvania," but Kane knew very well that the law of Pennsylvania did just that. Kane and Wheeler decided, therefore, to take the perhaps surprising step of issuing a writ of habeas corpus, demanding that Williamson "produce the bodies" of Jane Johnson and her two sons. This was surprising because it had generally been abolitionists who had used such writs in order to free fugitive slaves from imprisonment. Now, in a sinister mirror image of abolitionist tactics, Kane hoped that if they could force Johnson into court, they would be able find some legal pretext to return her to Wheeler.[27]

Williamson's case would have to wait for his return to Philadelphia, but in the meantime, Wheeler swore out a complaint against five Black men who had participated in the rescue of Jane Johnson: Isaiah Moore, William Custis, John Ballard, James Martin, and James Braddock (though, curiously, not William Still). Custis had actually been one of the men who rode in the carriage with Still and the Johnson family. The five men were arrested and thrown into jail overnight. The following day, they were brought before the magistrate and charged with highway robbery, riot, and assault and battery. Bail was set at an exorbitant $7,000 for each man and the five were committed to prison to await their trial.[28]

Once Williamson returned to town and faced the court, his response to the writ seemed irrefutable. "Jane Johnson, Daniel and Isaiah, or by whatsoever names they may be called," he testified, "are not now, nor was, at the time of the issuing of said writ . . . or at any other time, in the custody power or position of, nor confined nor restrained their liberty by him the said Passmore Williamson." He had not, Williamson insisted, ever been in a position to "produce" Johnson or her sons; he certainly was not in such a position now. Because Still had left him in the dark as to where the fugitives had actually gone, he could honestly claim that he did not even know of their whereabouts.[29]

Judge Kane, however, was unpersuaded by this claim. Williamson and his attorneys seem to have assumed that the hearing was to be perfunctory; they planned to submit his response to the writ and that was all. Judge Kane, however, and United States Attorney James Vandyke had other plans. Without allowing Williamson's attorneys time to prepare, the judge called Wheeler to the witness stand to offer a rebuttal to Williamson's testimony. They aimed to demonstrate that Williamson had substantially misrepresented his actions, to show that he was in fact guilty of perjury and contempt of court. Wheeler insisted that Williamson and Still had forced an unwilling Jane Johnson to leave her master, and that they had also assaulted Wheeler in the process. Several witnesses supported Wheeler's version of the events. Williamson stood by his story. Judge Kane decided to adjourn for a week, "to have time for reflection," though he warned Williamson that "if it is in the power of the defendant to produce the bodies of the three persons, it would be better for him to do so."[30]

Williamson, of course, had no intention of "producing" Jane Johnson or her sons. Neither did William Still, who actually knew where to find her: she and her sons had already made their way to New York City, where they had found refuge with allies of Still. These allies had subsequently provided her with passage to the relative safety of Boston.[31] When the court reconvened on July 27, Judge Kane found Williamson in contempt of court, though he reserved judgment on the charge of perjury. Williamson was remanded to Moyamensing Prison.

Kane's decision made it clear that he held Williamson, as the only white person involved, responsible for the entire affair. "Of all the parties in the act of violence," Kane wrote in his decision in the case, "he was the only white man, the only citizen, the only individual having recognized political rights."[32] Still and the other Black men involved might be responsible for their own behavior in certain respects, but they were not capable of independent action; in Kane's eyes it was Williamson who was the ringleader, the instigator, despite the fact that, as the evidence in court had shown, it was Still who had initiated the rescue. Here, Kane's opinion reflected a position that was extreme even among white Pennsylvanians, who more than a decade earlier had formally disfranchised the state's Black residents. At the time, even many of those who advocated for disfranchisement admitted that Black Pennsylvanians were citizens in some respects. Kane's position anticipated the more absolutist argument later infamously embodied in the *Dred Scott* decision, that Black men had "no rights the white man is bound to respect."[33]

This did not let those Black men off the hook entirely, however. On July 27, the day after Williamson was found in contempt, Moore, Custis, Ballard, Martin, and Braddock, the five men who had been charged with "riot," "assault," and "highway robbery," came before the court of quarter sessions. Attorneys working for the Anti-Slavery Society had employed a writ of habeas corpus to bring them before the court, hoping that a somewhat more favorable judge might be willing to reduce their bail. They found that more favorable judge in William Kelley. The judge had begun his career as a Jacksonian Democrat, but in 1854 he joined the newly established Republican Party. As a Republican he would go on to serve several terms in Congress and would become one of the city's most outspoken critics of slavery. Kelley's courtroom proved more favorable to abolitionists than Judge Kane's. The district attorney admitted that the highway robbery charge was unsustainable according to the laws of Pennsylvania, and Kelley reduced the bail for all the men: to $1,000 for Ballard and Custis (the two who had been most directly involved) and $500 for the other three. According to Wheeler, Ballard had been the man who threatened to "cut my throat," and Custis was, along with Ballard, the man who had taken hold of him on the boat.[34]

Wheeler continued to press the case. Williamson, the man he deemed to be most responsible for the assault on his property, was in prison, but he wanted to be sure that the other men involved, including Still, were also punished. He went before the grand jury on August 7, and on the following day Moore, Custis, Ballard, Martin, and Braddock were arraigned on the charge of riot and of assault and battery. Now, though, they were not the only ones Wheeler was accusing of these crimes: William Still was also named as a defendant. This seems to have been something of a surprise to William Pierce, the attorney defending the five men. Still was not even present in court. Due to Still's absence, and due to the need to prepare for this case, Pierce asked for and received a postponement of the trial. Most intriguingly, Pierce hinted that vital witnesses, perhaps even Jane Johnson herself, needed to be brought in from New York.[35]

By this point it was public knowledge that Johnson had fled the city. On August 1, the *New York Tribune* reported that "the former slaves of Mr. Wheeler, recently liberated at Philadelphia, were in this City yesterday." She had even given sworn testimony, witnessed by a judge in Brooklyn, refuting Wheeler's version of the events of her rescue. Johnson insisted that she had not been taken against her will, "nobody forced me away, nobody pulled me and nobody led me." Williamson and Still had offered her an opportunity but nothing more. "I always wished to be free," she testified, "and meant to be free when I came North." She made no mention of any violent acts, but made it clear that Williamson had merely extended a hand to her.[36]

On the morning of August 9, Still was in court, along with his five co-defendants. All pleaded not guilty. When he was examined by his attorney, Still reiterated his argument that he had important witnesses that were still absent from the court. In support of this notion, Miller McKim presented to the court telegraph dispatches to New York, seeking testimony relevant to the case. Despite the protestations of the district attorney, who was willing to try the other five defendants without Still, the judge postponed the entire trial until the end of August.[37]

Still was not, however, merely content to bide his time until the trial—he went on the offensive. Two days after the postponement of the trial, Still, accompanied by McKim and the abolitionist lawyer George Earle, went before an alderman, William Hibbard, and swore out his own complaint against John Wheeler. Still claimed that Wheeler did "violently and tumultuously seize upon Jane Johnson and attempt to carry her away contrary to her own wish, claiming her as a fugitive from servitude or labour." In doing so, he insisted, Wheeler had violated the anti-kidnapping provisions of the Personal Liberty Law of 1847. Evidently Still could not find a constable willing to serve the warrant to Wheeler and so as a legal matter this accusation went nowhere, but certainly it sent a message. Still and those who had helped Jane Johnson to escape were unrepentant, and they were willing to use their ample connections in the city and their knowledge of the law to their advantage.[38]

In the midst of all this controversy, Still had continued his Vigilance Committee work. On the same day that he and Williamson aided Johnson in her escape from Wheeler, Still recorded in his Vigilance Committee journal the arrival of Henry Crummell (Cromwell) from Baltimore County. "Walked to Harrisburg," Still recounted, "from thence came on the Burthen [freight] train." Even as his own trial dragged on into August, Still recorded one of his busiest months as chair of the Vigilance Committee. Fugitives from Virginia, Georgia, Delaware, Maryland, North Carolina, and Kentucky arrived, were welcomed by Still and sent along their way. Still provided them room and board, he paid for their transportation, he supplied them with shoes, clean clothes. Despite the fact that Still knew he was under more scrutiny than usual, the business of the Underground Railroad went on as before.[39]

While Still continued aiding fugitives, and while he prepared for his own trial, he also took an active role in publicizing the events surrounding the escape of Jane Johnson. The case had received wide coverage in the press across the nation, but Still realized that it was important to get his and Williamson's version of the story out. On July 30, he wrote a letter to the Republican Party organ, the *New York Daily Tribune*, laying out his own account of the events. The *Tribune* was the largest-circulation daily in New York at the time, and his piece would be widely reprinted in Republican and abolitionist newspapers across the country. Williamson, who still languished in Moyamensing Prison, had already become something of an abolitionist cause célèbre, but Still's letter was careful to highlight Johnson herself as the prime mover in all of this; he also celebrated his own role and the role played by Moore, Custis, Ballard, Martin, and Braddock. While much of the coverage around the country focused on the white hero, Passmore Williamson, Still wanted to be sure that he provided a counterpoint, that he made readers aware of the often unacknowledged labor of Black men and women in the Underground Railroad.[40]

Not incidentally, sharing his story also significantly raised

Still's own national profile. He had already built a national reputation among those who aided fugitive slaves, and his letters to
the *Provincial Freeman* and other abolitionist newspapers had made
him known to others who might not have actually met him, but
the attention he received as a result of the Jane Johnson affair was
of a different magnitude. In late August, *Frederick Douglass' Paper*
printed a "letter of sympathy" for Still and the five Black porters
who had been charged in the case, signed by James Pennington
and the elders and trustees of Shiloh Presbyterian Church in New
York City. Pennington, of course, was a fellow worker on the
Underground Railroad, and perhaps even the man to whom Still
had sent Jane Johnson.[41]

Whatever sympathies they might be receiving from abolitionists around the country, however, Still realized that at the moment
the most important sympathies they needed to cultivate were
those of the men who would sit on the jury when it convened at
the end of August. As the Philadelphia *Sunday Dispatch* noted, the
case had excited great interest, "but in most quarters it is discussed
in the spirit prompted by the feelings elicited upon the abstract
questions of slavery and abolition."[42] At this trial, Still would be
represented by veteran antislavery lawyer Charles Gibbons; the
other five men would be represented by William S. Pierce and
William Birney. While the legal team went about putting together
a collection of witnesses who would testify that Johnson had left
Wheeler of her own free will and that the men had only used force
to restrain the slave master *after* he attempted to restrain Johnson,
they knew that the most compelling witness they might call was
Johnson herself. There was risk in bringing her to Philadelphia,
however. Abolitionists firmly believed the law was on their side,
but surely Judge Kane had shown that he was willing to go to great
lengths to defend the rights of slaveowners like Wheeler.[43]

The trial was to have begun on Monday, August 27, but after one
more postponement it finally got underway in the court of quarter sessions two days later, with Judge Kelley presiding. The first
day's witnesses, including Wheeler himself, substantively repeated
the account that they had offered before in Judge Kane's court.

They depicted an aggressive Passmore Williamson, an unwilling Jane Johnson, and a violent Black mob attacking the defenseless Wheeler. The second day of the trial, however, saw the real fireworks. The first witness called by the defense, a plumber named George Sandgram, contradicted the prosecution on a number of facts. According to Sandgram, while Williamson had gently laid hands on Johnson while he appealed to her to come ashore and claim her freedom, it was Wheeler who had first put his hands on Williamson, and shortly thereafter it was two white men who had seized Williamson and asked him "would you rob a man of his property?" Soon after, he insisted, Wheeler had grabbed hold of Johnson, holding her around the waist, he thought.[44] This testimony certainly called into question the case that Wheeler and his attorneys had made, but it would be the next witness who would provide the most persuasive refutation.

When Jane Johnson was called to the stand to testify, "considerable surprise was manifested" by the crowd gathered in the courtroom. Perhaps many of these men and women were surprised that Jane had been called, or perhaps it was simply shocking to actually see, in the flesh, the woman who had been at the center of all this. In any case, it was not a surprise to Wheeler and his attorneys that she had been called. Johnson had been staying with sympathetic abolitionist families, at least part of the time with James and Lucretia Mott, so certainly some of those in the courtroom were aware of her impending testimony. Rumor had it that two warrants had been issued for Johnson's arrest, one claiming her as a fugitive slave and the other accusing her of larceny, of having literally stolen the clothes on her back. In any case the United States attorney, Vandyke, had every intention of seizing Johnson if she dared to appear in court. One correspondent noted that "the Courtroom was infested by the ill-favoured slave-hounds kept about the U.S. Marshal's office for dirty business." When Johnson was finally called, she was escorted into court by a city police officer and some of the most prominent abolitionist women in Philadelphia: Lucretia Mott, Rebecca Plumly, Sarah McKim, and Sarah Pugh. Johnson's appearance sent an electric charge through the courtroom. It was several minutes before the judge was able to bring order and silence to the room.[45]

"I can't tell my exact age," began Johnson. "I guess I am about twenty-five; I was born in Washington City; lived there this New Year's, if I shall live to see it, two years." Johnson's testimony served as a clear refutation of many of the major points of Wheeler's account, but it also served to humanize her, perhaps to tug at the heartstrings of jurors. She largely repeated the account she had sworn before a New York judge, but delivering it in person surely had an influence on the jury. "Jane is a fine specimen of the best class of Virginia housemaids," remarked one observer, "with a certain lady-like air, propriety of language and timidity of manner that prepossesses the audience in her favour." As she began to speak, Wheeler "laughed immoderately and nervously. "He was unaccustomed to being publicly contradicted by his property.[46]

As Johnson reached the climactic moment of her testimony, her former master began to turn pale. "Mr. Wheeler tried to stop me," she said. "I did not say I did not want my freedom; I have always wanted it; I did not say I wanted to go with my master; I went very willingly to the carriage, I was very glad to go; the little boy said he wanted to go to his massa, he was frightened; I did not say I wanted to go to Colonel Wheeler; there was no outcry of any kind, my little boy made all the noise that was made." She denied that it had been Williamson, or Still for that matter, who had enticed her to leave her master; she had already planned to flee from Wheeler once they got to New York. "I had made preparations before leaving Washington," she told the court. "I made a suit to disguise myself in—they had never seen me wear it." Apparently recognizing that Johnson's testimony had undermined Wheeler's, in his cross-examination Vandyke, the district attorney, turned instead to asking about Johnson's whereabouts since her escape. Johnson's attorney, Gibbons, objected to these questions, and his objections were mostly sustained by the judge. She did admit that she had met briefly with Still on Monday before the trial.[47]

Once Johnson had completed her testimony, she was escorted out of the courtroom by a Philadelphia police officer. Her path to the waiting carriage was "lined by a strong body of policemen, placed there by order of" friendly local authorities, including Judge Kelley. For a moment it seemed that there would be a stand-off between the local police and forces of the United States marshal, but in the end, Vandyke was forced to relent. Perhaps, as one observer suggested, "If an attack had been made by Kane's bloodhounds, it would have been received by one hundred as true hearts and manly breasts as exist in the old Keystone State" and he realized that doing so risked raising a bloody mob. The city where violent mobs had once been infamous for assaulting abolitionists now seemed more threatening to slave catchers than to the defenders of slaves. In any case, Johnson rode off in the carriage, accompanied by Lucretia Mott.[48]

A few days later, the courtroom was packed again, awaiting the jury's verdict. The day before, Judge Kelley had given his instructions to the jury. The defense had attempted to make the legal status of Jane Johnson irrelevant to the case. In charging the six men with riot and assault, attorneys for the United States government were prosecuting the manner in which they assisted Johnson, but Kelley, clearly friendly to the defendants' cause, was sure to remind the jury that "the law of Pennsylvania recognizes no slavery upon her soil . . . Jane Johnson and her sons were free when they sat on the steamboat where the circumstances that gave rise to this prosecution occurred." After deliberating for another day, the eleven-man jury found all the defendants not guilty of the charge of riot. On the charge of assault and battery, they found Custis and Ballard guilty and the others, including Still, not guilty. Custis and Ballard were each fined ten dollars and imprisoned for one week.[49]

William Still walked free that day. Jane Johnson returned to Boston. Passmore Williamson, however, remained in Moyamensing Prison, still subject to Kane's finding that he had been in contempt of court. While he was imprisoned, though, Williamson became a symbol of abolitionist resistance to the Slave Power. Abolitionist luminaries, both those from Philadelphia and those just passing through, continued to visit him to pay their respects. Still and Miller McKim visited their comrade, of course, but so did Harriet Tubman and Frederick Douglass.[50] Pennsylvania Republicans even ran him, unsuccessfully, for the statewide office of canal commissioner.[51] More than two years before the infamous *Dred Scott* decision, Judge Kane had become a symbol of how the power of slavery was not content to simply dominate Southern slaves; it also sought to subjugate white Northerners like Passmore Williamson. Not until November would he finally be released from prison, an abolitionist hero.

Perhaps Still was frustrated that the coverage of the entire affair focused so much upon Williamson. Certainly he did what he could in his own account of the events to give Johnson herself the starring role in the drama of her own liberation, and he had praised the "five colored porters who appeared, with warm hearts throbbing in sympathy with the mother and her children."[52] Nevertheless, the coverage of the events in newspapers across the country invariably focused on Williamson. In the North he was praised for his "integrity, truth, courage, and goodness" or denounced as a "seditious kidnapper" depending on the political orientation of the newspaper. Southern papers uniformly denounced him. He was, according to one North Carolina newspaper, "one of those fiery zealots in the cause; who would make a saint of a runaway negro, no matter how worthless and degraded."[53]

Whatever his frustration with how the Black participants in the affair were neglected, Still doubtless understood the political utility of Williamson's story. As he would later recall, "Every day he remained [in prison] would make numerous converts to the cause of liberty."[54] The sheer volume of coverage, long after Johnson had made her way to freedom, suggested an appetite for stories of white heroism, even white martyrdom. Williamson could serve as a symbol that slavery was a threat to the liberties of decent white men. This was a powerful message for the antislavery cause, which sought to expand its appeal beyond the hard core of abolitionists.

Still had not received quite the same attention that Williamson had, but he too emerged from the Johnson affair as a national figure, not just within the Underground Railroad community, not even just among abolitionists, but among the wider reading public. Indeed, the facts of the case, in many cases naming Still himself, had been widely reprinted in Southern newspapers as evidence of the rot within Northern communities, of the Black and white abolitionists working tirelessly to protect fugitive slaves. Following the trial, Still would continue his Vigilance Committee work, but now he did so as one of its public faces.

CHAPTER SEVEN

"YOUR NATIONAL SHIP IS ROTTING"

Even as the excitement of the Jane Johnson trial continued to roil Philadelphia, William Still made plans to leave the city, if only for a short time. For years he had been sending fugitives to the growing Black communities in Canada. There he knew they would be largely safe from slave catchers, but beyond the occasional letter from men and women he had helped on their way to freedom in Canada, Still had little direct knowledge of what life was actually like for these emigrants. In his years helping fugitives escape to the North, Still had received largely flattering accounts of Canada. "Our masters have told us there is no living in Canada for the Negro," wrote John Henry Hill, who had fled from a Richmond auction house less than a year earlier, "but I say give me freedom, and the United States may have all her money and her Luxtures [*sic*], yeas give Liberty or Death." There was, he assured Still, plenty of opportunity for those willing to make the journey.[1] The abolitionist press spoke of these settlements in glowing terms. Thriving Canadian settlements of free Blacks allowed abolitionists to both criticize the corruption of the United States by the nefarious Slave Power while also challenging the racist assumption that Black people could never prosper outside the system of slavery. Still was, of course, broadly sympathetic to both of these aims, but at the same time he could not help but wonder what conditions were actually like in Canada for the men and women who had left American slavery behind.

Still, ever the voracious reader of newspapers, would surely have seen plenty of negative accounts of these Canadian settlements. In one account of a Black settlement in the township of Elgin, along Lake Erie, the *New York Herald* describes Black emigrants as "idle, vicious, and turbulent," and noted that many "were actually relapsing into their native barbarism." White neighbors were rebelling against the presence of these newcomers and had, the article reported, elected a man as their representative to Parliament who pledged to "relieve the country of the plague of the negroes."[2] Such openly racist accounts might be easy to dismiss, but even the abolitionist press provided hints that white Canadians were not free of racial prejudice. *Frederick Douglass' Paper* noted that a Black pastor named John Garrow, visiting the town of St. Catharines from his home in New Orleans, had been denied admittance to an omnibus and had "met with some insults from carriers."[3] Still wanted to see for himself what conditions were like for emigrants from the United States and whether or not American benefactors might be able to aid them.

The years following Still's involvement in the rescue of Jane Johnson saw him wrestling with his increasingly public profile. Locally, he was well enough known that the manufacturer of a pain remedy included a testimonial from Still in a print advertisement.[4] These were also among the busiest years of his Vigilance Committee work as a growing number of fugitives passed through Philadelphia and Still's home. He found himself concerned with the sort of future that these fugitives might enjoy, whether in the Northern states or in Canada, and in the broader questions raised by this Vigilance Committee work. Would free Blacks be able to find work? Would they be able to prove themselves to their white neighbors as "respectable"? Would they ever be welcomed as full members of the nation, as equal citizens? What did the work of the Underground Railroad mean for the growing political conflict over slavery?

. . .

Before Still set out for Canada, he was sure to solicit letters of introduction from some of the most prominent abolitionists in Philadelphia. The letters provide some indication of the esteem in which he was held by the abolitionist community. Henry Grew introduces Still as "my esteemed friend and a sincere practical advocate of the cause of human rights against the oppression of a selfish world."[5] Samuel Rhoads assured his readers that Still "goes to visit our brethren and sisteren who have escaped from a land of wrong and oppression to one of freedom and security, and to many of them he will not be a stranger."[6] Still was, confirmed Dillwyn Parrish, "an intelligent and worthy citizen whose statements may be relied on and whose interest in the cause of his oppressed people entitles him to the favorable consideration of all with whom he may be associated."[7]

Clearly Still had the respect and admiration of prominent white abolitionists, but as a traveling companion he had someone even closer: his brother James Still. Nine years older than his brother, James had remained in rural New Jersey, settling not far from where the boys had grown up. James, like his brother, received minimal formal education, but he had developed an interest in medicine and eventually became a self-taught healer and physician. He seems not to have had much to do with his brother's abolitionist work, so it is unclear what led him to join William on this journey. In his published memoirs he notes simply that "I made a trip to Canada West for recreation. I was gone from home about three weeks." The fact that the two brothers chose to undertake this journey together, though, suggests something of the bond between the two.[8]

There had been people of African descent in Canada since the seventeenth century, but their numbers were relatively few. The legislative assembly of Upper Canada (what would later become Ontario) banned the importation of slaves in 1793 and began the process of gradual abolition. Small numbers of refugees from the United States settled in Canada in the early decades of the nineteenth century, but the first significant influx of Black migrants from the United States came in 1830, sparked by a racial pogrom in Cincinnati. These Black immigrants tended to settle in communities not far from the border. At first this was because many lacked the means to settle further into the interior and because a significant portion planned to eventually return to the United States. Subsequent waves of Black migrants tended to settle where they found existing Black communities. Some were drawn to settlements, like Wilberforce on the shores of Lake Huron, established specifically as refuges for American free Blacks.[9]

Black Canadians faced little of the legal discrimination experienced by free Blacks in the United States. Black men were allowed to serve on juries, they could vote, and they served in the military. Black emigrants from the United States, like Still's friend and ally Mary Ann Shadd, had trumpeted this legal equality both as an inducement for further emigration and as a way to shame the government of the land of her birth, which denied these rights to most of its Black citizens. What was less clear was just how these Black refugees fit in a society in which they remained a tiny minority and what sort of economic opportunities they enjoyed in their new home.[10]

William and James Still set out from Philadelphia in the second week of September 1855. Still left no record of how he got to Canada, but he likely used one of the routes along which he had sent fugitives, a train to New York City, then another headed for Canada. A train leaving New York at noon arrived at Albany at 5:30 that afternoon, and then at Buffalo at 6:30 the next morning. From there perhaps Still crossed over into Canada via the suspension bridge across the Niagara River that had been completed earlier that year.[11]

Just across the Niagara River from Buffalo lay what was likely one of Still's first stops, the town of St. Catharines, a "refuge for the oppressed," one visitor from the United States described it, "rest for the travel-soiled and foot-sore fugitive." The town was a thriving commercial center, situated along the Welland Canal. The houses of its Black residents were "neat and plain without; tidy and comfortable within."[12] Still spent the next several weeks traveling through the Ontario Peninsula, inspecting the communities where significant numbers of African Americans had settled. He visited the "wealthy, enterprising, and beautiful city" of Toronto where one visitor estimated that Black residents, who were "remarkably industrious," mostly resided in the northwestern section, and constituted about 1,000 out of a population of 47,000. Still also visited Black communities in Hamilton, Kingston, Buxton, and Chatham. He made a particularly close study of Chatham, noting that "nowhere in Canada do [Black residents] approximate in number so near the whites as there." This relatively high Black population led to some allegations that Black residents were disruptive, but Still disputed this. "The truth is," he wrote, "the colored people of Chatham, as a general thing, are industrious, peaceable and prosperous."[13]

Wherever he went, Still found the communities of fugitives to be prospering. Of course there were among these settlements those who were lazy, criminal, or intemperate, but, noted Still, "may not the same be said of white people?" In general, though, he found these settlers "in good spirits, well cared for, and evincing a disposition to care for themselves by industry and frugality." James Still agreed, recalling that "the people seemed as happy under the rule of the British lion as under that of the American eagle; indeed," he wrote, "I thought the colored people much happier."[14] The condition of these settlements fulfilled the Stills' hopes that refugees might find in Canada what was denied to them in the United States.

As they traveled, the brothers found that William was something of a celebrity among the refugee communities. "Our great and good Wm. Still," remarked one Black Canadian, "the fugitives know him well, as one of the greatest friends and helpers they have." No doubt this pleased William. James did not record what he thought of his famous brother, though later he would recall the trip as an unpleasant one, "owing to personal difficulties." Wherever they went, people they met asked for news of loved ones left behind. Many of these refugees knew William already, from having passed through Philadelphia or even staying under his roof. Even those who had not come to Canada through the Still household, though, seemed to have heard of William Still. To Still's amusement, though, these Black Canadians seem to have expected a "hoary-headed, wrinkle-visaged and bowed old patriarch" and were surprised to see the still young and vigorous man in the flesh.[15]

Still found not only that these settlements were thriving, but that they were, in his estimation, doing so without much aid from white Canadians. "It is an undeniable fact," wrote Still, "that white Canadians manifest no particular sympathy for the negro. They neither encourage his coming, nor offer objections against it." This was an important point for Still, because the Canadian refugee settlements were an important symbol of Black achievement. These settlements showed not only that free Black people were capable of prospering but that they could do so without white support. Here Still was echoing the argument made by Shadd several years earlier in her pamphlet "A Plea for Emigration," in which she trumpeted Canada as an alternative to the white-dominated (and therefore suspect) colonization schemes, the most prominent of which was the American Colonization Society's plan to colonize free Black people in Liberia. For Shadd and Still, the black settlements of Canada West were a celebration of Black autonomy and self-reliance.[16]

Still's visit to these Black Canadian settlements was also part of a larger project: the construction of a transnational Black community. These settlements were a refuge for fugitive slaves, but they were not simply a refuge. Still's public engagement with Shadd and her newspaper, the *Provincial Freeman*, his private correspondence with Canadian emigrants, and now his journey among these settlements helped to solidify the connection between free Black communities across North America. Black abolitionists had long noted the irony of the fact that the British crown offered them protections that the American republic did not. "The English," David Walker had insisted, "are the best friends the coloured people have upon the earth." Still's connection to these Canadian settlements, however, said little about the virtues of the British monarchy. He was far more interested in building and maintaining connections with the fugitives he had helped to flee to Canada, and with the communities they had built there. Still was constructing a Black abolitionist network, a community of fugitive slaves, that crossed borders.[17]

Only days after Still returned home to Philadelphia, he had a visitor, "a man of unmixed blood, well-made, and intelligent," who seemed more than willing to join the Black Canadian settlements Still had just left behind. His name was Pete and he had been enslaved to a William Matthews on the Eastern Shore of Virginia. While his master was "not a hard man," according to Pete, the man he hired as an overseer, George Matthews, was "a very cruel man." One day, displeased with Pete's treatment of an ox, Matthews became furious, threatened Pete with a pistol, and then took out a "large dirk-knife" and attempted to stab him. Pete was able to evade the knife, but the overseer beat him severely. The following day Pete took the four dollars he had been able to save up, used part of it to buy a pistol of his own, and set out "to follow the North Star." At some point during the nearly two-hundred-mile trek north, Pete came face-to-face with his former master. Pete held tight to his pistol but decided against using it; he ran as fast as his feet would carry him and was successful in eluding all attempts to recover him. Once he got to Philadelphia, he handed off the weapon to Still, recognizing "he had more confidence in his 'understandings' than he had in his old pistol." Pete, cleaned and renamed Samuel Sparrows, headed north for Canada, "looking quite respectable." Still kept the pistol as a souvenir, as "a relic of the Underground Rail Road."[18]

The fact that he retained this memento hints at the increasingly violent tenor of the antislavery conflict. Still remained an admirer of William Lloyd Garrison and ostensibly a supporter of Garrison's doctrine of nonresistance, and yet Still's work on the Vigilance Committee had forced him, perhaps even more than most Black abolitionists, to confront the reality that violent resistance was sometimes necessary. Still celebrated the success of men like Sparrows who "bade farewell to Slavery" without bloodshed, but he also recognized, and indeed admired, the willingness of the same men to hold on to the pistol as a last resort.[19]

Not long after Still returned from his tour of Canada, his ally Mary Ann Shadd also traveled from her home in Canada West to Philadelphia. The trip was a part of a larger tour that Shadd had undertaken as part of her effort to cultivate support for the *Provincial Freeman,* but she was also in Philadelphia to attend the National

Convention of Colored Americans held in Franklin Hall in the middle of October. The stated purpose of the convention was the resolution that free Black people should take greater responsibility for their own uplift. "That so far from being mere aids and lookers-on," read the call for the convention, "the time has fully come when they must be the guides, leaders and active operators in this great Reform." This sentiment fit nicely with Shadd's commitment to Black autonomy, and yet she found herself marginalized by the leaders of the convention. She was admitted to the convention as a delegate from Canada but was closed out of most of the official business. Still did not participate in the convention, though some of his closest allies on the Philadelphia Vigilance Committee did. Most of the leading figures of the convention, Frederick Douglass among them, rejected Shadd's appeals for Canadian emigration as an expression of Black autonomy and uplift. For some abolitionists, even voluntary emigration was an implicit acceptance of the colonizationist logic that insisted no African American could be a citizen in the land of their birth. Nevertheless, Shadd was able to speak in favor of Canadian emigration, impressing even those she did not convince. "However much we may differ with her on the subject of emigration," wrote one correspondent to *Frederick Douglass' Paper*, "she obtained the floor and proceeded to, and succeeded in making one of the most convincing and telling speeches in favor of Canadian emigration I ever heard. It was one of the speeches of the Convention." Nevertheless, Shadd deemed the convention "a great failure."[20]

Still, though not a full-throated advocate for Canadian emigration, was far more sympathetic to Shadd's cause than many other Black abolitionists. Though committed to fighting for full equality in the United States, Still's tour of Canadian settlements and his daily battles with slave catchers helped him to understand the emigrationist impulse. Shadd had remained in Philadelphia following the convention and continued her fundraising efforts. At the beginning of November, she took part in a public debate on the merits of Canadian emigration; her opponent, arguing "that it was not the business of the colored man to emigrate under any circumstances," was Josiah Wears, onetime member of the Philadelphia Vigilance Committee. A few days after this, Still was at the head of a committee hosting a meeting to celebrate and raise funds in support of Shadd and her work. The meeting did not explicitly endorse Shadd's call for free Black emigration (and in fact one participant, John C. Bowers, expressed his opposition), but the meeting clearly expressed the strength of support that Shadd enjoyed within the Black community of Philadelphia.[21]

Whatever sympathy Still may have had for Shadd's arguments, he remained committed to the fight for Black progress within the United States. Shortly after his return from Canada, Still began advertising a new boardinghouse at South and Ninth Streets, just about a block from the home on Ronaldson Street where his family had lived for a few years. "Respectable persons," read the advertisement, "can be accommodated with genteel transient or permanent boarding."[22] An account in the *Liberator* described the establishment as "large, clay, and situated in a respectable part of the city," adding that "Mrs. Still is an excellent housekeeper."[23]

Boardinghouses, like the one operated by the Stills, were an essential and ubiquitous part of the nineteenth-century American urban landscape. As the population of American cities ballooned, perhaps a half of these urban newcomers found lodging not in private residences but in some form of boardinghouse. These ran the gamut from what were essentially small hotels to private homes that simply took in additional lodgers. Those who came to cities like Philadelphia in hopes of work needed a place to live, and even as moralists were defining the "home" as the defining feature of American middle-class respectability, and using boardinghouses as the antithesis of their conception of domesticity, for many Americans the boardinghouse was in fact their home.[24]

For African Americans, these notions of respectability and domesticity were especially tricky. For most white-run boardinghouses, running a "respectable" establishment meant excluding Black people. "In Pro-slavery places like New York and Philadelphia," noted one of the visitors to the Stills' house, "colored people are universally excluded from places of entertainment for strangers."[25] African Americans who needed lodgings, then, needed either to stay with someone they knew or to resort to less-respectable accommodations. The latter option only reinforced the notion that Black people were unfit for better establishments, confirming white notions of Black inferiority. The Stills intended to counter these notions by running a "respectable" boarding-house, one that would be open to those of all races who were will-ing to conduct themselves decently. At the same time, the always frugal and upwardly mobile Stills could use the additional board-inghouse income to further their own ascent into the Black middle class. Still's salary at the Anti-Slavery Society had been raised from $30 a month to $35, but income from the boardinghouse surely helped the Stills support their family.[26]

For Still, running a boardinghouse had an additional ben-efit: it allowed him to expand the number of fugitives that he and Letitia could accommodate under their own roof. It is perhaps no coincidence that the years in which Still aided the largest number of fugitives coincided with his family's move from the home on Ronaldson Street to the more spacious boardinghouse on South Street. The coming and going of so many fugitives was likely less conspicuous in a boardinghouse on commercial South Street than it would have been on the residential side street where the Stills had lived previously.

Still was not home when a man he would later identify only as "the Doctor" knocked at the door of their boardinghouse. Letitia Still answered in her husband's stead. "I wish to leave this young lad with you a short while," he said, "and I will call and see further about him." With that, he stepped into his carriage and was gone. When Still returned home he found the young lad, cap on, sitting in his dining room. Letitia informed her husband that "the Doc-tor" had been there while he was gone and that he promised to return shortly.

"I suppose you are the person that the Doctor went to Wash-ington after, are you not?"

"No," replied the boy, who insisted he was from York, not Washington.

"From York? Why then did the Doctor bring you here?" asked Still. "The Doctor went expressly to Washington for a young girl who was to be brought away dressed up as a boy, and I took you to be that person."

Without a word, the boy stood up and walked out of the house. Still followed him out to the street. Once they were alone, the boy confessed that she was the girl from Washington. The Doctor had made her promise that she would only confess her true identity to Still himself and she had worried about revealing herself in the presence of Letitia. The girl's name was Ann Maria Weems, and her journey was an exceptional one. While Still and the Vigilance Committee only rarely sent agents into slave states in order to rescue fugitives, Weems's was one of these rare cases. Her father, John Weems, was a free Black resident of Rockville, Maryland, and her mother was enslaved to a man who, for an annual fee, allowed her to reside with her husband. This master had also promised to allow John Weems to purchase his wife and their five enslaved children (a sixth child, Stella, had escaped north years earlier). Such promises, however, were often betrayed once an owner found himself in difficult financial straits or when he simply received a better offer from a slave trader. John Weems had traveled north in order to raise funds for the purchase of his family, but ultimately was able to purchase only his wife and his youngest daughter, leaving the rest in bondage.[27]

In June 1854, Still had received a letter from Jacob Bigelow, a Washington, D.C., lawyer, asking for help rescuing Ann Maria Weems. Bigelow, who would use the pen name "William Penn" when corresponding with Still, wrote that the girl's owners had refused an offer of $700 to purchase her. Bigelow seemed confident that he would be able to help the girl escape from her master outside Washington, and that he could hide her for a time in his home, but he needed Still's help to get her to the North. They seem to have considered securing passage for the girl on a ship with one of Still's trusted allies, but nothing came of this for over a year.[28]

In the fall of 1855, they concocted a new plan. Still sent a man identified only as "Dr. H" to transport Weems to Philadelphia. Dr. H may well have been Samuel Hollingsworth, a physician and professor at Girard College who lived not far from the Stills, but even years later Still remained silent on the identity of this agent. The doctor seems not to have been a regular ally of Still's, and in this case there was a financial incentive to take on this dangerous case:

Lewis Tappan, the wealthy New York merchant and abolitionist, had promised $300 to the man willing to transport Weems from Washington to Philadelphia. In any case, Bigelow was impressed by Dr. H, a man he had never met before. He was, wrote Bigelow, "cool, quiet, thoughtful, and *perfectly competent to execute his understanding*." Within minutes of meeting him, Bigelow was sure that Dr. H would be able to handle this dangerous task, "that it would be alright."[29]

The problem was that as soon as Weems's master noticed her missing, he would immediately come looking for her. The road north would take her through miles of slave territory where authorities and hired slave catchers would be looking for her. Still had a solution, though. They would be looking for a young girl, so, perhaps inspired by Ellen Craft's escape a few years earlier, Ann Weems became Joe Wright. Dressed as a boy, she and Dr. H set out, with "Joe" driving the carriage. The journey would take more than a day, but Dr. H. had an old friend, a farmer, who lived in Maryland and they stopped at his home in hopes of staying the night. To the Doctor's relief, the slaveholding farmer not only welcomed him but was taken in by the ruse. Joe slept on a blanket on the floor in the corner of the room where Dr. H. slept. The two set out the next day and arrived in Philadelphia on Thanksgiving Day. Weems stayed a few days in Philadelphia, after which Still sent her on to the care of Lewis Tappan in New York City, after which she traveled on, ultimately to Buxton in Canada West.[30]

By 1855 Still had resumed forwarding fugitives to New York City. While in Philadelphia the work of aiding fugitives was focused in the Vigilance Committee, in New York there were a few competing organizations devoted to the protection and aid of fugitive slaves. The first group was the New York State Vigilance Committee, which was associated with Lewis Tappan and connected to the American and Foreign Anti-Slavery Society. It was most active in the early 1850s. A second group, the Committee of Thirteen, organized by Black abolitionists including Dr. James McCune Smith and formed in the wake of the passage of the Fugitive Slave Law of 1850, also provided aid to fugitives in New York and Brooklyn.[31]

It was a third group, however, that would prove to be the most important allies Still and his co-workers would have in New York City. This was the organization centered on Sydney Howard Gay, the Garrisonian editor of the *National Anti-Slavery Standard*. Gay employed two Black men in his office who assisted him in this work: Louis Napoleon and William Leonard. Typically, one of these men would meet fugitives at the docks or at the train station in order to ensure that they arrived safely. Then they would guide them to a safe place where they could stay until they were sent on their way. Still forwarded enough fugitives to Gay and his organization that the two men developed a code to facilitate their collaboration. "When it is possible," Gay wrote to Still in August of 1855, "I wish you would advise me two days before a shipment of your intention, as Napoleon is not always on hand to look out for them at short notice. In special cases you might advise me by Telegraph thus: 'One M. (or one F.) this morning. W.S.' By which I shall understand that one Male, or one Female, as the case may be, has left Phila. by the 6 *o'clock train*—one or more, also, as the case may be."[32]

Once fugitives could safely move on from New York, Gay and his organization ensured they were able to do so. Sometimes this meant they went to Gay's contacts in New England, to Boston or New Bedford, as had been the case with Jane Johnson; Gay had paid her passage on July 31, 1855. Often they headed toward Canada, like Laura Lewis, a fugitive from Louisville, Kentucky, who had been promised her freedom only to find that her owner reneged on the agreement after she died and left Lewis to her heirs. She escaped and made her way to Still in Philadelphia, who forwarded her on to Gay in New York. Gay sent her to live with friends who had already escaped to St. Catharines in Canada West. Gay maintained an extensive network of allies along this route, especially in Albany and Syracuse.[33]

Still also continued to cultivate the series of networks, through Delaware and southeast Pennsylvania, that helped funnel fugitives toward him in Philadelphia. Elijah Pennypacker continued to send fugitives to Still via the train from Norristown near his home; Still or one of his allies would meet them at the station to be sure they arrived safely.[34] Others came from further west in Harrisburg, where Joseph C. Bustill wrote to Still in March 1856 to inform him that he had sent "five large and three packages" to him via the Reading Railroad.[35] Still also continued his fruitful partnership with Thomas Garrett. In December 1855, Garrett sent Still one William Jordon who had escaped from North Carolina a year earlier, after spending months on the run in the swamps near his former home. Jordon had been working in the area around Wilmington for some time, but wanted to join friends of his who had settled in New Bedford. Garrett had furnished him with a new pair of boots and money enough to cover his passage to Still in Philadelphia.[36]

Still allies like Pennypacker and Bustill faced significant danger in the form of slave catchers and the Fugitive Slave Law, which bent the will of local authorities to the recovery of fugitives, but this was nothing compared to the increased pressure that confronted those working to aid the fugitive deeper in slave country. One of the most important of these was Captain Albert Fountain, who for years worked with Still to bring fugitives from Virginia port cities, Norfolk, Richmond, Petersburg, secreted aboard his ship, the *City of Richmond*. Fountain was a romantic, swashbuckling figure; Still would later recall "his rough and rugged appearance, his large head, large mouth, large eyes, and heavy eye-brows, with a natural gift at keeping concealed the inner-workings of his mind and feelings." Fountain was happy to accept compensation for work transporting fugitives, but he also faced great danger in doing so. "His deeds," wrote Still, "proved him to be a true friend of the Slave."[37]

Local authorities in the cities along the Atlantic coast looked to thwart the traffic in fugitive slaves, and they knew that men like Fountain were a critical part of the Underground Railroad. In November 1855, Captain Fountain's schooner lay at the wharf in Norfolk, loaded with wheat, but also with twenty-one slaves secreted below deck. Word had spread throughout the city that a large number of slaves had escaped and the mayor of the city, along with a posse armed with axes and spears, boarded Fountain's ship, convinced that they had caught him in the act. The mayor commanded his men to spear the wheat, but when "the spears brought neither blood nor groans," he instructed his men to "take the axes and go to work" on the deck and other parts of the boat. Fountain,

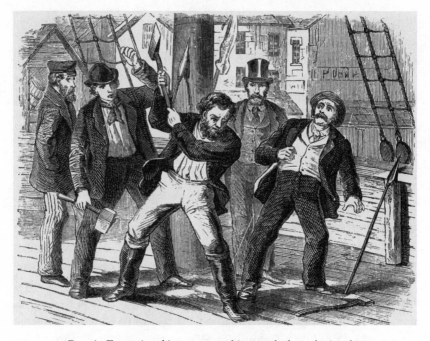

Captain Fountain taking an axe to his own deck, as depicted in
Still's *Underground Railroad*
(Library Company of Philadelphia)

presumably confident that the hiding place he had used to conceal
the fugitives was safe, all the while affected an air of indignance
and defiance. Eventually he lost his patience. "Now if you want to
search," he cried, "give me the axe and point out the spot you want
opened and I will open it for you very quick." Fountain brought
the axe down on his own deck, splintering the boards but revealing no hidden slaves. The mayor and his posse were confounded
by Fountain's performance, and shortly gave up on their search.
Fountain promptly sailed north, where he delivered his cargo to
Thomas Garrett in Delaware, who then forwarded them to Still
and the Philadelphia Vigilance Committee.[38]

It was not practical to thus splinter the deck of all such suspected smugglers and so authorities in North Carolina developed
a different means of preventing the escape of fugitive slaves. The
state passed a law requiring that all vessels headed north from the
state be "smoked" with noxious fumes prior to leaving port. Any

slave hidden aboard the ship would be forced to reveal themselves or they would die hiding. This did not deter all fugitives, though. Two enslaved men, Abram Galloway and Richard Eden, had found a ship captain willing to transport them from Wilmington, North Carolina, to Philadelphia. They made for themselves two silk oil-cloth shrouds, pulled tight around their waists with drawstrings. They also concealed within these shrouds bladders of water and towels, so that when the smoking began the two could hold the wet towels to their faces as a further protection. The day of departure came, and the two prepared themselves, but as luck would have it, the authorities failed to smoke the ship as required by law, and the two sailed for Philadelphia, where Still would ultimately assist them in moving on to Kingston, Canada West.[39]

Still's fame in abolitionist circles had steadily grown over time, and his role in the Jane Johnson affair had widened his notoriety even further, as did the publication of *The Kidnapped and the Ransomed*, a book written by Kate Pickard, a white woman who had met Peter Still while she was a teacher in Alabama. The book recounted Peter's ordeal, and depicted his meeting with his brother in Philadelphia, but William Still had largely remained mum about the specifics of his work in the Vigilance Committee. True, from time to time antislavery publications would note cryptically that the Underground Railroad was thriving, reports likely based on tips from Still, but there was little detail beyond this. Still's reticence began to change, though, with a letter published in the *Provincial Freeman* in January 1856, and shortly thereafter republished in the *National Anti-Slavery Standard*. The letter was a response to a request from Mary Ann Shadd for details on Still's work, his "labours in the cause of the oppressed," which she planned to publish for her readers' benefit. After years of reticence, Still was finally ready to open up.[40]

Certain elements, Still noted, he must "keep dark," for example "the place whence passengers come, the mode of their escape, &c.," yet even with these strategic omissions Still's letter includes some of the most vivid detail yet published concerning the escape of fugitive slaves. He writes of a man swimming across the Potomac River on horseback, his wife having been sold into slavery just a few days earlier. Another man, son of a "full-blooded Indian" from South Carolina, escaped in part by making use of a liquid he used to "prevent hounds from scenting him." Perhaps most provocatively, Still recounts the tale of a man who had been enslaved by the governor of North Carolina, who had separated him from his wife and then denied him the right to visit her. The man fled shortly thereafter, braving swamps and living in a cave for ten months before he was able to find a way to get to Philadelphia. Still's letter celebrates the fugitives themselves, their bravery and resourcefulness, rather than those who helped them along the way. "With but rare exceptions," he writes, "they have been of the most valuable, able-bodied, intelligent and brave of their class." Still seems intent on proving to his readers that these are not pathetic figures in need of pity; they are instead men and women who have largely won their own freedom. If they needed aid, it was not because of any failing of their own.[41]

Still's letter also seems written to provoke. He closes with what reads almost as a boast or a challenge. "In Virginia, they are as savage as wolves," he writes, "and threaten with annihilation every man that may be found aiding the Underground; but, nevertheless, they cannot stop the cars. The slaves, from the youngest to the oldest, have of late years got a thirst for liberty, and they are bound to have it, come what may." While the letter includes little in the way of detail about the operation of the Vigilance Committee, Still surely knew that his words would bring attention to the committee's work, for good or ill. By this point it seems that Still had weighed the risks and benefits of this sort of publicity and determined that the benefits outweighed the risks. Increased attention might bring unwelcome attention from law enforcement, but it could also help the chronically underfunded Vigilance Committee raise needed funds. It could also redirect the antislavery debate onto grounds that by 1856 seemed to favor abolitionists. Between June 1851 and April 1852, Harriet Beecher Stowe had published *Uncle Tom's Cabin* in the *National Era* in forty-one weekly installments, creating a sensation. White Northerners who had previously shown little sympathy for the abolitionist cause were moved by Stowe's tale, including her stirring account of the fugitive Eliza's flight across the frozen Ohio River. In the years that followed the book's publication, sympathy for fugitive slaves grew dramatically among white Northerners. By 1856, Still likely wagered that while the Vigilance Committee's work remained illegal, it was increasing popular at the same time.[42]

Still's confidence in the moral appeal of the fugitive slave cause is illustrated by another incident from roughly the same time. In Still's account of his Underground Railroad work, published years later, he noted that Alexander Cummings, the publisher of the *Evening Bulletin*, one of the city's most widely read newspapers, had expressed to Miller McKim his opposition to the work of the Underground Railroad. McKim invited Cummings to accompany him to see a group of fugitives, assuring him that if he would simply see the work itself, come face-to-face with these men and women and children as they passed through the city on their way to freedom, he would change his mind. Cummings took McKim up on his offer and the effect was dramatic. After seeing these fugitives in person, not only did Cummings withdraw his opposition to the work of the Vigilance Committee, but the publisher pulled a twenty-dollar gold piece out of his pocket and handed it to McKim. The anecdote seems a little too convenient, but it surely captures the abolitionists' broader sense that there was a latent sympathy for the fugitive slave among white Northerners that only needed to be drawn out.[43]

In general, Still's public writing had also begun to show a more explicit engagement with the world of electoral politics and commitment to the struggle to build a broader coalition of antislavery voters. In a February 1856 letter to the *Provincial Freeman* he noted the increasing willingness of Southern intellectuals to make the case that "the poor white man, as well as the black, is fitted only for slavery." Still applauded this honesty and hoped that it would lead to an alliance between Black slaves and poor whites. Too many whites, Still argued, "thinking themselves free and of the approved and favored race," were indifferent to slavery. In the same letter, he celebrated the election of Nathaniel Banks as Speaker of the U.S. House of Representatives after more than a hundred ballots. Banks was a member of the anti-immigrant Know Nothing Party (though he would shortly thereafter join the Republican Party), but as Still noted, he was also "the anti-slavery candidate" and a representative from Massachusetts, "the bulwark of the 'Personal Liberty Law.'" The man he had defeated, William Aiken, was a proslavery Democrat from South Carolina and, as Still reminded his readers, "the owner of two thousand slaves."[44] Banks's victory was surely something for abolitionists to celebrate.

As many abolitionists, Still among them, had foreseen, the Northern backlash against the Kansas-Nebraska Act had led to a reorganization of the politics of slavery and to the ultimate ascendance of the Republican Party. Antislavery Whigs and antislavery Democrats had fled their parties in the wake of the crisis over Kansas, though the exact route they took varied from state to state. Some joined what was called the People's Party. Others termed their party "Fusion" or simply "Anti-Nebraska." Some even saw the anti-immigrant Know Nothing Party as a vehicle for antislavery politics, but what united them all was a sense that the Kansas-Nebraska Bill had revealed the face of what they increasingly called the Slave Power: an aggressive political force, seeking to control the government of the United States in order to serve the interests of slaveholders. Eventually this disparate political coalition would become the Republican Party, which would hold its first presidential nominating convention in Philadelphia in 1856.[45]

Still, like many abolitionists, was both heartened by the rise in antislavery sentiment represented by the Republican Party and disappointed by its limitations. "Politically the numbers representing the Anti-Slavery sentiments will be far greater this year," noted Still, but he worried that "the number standing on genuine Anti-Slavery principles will be too few, obviously, to wield an influence sufficiently potent to effect in the coming National Convention of the Republican Party." Still's employers, the leaders of the PASS, remained allied with the Garrisonian branch of the abolitionist movement and in general were skeptical of voting as an effective means of advancing the cause, but by 1856 even Garrison himself had begun to soften his opposition to voting in light of the emergence of the Republican Party.[46]

Still remained mum on his own position in regard to voting, a right denied to him and all black Pennsylvanians by the state's 1838 constitution, but his extensive report on the Republican convention shows that he was genuinely excited by what he saw. He admitted that "the millions of slaves now groaning for deliverance all over the South receive no pledge from this Convention," which focused on checking the aggressive expansion of slavery and which frankly admitted the constitutionality of slavery where it currently existed. This was certainly a disappointment to Still, though not a surprise. What most pleased him, though, was the animating spirit that he saw in the convention. He praised the staunch antislavery men who were leading spirits of the party, William Seward, John P. Hale, Joshua R. Giddings, and Charles Sumner, and remarked that the speeches of these antislavery stalwarts were the "most cordially received and enthusiastically applauded and endorsed throughout." If the Republican Party as it stood in 1856 failed to live up to the hopes of Still and most abolitionists, its advent, the willingness of its leaders to cast aside their old party distinctions in order to establish "a strong Northern party," was something to cheer. Even if John C. Frémont, the Republicans' candidate for president, were to fail, Still predicted that the party itself would have a positive effect on the Northern public.[47]

Perhaps Still's optimism concerning the political future of the Republican Party had something to do with the flow of fugitives through the Anti-Slavery Society office and the increasing frustration of slave owners in their attempts to recover them. In March 1856, three enslaved brothers, Owen, Otho, and Benjamin Taylor, fled from slavery near Hagerstown, Maryland. The brothers harnessed two horses to the carriage of their master, loaded their wives and children into it, and fled north. In Chambersburg, Pennsylvania, they ditched the carriage and took cars to Harrisburg, where they sought the help of the vigilance committee there. Joseph Bustill, a member of the committee, then sent them on to Still in Philadelphia. Shortly thereafter, Still received a letter from Bustill. The former master of the Taylors, Henry Fiery, had contacted Bustill and offered to grant the group their freedom, eventually, if they would only come back to him. If they preferred, he added, Fiery would be willing to "sell them their time for $1300." The Taylor brothers, by this point well on their way to Canada, were hardly interested, but the fact that Fiery's first recourse was to negotiation, rather than to hire a slave catcher, suggests how little confidence that border-state slaveholders like Fiery had in the ability of the Fugitive Slave Law help them in recovering their former property.[48]

Of course, not all slave masters were as willing as Fiery to give up on recovering slaves who had fled from their possession. Slave-catching had always attracted the interest of unscrupulous, entre-preneurial policemen, looking to supplement their wages with extra work. Increasingly, though, the possibility of great profit and competition with men like Still led to greater sophistication on the part of slave catchers. In 1854, for example, a Maryland police officer, John Pope, helped to create an "Independent Police and Detective" force, an organization that claimed to have spies scat-tered across the Northern states and that offered a host of services which would help masters in search of absconded fugitives.[49] In Philadelphia, the notorious slave catcher George Alberti, who had been tried and convicted under Pennsylvania's anti-kidnapping law, had been pardoned by the state's governor, William Bigler, and almost immediately went back to work hunting slaves. Alberti cultivated a vast network of informants, many of them Black, who helped him track down fugitive slaves.[50]

This desperate struggle between slave catchers and those who would aid fugitives led both sides to look for advantages. Recog-nizing the importance of swift communication, both sides turned to the new technology of the telegraph. Samuel Morse had shown the effectiveness of the new technology with his famous demon-stration in 1844, and within a few years networks of wires were extensive enough that the telegraph had become an essential tool in the fight over fugitive slaves. Upon learning that a fugitive had escaped, masters would wire ahead to places where they thought they might have gone, sending word to men like Alberti to be on the lookout. For Still, the telegraph became a means to stay one step ahead of slave catchers, to receive and send word of the com-ing and going of passengers on the Underground Railroad so that agents could ensure their safe passage.[51]

Sometimes, however, telegraph messages fell into the wrong

hands. One day in May 1856, Still returned to the office to find an unfamiliar police officer waiting for him. "I have just received a telegraphic dispatch from a slaveholder living in Maryland," he told Still, "informing me that six slaves had escaped from him, and that he had reason to believe that they were on their way to Philadelphia." The slaveholder had offered a reward for their recovery. "I am not the man for this business," the officer confessed to Still, "I would have nothing to do with the contemptable work of arresting fugitives."

Still eyed the police officer warily, but listened. He had never met this officer before, and Still knew that things were not always what they seemed. In this case, though, Still had his own telegraphic dispatch, sent to him earlier that day by Joseph Bustill. It read: "I have sent via at two o'clock four large and two small hams." Now Still knew not only that six fugitives would be arriving from Harrisburg; he also knew that they were being hunted. He made sure that an agent of the Vigilance Committee met these fugitives at the depot and that they had a safe place to stay for a few days, "long enough to give the slave-hunters full opportunity to tire themselves, and give up the chase in despair."[52]

Of course, not all such cases ended well for those seeking to aid fugitives. Years earlier, Samuel Smith had participated in the escape of Henry Brown, sealing him in a box and shipping him to Philadelphia. Smith was so thrilled by the success of this endeavor that he sought to duplicate it. Two young men came to Smith and asked his help in fleeing to the North. This time, however, they were thwarted "through the agency of the telegraph." Their plan was uncovered by authorities in Baltimore, and word was relayed to Philadelphia before the men could be unboxed. The two fugitives were captured and dragged back into bondage. Smith was arrested, tried, and convicted, and sent to a Richmond penitentiary. On July 21, 1856, three days after he emerged from his near-eight-year term, Smith was given a hero's welcome in Philadelphia, at least among the city's Black community. Several Black leaders, Still among them, organized a mass meeting, held at Israel Church, to thank Smith as "a martyr to the cause of Freedom." Smith stayed with the Still family for a few weeks before departing for western

New York, where he began his life anew. The grateful Black community of Philadelphia sent him on his way with funds they had raised to help him do so.[53]

It is possible that Harriet Tubman was among this group. In the spring of 1856, Tubman had returned to Philadelphia. After helping her brothers escape from slavery in 1854, she had accompanied them on their journey to Canada, where they settled in the Black refugee community of St. Catharines. Tubman stayed in Canada for several months, but returned to Philadelphia in the late summer or early fall, in order to earn money for another foray into Maryland. While there, she immersed herself in the city's Black abolitionist community, likely attending the Colored National Convention held in Philadelphia that October; she visited Passmore Williamson in his Moyamensing cell on October 20. Later that fall, though, she returned to her old home on the Eastern Shore of Maryland hoping to guide more of her family and friends to freedom in the North. In early December, she brought north a man named Henry Hooper, who arrived in Philadelphia on the sixth after a short stop at Thomas Garrett's home in Delaware. Tubman immediately returned to Maryland, this time hoping to rescue her sister, Rachel. Unfortunately, at this time Rachel's master had separated her from her children and she was unwilling to leave without them. Tubman was forced to head north without her sister, but she did forward another man, Joseph Cornish, who arrived at Still's home on Christmas Day, 1855.[54]

Tubman remained in Philadelphia, saving money for another trip into Maryland in the spring of 1856. Once again, she was unable to bring her sister with her when she returned north, but she did bring four men, "young and able bodied." Once again, the group stopped first with Thomas Garrett in Wilmington before proceeding on without Tubman to Longwood, the home of John and Hannah Cox, in Chester County, Pennsylvania. Tubman followed the next day, and from there the group proceeded to Philadelphia, where on May 13 they were welcomed by Still and Nathaniel Depee, and then forwarded on to Canada.[55]

. . .

Even as Still and his allies continued their work ferrying fugitive slaves, Philadelphia, along with the rest of the nation, geared up for a presidential election. While the ongoing crisis in Kansas had driven many Americans into the arms of Frémont and the Republican Party, for others the civil war in "Bleeding Kansas" raised the ominous specter of disunion. The Democrats sought to portray their opponents as "Black Republicans," in league with abolitionists, and themselves as the only truly national party, emphasizing their fundamental conservatism by nominating Pennsylvanian James Buchanan, a longtime party loyalist and classic example of what antislavery Northerners called a "doughface": a Northern man with Southern principles. Buchanan was generally seen as a defender of the rights of slaveholders, but as minister to Britain he had been out of the country for most of the Kansas-Nebraska crisis so he could plausibly claim to be above the fray of what was increasingly a drag on the appeal of the Democratic Party.

For many voters, however, both the Republican and Democratic Parties seemed responsible for the growing sectional strife; such voters turned instead to former president Millard Fillmore as the representative of the American Party, still a home to many anti-immigrant "Know-Nothings," but increasingly depicting itself as the party of sectional compromise. In Pennsylvania, voters were presented with a complicated array of choices on election day, including two "fusion" tickets combining the Republican and American Party vote, one with Fillmore and the other with Frémont as the candidate, as well as straight Democratic and Republican tickets. In the end, Buchanan's reputation as a defender of slavery and the increasing frustration of Northerners at the events in Kansas led much of the North to vote for Frémont and the Republicans, but Buchanan maintained enough support to win his home state, as well as every slave state except Maryland, which went for Fillmore; this secured the presidency for the Pennsylvania Democrat.[56]

Many abolitionists had held out little hope that "the late Republican farce," as one of Still's correspondents termed it, would succeed in electing Frémont. And yet, as Still had noted in his report on the Republican convention that summer, a Republican campaign was not to be measured simply in its success or failure in electing its chosen candidate. "We have had much of genuine anti-slavery preached during this campaign," noted one Philadelphia abolitionist, "and numbers have been carried beyond 'freedom for Kansas' to an examination of the whole subject of American slav-ery, and have arrived at the conclusion that slavery and freedom cannot exist in the same body politic or social organization with-out the one encroaching upon the other." Abolitionists hoped that the campaign had awakened vast numbers of previously apathetic Northerners to the evils of slavery and the threat that it posed not just to the enslaved but to the rights of white Northerners.[57]

All recognized that Pennsylvania had been the lynchpin of Buchanan's success, and the state's antislavery Pennsylvanians were particularly ashamed by the failure of their state to rally to the Republican cause. Abolitionists attributed Buchanan's success in their state to a number of different factors. Some attributed Dem-ocratic victory to "our merchants and manufacturers," who, they argued, "were stricken with fear for their trade with the South." Others saw Frémont's failure as a product of the "fusion" effort, which had tainted Republicans with the stain of nativism and ruined their appeal with immigrants. For some, the Republicans had simply failed to offer a full-throated antislavery case. "Had the Republicans there, that is to say, been true to Republican-ism," noted one commentator, "there would have been a different result." Others insisted that Buchanan had won in Pennsylvania by misrepresenting his true intentions in regard to the issue of the extension of slavery.[58] Whatever the cause of Buchanan's vic-tory, abolitionists were sure that once he assumed the office of the presidency he would be sure to show his true colors and reward his Southern supporters.

Validation of abolitionist fears would come swiftly, though not through the actions of Buchanan, at least not at first. Two days after the president was sworn into office, the Supreme Court handed down its decision in the case of *Dred Scott v. Sandford.* The case had been long in germinating. John Emerson, an army physi-cian, had purchased Dred Scott and his wife, Harriet, and taken them from Missouri to his posting in Illinois and later to what was then the Wisconsin Territory. Slavery was illegal in both places.

After several years, Emerson returned to Missouri, bringing the Scotts with him. After Emerson's death, the couple and their two daughters were eventually passed on to Emerson's wife, Irene. In 1846, Dred and Harriet Scott brought suit against Mrs. Emerson claiming that their residence in the free state of Illinois and the free territory of Wisconsin had made them legally free. They initially lost their case but were granted a retrial, which declared them free. Mrs. Emerson appealed the decision to the Missouri Supreme Court, which overturned the decision, setting up a showdown in the U.S. Supreme Court.[59]

While on its face the case was about the legal status of one family, all recognized its larger significance. At its core the case addressed the right of Congress to exclude slavery from the territories. Even so, the Supreme Court might have evaded these larger questions and rendered a much narrower decision, simply rejecting Scott's specific claims and leaving it at that. There was precedent for such a decision. In the 1851 case of *Strader v. Graham*, the Court had decided that it was the right of each individual state to determine whether or not residence in a free state rendered a slave free. In the eyes of the chief justice of the Court, Roger Taney, though, this would have been a missed opportunity. The "fervently proslavery" chief justice, committed to saving the union from the threat of abolitionism, decided to write a decision he believed would place the contentious issue of slavery beyond the control of Congress. It consisted of two major parts. The first, the most infamous element of the decision and the one we most remember today, declared that Black people had never been and could never be American citizens, that they "had no rights which the white man was bound to respect." Since this was the case, Taney argued, the Scotts had no right to bring the suit. Taney might have ended his argument here, but he went on to insist that Congress had no right to outlaw slavery in federal territory. Since slavery was legal under the law of many states, he argued, the exclusion of such property from federal territory constituted a violation of the Fifth Amendment's guarantee that no one be denied "life, liberty, or property without due process of law."[60]

Unsurprisingly African Americans saw this decision, particularly its denial of Black citizenship rights, as an abomination and as a personal affront, but how would they respond? In a letter to the *Provincial Freeman*, William Still attempted to capture what he had learned of the views of Black Philadelphians he had spoken with "in my walks around the city." He admitted that there remained a diversity of opinion concerning the *Dred Scott* decision, but insisted that "its influence has been more discouraging and prostrating to the hopes of the colored man, than any preceding act of tyranny ever perpetrated upon him by this nation." One "leading (colored) Rev. gentleman of the city" told Still that he was actually glad that the Supreme Court had acted so boldly since in doing so it would only precipitate the Northern backlash to the Slave Power. Some, Still noted, were now more than before open to emigrating to Canada, though there were others who felt that Canada would be no better than the United States. Still others felt that it was a moral responsibility to remain in the United States to fight; as Isaiah Wears put it to Still, "not a free man can be spared." As for himself, Still remained somewhat vague, though he admitted that given the circumstances he had become somewhat less optimistic. "I confess I see but a faint prospect of any very great change for the better, at least in the present generation," he wrote. "Therefore I am not of the number any longer to subscribe to the above 'staying' &c. doctrine; and verily hope never to again as long as this abominable decision and pro-slavery constitution remains." And yet, the balance of Still's letter suggests he had not yet given up on the land of his birth. He continued to call out his fellow Black citizens for their insufficient zeal in fighting for the cause of the slave or for the struggle for equal rights. Still's letter expresses his deep pain, but that pain seems to lead Still to a call for action rather than to resignation.[61]

In Philadelphia, Black leaders organized a meeting at Israel Church, with Still as secretary, to express their outrage. In a series of resolutions, and then in a series of speeches, the meeting denounced the *Dred Scott* decision and refuted its historical claims that Black men had never been considered citizens of the United States. Despite rejecting Taney's historical claims, the meeting insisted that the decision invalidated any claims that the Constitution could be considered an antislavery document, an argument that many abolitionists, including Frederick Douglass, had come to embrace. Black men, they maintained, could owe nothing to such a government, a government that saw them as "nothing but an alien, disfranchised and degraded class." To continue to support such a government would be "the height of folly." In place of the feeling of optimism that many abolitionists, Still included, had expressed before the presidential election of 1856, the meeting offered a deep sense of pessimism, a feeling that the nation was in decline, and that any rights they had been able to enjoy were vulnerable to the whims of "the slave power." Free Black Americans had only been fooling themselves into thinking that the white majority considered them a part of the nation. "The only duty the colored man owes to a Constitution under which he is declared to be an inferior and degraded," they argued, "is to denounce and repudiate it, and to do what he can by all proper means to bring it into contempt." Even among those Black leaders most skeptical of the United States and its government, the *Dred Scott* decision was an outrage.[62]

The anger of these Black leaders resonated beyond Philadelphia and raised larger questions about what was to be done. Mary Ann Shadd Cary (she had married Thomas Cary in January 1856), writing from Canada West, remarked upon the meeting, but asked why these incensed abolitionists would go no further. "This is not the time for strong words only," she insisted. She called out many of her close allies, Still among them, by name. "Your national ship is rotting," she told them, "why not leave it, and why not say so boldly, manfully?" For years, she had been trumpeting Canada as a refuge not just for fugitive slaves but for free Blacks as well, for men and women who desired to be treated as full citizens, who desired the rights that were denied them in the land of their birth. *Dred Scott* seemed to confirm her argument that such rights would never be granted in "that slavery-cursed republic." Whether they wanted to admit it or not, she said, the United States was not their home.[63]

CHAPTER EIGHT

DARK DAYS

Early in 1857, William Still signed a petition calling for a convention that would "consider the practicability, probability, and expediency of a Separation between the Free and Slave States." To a certain extent, this was in keeping with the abolitionist doctrine of disunion that Garrison had been advocating for more than a decade. For Still, though, and for the men who signed the petition with him, this was a call born of a particularly desperate moment. "It must be obvious to all," they wrote, "that the American Union is constantly becoming more and more divided, by Slavery, into two distinct and antagonistic nations." Slaveholders had seized control of all three branches of the national government, and they were using it to roll back any protections that free men had once had. They had "removed all legal protection from a large portion of the people of the free States. As if to reinforce the second-class status that this slaveholders' union had placed upon Black citizens, the signatures of the petition were divided into two columns, one for "legal voters" and a second for "other persons."[1]

Nothing came of this particular call for disunion, but the call itself is a significant expression of the mood of abolitionists in the late 1850s. These were dark days. Not only had the Supreme Court declared that "the black man has no rights which the white man is bound to respect," and that the Congress had no right to ban slavery in the federal territories, but the Slave Power seemed ascendant everywhere. The bloody civil war between free-state and proslavery settlers seemed to have yielded the blatantly proslavery Lecompton Constitution in Kansas. Southern "filibusters" like William Walker were seeking to set up proslavery colonies in Central America, and slaveholding politicians greedily eyed a Caribbean empire. White Southern intellectuals were openly arguing that slavery was a positive good, that it was the only natural status for the descendants of Africans, and some were even advocating for the reopening of the Atlantic slave trade. And of course, the Fugitive Slave Law remained in force.[2]

At about four o'clock, January 15, 1857, two U.S. deputies, James Crossin and John Jenkins, accompanied by John Graham, a detective from Baltimore, seized a Black man named Henry Tiffney at the corner of Lombard and Ninth Streets in Philadelphia, in what was the city's residential and institutional Black center. These officers believed Tiffney was in fact Michael Brown, for whom they had an arrest warrant, issued at the request of his alleged owner, William Gatchell of Baltimore. The deputies, however, arrested him not as a fugitive slave but on the charge of theft. These two had encountered difficulties in fugitive cases before; three times they had been charged with assault and battery in the course of capturing fugitive slaves. In each case they had been acquitted, but through subterfuge they hoped to avoid any unpleasant reaction that might result from their actual work. Only when they got him before the court did they claim him as a fugitive slave. The commissioner in the case, David Paul Brown, Jr., who had succeeded Edward Ingraham when the notorious commissioner died, placed the defendant in custody and scheduled the hearing for the following morning.[3]

Tiffney's lawyer, William Pierce, requested that Still interview his client, and by Still's admission he was eager to "show my sympathy for the unfortunate man." Unfortunately, when Still arrived the deputy marshals forbade anyone but the counsel for the defense from visiting him. Tiffney did tell Still that he "had rather die than go back." In the hearing, which extended for two days, the defense sought to prove that Tiffney was, in fact, a free man. They produced a series of witnesses who testified that they had known Tiffney for some time, in some cases for years, and that he was free. There may also have been some plan among the city's Black community to take matters into their own hands in case the court decided against Tiffney. On the first day of the hearing the courtroom was packed with Black observers, Still among them, but on the second day Commissioner Brown restricted access to the room, citing "threats of a Rescue." Ultimately, the commissioner was unconvinced by the extensive testimony of Black Philadelphians. Brown remanded Tiffney to the hands of his alleged master. The authorities remained fearful that "colored friends" who surrounded the Court building were planning to intervene, but nothing came of this threat. Tiffney was handcuffed and taken to Baltimore by the eleven o'clock train.[4]

The outcome of the case was, perhaps, no surprise to Black Philadelphians. While fugitive slave cases had been uncommon in recent years, all knew the Fugitive Slave Law loomed over Black Philadelphians, whether they were legally free or not. What most shocked them was the name of the commissioner who had remanded Tiffney to bondage: David Paul Brown, Jr. This was shocking because the commissioner's father was a well-known abolitionist, a man who had *defended* accused fugitives on numerous occasions. While some wished to believe that the tide of popular opinion was turning toward the abolitionist cause, here was evidence that even sons of abolitionist fathers might be seduced by the Slave Power.

A few weeks after the trial a group of Black leaders, Still among them, organized a meeting, held at the new Masonic hall, to express their outrage. George Goines was called to the chair, and Still was appointed secretary. The meeting adopted a series of resolutions, including one stating "That henceforth the coloured citizens of Philadelphia look upon David Paul Brown, Jr., as being linked with our worst oppressors." Leading Black orators, including Robert Purvis and Frances Ellen Watkins, offered their words of condemnation. "If he had been present," noted Still, Commissioner Brown "would have been fully convinced, by the large and respectable audience, the tone and firmness of the speakers, and the intense indignation manifested throughout, of the inexpressible contempt felt for him by every lover of freedom amongst the coloured people of Philadelphia."[5] Black Philadelphians had always relied on white allies in their struggle against the Fugitive Slave Law, but many Black leaders were feeling increasingly that white allies were failing them. They could only truly rely on the solidarity of the Black community and its commitment to protecting its members.

Still took great pride in the fact that no traveler on the Underground Railroad had died while passing through the region around Philadelphia, but in early 1857 it looked like their good fortune had run out. One March night, a man came to Still's door, suffering from extreme frostbite to his feet and legs; he had lost all feeling in his extremities. Still immediately called for two doctors who had been helpful before. They removed the man's toes, hoping this would be sufficient to stop the mortification of his tissue. At first it seemed to be working, but then his symptoms changed for the worse. He spent thirty-six hours in extreme agony, fighting severe spasms and lockjaw. Still spent much of this by his side, comforting him and hoping to learn something of his story.

His name was Romulus Hall, and he had fled from bondage in Charles County, Maryland, with a friend named Abram Harris. They had set out together, but being ignorant of the distance before them or the paths they should take, all they could do was trust in God and keep "the North Star in view." It was bitterly cold and they went for days without food. Eventually Hall, who was the older of the two at about fifty years of age, could not go on and his friend was forced to leave him behind. Harris made it to the Vigilance Committee in Philadelphia and could only hope that his friend would be able to follow him to Canada. Later, once he had settled in his new home, Harris wrote to Still inquiring about his old friend. Still sadly reported that Hall had died in Philadelphia, "the first instance of death on the Underground Rail Road in this region." Of course, he knew that he could not save every slave who sought his freedom, but the sight of Hall on his deathbed seems to have shaken him. "Only think how this poor man," he later wrote, "in an enlightened Christian land, for the bare hope of freedom, in a strange land among strangers, was obliged not only to bear the sacrifice of his wife and kindred, but also of his own life."[6]

Surely this death weighed on him, but Still also had grown increasingly concerned about traitors within the extensive network of the Underground Railroad. In March 1857, Still's ally Thomas Garrett warned that "a colored man named Thomas Otwell" had betrayed a group of fugitives who were traveling through Delaware, working in partnership with "a *white scamp*." Fortunately, the group escaped jail and then, after hiding out for some time, made their way to Philadelphia.[7] There was little that Still could do in such circumstances but get the word to his allies to be on the lookout for this particular scoundrel, but he knew there would be others. Later that year, Still once again received word from Garrett that he and his agents should be on the lookout for a traitor. This time the traitor was in Philadelphia. Garrett had been informed by a constable who was sympathetic to the Underground Railroad that a Black man in Philadelphia "who professed to be a great friend of the colored people" had relayed information to him about a group of fugitives passing through Maryland, intending to help apprehend them. Still was never able to determine the name of the man in Philadelphia, nor was he even sure of the veracity of this tale of betrayal, but it surely worried him that his fugitive network might be compromised.[8]

Of course, Still and the other members of the Vigilance Committee were known to engage in some subterfuge of their own, and many slaves were only able to escape through swindling their masters. One such case found its way to Still in the summer of 1857. James Conner was enslaved to a man in Point Copee, about 150 miles from New Orleans. His master, Charles Parlange, had promised Conner his freedom years earlier but had never followed through on his promise, and so when his master made plans to travel to Virginia to purchase slaves and planned to bring Conner with him, Conner decide that this was his chance to escape. He reassured his master and mistress that he had no desire to escape. "They hated the North," he told Still, "and I made believe that I did too." Parlange and Conner traveled north to Baltimore before engaging in their slave-purchasing business in Virginia, and before they headed south, Parlange decided to take Conner with him on a short trip to Philadelphia. Conner grabbed his chance. Once left alone at the Girard Hotel, where he was staying with his master, Conner approached a Black man who told him about the Vigilance Committee and then took him to the Anti-Slavery Society office. Once there, Still assured him that he was, in fact, now a free man, and he even suggested that if Conner were to testify to a judge that he had been held illegally as a slave in Philadelphia, he might have his master arrested. Not sure that he would be able to face his master in court, Conner decided he was content with his freedom.

His master, however, was not as willing as Conner to spare them all a court date. Upon discovering that Conner had fled, Parlange went to the authorities. He knew that he had no claim on Conner under the Fugitive Slave Law, since he had brought him willingly into Pennsylvania, but he hoped he might use other means to recover his property. He claimed to the police that when Conner left, he had taken with him two boxes, one filled with money. In this way, Parlange hoped to use the Philadelphia police as his personal slave hunters, under the guise of tracking down a thief. Fortunately, the Vigilance Committee had secured Conner a ticket north; a few weeks later Still received a letter from St. Catharines, informing him of Conner's "safe arrival in the glorious land of Freedom."[9]

Some of the most dramatic examples of Vigilance Committee subterfuge emerged from its ongoing competition with the slave catchers prowling the streets of Philadelphia. One afternoon, a supporter of the Vigilance Committee's work brought into the Anti-Slavery Society office a letter that had been misplaced. The letter, addressed to George Alberti, stated that a woman from Maryland was then in Philadelphia and was interested in securing the services of the infamous slave catcher. At the request of the Vigilance Committee, Cyrus Whitson then went to the woman claiming to be an associate of Alberti's and agreeing to aid her in her effort to recover a man who had fled to Philadelphia. The woman, who seemed to want to avoid undue attention, was pleased that this matter was to be handled with discretion. Under this ruse, the woman revealed crucial information, "the name of the fugitive, his age, size and color, and where he may be found." With this information, the committee was able to alert the fugitive, a man named Butler, from the danger he faced at the hands of would-be slave catchers. They also printed a large number of handbills, three feet square, warning that "Miss Wilson, of Georgetown Cross Roads, Kent County, Md., is now in the city in pursuit of her alleged slave man, Butler." Shortly thereafter she slunk back to Maryland, without Butler.[10]

Other times, Still relied on former fugitives to supply him with information. Oscar and Montgomery Ball escaped from Alexandria, Virginia, early in 1857. They passed through Philadelphia with the intention of continuing on to Canada, but ended up finding work in Oswego, New York. Oscar remained in contact with Still in hopes that he might coordinate the escape of several others from Alexandria, including another brother of his. Oscar encouraged those friends and family members he had left behind to take the same route he had taken, even sending them money to help them on the way. "I am glad to hear that the Underground Rail Road is doing so well," he wrote to Still. "I broke the ice and it seems as if they are going to keep the track [in Alexandria] open." Still's sprawling Underground Railroad network often worked this way, relying on personal connections to bring people into contact with Still and the Vigilance Committee.[11]

These connections also served to bind together families and communities that had been severed by slavery and by the flight from slavery. Still's correspondence is filled with letters from those who had passed through his office and were now looking for information about loved ones they had left behind. Sometimes they simply wanted news, to find out if a wife had sent word, or if a mother was still living. In other cases, though, they were looking for Still's help in bringing family members north. Sometimes Still helped to coordinate the purchase of family members of those who had themselves escaped bondage but who had left loved ones behind. Such was the case of Arabella Weems (Still recorded her name as

"Earro"). Her freedom had been purchased in 1852 through the work of Jacob Bigelow in Washington, D.C., and Still and Bigelow had helped smuggle her daughter Ann Maria out of bondage in 1855, but in 1857 Arabella wrote to Still, asking for his help in purchasing the freedom of her son Augustus who was enslaved in Alabama.[12] On other occasions, Still's correspondents wanted help of a more direct sort. John Wood had run away from slavery in Maryland in 1857, but the next year, "not contended to enjoy the boon alone," he contacted Still looking for advice on how he might liberate his family. "I have made up my mind to make an adventure after my family," he wrote, "and I want to get an answer from you and then I shall know how to act." Still's records do not indicate whether or not he was able to help Wood, but it is clear that fugitive slaves continued to look to Still for help, even long after they had secured their own freedom.[13]

Still was often called upon to participate in schemes of various sorts to liberate the enslaved from bondage, but other fugitives continued to come to Still through means entirely outside of his control. Such arrivals were far less predictable than those who came to Still via his established networks. Alfred Thornton, for example, who "found no fault with the ordinary treatment received at the hands of his master," was surprised one day by the appearance of a slave trader; Thornton had been sold. The man approached Thornton and tried to take hold of him, but the young man was too quick. "I flew," he later told Still. "I took off my hat and run, took off my jacket and run harder, took off my vest and doubled my pace." The trader emptied his revolver in his direction, but he missed his mark. At first Thornton intended just to evade the slave trader with no intention of fleeing north, but before long he realized he had no choice but to "try and get to a free State." He did not know the way, and he had the misfortune to take flight in the midst of a rainy season; not only was he cold and wet, but he had no way to find the North Star. Nevertheless, Thornton eventually found his way to Still and the Vigilance Committee in Philadelphia.[14]

· · ·

Along with his brisk business in helping fugitive slaves, Still remained committed to the elevation of Black Americans. Still had long believed that cultivating an independent Black literary culture played an essential role in promoting the respectability of Black people. From his earliest days in Philadelphia, he had sought to improve himself and to provide opportunities for the like-minded to do the same. Still had championed the work of Black authors, like William Wells Brown and Frances Ellen Watkins, and he had served on the board of institutions such as the Library and Reading Room that operated out of the Institute for Colored Youth. At times Still was frustrated with the lack of support such institutions often received in the city, but he himself never wavered in his advocacy of Black literature.[15]

Still and William Wells Brown had bonded years earlier when Brown stayed in Philadelphia for several weeks on one of his speaking tours. Brown, who had been born in Kentucky to an enslaved mother and a white planter father, escaped from a steamboat docked in Cincinnati in 1834. He settled in Buffalo, New York, for a number of years, where he helped ferry fugitive slaves across the lake to freedom in Canada. He would go on to become an abolitionist orator and one of the most celebrated and prolific Black authors of the nineteenth century. In 1853 he published the first novel by an African American, *Clotel: or the President's Daughter*, a fictional account of two daughters born to Thomas Jefferson and an enslaved woman, loosely based on the actual Hemings family. Brown seems to have seen Still, the self-made son of former slaves, as a kindred spirit. A few years later, when he published his compendium of great Black leaders, *The Black Man: His Antecedents, His Genius, and His Achievements*, he included a glowing portrait of Still.[16]

Brown spent several weeks in Philadelphia in 1858, traveling around the region, delivering antislavery lectures, and generally promoting the abolitionist cause. Still coordinated Brown's appearances through the Anti-Slavery Society office, and it is likely that Brown stayed with the Still family for much of this month. Brown was an experienced orator, comfortable speaking on a multitude of antislavery themes, but in general his public speaking returned to his own story, his life as a slave and his escape from bondage—

slavery as he knew it. Over years on the lecture circuit, Brown had developed a style and tone that most effectively moved his audience. In clear and forceful language, he painted vivid pictures that made slavery immediate to his often largely white audiences. Like many antislavery lecturers, he paid particular attention to the toll that slavery took on Black families, its role in tearing mothers from children, husbands from wives. Brown's stories of Black life, their emphasis on the fundamental humanity of the enslaved, targeted white notions of Black inferiority.[17]

Still certainly admired Brown, and in their weeks together perhaps the two discussed Still's own ambitions to fashion an antislavery, antiracist literature from the raw material of his Vigilance Committee work. At the end of 1857, Still had written another extensive "report" on the Underground Railroad, published in the New York *Tribune* this time. As before, Still's account celebrates the vast number of fugitives making their way to Canada. He adopts the device of giving each fugitive a number in order to hammer home the scale of this mass migration. As before, the actual mechanics of fugitive escape are largely omitted. "As usual," writes Still, "many of the most thrilling and interesting incidents indispensable to the safety of the road must be kept concealed." Instead of focusing on the flight of these individuals, Still uses their escape as an opportunity to illuminate the lives of the enslaved. There is extensive discussion of what he termed "his or her impartial experience of Slavery." What Still also provides in this report, and here we can see a similarity to William Wells Brown's antislavery writing and oratory, is a particular emphasis on the remarkable character of those who escape from slavery. One example of this can be seen in his account of one particular fugitive from Cambridge, Maryland, a man named Nat. "Nat is no ordinary man," writes Still. "Like a certain other Nat known to history, his appearance and independent bearing in every respect was that of a natural hero. He was full black, and about six feet high; of powerful physical proportions, and of more than ordinary intellectual capacities."[18] For Still, fugitive slaves were to be seen as natural leaders, as exemplars of the "colored race," and as definitive refutation of pervasive notions of white supremacy.

Despite Still's continuing tendency to leave his own actions out of his accounts, others looked to him as a representative of the Black community in Philadelphia and as an indispensable leader of the abolitionist underground. On March 10, 1859, Still was one of a small group of Black leaders who came together for a secretive meeting in the Philadelphia home of the Black businessman, abolitionist, and Underground Railroad activist Stephen Smith at Ninth and Lombard Streets. Most of the men there were Black Philadelphians who, like Still, were involved in the Vigilance Committee, but there were out-of-town visitors as well. Frederick Douglass and Henry Highland Garnet were there. Most of the time Douglass would be unquestionably the most notable man present in any room where he found himself, but on this occasion the man they had all come to meet was one who had become even more famous, or notorious depending on how you felt about him, than Douglass: John Brown.[19]

Brown had distinguished himself as a fierce enemy of slavery and as a radical advocate for the rights of African Americans. Born in Connecticut in 1800, descended from early Puritan settlers, Brown moved with his family to the Western Reserve of Ohio in 1805, part of the larger migration of Yankees from New England to the states of what we now think of as the Midwest. Brown's family was both intensely pious and profoundly opposed to slavery. His family sheltered fugitive slaves, and his father withdrew his support for Western Reserve College in Ohio because it denied admission to Black students. In other words, the Brown family provided fertile soil for the growth of a young abolitionist, and Brown would continue to support the abolitionist cause after he left home and started his own family, but what seems to have truly radicalized him was the 1837 killing of abolitionist editor Elijah Lovejoy. Following the murder of the Illinois-based Lovejoy, Brown and his father attended a memorial prayer meeting where the younger Brown rose and, raising his right hand, declared, "Here, before God, in the presence of these witnesses, from this time, I consecrate my life to the destruction of slavery!" In the 1840s, Brown moved his family to Springfield, Massachusetts, where he became an integral part of the city's abolitionist community. Later he moved his family to North Elba, in upstate New York, purchasing

244 acres of land from the abolitionist Gerrit Smith, who had been encouraging African Americans to move to the region, offering fifty-acre homesteads without charge to many poor Black families. Here Brown continued his antislavery work, and here he especially developed close working relationships with Black abolitionists.[20]

All of this would have made Brown a trusted ally of Still, but none of it made him particularly well-known; what made Brown a household name was his work in Kansas. In the summer of 1854, as tensions over slavery escalated, a number of Brown's grown sons moved to the Kansas territory in order to swell the free-state population and to fight against the encroachment of proslavery settlers. After consulting some close Black allies, including Frederick Douglass and James McCune Smith, Brown himself joined his sons. In Kansas, the Browns became renowned for their fierce opposition to slavery and their willingness to meet proslavery violence with a violent response of their own. Most famously, in the spring of 1856, in the midst of rising, widespread violence, and in particular in response to the brutal proslavery sack of the free-state city of Lawrence, Brown led a group of men, including his sons, to seek vengeance. On the night of May 24, Brown and his small band visited the homes of a number of men they knew to be among the most proslavery settlers in the area near Pottawatomie Creek, dragged them from their beds, and executed them. A proslavery court issued an indictment for murder, but due to the chaotic state of the Kansas legal system, the case was not taken up immediately. In the meantime, Brown and his band hid out as news of the killings spread. Southerners in particular came to see John Brown as the violent face of abolitionism, and moderate Northerners distanced themselves from him, but for many Black abolitionists, even those like Still ostensibly committed to the doctrine of nonresistance, Brown's bold actions had proven him to be an ally.[21]

While in hiding from the authorities, Brown slipped out of Kansas and began traveling the country, sometimes crossing over into Canada, building support for a new plan. This plan had the financial backing of a small group of white radicals, but Brown knew that his most important allies would be Black abolitionists and so he carefully cultivated the support of those he felt would be most useful to the cause and most likely to support it. In May 1858, in Chatham, Canada West, he revealed his plan to a group that included mostly Black Canadians. Brown intended to capture the federal arsenal at Harpers Ferry in western Virginia and then use the arms and ammunition he seized there to lead a slave rebellion. His plan received warm support from many who attended the meeting, and he left feeling that many would be willing to join his assault. While he was in Canada, he met with Harriet Tubman, who also expressed interest in the plan. Douglass supported him too.[22]

Brown knew that Black allies in general would be essential to the success or failure of his project, but the Black Philadelphians he gathered together at the home of Stephen Smith, a group which included Still, were perhaps most important of all. Better than anyone save perhaps Tubman, these veterans of the Underground Railroad, Still most of all, understood how to navigate the dangerous borderlands of slavery. There is no record of what the group discussed, but surely Brown hoped that Still would be willing to support the plan, that he would be able to lend his expertise. John Brown, Jr., joined his father at the Philadelphia meeting; just a few months before, Brown had instructed his son to explore the region of Pennsylvania that lay just north of Harpers Ferry, the area around Chambersburg, Gettysburg, and Uniontown. This was a little beyond Still's usual Underground Railroad network, but Brown knew that Still had extensive connections throughout Pennsylvania and Maryland, even into Virginia. The two likely discussed how these connections might be used to plan the assault. Perhaps Brown even asked Still to join him. If he did so, Still declined.[23]

In early 1859, the Fugitive Slave Law threatened to claim another Black man who had been living in the free state of Pennsylvania for years. On the morning of April 2, 1859, less than a month after Still met with Brown, a deputy marshal by the name of Jenkins, acting under the authority of a warrant issued in Philadelphia, seized a man named Daniel Webster in Harrisburg. Jenkins was acting at the behest of Elizabeth Simmons of Loudoun County, Virginia, who believed that Webster was actually Daniel Dangerfield, an enslaved man who had run away in November 1854. Shortly before noon the Anti-Slavery Society office in Philadelphia received two telegrams, one from a member of the Harrisburg Vigilance Committee and the other from a congressman (possibly Thaddeus Stevens), informing them that Jenkins was on his way to Philadelphia with the prisoner. "Do what you can for him," asked the second of the two.[24]

The Philadelphia committee immediately set about securing counsel for the accused fugitive, and their allies in Harrisburg scoured the area for witnesses who could help Webster's case. When a member of the Philadelphia committee visited Webster upon his arrival in Philadelphia, he found him shackled. "Who put these manacles on you?" the committee member demanded. "I did," responded the gruff voice of the deputy marshal. "We were afraid of a rescue," he insisted. "He cried 'help!' 'help!' and brought about a hundred n—s around us. He *did* try to grab a butcher-knife off one of our stalls."[25]

The authorities and the claimants believed that the law was on their side, and the recent past suggested that their claim on Webster was likely to be upheld. Since the passage of the Fugitive Slave Law, case after case had been decided in favor of slaveholders. "We had no hope," admitted Miller McKim. "The most we expected to do was to make a good fight; to protract the issue." The commissioner in charge of the case, J. Cooke Longstreth, was a bit of a mystery. He came from an old Quaker family, but he had given every indication of sympathy with those who claimed Webster as a slave. The defense planned to call witnesses who would testify that Webster was not, in fact, Dangerfield, that they had known him in Harrisburg before the real Dangerfield ever fled from Virginia, but it was unclear whether or not the commissioner would be swayed by this evidence: all the witnesses for the defense were Black.[26]

If the claimants expected a friendly hearing in court, they still feared public sentiment on the streets of Philadelphia, and in particular they feared the anger of the Black community, which almost immediately began mobilizing to demonstrate its support for Webster. Well before the trial was set to begin, the small room that had been appointed for it was packed, so that only a fraction of those who wished to attend were able to fit inside, leaving a large crowd in the halls outside the courtroom, spilling out into the streets. Police attempted to remove from the Old State House those who were waiting out in the hall. "Colored people and some whites," recalled Miller McKim, "were collared and rudely thrust out." Nevertheless, the halls remained crowded and eventually the trial was moved to a larger room, which still could not come close to accommodating the crowd. Finally, a strong guard of deputy marshals forced their way through the throng, bringing the prisoner to the courtroom. Outside, a large crowd blocked Fifth Street, anxiously awaiting news of the trial. According to an account in the *Philadelphia Inquirer,* "the Fugitive Slave Law was more thoroughly abused than ever since the famous excitement in 1850, when it was passed by Congress." There were rumors of rescue plans in case the court decided against Webster. A large number of special officers had been sworn in in case there was trouble.[27]

Ultimately there was no need. The trial extended for three days, but eventually Commissioner Longstreth decided that the claimants had not proven the identity of the accused fugitive. This was somewhat puzzling. Perhaps he truly found the evidence inconclusive, though similar cases had been decided in favor of the claimants despite evidence calling the defendant's identity into question. Some speculated that Longstreth's Quaker wife had influenced him. Many, though, felt that the crowds had ultimately swayed him. "Others are inclined to believe that the pressure of public sentiment," noted Charlotte Forten, daughter of the esteemed Black abolitionist and businessman James Forten, "was too overwhelming for the Commissioner to resist." Following the announcement of the verdict, "the colored people called for Daniel and he was handed out to them, a free man." A jubilant Black crowd carried Webster down the street in "a perfect delirium of joy." Despite the jubilation, however, Webster's allies in Philadelphia warned him that he was not safe; with the aid of the Vigilance Committee, he left the city behind and settled in Canada West.[28]

If there was a single lesson for Still to draw from the Daniel Webster case, it was that public opinion was a crucial tool in the fight to protect fugitives. With this in mind, Still traveled north in the summer of 1859 in order to participate in the New England Colored Citizens Convention. The organizers had proposed the meeting as a way to discuss the "elevation" of Black people, with a particular emphasis on the role of Black voting rights in securing that elevation. The bulk of the attendees were, unsurprisingly, from the New England states, but a handful of Black leaders came from states outside the region. Still's attendance, and the fact that he was elected one of the convention's vice presidents, suggest that he was by this point unquestionably a figure of national importance.[29]

Still's good friend William Wells Brown set the tone for the meeting with his opening address. Brown urged his fellow attendees to commit themselves to making sure that all Black people enjoyed the rights of American citizenship. "Let us," Brown exhorted, "claim our rights upon the soil where our fathers fought side by side with the white men for our freedom. Let us remain here, and labor to remove the chains from the limbs of our brethren on the banks of the Mississippi." The convention unequivocally endorsed the vote as an essential means of advancing the antislavery cause. "It is our duty and interest," resolved the convention, "on all occasions to exercise at the polls the political franchise that is ours." This came despite that fact that this was largely a convention of Black men who had aligned themselves with Garrison and the non-voting wing of the abolitionist movement; these were not the "political" abolitionists like Frederick Douglass, who for years had been advocating for the support of antislavery political parties. Black abolitionists had long seen the sectarian divisions within the abolitionist movement as a distraction from the true goal of fighting slavery, but the fact that Garrison himself spoke briefly at the convention underscores the fact that by 1859 the political context of abolition had shifted.[30]

What is perhaps most striking about the convention is its explicit discussion of the Republican Party as a tool for advancing the abolitionist cause. In fact, one observer lamented what he deemed to be the convention's overemphasis on "political subjects" to the detriment of other avenues for "the social advancement of the free blacks."[31] The convention urged its members to pressure the Republican Party to "take a manly position" in regard to the extension of voting rights to Black citizens, and it also pointed out that in places where Black voters remained disfranchised, as was the case in Still's home state of Pennsylvania, Black abolitionists should appeal to the party's self-interest: if the Republican Party were to help enfranchise Black voters, those voters would reward the party for having proved itself deserving of their votes. Beyond this, the convention endorsed the notion that the Republican Party was on the verge of turning Northern states, or at least the states of New England, into an effective defense against the Fugitive Slave Law. Garrison himself "thought it time to put a stop to the 'Underground Railroad,' and was for making Canada of all the Northern States," that is, for making it as difficult to recover fugitive slaves there as it was to recover them from Canada. Northern states, not only through the passage of Personal Liberty Laws, but through the election of Republicans who were opposed to the implementation of the hated Fugitive Slave Law, would be a powerful check on the Slave Power.[32]

Despite Still's official position, he remained largely an observer; his office of vice president was largely an honorary one. Almost certainly, however, he was active behind the scenes. Many of the leading men of the convention were close allies, and he was certainly cheered by the prospect that elected officials might be turned into allies of the Underground Railroad. Pennsylvania was, of course, significantly more friendly to the Fugitive Slave Law and more hostile to the rights of Black citizens than were the states of New England, but if Massachusetts were to become "Canada" in its protection of fugitive slaves, then it would become a much more attractive destination for the men and women whom Still aided in their flight from slavery. After all, Still's commitment to sending fugitives to Canada was always contingent on the belief that it was the safest place for them. If fugitive slaves could be protected from slave catchers *and* remain in their native land, that was even better.

While Still remained a behind-the-scenes figure at the convention, he used his presence in Boston to more publicly promote the work of the Vigilance Committee and to share stories of the Underground Railroad. On the evening of August 2, after the convention had adjourned for its second day of meetings, Still delivered a lecture before an "interested crowded audience" at the Twelfth Baptist Church in Boston. Without direct accounts of his address, we cannot know for sure what Still specifically spoke about, but we can assume his "numerous thrilling and romantic cases" drew upon the written accounts of the Underground Railroad that he was increasingly sharing in print, and that he continued to use his stories of fugitive slaves both to demonstrate the inherent capacity and value of Black people in general and to build sympathy for the plight of the fugitive slave. He also took the opportunity to report on the status of a number of fugitives he had helped to resettle in the area; Still published his account of these investigations in the *National Anti-Slavery Standard*.[33]

Still's time in Boston also gave him a chance to reconnect with friends and allies whom he saw only infrequently. He likely enjoyed the camaraderie he experienced there, and he surely appreciated the confirmation of his growing national stature, but he had reason to hurry back to Philadelphia: Letitia was expecting. On September 15, she gave birth to a daughter. She and William named her Frances Ellen Still, after Frances Ellen Watkins, who had become a close friend of the family.[34]

Still had not heard from John Brown since the meeting months earlier, or at least he makes no record of having heard from him. Later Still would write that he "could not see that [the Harpers Ferry assault] was feasible, regarded it as a venture sure to end in disaster, and as an attempt involving more of desperation than valor, more of precipitation than prudence." Still had advised Frederick Douglass against involving himself in John Brown's plan, and he likely shared his concern with Brown, though probably in more measured language, so perhaps Brown discarded any hope that Still might be enlisted in the effort. Given Still's responsibilities with the Vigilance Committee, his travels, and the birth of

Frances, John Brown's plans were likely far from his top concern. When, on October 14, 1859, a letter arrived in the Anti-Slavery Society office addressed to "Captain Watkins," Still regarded it as suspicious, but he put the letter aside without opening it.[35]

On the morning of October 17, word began to trickle into Philadelphia that John Brown and a small group of followers had seized control of the federal arsenal at Harpers Ferry the night before. Initial reports were disjointed but gradually the picture became clearer. On the evening of October 16, Brown, along with eighteen followers, a mix of white and Black men, left the farmhouse where they had been conducting their final preparations and marched down to the Potomac River, toward Harpers Ferry; three others remained behind as sentinels. The small group easily captured the arsenal, rifle works, and armory, which were lightly guarded. Brown sent a small party, three Black men and three white, out into the night to begin spreading the word to Black residents of the region that the rebellion had begun. Brown had long hoped that slaves in the region around would quickly join his fight, that as he put it "when I strike, the bees will begin to swarm," but in the early hours of the 17th, few were swarming. Some of his men urged Brown to flee the town of Harpers Ferry, which they viewed as a death trap, to seek refuge in the nearby Blue Ridge Mountains, but Brown waited.[36]

Still and the abolitionist community of Philadelphia followed the news eagerly, but within days it was clear that Brown's raid had failed. While Brown and his men lingered in Harpers Ferry, a militia force assembled and took back some of the town, including two key bridges that Brown's men had captured in their initial assault. After nightfall, a company of marines, ninety men, under the command of Colonel Robert E. Lee arrived in Harpers Ferry. At dawn, Lee sent his aide, Lieutenant J. E. B. Stuart, to parley with Brown. Unsurprisingly, despite his hopeless position Brown had no interest in surrendering. Lee had anticipated this, and following his short meeting with Brown, Stuart stepped aside and waved his hat, the signal to attack. It was all over in just minutes. Of Brown's force, ten were either dead or dying, five had escaped the previous day, and seven, Brown among them, were captured.[37]

As news of the Harpers Ferry assault spread out across the nation, it created a firestorm. In Philadelphia, newspapers breathlessly reported details of what many of them were calling the "Negro Insurrection."[38] Still had held out little hope for Brown's project, but now he wondered what unintended consequences it might have for the Vigilance Committee. His worst fears were confirmed a few days later when newspapers began to publish descriptions of some of the materials found on Brown and his men at the time of their capture. In the pocket of Brown's top lieutenant, John Henry Kagi, was a diary, found after he fell during the defense of the arsenal. It included the following notation: "Wednesday.—Wrote Wm. Still." Still realized that his Vigilance Committee records, if discovered and seized by the authorities, might compromise the entire organization. He quickly gathered his papers together and hid them, in an out-of-the-way place in a loft of the Lebanon Cemetery, a cemetery in South Philadelphia where Black families were permitted to bury their dead. Frederick Douglass had also been mentioned in the materials found on Brown and his men. Douglass had actually been in Philadelphia the night of Brown's raid. Realizing his danger, and knowing that there were papers in his desk in Rochester that connected him to Brown, Douglass quickly fled Philadelphia and via a succession of trains made his way back home. With publication of Brown's papers in the newspapers, however, Still worried that Douglass would not be safe in Rochester either. Fearing that a letter sent directly to Douglass might be intercepted, Still sent warning by way of a mutual friend, Amy Post, who got the word to Douglass. Shortly before federal marshals were to raid his home to arrest him, Douglass slipped across the border to Canada, driven to the docks by Amy and Isaac Post.[39]

Still knew that while many white Philadelphians tacitly approved of his work aiding fugitive slaves, the Harpers Ferry raid was a different matter entirely. He feared that Brown's bold stroke would provoke a backlash against abolitionists. "For years past," insisted the nonpartisan *Public Ledger*, "war has been preached against the Southern institutions from pulpit and forum, and every effort has been made by demagogue politicians and political

presses to awaken sectional strife." According to Philadelphia dia-
rist Sidney Fisher, most Philadelphians opposed extremists of all
sorts, and "the mass of public opinion is sound & loyal." In such an
atmosphere Black Philadelphians were particularly suspect. While
Philadelphia's response to the Harpers Ferry raid was relatively
sedate compared to the reaction in slave states, there was enough
anxiety among whites in Pennsylvania that, according to some
reports, the adjutant general, who commanded the state's militia,
disarmed a volunteer militia company of Black men in Philadelphia, the "Frank Johnson Guards." Still knew that he was being
watched more carefully than usual.[40]

The Stills spent a few days of "terror and suspense," but after
a time, the mood of the city seemed to relax. Brown had been
captured, along with most of his men, at least those who had survived the assault. But just as soon as Still let down his guard he had
a visitor, "a tired, foot-sore, famished, powder-begrimed fugitive,
whose waist was encircled with a belt filled with revolvers." It was
Francis J. Meriem, a white man who had fought with Brown at
Harpers Ferry. Meriem had escaped with a small group of men,
evading bloodhounds by wading up streams, traveling at night, but
eventually he separated from them. While the others continued
on foot, Meriem risked a train to Philadelphia. Once he got there,
he knew that Still's house was the safest place for him to go. Still,
however, knew that his home was not safe at all. He quickly found
a trusted ally, Dr. I. Newlin Pierce, who was willing to help Meriem make his way from Philadelphia to Canada, with the help of
money furnished by Still and the Vigilance Committee.[41]

No sooner had Meriem departed then Still had another visitor, also fleeing the Harpers Ferry disaster. Osborne Anderson
was a free Black man, born in Chester County, Pennsylvania.
He escaped from Virginia with another member of John Brown's
band, a white man named Albert Hazlett, but Anderson had been
forced to separate from his companion; Hazlett was later captured
and executed. Anderson was himself almost captured by federal
marshals in Chambersburg when he stopped at a friend's house,
looking for some food, but narrowly escaped. He then made his
way, by foot and then by train, to Philadelphia. When he arrived

at Still's house, "he was literally in rags" and had no money. Still provided him with a new suit and tickets to get him to Canada. He took a day to hide out and rest and then he, too, was on his way.[42]

In the weeks between the Harpers Ferry raid and the trial and execution of John Brown, the Still home continued to be a center of activity for Brown's allies and family members. Brown's wife, Mary, stayed at the Still home and received admiring visitors while stopping in Philadelphia on her way to visit her condemned husband, a trip she eventually abandoned at the urging of well-wishers in Philadelphia. Mary was appreciative enough of Still's kindness that she sent him a lock of Brown's hair as an abolitionist relic. For a time, some supporters and allies of Brown, including his son, John Brown, Jr., met in Still's home as they formulated a plan to rescue Brown before his execution. Though the plan came to nothing, Still realized that the presence of such men under his roof, men "fully armed and resolved to die rather than submit to arrest and ignominious death on the scaffold," put his household in a tenuous position. Nevertheless, Still was grateful to contribute what he could to the Brown family in its time of need. Still wrote, on behalf of Black Philadelphians, to Brown's son, Salmon, expressing the love felt "for your noble hearted father + his beloved family," and sharing money that had been raised for the purpose of "aiding them in their distress."[43]

In Philadelphia, as was the case across the North, African Americans came out in large numbers to express their sympathy for Brown and his followers. Black ministers issued a call for prayer to be held at Shiloh Church on the day of Brown's execution. The same day, "an immense Anti-Slavery gathering was held in Brown's honor at National Hall. The day before Brown's execution, a group of Black men issued a call "that as a mark of respect and esteem we will, and do recommend to all, to close their places of business on Friday the 2nd of December, the day of execution." Another group wrote to Henry A. Wise, the governor of Virginia, asking for clemency for two of the Black men who had been arrested alongside Brown, or, if that request should be denied, that their bodies be returned to "us their *friends and brethren.*" Some white Philadelphians joined their Black neighbors in celebrating Brown and the martyrs of Harpers Ferry, but many did not. Black pastor Jonathan Gibbs was to have delivered a eulogy on the "Harper's Ferry heroes," but was prevented from doing so when the janitor of the hall they had rented expressed his apprehension that "the hall should be burned."[44]

These demonstrations of support for John Brown and followers, and those like them across the North, greatly contributed to the rising sectional tensions. Church bells tolled in honor of Brown, and abolitionists praised his bravery and commitment to the fight against slavery. The transcendentalist essayist Ralph Waldo Emerson famously declared that Brown would "make the gallows as glorious as the cross." While Republican politicians like Abraham Lincoln and William Seward sought to distance themselves from Brown and the Harpers Ferry raid, Southern politicians seized upon Northern support for Brown to cast Republicans as the fomenters of rebellion and disunion. Earlier claims by Lincoln that "a house divided against itself cannot stand. I believe this government cannot endure permanently half slave and half free," and warnings by Seward of an "Irrepressible Conflict," took on an ominous new significance in light of Brown's raid.[45]

The broad praise that Brown received from Black Northerners was particularly disturbing to slaveholders, who raised militia companies and cracked down on free Blacks who they increasingly saw as an abolitionist fifth column in their midst. Under the leadership of radical proslavery state legislator Curtis Jacobs, a serious effort was made in Maryland to re-enslave the state's sizable free Black population. Southern newspapers were suffused with stories of lynching and torture of Black Southerners, a desperate attempt to stem what many believed were imminent slave rebellions, inspired by the example of Harpers Ferry.[46]

In the midst of the drama surrounding the Harpers Ferry raid, the Vigilance Committee continued its work and the Still family hosted a series of fugitives from slavery. Increasingly, though, Still had grown worried that the generosity of the committee had led the unscrupulous to take advantage of it. To an extent the Vigilance Committee was a victim of its own success. It had become so adept at raising and distributing money to fugitive slaves that it must have been tempting for free Black Philadelphians, or for those passing through Philadelphia, with severely constrained economic opportunities, to appeal to the committee under false pretenses. Nor was this an issue faced only by Philadelphia abolitionists. In September, the *Liberator* printed an account under the title "Beware of an Imposter," citing Still as an authority, and advising those who aided fugitive slaves to be on the lookout for a man calling himself Thomas and claiming to have escaped from slavery in Baltimore. The man was asking for money that he claimed he needed to get to safety in Canada.[47]

In the eyes of some, this caution on the part of Still and other participants in the Underground Railroad went too far. Some even suspected that Underground Railroad agents might be personally profiting from their work. A letter, published in the New York–based, Black-edited newspaper, the *Weekly Anglo-African*, and signed "Many Stockholders of the U.G.R.R. Company," made just such an allegation. "It has become absolutely necessary," they argued, "to examine and overhaul the books and the management of this company." The letter names no names, though it suggests several places, Philadelphia among them, that needed to be investigated. "Several agents, conductors, and stationmasters," the letter warned, "have grown fat and proud, and behave in a very overbearing manner towards stock-holders and passengers."[48]

Even though there were no specific allegations leveled at the Philadelphia Vigilance Committee, merely a suggestion that "Philadelphia must be glanced at," Still seems to have taken this letter as a personal attack. He responded with a letter of his own to the *Anglo-African*. Still assured his readers that the Philadelphia Vigilance Committee would soon be presenting a full accounting of its actions to any "true friend of the cause," by any "genuine 'stockholder.' " He reserved special venom, though, for the writer (or writers) of the letter, for these supposed friends of the cause, and he derided them for hiding behind anonymity; Still proudly signed his letter with his own name. "It is believed here," wrote Still, "that 'Many Stockholders' are in no sense aiders of the vigilant cause, that they are maliciously disposed towards the committee, and have been actuated by the vilest motives in their secret and unscrupulous efforts to cast odium upon the cause." He also hinted that these allegations might be linked to an ongoing conflict related to a man named Dimmock Charlton.[49]

Charlton was born in West Africa, in what is now the Republic of Guinea. In his own telling, he was kidnapped at the age of twelve and sold into slavery, but when the slaver on which he was being transported was attacked by British forces, Charlton eventually came to serve as a cabin boy on a British warship. When that ship was sunk during the War of 1812, Charlton was again claimed as a slave, this time by a series of Americans, despite his insistence that he was a British subject and legally a free man. Charlton attempted to purchase his own freedom on a number of occasions but was repeatedly swindled by his masters, before he was finally sold to a master who made good on his promise. After acquiring his own freedom, Charlton set out to purchase the freedom of family members, and it is in this way that he eventually came to the attention of abolitionists in the Northeast.[50]

At some point in 1857, Charlton had appealed to abolitionists in Philadelphia and elsewhere for support in his effort to free his family members. Initially he received favorable reaction, but at some point, abolitionists in Philadelphia, including Still, began to sour on Charlton's cause. The *National Anti-Slavery Standard* went so far as to publish a warning to those who might be tempted to offer aid to Charlton: "Our friends in that city were privately advised, some time since, of his want of principle, but they did not give heed; now, after observing his conduct for themselves, they ask us publicly to denounce him." They warned that Charlton was "utterly untrustworthy, and money given him is worse than thrown away." Still penned a letter, published in *Frederick Douglass' Paper*, expressing a similar sentiment. According to Still, Charlton had substantially misrepresented his life story in order to cultivate greater sympathy among abolitionists; Still had been told by what he deemed reliable sources that Charlton had been free for more than twenty years and in that time had been working as a boss stevedore in Savannah. Perhaps most damning, Still's source had insisted that Charlton "associated but very little with his own color (felt above them) and was not infrequently instrumental in having them taken up, put in jail and whipped severely on very trifling pretext." To Still this was not the sort of person whom abolitionists would want to help. Charlton defended himself against what he deemed to be slander, and many abolitionist publications seemed sympathetic to Charlton rather than to the Philadelphians who had denounced him. Charlton published in *Frederick Douglass' Paper* a four-column defense of his own conduct, specifically attacking Still, claiming he had overcharged him for staying in his boardinghouse. Charlton even suggested this was a pattern whereby Still siphoned into his own pockets money that was to go toward fugitive slaves.[51]

Still understandably took these accusations personally. Beyond this, though, he knew that only a public refutation of Charlton's account would repair the damage done to his reputation, and, given how closely Still was associated with the Vigilance Committee itself, perhaps to the entire Underground Railroad network of Philadelphia. Even some of those inclined to trust Still felt that he needed to publicly answer such serious charges. Still himself wrote to the *Weekly Anglo-African*, defending himself against accusations that he had acted improperly, and he asked *Frederick Douglass' Paper*, the original source of Charlton's accusations, to reprint his letter. All of this was important to repairing Still's national reputation, and presumably the willingness of donors and co-workers on the Underground Railroad to trust him, but it was equally important for him to reassure local allies of his character. To this end, a number of friends of Still's organized a meeting, held on October 31, 1859, to provide a forum for Still to defend himself and answer his critics; the call for the meeting was signed by fifty of Still's friends and allies. Still, of course, kept meticulous records of his Vigilance Committee work, and he drew extensively upon these records in order to exonerate himself. While the meeting was undoubtedly stacked in Still's favor, his evidence seems to have been persuasive. The attendees unanimously resolved that "Mr. Still's defense be considered perfectly satisfactory." Some of Still's defenders went beyond this and expressed their contempt for Still's accusers, especially Charlton, who William H. Johnson, a Black abolitionist and Still ally, called "base and unscrupulous."[52]

Still might have dismissed the accusations made by Charlton as simply the product of resentment, the words of a disgruntled man who had been thwarted in his efforts to exploit the generosity of friends of the fugitive slave, but he could not help but feel that the publicity given to Charlton's claims hinted at an underlying resentment toward Still among some portion of the abolitionist community. Still concluded his defense of his personal integrity, with yet another letter published in *Frederick Douglass' Paper*, by calling out those who had conspired against him. "In conclusion," wrote Still, "who was the writer of the three columns of slander against me? Of course Dimmock never wrote a word of it."[53] Perhaps Still's rising national reputation had provoked resentment. Perhaps Still's high-mindedness and his personal rectitude had rubbed others the wrong way. Certainly by the late 1850s, Still had grown more confident in his own opinions and his own sense of how the Vigilance Committee should be run, and perhaps he had become less tolerant of those who disagreed with him.

In any case, the accusations of Dimmock Charlton were only the first of a series of challenges to Still and the way he operated the Vigilance Committee. A second, even more serious, incident involved a woman named Ellen Wells. She had been enslaved in St. Louis, where she had been able to acquire her freedom in 1853. Upon her release from bondage, she began traveling the North seeking funds to purchase various family members. She came to Philadelphia for a time, in June 1859, where she stayed in Still's boardinghouse. While she was in Philadelphia, some conflict arose between the two of them. In part the disagreement would deal with Still's insistence on Wells paying rent for her stay at his establishment. Later, Wells would claim Still grew difficult with her after she accused him of allowing "colored slaveholders" to stay in his boardinghouse. Though she may have made these accusations, it seems unlikely that there was any truth to them. For his part, Still seems to have grown suspicious of Wells. Some reported that they had seen her spending frivolously, on shoes and clothes for herself and on expensive cigars for her son. Other reports called into question her chastity. After departing Philadelphia, Wells traveled to Boston where she resumed her efforts to raise money among abolitionists. By chance, Mary Ann Shadd Cary was in Boston at the time, and after hearing Wells malign Still, she wrote to him asking about his impressions of Wells. Still replied with a letter in which he expressed his distrust of Wells and his low opinion of her character, labeling her an "imposter" and "a bad woman who ought to be exposed." Unfortunately for Still, the letter fell into Wells's hands.[54]

Wells returned to Philadelphia and in late 1859 brought suit against Still for libel, and the suit came before the Court of Quarter Sessions on March 14, 1860. Wells produced a copy of the letter and claimed it as evidence that Still had libeled her in order to prevent her from raising money among abolitionists. Still's legal strategy was to cast doubt on her character, presumably in order both to call into question the veracity of her testimony in court and to justify his treatment of her. In order to build his case, he had drawn on his vast abolitionist network in order to uncover evidence to support his depiction of her character, hoping that this evidence would be able to disprove some of the statements he expected her to make in court. "Be assured," he wrote to abolitionist Samuel May, "I shall leave no stone unturned to convict her out of her own mouth." The court returned a verdict of not guilty, but it was hardly the vindication that Still had hoped for. The decision was rendered on a technicality, due to an irregularity in some of the evidence Wells and her lawyers presented. There would be a retrial.[55]

Still was concerned about the retrial, and he continued to correspond with May concerning his strategy. Both Still and Wells called upon witnesses to testify to their character, and at some point, Still and his counsel began to have doubts about the likely success of their efforts to cast doubt on her veracity. In public Wells denied she was looking for "any severe punishment to be inflicted," that she simply wanted "public vindication." On the stand she broke down crying, lamenting that due to the money she was spending on the trial she would never be able to free her sister from slavery. In private, Still believed that she harbored a vendetta against him and the Vigilance Committee. In a letter to May he claimed that "she has made her boast that she is 'going to brake [sic] up the Underground Rail Road here.'" Most worrisome to Still, though, was the fact that the "Democratic Judge" in the case, Oswald Thompson, was prejudiced against him and that Wells and her lawyers would "avail themselves of extra Proslavery Counsel."[56]

On one hand, this sentiment seems somewhat overblown, especially considering the fact that Wells's attorneys were actually well-known lawyers who had defended fugitive slaves in the past. Certainly, Still was under great stress; while he was preparing for the Wells case he was still in the middle of defending himself from the accusations of Dimmock Charlton. However, issues of race and slavery were never far from the surface in the case, despite the fact that it was ostensibly a matter between two Black litigants. Whether or not the judge was "proslavery" as Still suggested, he clearly was no friend to Still's cause. By 1860 Still had become, in the words of the judge, "a man who has enjoyed the confidence of the public" due to his antislavery work, and Still's public status loomed large in the case.[57]

Beyond this, it seems likely that attitudes toward Wells's accusations, perhaps including the attitude of Judge Thompson, were influenced by the relative appearances of the litigants. Nearly every published account of the case referred to Wells's very light skin. "An intelligent looking woman, almost white," is how the *Public Ledger* described Wells. Still, on the other hand, is described in the same article as simply "colored" and was by all accounts fairly dark-skinned. This racial dimension of the case was accentuated by the fact that in the letter at the center of the case, Still had written "she is well calculated to make an impression upon the unsuspecting; upon such, especially, whose sympathies can only be fully awakened by that fact that the victim was a female, so near white that the agency of a telescope would be needed to detect that she had colored blood in her veins." It seems that part of Still's initial suspicion of Wells was connected with the way she used her light skin in order to play the victim. In the trial, the image of the dark-skinned Still and the "nearly white" Wells may have ultimately doomed Still.[58]

At some point, Still and his counsel seem to have realized that their case was likely to fail and he entered a plea of guilty. At the sentencing, the judge scolded Still for the "wicked and scandalous libel which you published." The fact that Still had not published it at all, that the words in question were in private correspondence, the judge dismissed. "All things of that kind," he maintained, "do find their way into circulation." He sentenced Still to ten days in the county prison and a fine of $100. This was surely humiliating to Still, which was the point. It was not enough for Still to be punished, insisted the judge. Since the injury to Wells had been public, so too "the vindication must be public." Still was handed over to the jailer, though after he had served four days of the sentence, the judge "reconsidered his judgement in the case" and released the prisoner. Perhaps Still had already been humbled enough in the judge's estimation.[59]

Shortly after his release, Still set out to defend himself against the public dishonor that had fallen upon his reputation. In a letter to the *National Anti-Slavery Standard*, Still insisted that his guilty plea was a mere technicality, an admission that he had written the letter at the center of the case. He denied that he had pled guilty to the broader implications that the judge had drawn from this letter. Still was especially keen to defend himself against the suggestion that his actions had harmed the antislavery cause. In court, Wells had claimed not only that Still had besmirched her character, but that in undermining her ability to raise money he had doomed those she was looking to purchase to a lifetime of slavery. On the witness stand, Wells had tearfully claimed that her sister was so affected, and Judge Thomson hinted that Still's actions had betrayed the cause to which he was supposedly devoted. An account of the trial in the *Public Ledger* went even further. "The Anti-Slavery Society," reported the paper, "would have the proud satisfaction of knowing that through the instrumentality of their accredited agent, two children were left in bondage and likely so to remain the balance of their lives." Many opponents of abolitionism could hardly contain their glee over Still's humbling.[60]

Still's allies in Philadelphia organized a public meeting intended to express their confidence in the beleaguered head of the Vigilance Committee, but conflict at the meeting suggests that criticism of Still was not limited to the enemies of abolition. The call for the meeting "of public sympathy with Wm. Still" was signed by "twenty-nine of our most respectable and influential colored citizens." The meeting itself was largely controlled by those sympathetic to Still. Still's pastor, the Rev. Jonathan Gibbs (who was actually living in Still's boardinghouse at the time), and long-time ally Isaiah Wears were on a committee that drafted a set of resolutions which defended Still and denounced the legal process, which they claimed was characterized by "sweeping tirades against abolitionists, and the gross perversion of truth and misconstruction of motives, so often indulged in by men who, having drawn largely upon the resources of anti-slavery men in times gone by, when they were proud to be thought allied to them through professed unison of sentiment, now make haste to ally themselves to the slavery propagandists of the times." Those who would criticize Still, they insisted, were in league with slavery.[61]

Although friends of Still controlled the meeting, there were those in attendance who disapproved of Still's conduct and sympathized with Ellen Wells. William Douglass, pastor of St. Thomas African Episcopal Church, led a faction that attempted to prevent the leaders of the meeting from passing the resolutions vindicating Still. Douglass, who according to William Wells Brown, was generally "not active in public affairs," seems to have been angered by Still's treatment of Wells, and accused Still of "moral turpitude." A number of other attendees supported Douglass in his disapproval of Still, but the leaders of the meeting were able to pass the resolutions over the objections of the dissenters, though at least one conflicting account insisted that the resolutions were not passed at all, that the chair simply called for the "ayes" and then refused to call the "nays." This letter, published in the *Weekly Anglo-African*, sought to make it clear that Black Philadelphians were not, as the meeting sought to suggest, unanimous in their support of Still. The writer, who signed himself Justitia, insisted while many of this opposition faction respected Still, they refused to defend his behavior in this matter, and they objected to the manner in which he had tried to defend himself in the trial. Another, less charitable writer claimed that he would not "sympathize with a man that vilifies a woman's character in her absence."[62]

Even before he had resolved the issues around the Wells case, Still was embroiled in yet another controversy that damaged his reputation among the Black abolitionist community of Philadelphia. It is quite likely that the quick succession of these controversial incidents helps to explain why some Black Philadelphians turned against Still. As Justitia had put it in his letter about the Wells affair, "Mr. Still . . . seems to need "endorsing" two or three times a year lately." This third incident stemmed from a fugitive slave case. On March 26, 1860 (between the two Wells libel trials), a man named Moses Horner was seized near his home in Harrisburg as a fugitive slave. The U.S. marshals who seized him brought him to Philadelphia for a hearing before Judge John Cadwalader. Evidently the marshals were wary of the sort of crowds that had attended the Webster case a year earlier, and they made arrangements to bring Horner to Philadelphia surreptitiously, avoiding the usual trains. Despite producing witnesses who disputed that Horner was the man his supposed owner claimed him to be, Judge Cadwallader, a Democrat who was reputed to have slave-owning family members, decided that Horner's status as a slave had been proved. Before Horner could be taken away by the marshal, however, his lawyers served Cadwalader a writ of habeas corpus, issued by Judge Joseph Allison, a Republican and judge of the court of common pleas. This provoked a heated discussion as to whether a state court may interfere in a federal court in this manner, and ultimately Judge Cadwallader and the marshals decided to ignore the writ. While all this was happening, however, a large crowd had started to gather outside the courthouse. By the time the marshals emerged with Horner, "Fifth street, in the neighborhood of the Court room, was thronged with colored people." Before the marshals could leave with Horner, a group of men rushed the carriage they were in, attempting to liberate Horner, but they were beaten back by police. Ten Black men were arrested for their involvement.[63]

The disagreements started after the men were arrested. Supporters of the men who had been arrested called a meeting in order to raise funds to pay for legal counsel. The meeting appointed five men, Samuel Smith, George Stevens, brothers Thomas and John C. Bowers, and Franklin Turner, as a Committee of Five responsible for directing efforts to support the men's defense. A member of this committee went to Still to ask whether the Anti-Slavery Society would help. According to this member, Still assured him that the Anti-Slavery Society planned to pay the legal fees for the case, though Still later denied he said this. Once the committee had received this assurance, they ceased their fundraising, and once they were told that the Anti-Slavery Society was not, in fact, paying for the defense, they had difficulty resuming their fundraising. It seems that the momentum had been lost. There were a series of smaller meetings, but the defendants had difficulty raising enough funds for the trial. Many blamed Still, though other officers of the Anti-Slavery Society also came in for harsh criticism.

Still seems to have made things worse with his public defense. In a lengthy letter, almost four columns long, published in the *Weekly Anglo-African*, Still laid out an extensive explanation of his persecution at the hands of his enemies in Philadelphia. He made no specific reference to the dispute over the Horner meeting, but instead traced the story of his enemies back to a seemingly forgotten conflict during the trial that followed the Christiana fugitive slave rebellion in 1851, when Still had expressed his belief that those raising money for the prisoners were not actually doing so for the prisoners, whose defense had already been paid for by the Anti-Slavery Society and the old Abolition Society. This was likely a veiled reference to the more recent dispute in the Horner case, and also suggests something of Still's motivation. He went on to explain his role in the Vigilance Committee and what he considered its success in efficiently disbursing funds to fugitives in place of the piecemeal "begging operations" that had preceded its founding. He ended the article with an extensive denunciation of the different types of Black men who had become his enemies: idlers, rum sellers, people of "low and immoral habits," and false friends of the abolitionist cause. The true friends of the cause, "the entire mass of worthy men, white and colored, who sympathize with the U.G.R.R.," Still assured his readers, were still his allies.[64]

Just when Still needed all the friends he could get, Still's accusations, both direct and implied, provoked heated reactions from Black Philadelphians who felt slighted by his defense of his own behavior. The men who had served on the Christiana committee in 1851, men who were important leaders in their own right, John P. Burr, James J. G. Bias, Nathaniel W. Depee, and William D. Forten, published a lengthy defense of their actions in that case, going as far as to include receipts attesting to their scrupulous management of funds in that nearly decade-old matter. Burr, Bias, and Depee had at various times worked alongside Still in the Vigilance Committee. Still's disagreements with some of these men were not new. As early as 1854 Still had written confidentially to friends about his conflict with "Bill Forten + Dr. Bias," but these published accounts brought these conflicts out into the open. Similarly, Still had long resented the willingness of some Black men to waste their money and time on what he deemed frivolous pursuits, but now he was denouncing such behavior in public, and doing so at a time when he could least afford to alienate potential allies.[65]

These three disputes, coming in quick succession as they did, displayed for all to see some of the least appealing elements of Still's character. His actions in each case might have been defensible. Certainly he had good reason to be suspicious of both Dimmock Charlton and Ellen Wells. While each had their defenders, many of Still's allies shared his assessment of the two and his unwillingness to support them in their efforts to raise money. In terms of the Horner case, Still's behavior might make some sense in light of his long tenure at the Vigilance Committee, which had taught him the careful stewardship of scarce abolitionist funds. From a different perspective, though, Still's behavior betrays a sanctimonious streak, a willingness to denounce those who did not meet his exacting standards of behavior, and his absolute confidence in his own assessment of a given situation. Even worse, his public defense in all three cases seems to have struck even some of his supporters as mean-spirited and petty. None of this is to suggest that Still was unique in making enemies; abolition was well-known for its heated schisms, and Black abolitionists, none more so than Frederick Douglass, often found themselves under attack by other Black leaders. Perhaps the vehement public criticism coming in 1859 and 1860 is largely a product of Still's increased status. Now that he was a prominent public figure, private rivalries had become public feuds.

In any case, Still did not retreat in the face of such criticism. Publicly his friends assured readers that even Still's imprisonment did not dim his spirits. "We hear that our friend bears his misfortune joyfully," wrote the *National Anti-Slavery Standard* of Still's time in prison, "feeling assured that he is suffering for having performed, to the best of his knowledge and belief, what he regarded as his duty." Privately, it is difficult to know what Still felt. The Anti-Slavery Society paid the fine in the Wells case, but they could not pay Still's way out of prison time. Perhaps he was humiliated. Certainly he seems to have been embittered toward those who he blamed for his misfortune. None of these feelings, though, prevented Still from continuing his Vigilance Committee work and from continuing his public work in the abolitionist cause.[66]

CHAPTER NINE

THE WAR YEARS AND NEW CHALLENGES

Some of Still's correspondents, especially those writing to him from slave states, used pseudonyms to conceal their identity in case local authorities were to intercept a letter with incriminating detail. Perhaps no Still correspondent was more colorfully named than the enslaved man from Petersburg, Virginia, known to us only as "Ham & Eggs." In October 1860, he wrote to Still in order to "open our correspondence with one another again." Evidently there had been a break in their communication (perhaps due to the Harpers Ferry raid and the ensuing backlash), but now he was ready to resume his Underground Railroad work. "I have some very good hams on hand," he wrote Still, "that I would like very much for you to have." All this makes the letter relatively unremarkable, aside from its author's colorful moniker. After mentioning this Underground Railroad business, however, Ham & Eggs goes on to venture into the day's political scene. "I have nothing of interest to write about just now," he writes, "only that the politics of the day is in a high rage, and I don't know of the result, therefore, I want you to be one of those wide a-wakes as is mentioned from your section of the country now-a-days, &c." He went on to close the letter by noting once again, "No more at present, until I hear from you; but I want you to be a wide-a-wake. Yours in haste, Ham & Eggs."[1]

The reference to "wide a-wakes" might be obscure to present-day readers, but Still understood it perfectly. In 1860, across the North, and even sporadically in towns of the Upper South, young men took to the streets, marching, carrying torches, and wearing pseudo-military uniforms. First organized by a group of dry goods clerks in Hartford, Connecticut, in March 1860, by the fall the movement had spread across the country. Wide Awakes combined the form and spirit of the era's abundant militia companies and fused it with the partisan zeal of one of the most contentious and consequential presidential election seasons in American history. For young men disillusioned by decades of partisan wrangling that seemed not to have addressed the pressing issues of the day, the Wide Awakes provided a meaningful, partisan identity, a political awakening. They rallied thousands of men to the cause of the Republican Party and its standard-bearer: Abraham Lincoln.[2]

The Letter from Ham & Eggs provides us a tantalizing glimpse into the political consciousness of enslaved people. Historians have long known that while masters may have liked to imagine their slaves as entirely ignorant of the politics of the day, this was hardly the case. Well before the fall election, even those masters were forced to recognize the whispers of enslaved people, the hushed conversations, the suspicious looks. The specter of Haiti had long hovered over the South, and masters feared that the inflammatory words of Northern abolitionists would stoke a revolution on American soil. For this reason, they had desperately fought to silence those abolitionists and to keep their words out of the South. Now it was the "Black Republicans" who threatened to stoke the fires of slave rebellion. As historian Stephanie McCurry has noted, nearly every enslaved person who left a record demonstrated some knowledge of Lincoln's campaign and victory.[3]

The letter also suggests that people like Still helped to connect free Black Northerners and enslaved Southerners into a larger Black political community. This community would flourish during and after the Civil War, when thousands of Black Northerners went south and even more Black Southerners came north, but even before the war these two seemingly distinct communities were bound together both by psychic bonds of affection and by more tangible connections like Still's correspondence. We do not know what Still wrote in response to Ham & Eggs. Perhaps his response stuck to the business of moving those "hams." What we know for certain is that Still's correspondence with men like Ham & Eggs told him that enslaved people were watching the coming election.

Still seems not to have had much to say about the impending election, at least publicly or in private correspondence that has survived, but he surely watched it with interest. The Democratic Party had split over its inability to agree on a single presidential candidate to unite the party's Northern and Southern wings. Southern Democrats withdrew from the party's nominating convention, enabling Northern Democrats to prevail in nominating their man, Illinois Senator Stephen A. Douglas. Southern Democrats then turned around and nominated their own candidate, the sitting vice president, John C. Breckinridge. Another group of disaffected politicians, feeling that neither faction of the splintered Democratic Party, nor the nascent Republican Party, could represent the whole union, assembled to form the Constitutional Union Party, which nominated the relatively unexceptional John Bell of Tennessee. The Republican Party, looking past its most prominent leaders, settled on Abraham Lincoln, a one-term former congressman from Illinois. Lincoln had significantly raised his national profile during his unsuccessful campaign against Stephen Douglas for the U.S. Senate seat in Illinois and had emerged as an eloquent critic of the Slave Power. To party leaders, Lincoln also seemed the candidate most likely to win the critical states of the Midwest.[4]

Black abolitionists were divided on the question of whether or not the Republican Party in general, and Lincoln in particular, could be trusted, but most were cautiously optimistic about the developments they saw in Northern politics. Often, free Black Northerners seemed skeptical of particular Republican Party politicians while celebrating the revolution in public opinion that many of them felt the success of the Republican Party represented. Many of the leading Republican candidates for the presidency in 1860, Lincoln among them, had made rhetorical gestures toward moderation, distancing themselves from John Brown and other radical abolitionists, and reassuring voters that their hatred of slavery did not make them advocates for racial equality, but most Black abolitionists echoed the words of Still's longtime ally Isaiah Wears, who insisted that "the election of Lincoln will certainly benefit us." The difference between the parties could not be clearer.[5]

Many Black abolitionists, Still among them, saw the Republican Party, for all its faults, as the heir of the abolitionist movement for which they had struggled for so many years. "I respectfully differ with gentlemen who say there is nothing to hope for by the success of the Republican Party," pronounced Black Philadelphian David Bowser, "it is the legitimate child of the Garrisonian party." The party was filled with staunch, faithful antislavery men who had proven themselves to be worthy allies. Still wrote a letter of thanks to Senator Charles Sumner in the summer of 1860, praising his speech "the Barbarism of Slavery," which marked Sumner's return to the Senate following a long recuperation from the wounds he suffered at the hands of Preston Brooks, who had savagely beaten the antislavery senator on the floor of the Senate. Sumner's speech made a compelling case that the unavoidable, central political issue of the day was the fight between freedom and slavery. "In my humble opinion," wrote Still, "you so effectively laid the axe at the root of the tree that thousands + tens of thousands who have been indifferent or proslavery will henceforth work for the deliverance of the bondman—will labor to help cut the tree down." Whatever questions Still might have about Lincoln, he had the utmost confidence in Republicans like Sumner.[6]

Even before the election, Still's attentions had begun to shift somewhat. By Still's own account, the years between 1855 and 1859 were the most active ones for the Underground Railroad in Philadelphia, and the numbers of fugitives traveling through Philadelphia had diminished somewhat in 1860. Perhaps this had something to do with the backlash to the raid on Harpers Ferry, which stoked Southern fears like never before and spurred a crackdown on the free Black Southerners who were so important to the flight of fugitive slaves. Still admitted that in the wake of the Harpers Ferry raid his own records became, out of necessity, less organized, more likely to be jotted down on loose paper and lost. Fugitives continued to make their way to Philadelphia in 1860, of course. Harriet Tubman made her last foray into the South in that year, but there seem to have been fewer fugitives for Still to aid.[7]

While Still certainly understood the importance of national political developments, he was especially focused on local politics. Of particular interest to Still was the practice of segregation on the city's streetcars. Philadelphia had grown dramatically in the decade and a half that Still had lived there. While parts of the city were densely packed with residents, the city also grew outward. In the 1840s this sprawling population had created jurisdictional problems, as the population of Philadelphia County exploded, especially in the heavily populated municipalities surrounding the city itself, creating a patchwork government. In 1854, leading citizens of Philadelphia finally succeeded in a decade-long effort to consolidate all of these jurisdictions into one greater City of Philadelphia. While the smaller jurisdiction had been essentially a walking city, the residents of this larger jurisdiction were increasingly reliant on public transportation to move them about the city. For several decades this primarily meant omnibuses, large carriages drawn by horses. The cost of riding such omnibuses was relatively high, so the clientele was largely the middle class, who increasingly lived at some distance from their downtown work. In the late 1850s, though, omnibuses were rapidly replaced by streetcars, still drawn by horse, but now running along rails laid throughout the city. The rails meant that the cars could provide a faster, more comfortable ride. The fares were also somewhat lower, though still high enough that most Philadelphians continued to find them prohibitively expensive. For the city's Black residents, however, the cost was not the issue: they were excluded, or "as a measure of grace, allowed to stand on the front platform."[8]

On August 31, 1859, the *North American and United States Gazette* published a letter from Still decrying the segregation of the city's streetcars. Still began his argument by noting that in cities across the nation, streetcars were open to Black passengers. This was true not just of Northern cities, like Boston, where "there is no obstruction in the way of colored persons riding" in the cars, but in some Southern cities as well. "In New Orleans," wrote Still, "colored people—slaves as well as free—ride in all the city cars and omnibuses." In the previous decades, abolitionists had fought against discrimination in public accommodations. Several years earlier, Still's ally, the Black abolitionist preacher James Pennington, had championed the effort to desegregate New York City's public transportation, with little success. Perhaps Still hoped that in the political climate of 1859, with Republicans in ascendance and with Northern politicians decrying the backwardness of the slave states, such a comparison would persuade his readers.[9]

The bulk of the letter, however, was dedicated to a different theme. "But doubtless," continued Still, "on a hurried consideration of the claims of the colored people, serious objections would be found by railroad boards and others, under the erroneous impression that the vicinity of St. Mary, Bedford, Seventh and Lombard streets &c., furnishes a sample of the great body of colored people residing in Philadelphia." In other words, Still worried that all Black Philadelphians were being judged by the poorest, most notorious neighborhood in the city. Still went on to defend the character of the bulk of the city's Black population, pointing particularly to the stable, respectable neighborhoods like the one where he lived, and to the successful Black businessmen, their stores "neatly and well kept." Why, Still asked, were Black Philadelphians to be measured by the poorest, most degraded among them? Surely the Black middle class, "comfortably supporting their families, educating their children, and leading lives of respectability," deserved to be treated with respect.[10]

To our modern ears, this sort of argument sounds somewhat elitist. It certainly sounded that way to some of Still's Black contemporaries. It is worth noting, however, the context of this letter and its strategic intent. On one hand, Still was simply asking that Black Philadelphians not be treated as one undifferentiated mass. Just as white readers recognized that Philadelphia was home to all sorts of white residents, so too he wished them to recognize different classes of their Black neighbors. On the other hand, Still and his readers must have known that the Black Philadelphians likely to ride the streetcars were not the poor denizens of "St. Mary's Court." It was, instead, Black businessmen, pastors, and teachers, men like Still, who were most likely to do so. If his rhetoric tended to reinforce the worst stereotypes of poor Black Philadelphians, Still hoped that in doing so he might be able to make the case for the class of Black Philadelphians that was genuinely being excluded from the streetcars. Notably, Still chose to make this case in the *North American,* a newspaper with Republican leanings, but which largely appealed to the city's businessmen, not to radicals. Segregation on the streetcars was the policy of individual rail lines, not of the city of Philadelphia. Still was fashioning an argument that he believed would sway the people who were in a position to make the change he wished to see.[11]

As Still himself solidified his status as a respectable member of the Black middle class, he hoped that his example and the example of men like him would force white Philadelphians to recognize their claims for civil and political equality. At the same time, he hoped that these examples would also serve as an inspiration to Black children, encouraging in them good habits and good character. This belief in the virtues of respectability was nearly universal among Black reformers of the nineteenth century. It would be difficult to find a Black leader in this era who did not preach some form of the gospel of self-improvement.[12]

The need for African Americans to pursue various means of self-improvement was frequently emphasized in the state and national "colored conventions" that met periodically over the course of the nineteenth century. Black Philadelphians, including some of Still's closest friends and mentors, were prominent in promoting the gospel of Black moral reform and self-improvement. Men like Robert Purvis and William Whipper, men who had helped bring Still into the work of the Underground Railroad, were also advocates for various programs of Black moral reform as a means of promoting Black progress.[13]

Still made a signal contribution to this tradition when he was invited to address the Colored Evening School at Clarkson Hall, Sixth and Cherry Street, in March 1860. This was a natural place for Still to speak. He had long been a supporter and contributor to the cause of Black education, going back at least to his work in the Moral Reform Retreat after he first came to Philadelphia. Still began his speech by acknowledging the great barriers faced by Black people in the United States. It was understandable that they would doubt the value of education, given such circumstances. "Some may ask," he admitted, "what benefit will education be to me? What benefit is learning to any colored man in this country?" And yet, he insisted, Black people needed to resist such despair. He made the obvious case that education would help in practical ways, but Still also insisted on "preparing the mind for hungering and thirsting after learning." Such learning, Still argued, was of great value in the struggle for Black rights. In cultivating his mind, "taking an interest in the things of the world around him, whether pertaining to religion or politics, to nature or art," a Black person would be challenging "the dominant race." Not only would the cultivated mind provide evidence to refute the "oft-repeated taunt that the negro is naturally inferior to the other races of men," but education would enable Black people to challenge this idea directly, to formulate this argument in language that whites would be unable to refute. This brought him to his central argument. "It cannot be denied," he insisted, "that the main part of elevation must be performed by colored men themselves, and that by self-improvement." While there were certainly whites who sympathized with their Black neighbors, it was imperative that Black people not rely on such philanthropy. Their salvation lay in their own hands. Here Still surely had in mind the heroic labors of the fugitive slaves he had aided over the years, their brave flight, their willingness to face great odds, and their ultimate triumph.[14]

He followed up this effort a few months later with another address in which he hammered home some of the same themes. The occasion was the anniversary of West Indian emancipation, celebrated at Kennett Square, a small town about thirty miles west of Philadelphia and not incidentally a center of Underground Railroad activity. Befitting the occasion, Still devoted considerable time to convincing his fellow Black Pennsylvanians of the great responsibilities they bore in the struggle against slavery. "We are bordered by three slaveholding States," he reminded his audience, "where prejudice is engendered against us, and is liable to frequent occurrences of kidnapping and continual outrages from the slave-hunter under the operation of the infamous Fugitive Slave Law." As residents of a border state, not only did they bear a large share in the struggle to aid fugitive slaves, but they also stood as representatives of their race. The eyes of the South were upon them. And yet, he argued, Black Pennsylvanians were not doing enough. They had become too comfortable. "Have we given a hearty support to the anti-slavery cause?" he asked. "Do we take anti-slavery papers and make ourselves acquainted with the great struggle going on in all parties in regard to slavery and our own liberties?" He encouraged them to place themselves in the shoes of the enslaved, "just across the Mason and Dixon's line—only a few hours from this spot." Where in his speech before the Colored Evening School Still had been speaking of the responsibility that a free Black community had to better itself, here he expands the borders of that community and demands that his audience see themselves as inextricably bound to their enslaved brothers and sisters. Again, he insisted that while there were white friends of the cause, the greater share of the responsibility for the struggle lay on the shoulders of Black men and women.[15]

While Still urged his listeners in both cases to think about themselves as a part of a larger struggle, he may also have had more personal contexts in mind. In early 1860 Still was dealing with accusations that he had betrayed the trust of the Black abolitionist community in the cases of Ellen Wells and Dimmock Charlton. We might see these speeches as a part of a larger effort to make the case for Still's continuing leadership. Still's resistance to aiding both Wells and Charlton had boiled down to his estimation of their character, and so his emphasis on self-improvement among Black people might be seen as a reflection and reassertion of these concerns. On the other hand, Still's criticism of his fellow Black Pennsylvanians for their failure to adequately support the antislavery movement was both a call to action and perhaps a subtle reminder to his audience of all the antislavery work that Still himself had done over the years.

In the midst of Still's continuing struggle to promote the antislavery cause, he had personal reason to rejoice. In early summer, Letitia had given birth once again. She and William named the girl for her mother. Little Letitia joined a large extended household managed by her mother in the Still boardinghouse on South Street. In addition to the immediate Still family, which now included four children, the 1860 census lists eight boarders in the Still household. Most notable of these was Jonathan Gibbs, the thirty-year-old pastor of the Stills' own First African Presbyterian Church.

There were also four residents who had been born in Maryland, and one, nineteen-year-old Clara Boulden, who had been born in Georgia. Still's record keeping from 1860 was somewhat less scrupulous than it had been in previous years, so we can only speculate whether or not these were fugitives from slavery, taking shelter in the Still household.[16]

This growing family, though, hardly diverted Still from the struggle for Black progress. In his address on the anniversary of West Indian emancipation, Still had lamented the lack of "any Board, Committee or other organization, having the improvement of our people at heart." On September 5, 1860, Still hosted a meeting of some of the leading Black citizens of Philadelphia who sought to remedy this situation. Still's lodger, the Rev. Jonathan Gibbs, was named the chair of the meeting, though Still seems to have played a leading role. "Mr. Still claimed the attention of the meeting on the importance of making efforts to secure the right of suffrage, the right of riding on the passenger railways, and of obtaining statistical information . . . also of the importance of always being ready to repel injurious slanders." He mentioned an article that had been published the previous day in the Philadelphia *Press*, a Republican paper, attempting to paint a comprehensive picture of the city's Black population. The fact that Republicans, in the midst of this campaign season, were looking to connect the larger struggle against slavery with improving the status of free Blacks was, to Still, an opportunity. Gibbs called for a three-man committee to draft a plan for the proposed organization, naming Jacob C. White, Clayton Miller, and Morris Brown, though Miller and Brown declined, maintaining that "there were others present who had given more attention to the subject and were better qualified. After some discussion, Still and Isaiah Wears were named to take their places.[17]

The organization that this meeting spawned was the Social, Civil, and Statistical Association of the Colored People of Pennsylvania. Its constitution indicated that its goal would be "to labor earnestly for the right of Suffrage by the use of petitions, memorials, etc.," but its founders also clearly embraced Still's notion that the gathering of statistical data on the Black population and the publication of such data were critical to advance this cause. Still was not initially named one of the officers of the organization, but less than a month after its founding, Parker J. Smith resigned his post as corresponding secretary and Still took his place. Still was also chair of the subcommittee that focused on black suffrage, notable in the midst of a heated election in which Black Pennsylvanians were denied the right to vote. The committee itself was made up of a mix of the old guard of Philadelphia's Black leaders, men like Still, Wears, and White, and a younger generation, including Octavius Catto and Jacob C. White, Jr., both sons of important Black leaders.[18]

Even as these Black Philadelphians struggled for the right to vote, they also kept a close eye on the elections from which they were excluded. Nineteenth-century elections unfolded gradually, the way primary elections do today, rather than all at once. The election calendar spread elections out over the fall, so newspapers carried stories of elections from across the nation, and readers followed the electoral contest in what today would seem like slow motion. Republicans carried the Pennsylvania state elections in early October, placing Andrew Curtin in the governor's seat and dealing Democrats a serious blow in the state. This boded well for the party's chances a month later when the voters would cast their ballots for the presidency. Republican operatives built on this success, hosting public meetings, barbecue, and parades to continue the momentum through the presidential campaign. Many abolitionists looked on, warily, clearly preferring Lincoln to the alternatives but also suspicious of the westerner. Black abolitionists were particularly dismayed at Lincoln's support for the enforcement of the Fugitive Slave Law, yet well understood that he was superior to the alternative.[19]

Whatever ambivalence Black abolitionists like Still may have had about the election of Lincoln, slaveholders of the Deep South recognized the threat he posed to them. On December 24, 1860, months before Lincoln even took office, leaders of South Carolina met and declared that the bonds between their state and the United States had been dissolved. In justifying their decision, the secession convention particularly cited the failure of many Northern states to honor their constitutional obligation under the Fugitive Slave Law. "In many of these States," they argued, "the fugitive is discharged from service or labor claimed, and in none of them has the State Government complied with the stipulation made in the Constitution." Within weeks the other states of the Deep South followed suit; soon after they would join together to form a new union, the Confederate States of America.[20]

While the secession of the "cotton states" cheered many abolitionists, especially those who had long insisted that there should be "no union with slaveholders," many Northerners were horrified by the prospect of disunion. In Philadelphia, significant portions of the population, especially but not exclusively Democrats, organized to silence the abolitionist agitation that they felt had instigated the secession crisis and to send a strong unionist message to their wayward Southern brothers. Some Philadelphia Democrats openly sympathized with the South; a few even called for Pennsylvania to join the Confederacy. Most Democrats were unwilling to go this far, however, though they were open to making concessions they hoped would appease the seceded states, especially in regard to what one unionist meeting termed "the heedless legislation of some northern States in passing personal liberty laws." Most Republicans, however, resisted such measures; even those who had been most critical of abolitionists tended to balk at measures that would now be seen as appeasing the traitors of the Deep South. When Lincoln stopped in Philadelphia on his way to his inauguration, he was greeted with rapturous crowds. The Democratic newspaper, the *Pennsylvanian*, noted that "negroes were delighted and turned out in unusual numbers."[21]

Even if the number of fugitives passing through Philadelphia slowed during this time, Still continued to assist those who came to the Anti-Slavery Society office looking for his help. Those who did seek Still's aid often went unrecorded; Still noted that after the assault on Harpers Ferry he was more cautious in taking notes. In December 1860, Thomas Garrett wrote to Still notifying him that "Harriet Tubman is again in these parts." Tubman had helped an enslaved man named Stephen Ennets, his wife, Maria, and their three children to escape from bondage in Dorchester County, Maryland. From Garrett's home in Wilmington the group made their way north, first to Chester and then to Still in Philadelphia, where they were clothed and fed and sent on to Canada. This would be Tubman's last foray into her home state as an agent of the Underground Railroad.[22]

Still continued his correspondence with many of those he had helped on their flight to freedom in Canada, but many increasingly asked not just for news of loved ones they had left behind but for news of the growing conflict over secession. "We have read here of the great disturbance in the South," wrote John William Dungy, whom Still had assisted in his flight to Canada in February 1860. "My prayer is that this may be the deathblow of Slavery." For men like Dungy, escape to Canada had not severed their bonds to those left behind in slavery. While they worked to make a better life for themselves in Canada, they held out hope for the land of their birth. "I pray," wrote Dungy, "that the time may come when we will all be men in the United States."[23]

Though many Black Philadelphians were excited by the political change they saw around them, they were also persistently reminded of the desire of their white neighbors to keep them in their place. The struggle to secure equal access to the city's streetcars was dealt a serious setback by the Pennsylvania District Court when Judge John Innes Clark Hare decided in favor of a Philadelphia streetcar conductor who, following his company's policy, had "forcibly" ejected a Black man named George Goines from his car. Goines had sued the conductor, hoping to establish a legal precedent defending the rights of Black passengers. Unfortunately, the judge was more inclined to protect the right of the streetcar companies to establish their own rules. The question, insisted Hare, "is not whether the law does or should exclude negroes from the passenger cars," but rather "when a passenger railroad company thinks it proper to exclude them, the law ought to intervene." Hare attempted to thread the needle, maintaining that there was no positive law banning Black passengers from the cars, but defending the rights of companies to exclude them. The consequence was that streetcars would continue their policy of discrimination against Black riders. Still took to the pages of the *Christian Recorder* to attack the decision, calling it "a second edition of the Dred Scott decision."[24]

Yet, while Still reserved his harshest words for Judge Hare, he also criticized Goines and his supporters for what Still believed was a tactical misstep. "Many intelligent colored men," wrote Still, "predicted that the result would be as the verdict now proves." It was essential, he felt, that this sort of lawsuit be accompanied by a broad-based, coordinated effort to influence public opinion, to leverage Black economic power, and to appeal to powerful and influential friends. This was just the sort of work that the Social, Civil, and Statistical Association had been doing in its effort to challenge the discriminatory policies of the city's streetcars. From a certain perspective, this was simply a continuation of Still's insistence that his way of doing things was the right way. Surely some of his rivals saw this as Still defending his turf. From Still's perspective, though, it was fruitless, and perhaps even counterproductive, to simply entrust the fight to the hands of judges like Hare. "I do not wish it to be understood," concluded Still, "that I am not in favor of contending for our rights in the courts, for certainly this would be a mistake, but in doing so, I deem it highly important in a case that affects the entire colored community, as this case does, to bring to bear all the influence imaginable, to win the day." Despite his contention that the decision to bring the suit against the conductor was premature, Still was generally encouraged by the progress that movement for desegregating the streetcars had made in cultivating public opinion, noting that favorable articles had recently appeared not just in the newspapers where they might have been expected, but also in mainstream Republican papers like the *North American* and the *Press*.[25]

For many abolitionists, Still among them, this optimism in the progress of their cause was buoyed by the imminent transfer of the presidency from the hated proslavery Democrats to Lincoln's Republicans. For all his cautious, lawyerly talk, Lincoln seemed to be a genuine ally to the abolitionist cause, even if he was not himself an abolitionist. "I have always hated slavery," Lincoln had said in 1858 in a well-publicized speech, "I think as much as any Abolitionist."[26]

And yet, as he prepared to assume the presidency, Lincoln

faced the gravest crisis since the nation's founding, a crisis that threatened to grow graver if the slave states of the Upper South followed their Deep South neighbors in seceding from the Union. As much as he hated slavery, Lincoln's first priority was halting secession in its tracks. To do that, he needed to allay the fears of anxious Virginia politicians. He had long supported the mainstream Republican position that the federal government did not have the power to emancipate slaves in the states where slavery was legal. He reiterated this point in his inaugural address. "I have no purpose, directly or indirectly, to interfere with the institution of slavery in the States where it exists," he declared. "I believe I have no lawful right to do so, and I have no inclination to do so." Lincoln went on to specifically address the conflict over the return of fugitive slaves. He admitted that the Constitution was clear in its requirement that fugitive slaves "shall be delivered up on claim of the party to whom such service or labor may be due."[27]

If this right to recover fugitive slaves was troubling to Black abolitionists like Still, who had spent more than a decade thwarting the "rights" of slaveholders, in the very next line Lincoln undercut the reassurance he had just offered. "There is some difference of opinion whether this clause should be enforced by national or by state authority," he admitted, "but surely that difference is not a very material one. If the slave is to be surrendered, it can be of but little consequence to him, or to others, by which authority it is done." This is Lincoln at his cagiest. He knew very well that it absolutely mattered which authority was to be responsible for the return of fugitive slaves. The reason for the Fugitive Slave Law of 1850 was the frustration of slave owners with the intransigence of Northern state governments who had seized every opportunity to thwart the recovery of fugitive slaves. Now Lincoln was, at least theoretically, reopening the possibility that it would be states that would determine the manner in which fugitives would be returned. Of course, in part this was Lincoln the moderate, trying to suggest that sectional disagreements were not as insurmountable as they might appear, but it also offered clues as to which side he was on. "Again," he continued, "in any law upon this subject, ought not all the safeguards of liberty known in civilized and humane jurisprudence to be introduced, so that a free man be not, in any case, surrendered as a slave? And might it not be well, at the same time, to provide by law for the enforcement of that clause in the Constitution which guaranties that 'The citizens of each State shall be entitled to all privileges and immunities of citizens in the several States?'" Not only was Lincoln endorsing the position that Still and other Underground Railroad activists had been advocating for years, that free Blacks needed to be granted stronger protections from arbitrary claims that they were fugitive slaves, he was also implicitly recognizing African Americans as citizens of the United States.[28]

This should not suggest that Lincoln saw African Americans as *equal* citizens, nor that he believed their presence in the United States to be desirable. "I am not, nor have I ever been in favor of bringing about in any way the social and political equality of the white and black races," Lincoln had maintained during his 1858 debates with Stephen Douglas. "I will say," he continued, "there is a physical difference between the white and black races which I believe will forever forbid the two races living together on terms of equal social and political equality." Lincoln had long seen the colonization of free Black people as a solution to the dilemma posed by emancipation, as a way to oppose slavery while also continuing to distance himself from the radical abolitionist doctrine of racial equality. He continued to support colonization, and to commit his administration to carrying it out, well into his presidency.[29]

Abolitionists, then, Still among them, had reason both for cautious optimism and for skepticism about the new president. Lincoln continued to walk a tightrope in the first weeks of his presidency. He understood that the commitment of Upper South slaveholders to the Union was contingent upon his reassurance that he posed no threat to slavery and that he would not use the power of the federal government to coerce the Lower South states back into the Union. This balancing act became untenable when South Carolina forces in Charleston fired upon federal forces occupying Fort Sumter on April 12, forcing the garrison to surrender after a thirty-three-hour bombardment. Lincoln responded by calling for seventy-five thousand troops to suppress the rebellion. Unwilling to go along with what they saw as an effort to coerce the Deep

South back into the Union, four more states seceded: Virginia, North Carolina, Tennessee, and Arkansas.[30]

Almost immediately, the legal question of the status of fugitive slaves became a pressing issue for military authorities. In the weeks after Fort Sumter, as federal troops moved to secure the border states, the slave states that had still remained loyal to the Union, many federal officers remained committed to enforcing the laws of the states they were defending, which meant that in many cases enslaved people who fled to Union lines were returned to their masters. This was in keeping with the Lincoln administration's desperate need to maintain the tenuous loyalty of these states. As perilous as his situation already was in the spring of 1861, if Maryland, Kentucky, or Missouri joined the Confederacy, Lincoln knew that he stood little chance of preserving the Union.[31]

Abolitionists, Black abolitionists in particular, were critical of Lincoln's willingness to appease border-state slaveholders. Frederick Douglass openly criticized Lincoln's inaugural address, and the Philadelphia correspondent of the *National Anti-Slavery Standard* denounced the president's post-Sumter proclamation, which called for federal troops to avoid "interference with, property." The writer had little sympathy for the delicacies of Lincoln's border-state policies. "If Maryland, Virginia and Kentucky choose, whether in the Union or out of it, to hold slaves," wrote the correspondent, "let them do so at their own risk and on their own responsibility." Abolitionists might be optimistic about the promise of the Lincoln administration, but they were not about to stop holding his feet to the fire.[32]

While Lincoln worked to reassure border-state politicians that the Fugitive Slave Law would continue to be enforced, some federal officers took matters into their own hands. On May 23, 1861, three men, Shepard Mallory, Frank Baker, and James Townsend, ran away from their master, a recently appointed Confederate colonel, and sought refuge with federal forces at Fortress Monroe, which guarded the harbor at Hampton Roads in southeast Virginia. The commanding general, Benjamin Butler, a former Democrat who had recently been transferred to the post, decided to shelter the trio. When a representative of their owner presented himself the day after their arrival and demanded their return under the Fugitive Slave Law of 1850, Butler issued him receipts for the three men and told him that they could revisit the matter after the conflict was complete. Butler had realized that Confederate forces were making use of enslaved labor to build batteries not far from his own position. If he were to return these men, they might very well have been put to work helping the Confederate cause; this he would not allow. He seized them as "contraband of war," as property that might legally be seized in time of war.[33]

This was the policy of just one man, but the general almost immediately wrote to his superiors, asking for approval of his actions and for further instructions. Butler realized that while he had taken individual initiative in order to defend his own position, his actions had potentially broader consequences, that it was also "a political question and a question of humanity." On May 30, Lincoln's cabinet met to discuss the matter, and shortly thereafter Secretary of War Simon Cameron telegraphed Butler that his policy of claiming fugitive slaves as "contraband" was approved, but with some clarifications. Butler was to "refrain from surrendering to alleged masters any such persons who may come within your lines." However, his men were not to interfere with slaves "held to service under the laws of any State." What this meant was that federal troops were not to encourage enslaved people to flee, but if enslaved people chose to do so on their own, they were not to be returned. "The question of their final disposition," concluded Cameron, "will be reserved for future determination." This might not have been emancipation, but it was clear that federal forces would not be in the business of returning fugitive slaves.[34]

William Still surely followed these developments with interest. A significant number of the fugitives he had aided over the years had come via Norfolk, just across the channel from Fortress Monroe, and he likely still had contacts in the region. The Philadelphia newspapers followed Butler's actions closely. Many abolitionists watched the growing crisis, saw fighting men moving into the South, and anticipated a new phase of the antislavery struggle. In Philadelphia, the leadership of the PASS decided that it was time to refocus their efforts in light of these changes and cut back some of their expenses. They moved their office from its longtime location on North Fifth Street a few blocks away to North Tenth Street.[35]

This was a great time of transition for Still as well; he decided to step down from his position at the PASS. He submitted his letter of resignation to the executive board on May 29, as the drama over Butler's "contrabands" unfolded. "Dear Friends," Still began, "Understanding that you are contemplating some measures of retrenchment and believing that my service in the cause can now be dispensed with by the Society, I hasten to tender my resignation." For fourteen years he had served as a clerk in the PASS office, and in those years, which he termed "the pleasantest & most profitable of my life," he had helped hundreds of fugitive slaves. Now, he informed the board, "I expect to go into business immediately for myself, but I hope that however I may be engaged or whatever my lot, that I shall always be able to render service to the cause, to which you are all devoted." Even though Still planned to focus his efforts on his business endeavors, he was not about to turn his back on the struggle against slavery.[36]

Conveniently, Still had found a fine location for his new business: his old office. The now vacant space seemed perfect for Still's new stove business. Years earlier, before he had gone to work at the PASS, he had briefly worked at a stove store, and he seemed to feel that he could manage his own now. The middle decades of the nineteenth century had witnessed an explosion in the manufacturing and marketing of household stoves, for heating and for cooking. Manufacturers were able to drive down the price so that while stoves remained fairly expensive, more and more homes were able to purchase them. Retailers, like Still, also played an important role in popularizing and marketing stoves to people who previously would not have bought one. Still in particular hoped to use his connections and his stature in Philadelphia's Black community to market his goods to Black families. "He is as fully prepared to meet the demands of our people," read one notice in the *Christian Recorder*, the official newspaper of the AME Church, "or indeed the public generally, who may want good cook, parlor or chamber stoves, as the generality of stove dealers in this city." Still also repaired stoves and sold coal by the ton.[37]

Still's goal in opening this business was surely to better provide for his family, but he also hoped to live out the self-improvement doctrine that had come to be such an important part of his public rhetoric. The *Christian Recorder* piece that announced his new store's opening leaned into this notion. "Most assuredly we wish him success," it read, "feeling fully persuaded that the more our people can establish themselves in respectable business localities, and cope with white men in carrying on business, the sooner will the prejudice that has so long hindered our people from rising, be removed." For years Still had been reminding free Black people that they could not rely on white allies to help them; they needed to take responsibility for their own economic destiny. His business would help make this case.[38]

William and Letitia moved their family from their boarding-house on South Street and settled in the space above William's new office. The final advertisement for the Stills' boardinghouse appeared in June in the *National Anti-Slavery Standard*; Still's advertisements had been a regular feature in the back pages of the *Standard* for years. In its place was one advertising "COAL, STOVE, ETC., ETC." Still gave no indication of why he closed his boardinghouse, other than that he was moving on to new business ventures. Perhaps the work of keeping the boardinghouse was too much of a burden, given William's new business and the Stills' growing family. Perhaps there was another reason as well.[39]

Letitia, the Stills' fifteen-month-old daughter, died on October 11, 1861. Still seems not to have written about it; perhaps she had been sick for some time. Infant mortality was far more common in nineteenth-century America than it is today. In 1850, more than one in four children died before they reached their first birthday. Because of this, American families were more accustomed to dealing with the death of a child, and yet the loss could still be shattering. The most famous novel of the period, one that Still most certainly had read, Harriet Beecher Stowe's *Uncle Tom's Cabin*, played on these familial bonds in its depiction of the death of the angelic Eva. Despite the fact that Still did not leave a public record of his mourning, it is hard to imagine that the Stills, who had worked so hard to build a stable, middle-class life for their children, were not devastated. Perhaps we can see echoes of his own mourning if we read between the lines of his later depiction of the severing of enslaved families, which is such a common part of his writing about his Underground Railroad work.[40]

Still channeled his sorrow into his work; now more than ever he was committed to ensuring that his remaining family was secure. Still seems to have begun selling coal out of his stove store almost as an afterthought. Years later he recalled that since he could not raise the capital he needed to finance his stove business, he planned to use the coal as a way to gradually save the money he needed to build up his inventory of stoves. Selling coal was a difficult business, though. Dealers had to confront a brutally competitive market, selling a commodity that was largely undistinguishable from what was sold by their competitors. As it turned out, sales of coal rapidly outgrew Still's expectations. In the first month, coal sales netted him more than three times the cost of his rent, and his newfound prosperity helped convince others to extend him credit, which they had been reluctant to do for an unproven businessman. He worked alone, rising at four each morning to repair and service his stoves himself, before changing his clothes and managing the store.[41]

If most of Still's daily hours were now devoted to sales of stoves and coal, he also followed news of the growing crisis in the South. The months after Fort Sumter saw small-scale fighting across the South, but on July 21, a reluctant Union General Irvin McDowell, spurred on by President Lincoln himself, advanced on the Confederates' defensive line near a railroad junction in Manassas, Virginia. At first the fresh Union troops seemed to drive back their Confederate foes, but then, after rallying around Brigadier General Thomas Jackson, who earned himself the enduring nickname of "Stonewall," the Confederates launched a furious counterattack, driving their foes from the field and sending them retreating back to Washington in a panic. Philadelphia papers that Still might have read emphasized the brutality, "the infamous conduct of the traitors," and also noted the fugitive slaves who fled the Confederate army, seeking refuge in the North.[42]

There continued to be disagreement in the North about

what was to be done with such refugees. Butler's actions had been widely debated, with Democrats and a small number of conservative Republicans critical, but in August the Congress passed, and Lincoln signed, the first Confiscation Act, which essentially codified Butler's policies into law. "Any person claimed to be held to labor or service under the law of any State" who was compelled to serve the Confederate military effort, "the person to whom such labor or service is claimed to be due shall forfeit his claim to such labor." In other words, not only was that person not to be returned to the master who claimed him, he was free. This was not the broad emancipation that abolitionists wanted—it did not apply to all fugitives—and some leading abolitionists continued to criticize the timidity of the Lincoln administration, yet this was clearly a step toward emancipation.[43]

Many, though not all, young Black men in Philadelphia were eager to join the war, seeing it from the very beginning as a fight against slavery. Even though the state was not yet prepared to accept such service, Black leaders raised two regiments of Black troops in the spring of 1861, hoping that the patriotism of these volunteers would overcome the doubts of white leaders. "Peril and war," argued one such Black Philadelphian, "blot out all distinction of race and rank." Black Philadelphians had long been willing to put their lives on the line in defense of their own liberties and those of their friends and neighbors. Some hoped to channel the same spirit into the fight against the Confederacy. Others, though, were reluctant to join a war effort that was not explicitly dedicated to blotting out slavery. While Lincoln might have been slowly moving toward a more vigorous embrace of emancipation, and while that movement would be clear in hindsight, he continued to hold out olive branches to the seceded states. Why should Black men fight to rebuild a Union that had only ever treated them as slaves? Should they not at least wait, leveraging their service in order to force the administration to more aggressively pursue emancipation? Whatever Still thought of these debates, he was not one of those eager to enlist. At the start of the war, he was almost forty years old. He had a new business and a family to support.[44]

Despite his long hours at work, however, Still did find himself deeply involved in the effort to aid the increasing number of Black refugees from slavery. Like many abolitionists, white and Black, across the North, Still initially focused his efforts on the formerly enslaved people of Port Royal, South Carolina. The Union navy had occupied the area, which included a strategically important sound, early in the war, in November 1861. The area was also home to thousands of slaves who grew valuable Sea Island cotton on plantations scattered along the coast. When the Union navy occupied it, masters fled to the mainland, leaving behind their former slaves. Soon this land became a sort of laboratory for Reconstruction, and philanthropic Northerners, white and Black, poured into the area in order to help these men and women in their transition from slaves to wage workers.[45]

Across the North, philanthropic citizens rallied to support these efforts. At a mass meeting held in National Hall on March 1862, a number of the leading citizens of Philadelphia formed the Port Royal Relief Committee. A few weeks later, at Still's urging, the Social, Civil, and Statistical Association hosted a meeting to raise money for the "Port Royal Contrabands." The Hutchinson Family Singers, a famous abolitionist singing group, performed, and the committee passed a series of resolutions celebrating the "FREEMEN" of Port Royal and calling upon the people of Philadelphia to support them in their time of need. The association contributed $50 to this cause and Still added $5 of his own.[46]

Unsurprisingly, Still was also involved in the effort to support Black refugees who found their way to Philadelphia. This was a natural extension of his Underground Railroad work. While the bulk of his work in the 1850s had involved moving fugitives through Philadelphia to safer destinations, he had also occasionally helped Black refugees from the South find work in and around Philadelphia. In March 1862, the Pennsylvania Abolition Society, the "old" abolition society, asked Still to manage an agency that would help former slaves find work and housing in Philadelphia. Still initially balked at the request. "I do not know," he wrote Dillwyn Parrish, "that I could do very much in the way of serving the old abolition soc. in [managing] the kind of agency that you suggested." Though he admitted "that the cause requires such an agency," he insisted that his new business constrained his ability to take on this responsibility. Though in the same letter, he passed

along to Parrish letters from two individuals who had already contacted Still looking for such help, and he noted that others had
approached him as well. Despite his reluctance, two days later Still
accepted the position, with a salary of eight dollars per month. He
was reluctant to accept any salary at all, since "as a colored man
I feel that as far as possible I should aid for nothing the elevation of my race," but he also noted that as "a poor man" he could
only accept such a demanding job if he would be compensated for
doing so.[47]

Still was right to expect that this would be a demanding job.
Two months later, in a report on his work with the agency to his
employers at the Pennsylvania Abolition Society, he reported that
"193 persons have applied for help or servants." In fact, he noted,
"persons continued to apply daily for Contrabands," but there
were not enough coming into the city to fill this demand, at least
not enough that were coming to Still for such work. He suggested
that they advertise in order to alert more potential workers to the
demand for their labor.

Still also found that he needed to publicly reassure anxious
white Philadelphians who feared their city was being overrun by
desperate and impoverished contrabands. He denied the truth of
the rumor that "five hundred or a thousand were daily expected"
to flood the city. Those who had fled to Philadelphia had been
"welcomed to temporary homes in Colored families," and most
had been placed "in the country" where "occupations were found
for them." Only one of these was incapable of supporting herself,
said Still, and she, he noted "is 104 years of age." Still well knew
that even benevolent white Philadelphians were wary of any dramatic expansion in the city's Black population.[48]

While Still worked to ensure that emancipated slaves could find
work, the Lincoln administration and Republicans in Congress
took further steps toward embracing emancipation as an essential aim of the war. On July 17, 1862, Lincoln had signed into
law a second Confiscation Act, which broadened the power of the
Union army to emancipate; where the first act had applied only to
slaves actively employed in the Confederate war effort, the second

applied to all those claimed as slaves by rebels. A few months later, Lincoln took this one step further, and on September 22 issued the Emancipation Proclamation declaring that on January 1, 1863, all slaves in states that were still in rebellion against the United States would be "forever free." Though the Emancipation Proclamation was a part of a longer process whereby the Lincoln administration and the Republican-led Congress gradually embraced emancipation as a critical element of waging the Civil War, as James Oakes, the historian who has most closely studied this process, noted, the Emancipation Proclamation "struck like a thunderbolt." Across the North, supporters celebrated the president.[49]

Black Philadelphians were, unsurprisingly, ecstatic over Lincoln's proclamation. This seemed to be validation of the long-held view of many of the city's Black leaders that the war that had been precipitated by the conflict over slavery would inevitably lead to slavery's demise. As was the case across the North, Black Philadelphians prepared to publicly celebrate the final version of the proclamation when its provisions became official on New Year's Day 1863. Still and the leaders of the Social, Civil, and Statistical Association, however, were concerned that such celebrations might lead to a backlash against the struggle for Black rights in Philadelphia. They issued a call to their fellow Black citizens of the city to observe the date with sober discipline, rather than with raucous spectacle. They worried that if, in the midst of "the dark clouds of war and the violent ragings of our enemies," Black citizens were to be seen parading in the streets, celebrating the "jubilee," it would reflect poorly upon them. The best way to celebrate Lincoln's Emancipation Proclamation, they suggested, was not by feasting and drinking but by supporting the suffering contrabands of the South through donations of money, food, and clothing. "The time may come soon," they warned, "when we can publicly rejoice over the downfall of slavery and the rebellion together; but be assured it is not yet." Many Black Philadelphians shared this cautious approach, and observed the traditional New Year's Eve watch night services with solemn expectation.[50]

When New Year's Day finally came, Lincoln's final version of the Emancipation Proclamation gave Black men across the North an additional reason to celebrate: it lifted the long-standing restriction on enlisting Black men in the Union armies. The earlier debates about whether or not it was right for Black men to serve in the war seemed to have been swept away; for many the Emancipation Proclamation had made official what they had long hoped for, that this would become a war to end slavery. Massachusetts was the first state to raise Black troops, and Black men from across the North signed up to serve in the Massachusetts 54th Volunteer Infantry Regiment. Black Philadelphians met in March at Franklin Hall to celebrate and to encourage men from the city to join this pioneering regiment.[51]

Before long, though, Pennsylvania authorities began to worry that they were losing out because of this exodus of Black men to out-of-state regiments. This was especially problematic because states were given quotas of enlistments for which they were responsible, whether by volunteer or by draft. As the *Philadelphia Inquirer* noted, "Pennsylvania has already lost the credit for full fifteen hundred men, recruited here for Massachusetts regiments, who will be credited to the quota of the Bay State on the approaching draft." On June 13, the governor of Pennsylvania, Andrew Curtin, issued orders banning Black Pennsylvanians from enlisting in out-of-state regiments.[52]

Many Black Philadelphians were eager to enlist, both to strike a blow against slavery and to demonstrate their manhood and love of country. By June, leading citizens had formed a committee to raise Black regiments, recruiters were operating in the city, and the War Department had established a camp, which came to be named Camp William Penn, just north of Philadelphia, in what is now Cheltenham, where Black troops were to be trained. Handbills were appearing around town. "Men of Color, To Arms! To Arms!" "Come Forward!" "Now or Never." "Valor and Heroism." Most of these handbills featured the endorsement of many of the leading Black men of the city. In July 6, Frederick Douglass spoke at a mass meeting held at National Hall in order to promote the enlistment of Black troops. Stephen Smith, a wealthy Black businessman and longtime ally of Still's in the Underground Railroad, served as president of the meeting. The extensive list of vice presidents and secretaries included some of the most prominent Black men of Philadelphia.[53]

Still's name is conspicuously absent from these handbills and from the meetings promoting Black enlistment. He was surely not opposed to the enlistment of Black men and seems to have had some involvement with the raising of Black troops, or at least he maintained connections with those who did. When George Stephens, a Black man from Philadelphia who had enlisted in the Massachusetts 54th, grew frustrated with his inability to secure a promotion to the position of drill sergeant, he wrote to Still for help. Later, Thomas Garrett asked for Still's help in ensuring that a particular former slave who wished to enlist would receive the full bounty paid by the government, that it would not go to "land sharks," a reference to the abundant brokers and agents who profited from the complicated system of Civil War enlistment. Still also donated money to support a committee that was recruiting Black troops, though far less than he was regularly giving to support emancipated slaves.[54] Perhaps Still's absence from the enlistment handbills and meetings that called for the enlistment of Black troops reflects his own commitment to other means of serving the war and the fight against slavery. Perhaps he was uncomfortable asking others to do what he would not do himself.

In the spring of 1863, as many Black Philadelphians were preparing to enlist in the Union armed forces, the Still family once again was visited by tragedy. On April 15, 1863, Letitia Still gave birth to a stillborn daughter. As had been the case seventeen months earlier, when their daughter Letitia died, the Stills have left us little evidence to know how they dealt with the loss of a child. They buried her in Lebanon Cemetery, on the southern edge of the city, along with her sister. If they gave her a name it was not listed on the death certificate.[55]

In the summer of 1863, Still received a letter from his old friend William Wells Brown. Brown shared news with Still about his most recent book and joked about some of the criticism he had received about it. While Still was generally sympathetic to his friend's literary work, he also had a particular interest in this book. Earlier that year, Brown had published *The Black Man, His Antecedents, His Genius, and His Achievements*, a compendium of great Black

Americans, beginning with the Black scientist Benjamin Banneker and continuing up to the present day. Through these short biographical sketches, Brown hoped to challenge racist notions about African Americans and their potential. The bulk of the book was dedicated to Brown's contemporaries, men who were still engaged in the struggle for Black progress. Perhaps unsurprisingly, he included a sketch of his friend, William Still.[56]

The sketch presented a glowing picture of Still, a man who had distinguished himself as one of the most important abolitionists in the country and who now seemed on the verge of even greater things. "Mr. Still is somewhat tall," wrote Brown, "neat in figure and person, has a smiling face, is unadulterated in blood, and gentlemanly in his intercourse with society." He praised Still for his Underground Railroad work, quoting appreciative Canadian refugees who expressed their gratitude to their benefactor, but he particularly emphasized Still's polish and respectability. "He laughed at times," Brown wrote, "but never boisterously, and in profounder moments threw a telling solemnity into his tone and expression." Still is depicted as the pinnacle of Black uplift, as a man deeply committed to the progress of Black people and to the struggle to ensure that they be full citizens in the land of their birth.[57]

Still was surely proud to be so depicted by his friend. The short sketch was in keeping with how he viewed himself, but it also likely irritated those in Philadelphia who had become critical of Still's somewhat high-handed attitude toward those who failed to live up to his high standards. In a letter to the *Weekly Anglo-African*, Brown joked about tense encounters with acquaintances who had been left out of the book, and quoted "a friend in Philadelphia," most likely Still, who commented that "the greatest opposition [to *The Black Man*] comes from those who are left out."[58]

Whatever his rivals thought, Still was considered by many to be among the most trustworthy and respectable Black men in the city, and it was this reputation that led federal authorities to ask him to serve as sutler to Camp William Penn. The camp, which had grown to a sprawling twelve-acre complex in the hills northwest of Philadelphia, adjacent to the estate of his friends and fellow abolitionists, James and Lucretia Mott, hosted the training of nearly 11,000 Black soldiers over the course of the Civil War.

Sutlers were civilians attached to military units or posts who sold various goods to the soldiers. The sutler for Camp William Penn would be responsible for ensuring that enlisted men were able to purchase whatever goods they might need but which they were not supplied with by the army itself. If a soldier needed cigars, a toothbrush, pens, or razors, he went to the camp sutler.[59]

While many sutlers conducted their business with the utmost scrupulousness, it was not uncommon for others to take advantage of their position for personal gain. During the Civil War, sutlers were known for price gouging, offering inferior goods, and selling contraband and stolen goods, among other infractions. In the case of Camp William Penn, the initial decision of the War Department not to appoint a camp sutler had led to even worse abuses. In the absence of an official source for the sorts of goods that sutlers typically supplied, enterprising merchants entered the camp, claiming to have the authorization of the War Department, and sold their goods to Black soldiers desperate for everyday necessities. The camp commander, Lieutenant Colonel Louis Wagner, was most likely aware that such men were operating in his camp, but without an officially sanctioned sutler, he may have felt as though he had no choice but to look the other way. In December 1863, however, he was informed by the War Department that "two white men" were posing as sutlers and that he should have them removed immediately.[60]

For months the War Department had been ignoring Wagner's requests for a sutler, and in fact his requests for more staff in general seem to have fallen on deaf ears, but soon after these two imposters were ejected from camp, Still was offered the position. At first, he refused, fearing that he would not be able to manage the job alongside the work demanded of him by his growing stove and coal business, but shortly thereafter he reconsidered. Still's appointment seems to have been a part of a larger effort on the part of the Supervisory Committee for the Recruitment of Colored Soldiers, which had grown concerned about the drunkenness and prostitution that it believed to be rampant at the camp. Such concerns were likely overblown, but Still's reputation for honesty and respectability led the Supervisory Committee to see him as a good influence.[61]

While Still might have had the confidence of the Supervisory Committee and of the camp leadership, it seems that some of the enlisted men were suspicious of him. Within a month of his taking up the position, Still's operation was destroyed by members of the 25th Colored Regiment, who seem to have thought he was cheating them. What led them to such a conclusion, and whether or not there was any justification for them to have acted so, is unclear. The post of sutler was a potentially lucrative one, and Still surely operated with an eye on profit. He gave freely to charity but this was not one of them. Perhaps, as one historian has suggested, the assault on Still's operation was a product of class conflict, a largely lower-class group of Black soldiers who resented the prosperous Black merchant who was profiting off them. Perhaps they resented the fact that they would be going off to war while he would stay behind (in fact the job exempted Still from the draft). Much later, Still would suggest that his refusal to sell contraband and alcohol to Black soldiers and his unwillingness to accept counterfeit currency that had been passed off on the soldiers had been a source of resentment toward him. In any case, Still continued on as camp sutler and there is no indication from Wagner or from others who supervised the conduct of the camp that their confidence in Still's conduct had diminished.[62]

At some point that spring, Still brought on his brother John Still, older than William by six years, to work for him at Camp William Penn as a clerk. It is unclear how close the two brothers were, but it seems likely that John hoped to benefit from his more prosperous brother's connections. Perhaps William was eager to help his brother out. In March, a correspondent for the *Christian Recorder*, while visiting the camp, found John Still "a very intelligent man," minding the store. Intelligent he may have been, but it seems that John was not content with the money he made legally. Not long after this visit, John Still was arrested and charged with purchasing soldiers' clothing, which was the legal property of the United States, which he then resold, keeping the profits for himself. Perhaps some of these goods were stolen, though the reports of the case are unclear on this. Most embarrassing for his brother, John had some of these illegal goods transported to William's house, sealed inside barrels. Investigators entered Still's home and seized these contraband goods. John was tried and convicted by a district court.[63]

William was not charged in his brother's crimes, but he was certainly mortified by the entire ordeal. The day after his brother's conviction, Still published a notice in the *Philadelphia Inquirer* attempting to absolve himself of any involvement in or knowledge of his brother's wrongdoing. Still admitted that he knew his brother was conducting a side business out of the sutler's office, a business he permitted to continue because of "the pleas of poverty made by my brother," and because the Post Adjutant had given John permission to do so. Still denied that he had known the nature of the goods his brother was purchasing, that they were uniforms and the legal property of the United States government. He had believed them to be simply "citizens' clothing," meaning that soldiers were legally entitled to sell them. Despite any blow this might have given to his reputation, Still continued on as sutler for Camp William Penn, a position he would hold through the end of the Civil War.[64]

Camp William Penn had been situated a short distance from the city of Philadelphia, but soldiers from the camp sometimes found reason to be in the city itself, which often resulted in conflict with white Philadelphians. Many white Philadelphians were particularly incensed to see Black men in uniform, particularly those with a sergeant's stripes. In September 1864, a sergeant major of the 127th United States Colored Troops, then training at Camp William Penn, was assaulted while walking down South Street by "a number of ruffians," seemingly without provocation. When the sergeant major defended himself, he was arrested and taken into custody. On another occasion, a white mob chased a Black sergeant, Prince Rivers, who sought refuge in Still's stove store from "his howling and infuriate pursuers." Only the intervention of Still's friend the Rev. Jonathan Gibbs, pastor of the First African Presbyterian Church, prevented bloodshed.[65]

Ultimately, despite the concerns of some white Philadelphians, the Black men trained at Camp William Penn would go on to serve a critical role in the victory of the Union forces. Regiments trained at the camp would fight under General Ulysses S. Grant in the Overland Campaign through Virginia; they would take part in the assault on Wilmington, North Carolina; they were among those who marched into Richmond once it was abandoned by the Confederate government; and they were present at Lee's surrender to Grant at Appomattox Court House. The men of the camp were unsurprisingly proud of their contributions. A correspondent for the *Christian Recorder,* visiting Camp William Penn in April 1865, noted that "About midnight, the cry was heard in the camp, that Lee and his whole army had surrendered. You can judge the feelings among the soldiers when the distant sound of booming cannon was heard, and the ringing of bells throughout the town and country." Black men in uniform joined the rest of the nation in celebrating the victory that they had done so much to secure. Within days, though, their joy had turned to sorrow. With the rest of the nation, they mourned Lincoln's death, and when his funeral train passed through Philadelphia, instead of the victory parade that Colonel Wagner had planned, Black regiments joined the massive procession that honored the slain president.[66]

CHAPTER TEN

THE STREETCAR FIGHT

On a cold December day, shortly before he was appointed sutler for Camp William Penn, Still took the North Pennsylvania
Railroad from Philadelphia out to the camp, arriving at eleven in
the morning. He had business to attend to there, but he also had
an engagement back in Philadelphia in the early afternoon, so he
planned to complete his business at the camp quickly and then
head back the way he had come as soon as possible. Still had hoped
to catch a one o'clock train, but missed it by five minutes, and so
was forced to take a streetcar instead. This would take longer, but
he could not afford to wait for the next train.

As soon as a streetcar pulled up, Still and a man who worked
for him and who had been with him at the camp, a white man, got
on board. Still handed the conductor the fare for both men. The
conductor gladly took his money, but before he handed him his
change he asked Still to "step out on the platform."

"Why is this?" asked Still.

"It is against the rules," replied the man.

"Who objects?"

"It is the aristocracy."

"Well, it is a *cruel cult!*" countered Still, "and I believe this is
the only city of note in the civilized world where a decent colored
man cannot be allowed to ride in a city passenger car. Even the

cars which were formerly built in Philadelphia for New Orleans were not devoid of accommodations for colored people inside."

Still also had his doubts that "the aristocracy" was behind this policy. As a member of the Social, Civil, and Statistical Association (SCSA), Still had circulated a petition in favor of allowing Black riders on the streetcars, and it had received hundreds of signatures from the most respectable citizens of Philadelphia. The conductor insisted that while he had no personal objection to allowing Still to ride inside the car, he had to follow "the rules."

Still felt he had little choice but to accept this second-class citizenship, at least for the moment. He did not want to miss his meeting back in Philadelphia, and he had no other way to get there. It had been four years since he had publicly challenged the policy of segregation on Philadelphia's streetcars, and in those four years little progress had been made. As the car began to move, Still felt the cold wind on his face and he reflected on the indignity of being denied a space inside a nearly empty car on a day such as this. It was the perfect illustration of Judge Taney's *Dred Scott* decision, Still thought to himself. Truly "black men have no rights which white men are bound to respect." It began to snow.

That evening, Still penned a letter to the Philadelphia *Press*, a Republican paper, describing the experience and reminding the paper's readers that "every colored man, woman, and child" in the city was subject to the same treatment. Those who had attempted to cross this color line in public transit had been repeatedly put in their place by white conductors. It did not matter if they were "taxpayers, and as upright as any other class of citizens." The indignity was only compounded by the fact that Still had been compelled to travel out to Camp William Penn on U.S. Army business. Was a man doing his duty to his country to be treated this way? When the *Christian Recorder* reprinted this letter a few weeks later, it took this implication a step further, suggesting that the operators of Philadelphia's streetcars were traitors to the Union cause. "Are they Copperheads [a derisive term for those who were disloyal to the Union] that they treat us this way?" the paper asked.[1]

Still's frustration with the segregated streetcars of Philadelphia was not new, nor was his commitment to challenging that policy, but in the last year of the Civil War, he devoted himself to this struggle with renewed zeal. In part, this was a continuation of his long-standing fight for Black citizenship rights. This fight had taken many forms, but Still's efforts to promote Black uplift and to demonstrate the respectability of Black Philadelphians were part of a long tradition of Black activism. For Still, this struggle had also had a personal dimension. He saw his own rising status, the success of his business and the prosperity of his family, as an illustration of the capabilities of Black people.

At the same time, Still's fight for the desegregation of Philadelphia's streetcars was a part of a broader effort to "reconstruct" the city after the Civil War. As Black Southerners struggled to remake the region in the wake of slavery's demise, to secure political power, and to ensure their own economic progress, so too did Black Northerners seek to capitalize on the Civil War and its aftermath. Black Philadelphians had been instrumental in securing the victory of the Union, and they felt that in doing so they had definitively proven their status as American citizens. Increasingly, they depicted those who opposed these claims, who stood in the way of Black progress, as traitors to the cause, as "copperheads."

Since its founding, the SCSA had been committed to the desegregation of Philadelphia's streetcars, and Still had been particularly active in pushing action on this front within the executive committee. When the society formed a committee devoted to the issue, Still was appointed chair. There was some disagreement within the society as to tactics, but Still seems to have been committed to making direct appeals to prominent and influential Philadelphians. Still's work with the Vigilance Committee had brought him into contact with some of the leading men of the city, and his own business had only widened this network. He personally appealed to hundreds of prominent men; Still visited "the merchant in his counting-house, the minister in his sanctum, the judge on the bench, the lawyer in his office, members of Congress, bankers, presidents of railways, and editors of secular and religious papers." He was confident that he could appeal to such men; he increasingly felt that he was one of them.[2]

Still was particularly confident that he could turn the loyalty of Black citizens and their service to the Union cause into a potent tool for equality. The Car Committee drafted an appeal to the board of managers of various city passenger car companies that made this appeal clear. "The fifteen hundred wounded soldiers who lay in pain at the Summit and Sattelee hospitals a few weeks since," they lamented, "received but few visits from their colored brethren, simply because the rules enforced on these cars would not allow decent colored people to ride." Perhaps they hoped that these businessmen would be moved by patriotism, or perhaps they hoped to shame them into action. "Not a few of these brave men," they continued, "have already won imperishable honor on the battlefield," and yet still they were compelled to face the indignity of second-class citizenship.[3]

This combination of Black patriotism and Black respectability was, Still hoped, a potent means of molding white public opinion. At the same time, Still and the Car Committee continued to negotiate directly with the leaders of individual car companies, hoping that if they saw that public opinion had changed on the issue they would then be willing to change their policy, but these negotiations bore little fruit. In December 1864, the president of the Ridge and Girard Avenue streetcar line wrote to the committee promising to run one car per hour specifically for "colored passengers," and other lines made similar modest offers, but most lines refused to make even this sort of meager concession, and Black Philadelphians continued to be tossed from streetcars when they tried to ride inside with white customers.[4]

Still also realized that through his years of work in the abolitionist movement he had developed a network of relationships with some of the most influential white men in the city. He felt that this might be the time to draw on these connections. In January 1865, he suggested to his old employer, Miller McKim, the organization of a mass meeting to bring together many of the leading citizens of Philadelphia in order to express their support for the desegregation of the streetcars. The meeting, held on January 13 at the Concert Hall, likely exceeded Still's wildest expectations. "The platform was occupied," reported the Philadelphia *Press*, "by a number of distinguished gentlemen, among whom were represented the clergy, the legal profession, the mercantile interest, members of

Congress and others." The massive meeting appointed forty-five vice-presidents and twenty secretaries, including many of those who had been important Still allies over the years, not only Miller McKim, but Edward M. Davis, James Mott, Charles D. Cleveland, and others. Many of the leading Black citizens of Philadelphia also attended and, contrary to typical practice, were scattered throughout the hall rather than cordoned off into a separate section.[5]

The meeting adopted a series of resolutions, many echoing the arguments Still and the SCSA Car Committee had been making for years. They denounced the "exclusion of respectable persons" from the streetcars "on the ground of complexion." They lamented the fact that "decent women of color" were forced to walk long distances, often in bad weather. They reminded their audience of the service of Black men in the Union cause, and they linked prejudice in the North to slavery in the South. Finally, the meeting appointed a committee of men, led by Benjamin P. Hunt and filled with veterans of the antislavery movement, to continue to put into practice the principles laid out by the meeting and to continue to press for streetcar desegregation. This was a white counterpart to Still's Car Committee, made up of influential men who were sympathetic to the cause of Black rights.[6]

Many of the leaders of the city's streetcar companies continued to insist that opening their cars to Black riders would hurt their business. This was, of course, not an unreasonable assertion in a city where whites were well-known for their racism. Still might have hoped to dispel this notion with prominent display of white support, but the companies maintained that the bulk of the people who actually rode the streetcars on a daily basis remained opposed to sharing those cars with Black passengers. In January of 1865, the city's car companies attempted to take the pulse of their ridership by conducting a poll of riders, asking whether or not they were in favor of allowing Black passengers to ride in the cars with whites. Conductors distributed printed slips of paper to riders after taking their fare. Advocates for the desegregation of the streetcars were skeptical of this process from the start; some reported that riders had voted multiple times, and many "respectable" patrons refused to participate. Some wrote in additional opinions on the slips of paper, expressing their support for separate cars for Black riders or damning Black Philadelphians with a stream of vulgarities. When the poll, perhaps inevitably, showed that riders were opposed to the integration of the streetcars, advocates for desegregation dismissed it as a "subterfuge" and continued their advocacy.[7]

Despite the glacial progress of their efforts, Still remained committed to the slow work of changing public opinion and direct appeals to the streetcar companies themselves. Some Black Philadelphians urged the Car Committee to embrace a campaign of direct action, whereby significant numbers of Black riders would attempt to board streetcars in order to force a confrontation, but Still remained unconvinced of the wisdom of this strategy. The committee debated this proposal, but "after much discussion the motion was finally lost." Still seemed sure that his strategy was slowly gaining support, and while it had not yet borne fruit, he was fearful that a more direct strategy risked the progress that had already been made. The committee instead resolved to "exercise their best judgement to urge the rights of colored people on the cars." Perhaps this cautious approach was reflective of Still's hard-earned middle-class status and his growing business interests, but it also surely was reflective of his long career as an abolitionist and activist. He knew from experience that whatever gains Black Philadelphians had made were tenuous and that white support could always be withdrawn. He feared that the sort of confrontational tactics advocated by some of his colleagues would alienate moderate white supporters.[8]

More promising in Still's eyes was the possibility that the state legislature might compel streetcars to admit Black passengers. In January 1865, State Senator Morrow Lowry introduced a bill stating "That it shall not be lawful for any passenger railway company, within this Commonwealth, to make or enforce any rule, regulation or practice, excluding any race of people from its passenger cars on account of color." Lowry, from Erie County in the far northwest of the state, had already distinguished himself for his zeal in the antislavery cause and his advocacy of the rights of Black people. The bill passed the Senate by a narrow margin, but its success in the Pennsylvania House seemed less sure. The prime obstacle was the Passenger Railway Committee, eight of whose fifteen members were from Philadelphia. A number of organizations, including Still's Car Committee as well as the committee established by the Concert Hall meeting and headed by Benjamin Hunt, lobbied the legislature to no avail. The bill never even made it to the full House for a vote. Despite the fact that twelve of the fifteen committee members were Republicans, they were afraid of the consequences of supporting such a bill. Philadelphia Republicans were convinced that the bill was electoral poison, and even many of those who had agreed to serve on Hunt's committee were reluctant to push too hard, fearing the consequences of moving too far in advance of public opinion.[9]

Still was surely disappointed in the failure of Morrow's car bill, but likely unsurprised. As the Civil War drew to a close, Still continued his cautious strategy, cultivating alliances with political allies and sympathetic businessmen, but he and the SCSA increasingly coupled this with a renewed emphasis on the promotion of public discussion of issues that were vital to the Black community. Starting in January 1865, Still, as chairman of the SCSA's Committee on Lectures, organized a series of public addresses by leading figures of the abolitionist movement and other supporters of the cause of Black rights. The opening lecture was delivered by William Lloyd Garrison on January 16 at the Concert Hall. Tickets were twenty-five cents and proceeds were to be used by the SCSA "towards procuring the rights of colored people on the city passenger rail-ways, for the benefit of the freedmen, and to aid sick and wounded soldiers." At the same time, Still and the SCSA certainly saw these lectures as a part of his broader effort to promote Black respectability. Among the first group of speakers were such Black intellectual luminaries as Frederick Douglass, Francis Ellen Watkins Harper, and John Mercer Langston.[10]

Meanwhile, the SCSA became increasingly focused on the effort to secure voting rights for Black Pennsylvanians. Still had been the chair of the Suffrage Committee since the founding of the SCSA and he took the lead in the organization's efforts in this area. On July 10, 1865, Still introduced to the executive committee of the SCSA a resolution calling for "increasing efforts to promote" suffrage, and a week later, when the SCSA hosted a public meeting at Sansom Street Hall to promote this effort, Still was one of the secretaries. In his opening address, sometime Still ally Isaiah Wears tapped into the still raw feelings of the recently concluded Civil War. As reported in the *Christian Recorder*, he noted that "the present action of the Government tended to hand over the colored man of the North, as well as of the South, to the will of those who oppressed him before the war. He believed that gratitude, if nothing else, should prompt the nation to reward the faithfulness and bravery of this class, in the hour of its sorest need, by giving to them the right to use the ballot as the only sure means of self-protection." The meeting adopted a series of resolutions reminding listeners of the service and loyalty of African Americans and linking those who would deny Black voting rights with the enemies of the nation.[11]

Notably, the meeting also expressed its desire to cooperate with a coming convention to be held in Harrisburg that also intended to promote Black suffrage. This meeting was organized by the Pennsylvania State Equal Rights League (PSERL), a branch of a national organization founded a year earlier at a national convention in Syracuse. The national organization and its state and local affiliates were dedicated to the fight for Black citizenship rights. While some members of the SCSA would become active in the PSERL, others, Still among them, resisted some efforts to promote overt cooperation between the two organizations. On September 4, 1865, for example, when some members of the executive committee of the SCSA pushed for the organization to make a financial contribution to the PSERL, Still and Wears opposed doing so, on the grounds that it would take away from their own efforts. Perhaps they were hesitant to cede authority to an organization they were not able to control. It is also notable that while some of Still's allies worked in both organizations, the leadership of the PSERL also included such longtime Still antagonists as Alfred M. Green and William Forten, and others who would soon become critical of Still's leadership, like Octavius Catto and Jacob C. White, Jr. Nevertheless, even as they operated independently, the two organizations generally complemented each other's efforts.[12]

Increasingly, the SCSA seemed to operate as Still's personal vehicle for activism. Officially Still served as the corresponding secretary for the society, but the minutes of the executive committee seem to show Still as the driving force for much of the work that was being done. Since the larger committee met only rarely in these years, it was in the executive committee that the bulk of the work was done. As chair of the Committee on Lectures, Still occupied the most public-facing role in the organization. This work seemed to occupy an increasing proportion of the organization's funds. Still also chaired two of the other most active committees, the Suffrage Committee and the Car Committee. Other members continued to participate in various ways, but Still was at the center of almost everything that the SCSA did.[13]

A significant portion of that work was directed toward the aid of newly emancipated Black Southerners. Like many Black Northerners, the leaders of the SCSA saw their own struggle for citizenship rights as intimately connected to the struggle of freedmen and -women. During the Civil War, Still had taken an active role in the effort to support contraband communities. In 1864 he had urged the SCSA executive committee to support "a school in the district of Columbia for the benefit of the freedmen," and this effort continued after the war ended. In the summer of 1865, Still traveled to Virginia in order to observe firsthand the conditions of freed people. In keeping with his long commitment to Black uplift, Still was particularly eager to find ways to promote education among a population that had been largely denied formal schooling.[14]

Still himself had gone to school only sporadically as a child, but he ensured that his children were provided with the education he had been denied. Like many middle-class Black families in Philadelphia, the Stills sent their children to be educated at the Institute for Colored Youth, a school founded by Quakers in 1837, at which they received a classical, college-preparatory education under the guidance of a distinguished all-Black faculty. Caroline Still, their oldest child, graduated with distinction, and continued her education at Oberlin College in Ohio. The Oberlin Collegiate Institute had opened its doors in December 1833, and quickly became known as a hotbed of abolition; in 1835 it became the first

American college to admit Black students. Just a few years later, it began to enroll women as well. It was, therefore, a perfect place for the precocious daughter of a Black abolitionist.[15]

William Still was perhaps particularly honored, then, to be invited to address Oberlin's graduating class in 1865. As a part of the weeklong commencement celebration, the school hosted a celebration for returning Black soldiers. Still shared the platform with fellow Black luminaries John Mercer Langston and Alexander Crummell, and all three took the opportunity to hold up the service of Black soldiers to the Union cause as an argument for Black suffrage.[16]

Still's affection for his eldest child shines through in his letters to her while she was studying at Oberlin. They share with each other the mundane details of their day, details they once had been able to share over the dinner table. Caroline writes about her schoolwork and social life; her father writes of his business and of the rest of the family. Perhaps unsurprisingly, the most common topic of correspondence is money. Caroline frequently wrote to her father asking him to send more. Still felt compelled to lecture his daughter on the importance of frugality and prudence, on one occasion going into a long story about how "(Some 18 years ago) I applied to a gentleman for a small house he owned which was 'to let' and he told me imphatically [sic] that his "rule was unswervingly to receive his rents in advance." We can imagine Caroline rolling her eyes at her father's advice, but he almost always eventually sent her what she requested. For her part, Caroline was generally apologetic about her constant requests for money. "Everytime I write," she admitted, "it seems to me I write for money and I know you think I spend a lot but really I try to be careful and don't go into debt only when I can't help it."[17]

Caroline corresponded with her family frequently enough, but she also immersed herself in the social life of Oberlin. In particular, she drew the attention of a young man, Edward Wiley, a former slave who was also a student at the college. By January 1866, it seems that the two were quite serious. In a letter from Philadelphia, written while she was back home visiting her family, she wrote that she was "almost breathless" after reading the first few lines of his letter to her. Once she returned to campus, however, her letters reveal little about this relationship, though her family was clearly aware they were a couple. Despite her burgeoning love for Wiley, Caroline missed her family and even urged her father to move to Oberlin to be closer to her, though of course Still would hear nothing of it. He was, he told her, "more deeply involved in business than ever before."[18]

In fact, Still's business was doing quite well. In September 1865 he placed an advertisement for "good workmen on tin and sheet-iron in his stove store," noting that it was an opportunity for "freedmen or others deprived of following their trades, owing to the controlling prejudices of white mechanics, would do well to apply immediately." Nevertheless, the coal business, which had initially been only a supplement to the stove store, had increasingly become the mainstay of Still's operations. His business had prospered, so that by the end of the Civil War, when Still was mentioned in newspapers it was often in reference to his wealth rather than to his activism. The Philadelphia weekly newspaper, the *Saturday Night*, estimated that Still "could, we guess, muster twenty-five or thirty thousand dollars, and have enough left besides to get a dinner and buy a copy of *Saturday Night*."[19]

By this point, the coal business had outgrown the office on North Fifth Street, and Still began looking for a more commodious location. He sold off the stock of the stove store in order to focus on the coal business, though he kept the store itself to serve as an office. In 1866, he believed he had found a couple of suitable lots on Washington Avenue, between Twelfth and Thirteenth Streets in South Philadelphia. This wide avenue with a railway running down the middle of it was part of a burgeoning industrial area of the city. He approached the real estate agent who was handling the sale and made an offer. They agreed on terms, but when Still returned to the agent the following day in order to make payment and get the deed to the property, he was told that the deal was off. When pressed for reasons, the agent was evasive, but finally admitted that "it was feared the neighbors might give trouble." Still suppressed his frustration, and resolved that the lots would be his, neighbors be damned.[20]

This was not the first time that Still had faced discrimination
for being a Black man. Once again, as he had done with the streetcars, he drew on his connections with respectable white Philadelphians. In this case, he enlisted the aid of Dr. Samuel S. White,
who had an office near Still's, on Arch Street. They agreed that
White would purchase the lots in his own name and then transfer
them to Still. When he met with the agent, however, White was
informed that the lot had already been sold. There was, however,
a larger lot, adjoining the ones Still had hoped to buy, that was
available. The doctor purchased this one instead and transferred
the deed to Still.[21]

Still immediately began improving the lot, preparing it for his
coal business. This was all part of his plan, of course, but surely
Still also hoped to show his new neighbors, and the agent who
had been unwilling to sell the lot to him, the folly of their prejudice. He built sheds to protect the coal, stables for the horses that
would haul it, and tracks to connect his own establishment to the
main railway that ran down the middle of Washington Avenue. He
later remembered, with some pride, that the very agent who had
refused to sell him the lot later came by to congratulate him on
the improvements he had made and on the overall appearance of
his business. Still knew that in the competitive coal business such
appearances might prove critical, but he also had long hoped that
businesses such as his would help change how Black people were
viewed by their white neighbors.

He also, of course, would financially benefit from the desire
of other Black Philadelphians to support a business like his. Perhaps Still leaned on his connections to ensure that his business
received positive coverage in the Black press. In October 1866,
the *Christian Recorder* printed a letter in which Still's coal yard was
described as the "neatest and best arranged place that I have seen
anywhere." The writer celebrated Still as a model Black businessman. "What gives it most grace in my eyes is that it is owned and
carried on by a colored man," he wrote. "It would do your heart
good to go there and see Mr. Still's fine place of business. We con-
versed upon the propriety of colored men going into business, in
order to break down the silly and very unthinking prejudice of the
American people."[22]

With the increasing prosperity of his business, Still looked to move his family to a more suitable home. For a number of years, they had been living in the apartment above the old Anti-Slavery Society office, but in 1866, Still purchased a home on Lombard Street. The house had once belonged to Joseph Cassey, who had been one of the richest Black men in Philadelphia. Many of the leading Black families of the city lived on this stretch of Lombard Street, which Still described as "pretty genteel & quiet." It was, he wrote to his daughter Carrie, "a very nice house & just about the kind of a one I have been hunting for." Surely a part of Still was proud to move his family to this neighborhood. It would be a sign that they had made it, that they had ascended to Philadelphia's Black elite. But he had reservations as well. "Still I have some prejudices against Lombard St.," he wrote, "and may hesitate for sometime before consenting to move there." Still had had his differences with some of these leading Black families, and he seems to have been unsure as to whether he belonged among them. Whatever his reservations, he eventually moved his family to the new house, where the 1867 city directory listed him as residing.[23]

The years following the end of the Civil War also saw a deepening of Still's involvement in the Presbyterian church. Still had been renting a pew for his family at the First African Presbyterian Church since the mid-1850s, when the pastor was fellow abolitionist William T. Catto, father of Octavius. Still's connection to the church only seems to have deepened after his friend and ally Jonathan Gibbs took over as the pastor in 1859. In 1865, Still assumed the office of elder within the church, taking the place of Jacob C. White, Jr., who had declined the office.[24]

Despite the increasing demands of his coal business, Still remained active in the struggle for Black rights. In this regard, however, he was less successful. Little progress had been made in the struggle to desegregate the city's streetcars. The state legislature had failed to pass its streetcar bill, and the advocates for desegregation found few allies within the city government. "I am not with you, gentlemen," admitted the Republican mayor, Alexander Henry, "I do not wish the ladies of my family to ride in the cars with colored people." For the most part, the government of Philadelphia sided with streetcars who continued to bar Black passengers from riding inside streetcars. Benjamin Hunt, Still's ally and the head of the committee of respectable whites that had been established by the 1865 meeting at the Concert Hall, published a pamphlet in 1866 lamenting the failure of white Philadelphians to defend the rights of their Black neighbors.[25]

This is not to say that segregation in the cars went unchallenged. Individual Black Philadelphians had continued to board streetcars, confronting the injustice of the car companies with their own bodies. In March 1865, three Black men, Miles Robinson, James Wallace, and R. C. Marshall, in "a pelting cold rain," attempted to board a streetcar. The conductor immediately told them that they could not ride in the car. "You can draft us in the service and why can we not ride?" responded one of the men. "I do not care for that," replied the conductor, "you have to go out of this car." When the men stood their ground, the conductor called a police officer, who with the help of some white bystanders dragged the men off to jail, where they were charged and held until a friend was able to bail them out.[26]

A few months later, in May 1865, another Black Philadelphian, this time an elderly woman, attempted to board a streetcar on the Lombard Street Line. She had been at church, where she had been caring for wounded soldiers. In this case, the woman actually succeeded in boarding the car, but a few minutes after she sat down, the conductor confronted her, insisting that she could not ride in the car. The women protested. It was late, and there were very few other passengers on the car. Nevertheless, the driver stopped the car and the conductor, with the help of a few others, dragged the woman from the car, striking and kicking her, and leaving her at the side of the road. The woman then brought suit against the conductor for damages. She had the good fortune of drawing a sympathetic judge, Republican Joseph Allison, who instructed the jury that while cars could make individual distinctions as to who could ride the cars, they could not discriminate based on color. "The logic of the past four years," he pronounced, "has in many respects cleared our vision and corrected our judgement . . . men who have been deemed worthy to become defenders of the country, to wear the uniform of the soldier of the United States, should not be denied the rights common to humanity." The jury awarded fifty dollars in damages.[27]

Some advocates for streetcar desegregation hoped that this decision would lead companies to change their policy, if only to avoid future damages, but it did not. The companies seemed willing to pay the occasional price of continuing the policy that they believed their white customers preferred. By this point it had become clear that it was not enough to seek damages for individuals who had been mistreated. The only way to effectively desegregate the cars was to make it illegal to keep them segregated.

In February of 1866, at a meeting of the Statistical Association, Still introduced two men who believed they had found a solution. The two men, Benjamin Hunt and Philip Randolph, both members of the committee established by the Concert Hall meeting, informed the meeting of a case that they were pursuing, hoping to eventually bring it before the state supreme court. The plaintiff, a Black man named Martin W. White, had been denied passage on the Frankford and Southwark Philadelphia City Passenger Railroad Company the previous April. White had enlisted in a regiment that was then encamped at Camp William Penn, and he and a member of his company were seeking to take the last train back to their post that evening. After being denied access to the car, the two withdrew rather than make a scene, but subsequently brought suit for damages. White and his attorneys hoped that the case would finally compel the city's streetcar companies to change. At Still's urging, the Statistical Association agreed to donate $100 to support the effort.[28]

The results of the case, however, were disappointing. White's attorney, Charles Gibbons (a member of the Concert Hall committee and the man who had represented Still in the Jane Johnson affair), argued that because the streetcar company was publicly chartered, and because that charter had granted them a monopoly on carrying passengers on their particular route, it was limited in its right to discriminate against particular classes of people. "Their powers," he argued, "are limited by their charter, which confers upon them no right to make regulations whereby colored persons are excluded as passengers from particular cars." He echoed Judge

Allison's argument that companies could discriminate against individuals, but not against classes of people. Unfortunately, Judge James Thompson, an associate justice of the Pennsylvania Supreme Court, disagreed. He argued that since the company in question did provide separate cars for Black passengers, "it was within the power of the Company to confine colored persons to such cars." The conductor, therefore, had committed no offense in so doing.[29]

The frustration of activists in Philadelphia drew them closer to those who were fighting on a national level for the rights of African Americans. Radical Republicans in Congress found themselves in an escalating conflict with President Andrew Johnson. After ascending to the presidency upon the assassination of Lincoln, Johnson quickly dispelled any hope that he might be an ally to Radicals. He might have hated the slave-owning aristocrats he blamed for pushing the South into secession and Civil War, but his sympathies lay with the white people of the South. He had accepted the end of slavery as a necessary means of bringing down the Confederacy, but now that the South had returned to the Union, he felt that the states were ready to assume their former status. This meant, in effect, that he was ready to hand control back to white Southerners. Newly emancipated Black Southerners were left at the mercy of their former masters.[30]

Once back in control of state governments across the region, white Southerners wasted little time in passing a wave of legislation that detractors denounced as the Black Codes. These laws attempted to reestablish the white dominance that had been challenged by emancipation. Each state adopted its own set of laws, but in general they sought to deny political and economic rights to Black citizens of the South. Black men were denied the right to rent land; they were required to sign yearlong labor contracts; they were subject to vagrancy laws that often provided the pretext for a system of convict labor that acted very much like the slavery that had been supposedly abolished. Black men were barred from specific occupations and excluded from juries; they were denied the right to vote or to testify in court against whites.[31]

All of this was amply reported in the Northern press. "If this policy, which is here announced by Governor Perry," wrote one correspondent in the *Christian Recorder*, "which ignores our manhood, and denies us a place in the body politic . . . this policy is to be our reward, then have we bled in vain." White Northerners might be wary of granting rights to their Black neighbors, but the idea of the former rebels re-creating slavery by another name, the prospect of the fomenters of secession returning to power, provoked outrage across the North. Some even warned that another civil war was imminent. "If we don't protect the rights of these people," warned one Pennsylvania legislator, "in four years from now we will have another war upon us—a war of black against white." A defense of Black rights, then, became a defense of the Union itself.[32]

Radicals in Congress sought to secure these rights with a number of measures. Perhaps most significant, in January the House passed a Fourteenth Amendment to the Constitution, penalizing states that limited the right to vote based on "race or color," though it failed in the Senate. At the same time, Senator Lyman Trumbull of Illinois introduced a civil rights bill that stated that "all persons born in the United States and not subject to any foreign power, are hereby declared to be citizens of the United States." For the first time in U.S. history, the principle of birthright citizenship (later included in the revised version of the Fourteenth Amendment, which omitted the voting provisions of the earlier version) would be enshrined in federal law. While the Civil Rights Act was designed to remedy the abuse of freedmen and -women in the states of the former Confederacy, it was obvious that it would expand the rights of Black Northerners as well. The Philadelphia *North American* contended that "these black codes, north and south, are all alike inconsistent with the provisions of the national Constitution."[33]

While the Civil Rights Act would clearly apply to Northern states, what was not entirely clear was whether it would impact practices like segregation on Philadelphia's streetcars. Trumbull himself, the author of the bill, was not entirely consistent in his assertions of its reach. While the bill's focus was certainly on legal discrimination, Trumbull and others sometimes suggested that it might also apply to other means of depriving citizens of their rights. Would this mean that publicly chartered streetcar companies would be subject to prosecution under the bill? No one was sure.[34]

The bill passed both houses of Congress, but on March 27, President Johnson vetoed it. In doing so, he not only cast doubt on whether or not Black Southerners needed such extraordinary protection, but he warned of what the consequences of the law would be beyond the South. "By statutes of some of the States, Northern as well as Southern," he noted in his veto message, "it is enacted, for instance, that no white person shall intermarry with a negro or mulatto." This Civil Rights Act, Johnson warned, might invalidate such laws, opening the door for interracial marriages in places where it had been previously banned by state law. Beyond this, he cast doubt on whether most African Americans were equipped for the rights of citizenship. "Four millions of them have just emerged from slavery," he wrote. "Can it be reasonably supposed that they possess the requisite qualifications to entitle them to the privileges and immunities of citizens of the United States?" Despite Johnson's protest, Republicans in both houses of Congress mustered the two-thirds supermajority to override his veto, and the Civil Rights Act became law on April 9.[35]

The conflict between the president and the congressional opposition set the stage for an intense election season in the fall of 1866. Johnson took to the road in the summer and fall of 1866, in what came to be called the "Swing Around the Circle," an extended tour of the country in which he made the case for his own policies and denounced his Radical opponents. Democrats in Pennsylvania embraced the president's opposition to civil rights for African Americans, and warned of what Radical dominance in Washington and in Harrisburg would mean for the North. Figuring that moderate Republican voters who supported Black civil rights in the South had no stomach for providing those same rights to Black Pennsylvanians, Democrats ran one of the most racist campaigns in the history of the commonwealth. "Equality for the blacks of the North," insisted the Democratic Philadelphia *Age*, "and absolute dominion for them in the South are now openly demanded by the Radicals." Democratic handbills featuring grotesque caricatures of Black men denounced "The Freedman's Bureau" as "An agency to keep the Negro in Idleness at the Expense of the White Man," and boldly stated of Pennsylvania's two gubernatorial candidates, "Clymer's Platform [the Democratic] is for the White Man" and "Geary's Platform [the Republican] is for the Negro."[36]

Despite the fact that neither the Civil Rights Act nor the proposed Fourteenth Amendment would explicitly enfranchise Black men, suffrage became a key element of the election. Pennsylvania Republicans were generally evasive on the issue. General John White Geary, the party's candidate for governor, deemed "negro suffrage" to be a "false issue," misrepresented by Democrats in order to appeal to voters. He noted that in Pennsylvania the right to vote was denied to Black residents in the state constitution, ratified in 1838. The constitution could only be amended once every five years, and since it had been amended in 1864 to allow soldiers to vote, it was impossible for it to be amended again so soon. "Negro suffrage," he noted, "might be a very proper question to consider in 1870, but at present it was a myth." Despite these protestations, Pennsylvania Democrats continued to insist that their opponents sought "to organize a republic based on unlimited negro suffrage."[37]

Black activists, including Still and the leaders of the Statistical Association, recognized that the time was ripe for a broad-based push for Black citizenship rights. Some Republicans might be evasive on such issues, but others were forthright in their advocacy of Black rights. The most prominent Radical Republican in the city, William Darrah Kelley, was a longtime Still ally. He had been the favorable judge in the Jane Johnson affair. Still and the Statistical Association had invited Kelley, who had been elected to Congress in 1861, to deliver a lecture at the Concert Hall in March 1865, an occasion Kelley had used to advocate for Black citizenship. The denial of rights to Black Americans, Kelley had declared, was the cause of the war. "This war," insisted Kelley, "is but the penalty we are paying for violating a fundamental law of God—for violating a law of God that we all professed to believe—the law of human equality—(applause)—the law of the inherent nature and the indestructibility of man's rights." A year later, Kelley reached out to Still to ask for support for his effort to promote the movement for Black voting rights. Still and the Statistical Association agreed to raise $1,000 to pay for the distribution of materials supporting "universal suffrage" in Congress. This came at a time when even some Radicals in Congress were willing to put off their advocacy for Black suffrage out of expediency.[38]

The fall elections were a smashing success for the Republican Party. Republicans won governorships and state legislatures across the North, and they expanded their margin in Congress, where they now controlled more than two-thirds of the House. Even so, advocates for Black rights in the North wanted to be sure that these majorities would be put to good use. Much of the emphasis in the campaign had been on violence in the South, stoking resentment among Northerners against recalcitrant rebels. Many activists believed that the best way to ensure that this anger would be directed to the cause of Black rights in the North was to remind white Northerners of the vital role Black men had played in putting down the rebellion. When Governor Andrew Curtin visited Philadelphia on the Fourth of July, Still and the Statistical Association worked to ensure that when battle flags representing the regiments of Pennsylvania were presented to him, the flags of colored regiments were among them. Those flags were also displayed at the Freedmen's Fair, held on July 4, in which Frances Ellen Watkins Harper delivered a lecture on the colored troops and the freedmen. Letitia Still was among those who served on the organizational committee.[39]

This push to celebrate the contribution of colored soldiers and to use that contribution as an argument for Black citizenship rights would continue, when later that year an organization called the Colored Soldiers' and Sailors' League issued a call for all who "believe that in sustaining the Union with the musket they have now a right to the ballot" to attend a meeting in Philadelphia in January. When the meeting assembled, in National Hall at Thirteenth and Market Streets, it featured an impressive roster of Black leaders from across the country. Many of them had served in the Union armed forces, but other prominent Black leaders, like John Mercer Langston and Henry Highland Garnet, participated as well. William Still served on the business committee that was tasked with drafting a memorial for Congress. Overall, the meeting demanded full citizenship as the reward for Black military service. "It is the duty of every black soldier who fought for the Union," insisted Sergeant A. W. Handy of Maryland, "to ask the people, in the name of sympathy and the battles they had fought in defense of the country, to grant them all their rights." The meeting denounced President Johnson for his betrayal of those rights and invoked the spirit of the martyred Lincoln.[40]

Still himself was convinced that the service of Black men in the Union armed forces was the single most important factor shifting white public opinion in the matter of Black citizenship rights. "It must not be forgotten," he would later write, "that the slow and heavy car wheels of prejudice, after all, were moved mightily at Fort Wagner, Milligan's Bend, Allusta, &c." Activists have played an important role as "the axe which has been laid at the root of this accursed tree of prejudice," but that activism would have been ineffectual without the bravery and sacrifice of Black soldiers.[41]

There seemed to be an opportunity to capitalize on Northern support for more forceful Reconstruction of the South in order to bring citizenship rights to Black Northerners. Just over a week after the Soldiers' and Sailors' Convention, Still served on the executive committee of a meeting to establish "the Pennsylvania Equal Rights Society." Despite its similar name, this organization, made up of white and Black, men and women, was distinct from the Equal Rights League, though notably Octavius Catto, William Altson, and Elisha Weaver were members of both organizations. "Reconstruction should begin at home," declared the new organization, which committed itself to promoting the right of all American citizens to the ballot, regardless of race or sex. In order to secure this right, it proposed the creation of Equal Rights Clubs in every county of the state and to circulate tracts, pamphlets, and petitions in order to shape public opinion.[42]

In the early months of 1867, the Pennsylvania State Equal Rights League (PSERL) took the lead in renewed efforts to pass a bill in the state legislature outlawing racial discrimination in streetcars. The PSERL's Car Committee, William D. Forten, Octavius Catto, and David Bowser, had traveled to Harrisburg in order to personally lobby for the passage of a streetcar bill. Still was supportive of the bill, but was also skeptical that the lobbying efforts of the PSERL were doing any good. A number of Still allies had also traveled to the state capital in order to push for a streetcar bill, but all had returned feeling that such efforts were unlikely to bear fruit. Nevertheless, Still continued his correspondence with leading legislative supporters, supplying them with materials supporting their efforts to push the bill's passage.[43]

Whether or not the PSERL's lobbying made any difference, the bill, which the previous year could make no progress, now found significant support among the Republican caucus of the state legislature. What had changed? Democrats remained universally opposed to the bill. Republicans, however, had united around it. The reason for this shift seems to have been that Republicans increasingly saw the desegregation of Pennsylvania's streetcars not simply as a local matter but as a part of the larger process of Reconstruction. An early version of the bill, introduced by State Representative James Freeborn, Republican of Philadelphia, made this link explicit.

> Whereas, the recent just, humane, and politic legislation of Congress consequent upon the destruction of human slavery, and intended to secure all the people of the United States their civil rights without distinction of race, nationality, or color, renders it imperative upon the loyal States to conform their local legislation thereto.

Republicans also saw that it was increasingly likely Black men would soon be given the right to vote. "When negro suffrage is allowed in this state," commented the Philadelphia-based *National Baptist*, "the gentlemen [voting against the car bill] will be soliciting the votes of people they would compel to walk or ride on the outside of a car." Republicans, especially those in parts of the state with significant numbers of Black citizens, would be happy to be able to point to their support of the desegregation of streetcars as a reason for Black support come election day. The final version of the bill passed the Pennsylvania Senate and House by party-line votes and was signed into law by Governor Geary on March 22, 1867.[44]

The following Monday, March 25, a "mulatto woman, named Caroline R. Lacount [*sic*]," stood at the corner of Eleventh and

Lombard Streets where shortly after noon she attempted to flag down Car Number 24 of the Tenth and Eleventh Street Line. LeCount, twenty-one at the time, had been educated at the Institute for Colored Youth and by this point was teaching at the Ohio Street School in Frankford, in northeast Philadelphia. She was already well-known as an activist and would later become engaged to Octavius Catto. It was likely through her connection to Catto that she ended up as a test case for the new streetcar law. In any case, the young, educated, and unquestionably respectable LeCount was a perfect candidate for this role. Nevertheless, as the car rolled past her, the conductor, Edwin Thompson, "sneered at her," and the driver refused to stop. LeCount then proceeded to swear out a complaint against the conductor, who was later arrested, the first such arrest under the new law.[45]

While Caroline LeCount sought to make sure that the new law was enforced, other members of the city's activist community gathered to celebrate the law's passage. The evening after LeCount was denied passage on the Tenth and Eleventh Street Line, "a large and enthusiastic meeting of colored citizens was held at Liberty Hall" to celebrate "the grand result." Liberty Hall, at Lombard and Eighth Streets, had been opened a few months earlier as a venue for Black activists and organizations to meet; Still was one of its stockholders and managers. Presiding over the meeting were some of the longest-serving members of the city's Black leadership, including Still ally Stephen Smith, but the clear stars of the meeting were the members of the Equal Rights League Car Committee, William D. Forten, Octavius Catto, and David P. Bowser. The president of the meeting, F. P. Maine, read aloud a letter from a handful of members of the state legislature addressed to Forten, Catto, and Bowser, thanking them for their efforts on behalf of the streetcar bill. "The bill is essentially your own," insisted the legislators, "having been drawn by your chairman, Mr. Forten." The meeting adopted resolutions echoing this sentiment, and also thanking other individuals and organizations, including the Statistical Association, that had also contributed to the bill's passage.[46]

What might have been a celebration of collective victory by the Black community of Philadelphia, however, soon turned acrimonious. The favorable account of the meeting published in the

Philadelphia *Press* noted that "the meeting was eminently enthusiastic and orderly," but this told only part of the story. Jacob C. White, Jr., a close friend and ally of Octavius Catto, rose to speak, and took the opportunity to denounce William Still by name, contending that Still had been *opposed* to the bill. White alleged that Still had personally written to the governor asking him not to sign the bill because he was only in favor of allowing the most respectable Black Philadelphians to ride. Still surely resented the fact that his young rivals were being given the lion's share of credit for work that he had been doing for years. Perhaps he seethed as he listened to the encomiums to the PSERL while the contributions of his own Statistical Association received only passing mention, but now, to hear his name slandered, to hear allegations that he had actually opposed a bill he had done so much to support, this was too much. Still rose to defend himself but was shouted down. "Put him down!" someone yelled. As Still and his allies (who had been denounced along with him) continued to attempt to take the floor, the shouts turned personal, and violent: "Kill him!" "There will be a funeral in the coal yard now!"[47]

Still had surely had his differences with rivals before, but this was of a different magnitude and it seemed to genuinely shock him. Where did these allegations come from? Some of the animosity was purely personal in nature. Still had been privately, and perhaps publicly, dismissive of some of the men who now denounced him. He had long had his differences with William Forten, the oldest of the three (and only a few years younger than Still). The other two, Catto and White, had also had their differences with Still, who thought that both men, sons of fathers who had been important leaders in Philadelphia, were inclined to frivolity. Perhaps this reflected Still's resentment of men who had been given opportunities that were denied to him.

Still also had personal reasons that may have led to a chilly relationship with Catto. In 1861, Catto had fathered a child, out of wedlock, with Rebecca Underwood, who had been employed as a housemaid in the Stills' boardinghouse. The child, Elizabeth, died before she reached her first birthday. This surely did not endear Catto to the morally upright Still. In any case, both Catto and White seemed to have had a decent working relationship with Still as late as 1866, when both were listed as members of the Statistical Association. In December 1866, however, Still and White seem to have engaged in a heated exchange during a Statistical Association meeting, though the origins of the conflict are unclear. A few months later the two once again sparred at a meeting, this time over a resolution proposed by Still that the Statistical Association send a delegation to Harrisburg to support the streetcar bill. White opposed this resolution, perhaps because he felt that the Equal Rights League was already doing this work.[48]

As to the specific allegation made by White, that Still had been in favor of rights for the Black elite, but not for the Black masses, this seems to have derived from some of Still's writings protesting the segregation of the streetcars in which he emphasized the respectability of those denied access. Still's first published assault on this practice, in 1859, had argued that such discrimination was at least in part attributable to white perceptions of all Black people as "hopelessly degraded." In answer, Still held up the "genteel" Black class of the city, businessmen, churchgoers, taxpayers. Still's audience would clearly have understood this as a part of the long-standing Black tradition of respectability, but his rivals twisted this into a total abandonment of the Black lower classes. This allegation took on additional resonance in 1867, by which time Still, who had been moderately prosperous in 1859, was now quite wealthy.[49]

Still might have swallowed the bitter pill of these allegations, but evidently some of his critics attempted to organize a boycott of Still's coal yard. In response to this, Still resolved to clear his name and organized a meeting, held April 8, also held in Liberty Hall. It is unclear how large this meeting was, though Still's own account termed it "a large Public Meeting." It consisted largely of an extended address by Still, attempting to vindicate himself and his allies. "Misrepresented by some," Still began, "and willfully slandered by others, who for more than a dozen years have been my bitterest enemies, and have spared no pains in order to compass the destruction of my reputation in this city and with the public generally, I feel called upon, for the simple sake of truth and the cause of Equal Rights, to make a defense." In an address that would fill twenty-four printed pages, Still disputed the allegations that he had ever opposed the streetcar bill, which he labeled "the glorious bill which gives us our rights," and generally made the case that his efforts had been important to the bill's passage. He also celebrated other organizations that had contributed to the effort. It was his rivals, Still insisted, who had attempted to claim sole responsibility for the bill, which was the product of a vast network of groups that had been working for the same purpose.[50]

He closed with a call for unity within the Black community. "I know that it is no time for quarrelling amongst ourselves," he said. "I know we have had abundant cause for rejoicing over the passage of this bill." Even here, though, Still used this as an opportunity to contrast his own vision of disciplined, sober, rigid economy with his opponents, who he maintained were obsessed with "leisure" and "idle and frivolous society." Too few young men, in Still's estimation, were devoting themselves to building businesses in the Black community. While the allegations that Still had opposed the extension of rights to the Black masses did not hold up to scrutiny, nevertheless, even in refuting these claims, Still demonstrated a rhetorical style that continued to alienate some of those he hoped to win over. It also did not escape notice that on the back of the printed version of Still's version of the streetcar fight, he had included a full-page advertisement for his coal yard.[51]

CHAPTER ELEVEN

WRITING THE BOOK

William Still was clearly shaken by the conclusion of the streetcar campaign. In 1868, Still would leave behind his church of more than a decade, First African Presbyterian, joining instead Lombard Central Presbyterian. Still never explained the reason for the switch, but the timing suggests he may have been driven to leave behind a congregation of which so many of his fiercest critics, perhaps most notably Jacob C. White, Jr., were members. He was not, though, one to dwell on such feelings. "As regards the treatment of the S.C.& S.," he wrote to his daughter Caroline, "I am somewhat inclined to think a good providence will grow out of this movement. I look at this matter in this light. Possessing desires so ardent as I did to see our people moving in the direction and self elevation &c. in order to aid the good cause I was putting forth efforts far beyond my strength. You know every movement of my time was occupied with public and private business." The conflict had led him to a period of self-reflection, and it had given him an opportunity to step back from his public activism a bit. Truly, for the previous few years he had been a dynamo, committing himself to the growth of his business and to any number of causes. "If the Lord allows me in future," he wrote, "I shall have more leisure, rest & recreation—I shall have more time for reading and the improvement of my mind."[1]

Still being Still, however, such reading had a deeper purpose. "By the way," he continued,

I am now reading Macaulay's History of England with great interest. Several times before I undertook it but never managed to get through with it. This time I am taxing myself (one hour a day) and I think I shall finish it soon. As I am going to write the History of U.G.R.R. I must do a good deal of reading & thinking in order to be able to write well. I may commence my book this fall some time.[2]

The book Still was preparing to write would be one of the great achievements of his life. Unsurprisingly, he approached this preparation systematically, and with great seriousness. In a certain sense he had been preparing to write it for years, gathering sources, honing the tales of fugitive slaves that would make up the bulk of it, and developing his own voice as a writer. Now, though, he would begin writing in earnest, a task that would occupy the next several years of his life.

It is notable that Still cites Macaulay's multivolume history of England as the book he was reading in preparation for writing his own history. Though not much read today, in nineteenth-century America Macaulay was tremendously popular. Rising to prominence as a poet and essayist and later as a Whig member of Parliament and advocate for the Great Reform Act of 1833, in the 1840s Macaulay began writing his *History of England from the Accession of James the Second*. The work centers on the Glorious Revolution of 1688, depicting it as the triumph of progressive liberal values within the English constitutional system. What drew Americans, including Still, to Macaulay's work? On one hand, Macaulay's appeal to readers, and his appeal to Still as a model, lay in his lively prose. One scholar has compared the book to the fiction of British writers like Dickens and Scott that found a wide American audience. Macaulay wrote history like a novel, emphasizing vivid characters and attention to detail. These were elements that Still surely hoped to incorporate into his own writing.[3]

There was also an ideological element to Macaulay's work that helps explain its appeal to an American audience. The work embodies what is often known as the "Whig" school of history, an approach that sees history as the story of progress, perhaps inexorable progress. Macaulay's account of the progress of liberal values resonated with an American audience, and many American readers saw a clear parallel between Macaulay's celebration of the Glorious Revolution and their own understanding of the American Revolution (though Macaulay himself resisted such parallels).[4] Still had little to say about Macaulay's work beyond the fact that he was reading it as a model for his own book, but he clearly identified with the work's vision of history as the story of progress and he sought to emulate it.

Still understood that this book, his account of the hundreds of fugitive slaves who had passed through the Philadelphia Vigilance Committee, was itself a part of the struggle to which Still had devoted his life. Already by the late 1860s it had become clear that the memory of the Civil War, and the larger struggle over slavery of which it was a part, had become a front in the battle for Black rights. The stories that people told about that struggle had become potent weapons, as had been clear in the push for desegregation of the streetcars in Philadelphia. Still and his allies constantly trumpeted the loyalty and service of Black men who were denied the rights accorded to whites who had supported the Confederacy. Still's rivals would even turn this framing back upon him. When they were attempting to organize the boycott of his coal yard, they told him "they would prefer getting their coal from Copperheads." Better to buy coal from disloyal whites than from Still, they maintained.[5]

Despite Still's assurances to his daughter that he would "have more leisure, rest & recreation," the years which followed the streetcar victory only saw him refocus his long-standing commitments to Black uplift. The writing of his book was a part of this. He saw it as a testament to the capabilities of Black people and as an effort to ensure that the role of Black people in the long Civil War was not forgotten. So too was his business, which he saw both as a demonstration of Black excellence and as a platform for his growing philanthropy. But he also continued his public activism in a number of other ways, maintaining his commitment to the Black community of Philadelphia and to the larger push for Black rights.

. . .

The book was not his only foray into the struggle to shape how the Civil War would be remembered. Still was among a group of prominent Black men, including Frederick Douglass, William Wells Brown, and Charles Reason, who were raising money to pay for a "Freedmen's Monument to Lincoln." The monument was to be built on public grounds in Washington as a means of ensuring that emancipation and Black liberation remained at the center of public memory of the martyred president. Notably, the model that Still supported was much grander than the one that would ultimately be built. While the final version entailed the controversial image of a slave kneeling before Lincoln, the unbuilt version featured upright figures of African Americans, including a Black soldier, surrounding the president. This proposed version would have been a fitting monument not just to Lincoln, but to his Black allies.[6]

Despite Still's continuing activist commitments, he was first and foremost a businessman, and his coal yard was his primary concern. The boycott, or the threat thereof, had worried him for a time, but by the summer his fortunes seem to have rebounded. "I have no reason to complain," he wrote to Caroline, "for my business has been better this summer than any of my neighbors." His yard spread across three lots, fronting Washington Avenue, and he had continued to improve the multiple buildings in which he did his business. "The spacious premises are entirely floored with four-inch plank," reported the *Christian Recorder*, "and have all the solidity and neatness of a bowling alley. The stock of coal is covered by symmetrical and well-built sheds, while upon the front of the ground are two brick buildings of handsome exterior—the one a counting room, the other a stable."[7]

The coal business was extremely competitive, and it was important for Still to stand out if he was to continue to prosper. There were quite a few competitors on his immediate stretch of Washington Avenue, and throughout the city customers had any number of choices as to where they would buy their coal. This led to cut-throat competition among coal dealers. There were few ways to prosper in such an environment. Some sought to swindle their customers, selling a "ton" of coal that was a little short each time. Still went in the opposite direction, attempting to establish his business as more trustworthy, as more reliable than his competitors. He advertised extensively, building a clientele, and working hard to ensure that his business was as respectable as possible. This work kept him from writing as much as he would have liked, but Still's dedication to his business paid dividends. By the spring of 1868 he had weathered the storm of the previous year and felt confident in his future. "It is doing first rate," he wrote Caroline. "Sales are more than double what they were this time last year, and I have no fears if my success continues my yard will be decidedly the leading one on Washington Avenue."[8]

While Still weathered the personal and business aftermath of the streetcar campaign, the desegregation of the streetcars also had a profound impact on Philadelphia politics. Flush with the successful passage of the streetcar bill, Black Philadelphians, led by members of the state Equal Rights League, pressed on, urging the state to strike from its constitution the ban on Black voting. White Republicans, however, continued to be wary of fully embracing the rights of Black Pennsylvanians to vote. They downplayed "local" issues, and continued to emphasize the Reconstruction of the South and the need to enfranchise Black Southerners as a check on the power of former Confederates. "The election tomorrow," insisted the Republican *Press*, referring to a state judicial election, "is not so much to decide who shall receive judicial honors in the State, but rather whether the people approve the reconstruction policy of Congress." They continued to hope that outrages in the South could win votes for Republicans, despite the electorate's suspicion of Black Pennsylvanians.[9]

Democrats, convinced that Republicans and their Black allies had overreached in their fight against segregation, once again leaned into their race-baiting tactics of the previous year. This time, they emphasized the looming threat of Black voting. "They have declared that the negroes shall vote in the southern states," said the Democratic *Age*. "Proceeding upon this assumed power, they now declare their intention to force negro suffrage upon this state." Democrats denounced their Republican rivals as hypocrites for embracing Black voting in the South but not in the North, while at the same time warning that Republicans secretly planned to force Black voting rights on Pennsylvania just as they were doing in the South, at the point of a bayonet.[10]

The result was a smashing victory for Philadelphia Democrats, their first since the start of the Civil War. Republicans lost state-wide and they lost in Philadelphia; they lost elections across the country. Leaders of the party were divided in their assessment of the defeat. The *North American* attributed the loss to an almost inevitable decline in the intensity of the electorate in the wake of the cataclysm of the war years; many voters who had come out to vote when the fate of the nation was at stake "relaxed into their former apathy." Others pointed to divisions within the party. Sidney George Fisher, a Conservative Republican, attributed the loss to two factors, "Negro suffrage and Sunday liquor laws." Leading Democrats agreed with Fisher, at least in regard to the importance of the threat of Black suffrage in winning them the election. "The opposition to Negro Suffrage, in the South as well as in the North," declared former president James Buchanan, "has been the principal cause of our triumph everywhere." In Philadelphia, Democrats mocked their rivals with a political broadside that declared "The Great Negro Party—Born 1856—Died Oct. 8, 1867."[11]

Despite his longtime participation in the fight for Black citizenship rights, and his particular work as an advocate for Black suffrage, Still seems to have had little to do with the efforts to push for Black voting rights in this period. As he had promised to his daughter, he backed off somewhat on his public activism. Still continued his frequent correspondence with his eldest daughter, who was still away at Oberlin for most of the year. The Stills also still had three other children at home, Frances, William Wilberforce, and Robert (born in 1865). The burden of running this household continued to fall on Letitia, who was beginning to feel her age. "I hav bin very tired," she wrote to Caroline in March 1868, "so mutch so that when sunday comes I am too tird to go to church." She had hired a girl to help her, but it was unclear how much help she actually provided. "She is a quiet woman," Letitia confessed, "but not a fast one."[12]

The household would grow once again in the fall. Caroline Still graduated from Oberlin College in August 1868, and returned home. She was the youngest member of her graduating class, the only woman, and the only Black graduate out of twenty-five students granted the degree of bachelor of arts (there were an additional nineteen women who graduated from a specific "women's course"). During several days of commencement exercises, Caroline Still was granted the honor of presiding over the anniversary of the Ladies' Literary Society, an honor that had never before been granted a Black woman. She seems to have been eager to return to Philadelphia, though, where she hoped to join in her family's tradition of community service. "Oh if you only knew," she would write shortly after returning home, "the work to be done here the vast field for labor the greatness of the degradation which surrounds us." She took a teaching position, dismayed at how rare were Black teachers in Philadelphia; she was convinced that she could make a difference in the "ragged school" where she found herself.[13]

Her father was surely proud of this philanthropic spirit. Despite a respite in his public activism, William Still continued to show his commitment to serving the Black community of Philadelphia. His philanthropic work was increasingly dedicated to the neediest members of the Black community. Two institutions particularly benefited from Still's patronage and service. The first was the Colored Soldiers' and Sailors' Orphans Home Association, founded in 1868. The service of Black men in the Union armed forces had left a significant number of orphaned children across the country, and in Philadelphia this organization sought to care for those who were without support. Still was an early contributor. The second, which was to become one of Still's greatest commitments in the coming years, was the Home for Aged and Infirm Colored Persons. This organization, founded by a group of Black leaders and white philanthropists (mostly Quakers) in 1864, was committed to the care of the elderly of "that worthy class of colored people." Longtime Still ally Stephen Smith had been particularly instrumental in providing the funds for its establishment. Still was a member of the board of managers appointed at its initial meeting, and his role would grow over time; in 1874 he would succeed Smith as vice president of the organization.[14]

Still was also instrumental in the founding of the Philadelphia

Building and Loan Association in the fall of 1869. Typical of the period, the association was designed to help facilitate home ownership among working people. Members would pay a modest one dollar a month for a share, and then would have an opportunity to take out a loan from this capital. In this way, people gained access to capital who would not otherwise have it. These organizations also became a way of promoting thrift and savings, which certainly appealed to Still. Along with Still, longtime allies William Whipper and Isaiah Wears also took leadership roles in the association.[15]

Still also used his newfound prosperity to continue to patronize Black artists and intellectuals. The Statistical Association's lecture series ended after 1867, amidst some controversy within the association's leadership over the cost associated with its operations, but Still continued to host visiting luminaries, though he often did so in his home rather than in more public venues. The *Christian Recorder* reported on one such "parlor reading," in the summer of 1868, in which Still hosted old friend Frances Ellen Watkins Harper in an intimate gathering in his "double parlor." Harper recited from memory extensive passages from her poetic work *Moses: A Story of the Nile*. Harper, like many Black artists, was drawn to the figure of Moses as a liberator, a parallel to their own struggle against bondage.[16]

Harper remained in Philadelphia in the late summer and fall of 1868, living with the Stills. She planned to travel to England in the winter for a lecture tour, but in the meantime, she traveled around Pennsylvania and New Jersey, delivering several lectures and readings of *Moses*, which was soon to be published. Neither Still nor Harper left any record of what they talked about during this long stay, but it is hard to imagine that the two did not discuss Still's *Underground Railroad*, his work in progress. For years Still had been a patron and advocate of his friend; now Harper, who by this point was an accomplished author, was in a position to give Still advice on his writing. Much of her work, of course, had dealt with the horrors of slavery. While Still's prose does not resemble Harper's writing in any obvious way, the themes of her poetry—enslaved families, the auction block, fugitive slaves, freedom—surely resonated with Still.[17]

Sometime in the winter of 1869, Still's daughter Caroline

opened up to her parents about her renewed relationship with Edward Wiley, with whom she had been romantically involved while she was at Oberlin. Wiley was also a student, but his road had been quite different from Caroline's. He had been enslaved in Alabama and had fled his master when the Union army arrived in the state. He joined the army and then after the war came north. He enrolled at Oberlin, but while Caroline might rely on constant funds from her affluent family, Wiley was forced to support himself with "hard physical labor." Ultimately this proved too difficult, and Wiley left Oberlin after three years without a degree. Caroline wrote to Wiley, begging him to come to Philadelphia and promising that her father would help him secure employment.[18]

The two were married in December 1869 in the Still family home. The wedding became a veritable abolitionist reunion. Sixty or seventy guests attended, many of them friends from Still's years with the Vigilance Committee. Lucretia Mott, by this point in her mid-seventies, was there and the guests were delighted with the address the abolitionist legend gave. It was, of course, unusual for such an occasion but, as a reporter noted, "Lucretia Mott can do nothing that is not graceful and right." Miller McKim, Robert Purvis, Isaiah Wears, Sarah Mapps Douglass, Passmore Williamson, and William Whipper were also there. We can only imagine the reminiscing about the old days of the antislavery struggle. Did they talk about Still's in-progress book? It seems likely. Perhaps Still even gathered stories or clarified details of events in which they had all shared. After the ceremony, they were entertained by the renowned Black singer Elizabeth Greenfield, the "Black Swan," who had performed so often at abolitionist events.[19]

Black Pennsylvanians had made significant progress in their fight for full citizenship, but they still could not vote. They had been entirely disfranchised since the ratification of the state constitution of 1838. Efforts to push for enfranchisement on a state level had proved fruitless. After the setback in the fall elections of 1867, Radicals in the legislature had continued to push for a change to the state constitution that would have permitted Black voting (though adding a literacy test for both white and Black voters), but when this proposal came to a vote in January of 1868, it was resoundingly defeated, with a majority of Republicans joining Democrats in opposing it.[20]

The state politics of Black suffrage remained difficult. Pennsylvania Republicans feared that if they were to be seen supporting Black suffrage rights, that support would be used against them. Some hoped that action at a national level would take the responsibility from their shoulders, but in any case, after joining Democrats in rejecting the proposed constitutional amendment, most Pennsylvania Republicans sought to avoid the issue at a state level, and insofar as they supported Black suffrage, they framed it as a Reconstruction issue, as one that would help protect Black Southerners against unreconstructed white Southerners. Pennsylvania Democrats, on the other hand, put the issue front and center in their campaign in the fall of 1868. They warned that enfranchising Black men was but the first step in what they deemed more nefarious motives. "It is pretended," argued Richmond Jones, a Berks County Democrat, "by the eloquent advocates of negro suffrage, for the most part that political equality alone is sought to be established, and that no one contemplates social equality; but one follows the other as night follows day." Democrats, he argued, were pushing "to protect the race from ultimate extinction or complete amalgamation." The party would continue this line of attack in the fall elections, insisting that whatever their reticence on the question of Black suffrage, Republicans were the advocates of untrammeled social and political equality between the races.[21]

The results of this campaign were mixed. Nationally, Pennsylvania helped to elect General Ulysses S. Grant as president. Grant was no Radical, but he promised to be far more sympathetic to Black rights than his predecessor. At the state level, Republicans maintained their control of both houses of the legislature, though their margins in both declined somewhat. In the city of Philadelphia, Democrats triumphed once again. They took control of the mayor's office, electing longtime Democratic politician Daniel Fox, the first Democrat to be elected to that office in more than a decade. In what was surely a sinister omen for the city's Black citizens, a political cartoon printed after the election was captioned

"The Stampede from the Mayor's Office," and it depicted a white police officer chasing three Black men.[22]

Frustrated at their inability to sway Republican officials at the state level, and wary of local Republicans who seemed to be losing ground to Democrats, Black Philadelphians increasingly looked to the federal government for help in their struggle for voting rights. When the Pennsylvania State Equal Rights League convened for its annual meeting in the summer of 1868, it was clear that the organization saw national Republicans as natural allies. William Foster, a delegate from Philadelphia, submitted a resolution that "impartial justice demands that every voter, white or black, should vote solid for Grant and Colfax, and all the candidates, of which the great captain of the age, and great champion of equal justice, is our standard bearer." If Republicans were hesitant to embrace Black suffrage on principle, perhaps they would do so out of self-interest.[23]

In February of 1869, after a long and contentious debate, the U.S. Congress finally approved an amendment to the Constitution that would guarantee the right of Black men to vote. Congressional Republicans, no doubt buoyed by Grant's election and impending inauguration, passed the amendment with no Democratic support. The proposed amendment read simply that "the right of citizens to vote shall not be denied or abridged by the United States or by any State on account of race, or previous condition of servitude." Now it was up to the states to ratify. Pennsylvania Democrats hoped to thwart the amendment, but Pennsylvania Republicans, who had so recently shown little willingness to support Black suffrage, supported the amendment on a strictly party-line vote in March. It would be nearly a year before the requisite three-quarters of the states approved, but slowly, steadily, states fell into line. In February of the following year, Iowa ratified, crossing the three-fourths threshold, and making the Fifteenth Amendment official.[24]

The ratification of the Fifteenth Amendment produced an outpouring of jubilation among African Americans across the United States. In Philadelphia, Black leaders organized a spectacular program of celebration to commemorate their enfranchisement, on Tuesday, April 26, 1870. The Colored Union League and the

Equal Rights League collaborated to plan this massive spectacle. At sunrise on the appointed day, the city was bustling with Black people preparing for the festivities to come. One observer, traversing the section of the city west of Broad along Lombard Street where many Black homes and institutions could be found, remarked that his walk "disclosed a gala scene, and from every house-top, window, door-way, and every conceivable point floated the nation bunting." Black Philadelphians were ready to celebrate their full embrace by the nation they had long claimed as their own.[25]

Throughout the day, Black Philadelphians celebrated and commemorated the history that had brought them to this moment. There were two main religious ceremonies: the first at the Stills' Central Presbyterian Church, and the second at St. Thomas Episcopal. At Central Presbyterian, the Reverend J. B. Reeve (who a few months earlier had officiated at Caroline Still's wedding) closed his sermon by asking his congregation to honor Thaddeus Stevens, the Radical Republican congressman who had played such an important role in promoting the interests of African Americans. At St. Thomas, the Reverend William J. Alston reminded his listeners of "the negro Crispis Attux, whose blood was the first shed in the Revolutionary War." Throughout the day there were cries of celebration for Abraham Lincoln and John Brown, prayers of thanks for the service of Black soldiers and sailors, and calls to "remember Christiana." This joyous celebration culminated at noon in a massive procession, in which banners continued this celebration of the heroes who had fought for Black citizenship.[26]

It is unclear if William Still took part in these celebrations. Certainly, he shared in the jubilation, but massive, raucous spectacle was not his style. Likely he attended the service at Central Presbyterian. The extensive newspaper account of the day's events makes no explicit mention of his participation.

A week later, though, Still took part in a very different sort of celebration of the Fifteenth Amendment. He was asked to speak at the final meeting of the Pennsylvania Anti-Slavery Society, which was held May 5, 1870, at the Assembly Building, Tenth and Chestnut Streets. The meeting was called to order by President Robert Purvis, who had been there at the founding of the PASS. "Our idea was to overthrow slavery," he recalled, "we intended to labor until those in bondage were declared American citizens; these were our pledges; that they have been faithfully redeemed, who doubts?" The triumphalist pronouncements of many of the participants, however, were tempered by the understanding that there was still work to do. "We are fully aware," noted one resolution, "of the difficulties and perils which, for some time to come, will beset the colored men of the nation." This was a moment of triumph, to be sure, but it was also a moment of reflection and of renewed commitment to the fight for Black equality.[27]

When Still rose to address the meeting, his remarks reflected both the triumph of the moment and his resolution to use the memory of the Underground Railroad to inspire continued struggle. He opened with a personal note about what led him to write down these stories of fugitive slaves. Still recalled for the audience the story of his reunion with his long-lost brother Peter. No doubt every attendee already knew this story. Indeed, many of them knew both William and Peter Still, but this time Still revealed a detail that many of them had not known: their mother had been a fugitive slave. The public version of Peter's story, published in 1856 as *The Kidnapped and the Ransomed*, had been that he had been kidnapped from his parents' home in New Jersey. The truth, of course, was that Sidney Still and her two boys, Peter and Levin, had been seized as fugitives and returned to bondage. Later she fled once again, without the boys. The true story would have exposed the elderly Sidney, who had taken the name Charity as a fugitive slave, and placed her at risk. In some ways the truth was even more tragic than the published story, the story of boys being stolen away by kidnappers. Surely the idea of a mother, forced to leave her sons behind in bondage, touched the hearts of Still's listeners.[28]

This personal story, this family tragedy and the remarkable coincidence that brought Still back together with his brother, was what inspired him to begin collecting the stories of fugitives who passed through his office in Philadelphia, in hopes that he might be able to help other families reunite. He related for his audience the famous story of Henry "Box" Brown. He recalled the escape of Abraham Galloway, who had escaped from North Carolina hidden in a ship, but who now, Still informed his listeners, was a state senator in his native North Carolina. He pulled at his listeners' heartstrings with the story of Romulus Hall, who had escaped from Maryland fleeing in the freezing cold, only to arrive in Philadelphia near death. We can imagine the audience's rapt attention as Still described kneeling next to the man's bed, asking him "Do you regret having attempted to escape from slavery?" The man paused and coughed, and Still thought he was about to die. Instead, the man regained his composure. "Don't go out," he told Still. "I have not answered your question . . . I am not sorry I escaped slavery." Having made this declaration, Still told his audience, the man shortly passed away. "The sufferings and narrative of this bondman," declared Still in closing, "can never be effaced from my mind."[29]

Still hoped that the same would be true of his audience. He wanted to ensure that the lives of these remarkable men and women, the fugitives from slavery he always placed at the center of the story of the Underground Railroad, would never be forgotten. Still generally avoided explicit didacticism and preferred to let the narrative speak for itself, but his choices here reveal a larger message that he hoped his audience would draw from the stories. Yes, those who aided fugitives in their escape were to be honored, but Still's accounts tended to highlight the ingenuity and bravery of individual fugitives. They celebrated these individuals for seizing control of their own lives, for refusing to accept the bondage into which they were born. The meeting closed with a resolution calling on Still to "compile and publish his personal reminiscences and experiences relating to the 'Underground Railroad.'" Of course, he was already doing so, but this public call gave the official imprimatur of the PASS to Still's work; it was not just his own personal project, it was itself to be a part of the antislavery struggle.[30]

Still might have seen his book-in-progress as his primary political statement, but now that Black men were enfranchised in the commonwealth of Pennsylvania, they were drawn into partisan politics like never before. Democrats had warned that Republicans were only seeking to enfranchise Black men because they saw them as guaranteed Republican voters, and surely at least some Republicans had seen Black enfranchisement not as a matter of principle but rather as one of pure practical calculation. Now that Black men could vote, however, it was clear that Democrats were not simply going to roll over and accept this fact. Prior to 1838, that is prior to the legal disfranchisement of Black men, Black voters had been kept from the polls through violence, and many Democrats were ready to resume this strategy.

In April 1870, just days before the streets of the city would be flooded with Black celebrations of the Fifteenth Amendment, the Philadelphia *Press* printed a small notice informing its readers that "the Moyamensing Hose Company recently sent a complimentary ticket to their great ball to Mr. William Still. Mr. Still declines association with the class of people who attend the Moya's balls." This seemingly cryptic statement would have meant a great deal to the readers of the *Press*. Nineteenth-century fire companies were notorious; many of them were little more than street gangs. In Philadelphia, the Moyamensing Hose Company was one of the most infamous. Located in a neighborhood in South Philadelphia that was home to large populations of working-class Black and Irish residents (Still's home in the early 1850s had been on the northern border of the neighborhood), "the Moya" was also a political force. In an era where such street gangs often played an important role in the raucous and unruly world of partisan politics, members of the company helped get out the vote on election day and, if necessary, they helped keep rivals from the polls as well. The leader of "the Moya," William McMullen, had used his position to control the neighborhood and to get himself elected alderman. As an influential figure within the Democratic Party, and as a representative of his working-class Irish constituents, McMullen was ready to use his influence to counter the Black vote. In this context, the invitation of Still, one of best-known and most respectable Black men in Philadelphia, a man who operated a prosperous coal yard in the neighborhood, was at the very least a bit of mockery; likely it was also a thinly veiled threat. McMullen and "the Moya" had long been hostile to the Black residents of their South Philadelphia territory.[31]

The real test would come that fall, when Black men went to the polls for the first time. Democrats attempted to stir up suspicion

William Still Lehigh Coal Company Photograph

against newly enfranchised Black voters. "Beware of COLORED REPEATERS," warned one handbill. "They have been engaged to disfranchise you. They will vote early and often. Watch them! Challenge them!" McMullen himself confronted one Black voter and attempted to remove him from the polls, but the man fought back, knocking the political boss to the ground and then fleeing the scene. McMullen and his men continued to challenge Black voters, attempting to prevent them from voting. By some reports, they were soon joined by police officers, some of whom "removed the numbers from their caps for the purpose of identification." Some looked the other way while white toughs terrorized would-be Black voters; others joined in the mayhem.[32]

Fortunately, this election day violence was not unexpected. A force of U.S. Marines had been stationed just outside of Philadelphia in preparation for any such trouble; in the afternoon General E. M. Gregory, U.S. marshal for eastern Pennsylvania, ordered them into action, and they marched to Fifth and Lombard and promptly dispersed the rioters and permitted voters to go about their business. Notably, these marines were operating under the authority of the recently passed Enforcement Acts, which had empowered the federal government to intervene when state and local governments were incapable of defending the rights of American citizens, or unwilling to do so, especially those rights recently granted by the Fourteenth and Fifteenth Amendments.[33]

Perhaps unsurprisingly, the intervention of federal troops in an election in Philadelphia was controversial. Predictably, Democrats squealed about the actions of the troops, which they saw as purely partisan in nature. Mayor Fox called it "an unwarrantable infringement upon the rights of our State and particularly of this city." This sentiment echoed across the country as Democratic papers seized on the events in Philadelphia as evidence that their Republican rivals were preparing to subjugate the North with the same tactics they were using in the South. It was not, however, just Democrats who expressed uneasiness with the prospect of military intervention in Northern elections. In his New Year's address, the Republican governor of Pennsylvania, John White Geary, distanced himself from the deployment of troops in Philadelphia. It was done, he insisted, "without the consent or even the knowledge of the civil authorities of the city or state," and insisted it was "a measure which meets my unqualified disapproval." The use of federal troops had been critical to the defense of the right of Black Philadelphians to vote, yet there seemed little political will to continue to do so.[34]

This set the stage for tragedy the following year. In the fall of 1871, the only force that would be available to keep the election day peace was Democratic mayor Fox's police force, the very same police force that had joined in the rioting the year before. Democratic ward leaders like McMullen remained committed to keeping Black voters from the polls, with violence if necessary. Black voters fought back, and before long the violence spread and degenerated into general rioting. Without the help of federal troops, Black Philadelphians found they were on their own.

Octavius Catto, the civil rights leader and also a teacher at the Institute for Colored Youth, was in the thick of the fighting. The school, which was located in Moyamensing, once again the center of election day violence, closed at the first sign of trouble. Catto left the school and headed to the polls, walking up Ninth Street toward South. He carried with him an unloaded gun. A man came up behind him and called out his name. Catto kept moving, but the man, later identified as Frank Kelly, a known associate of William McMullen, shot him three times in the back. Catto died instantly. Kelly fled the scene. Two other Black men were also killed, as Democratic thugs ravaged the city. Northern Republicans frequently denounced the violence that plagued Southern states and disfranchised Black Southerners, but Philadelphia had shown that Northern Democrats were just as willing to terrorize Black voters as were their Southern allies.[35]

Still took little public role in the violent conflict of the first two years of Black voting in his city. Following the passage of the Fifteenth Amendment, and the official call of the PASS for him to publish his account of the Underground Railroad, Still seems to have redoubled his efforts to finish the book. His coal business was, of course, his first priority, but an extended strike in the coal fields of northeast Pennsylvania during 1871 had the unintended consequence of permitting Still some extra time for writing. He had his own voluminous records to draw upon. These included the official journal of the Vigilance Committee as well as letters, clippings, and other records Still had retained over the years. He also reached out to old co-workers, looking to fill in gaps in his own materials, in some cases traveling to procure the documents he needed when those records could not be sent to him.[36]

On January 29, 1872, Still signed a formal agreement with a Philadelphia firm, Porter & Coates, who promised to print ten thousand copies of *The Underground Railroad*. Still had very clear ideas about how he wanted the volume to look, and before approaching printers he had identified books whose appearance and binding he wished to emulate. The look needed to match the book's ambition. Porter & Coates would offer multiple bindings, ranging from "Fine English Cloth, extra gilt" for $4.50 to "Half Turkey Morocco" for $6.50. The firm would pay Still 62.5 cents for each copy sold. It would be available only by subscription.[37]

The final writing of the book would take place at a breakneck speed. Still agreed to produce four pages of the printed book each day, which the printer would set in type as they came in. William Henry Furness, the renowned antislavery theologian and longtime Still ally, agreed to read the manuscript, page by page, as Still finished it. Still rose at five in the morning and finished his day of writing at eleven in the evening. Daily pages would be taken to Furness at his country home outside the city and returned to Still promptly, whereupon they were sent to the printer for typesetting. At some point Furness had to leave town, and his son, Horace, a Shakespearean scholar, took over his duties as proofreader. For a first-time author, especially one with as little formal schooling as Still, the assistance of these two learned men was welcome and reassuring. Still also enlisted the services of a number of engravers in order to produce dozens of images that would illustrate the narrative, many of them depicting dramatic scenes from the text.[38]

The product of these labors is a remarkable book, perhaps the single most important source for historians' understanding of the Underground Railroad and an invaluable resource for those wishing to understand the lives of enslaved people in the decade before the Civil War. Still dedicated it "to the friends of freedom, to the heroic fugitives and their posterity in the United States." He promised his reader that he had taken "scrupulous care" in assembling the text, and that these stories of the Underground Railroad would be "artless stories, simple facts, —to resort to no coloring to make the book seem romantic." Still sought not just to entertain, but to instruct, and to do so he needed his audience to believe in his accounts, to see them as authentic. To ensure that his readers understood his authority to write this book, Still solicited dozens of testimonials from leading men (nearly all of them white), which he published at the front of the book. Supreme Court justices, senators, congressmen, and abolitionist luminaries all testified to Still's unique qualifications.[39]

In form the book is a bit odd, perhaps owing to the way it was put together, written in daily chunks and sent off to the printer to be set. It opens with a personal story, the account of Seth Conklin's doomed attempt to rescue the family of Peter Still. This is immediately followed by a chapter consisting solely of reproductions of letters written to the author by co-workers in the cause. Still likely hoped that by opening with these two chapters he would further establish his authority, his own personal stake in this story, though the two chapters certainly also serve to draw the reader into the dramatic world of the Underground Railroad. From here the book continues as a series of episodes, recounting individual fugitives or groups that arrived together. Each is labeled individually. Some, like the story of Perry Johnson, who fled from Elkton, Maryland, in November 1853, after losing an eye in a particularly brutal lashing at the "hand of his mistress," are brief, covering less than half a page. Others unfold over many pages, like the story of John Henry Hill, which includes not just Still's account of Hill's escape, but also incorporates copies of letters Hill wrote after escaping to Canada in which he seeks Still's aid in reconciling with the wife he left behind. These episodes proceed in roughly chronological order, but occasionally jump out of that chronology, so Still can provide important background, on the Fugitive Slave Law, for example, or on particularly important incidents like the escape of Henry "Box" Brown or the Christiana uprising. The book closes with about two hundred pages of profiles of individuals who had been particularly instrumental in helping the work of the Vigilance Committee.

What conclusions can be gathered from such a sprawling work? Perhaps the clearest message of the book is the need to keep fugitive slaves themselves at the center of the story of the Underground Railroad. Here Still was continuing with a theme that had long animated his oratorical accounts of the Underground Railroad. To be sure, Still's book gives those who aided fugitives, many of them white, their due as well, but the overwhelming majority of the text is dedicated to rich accounts of men, women, and children who escaped from "the prison-house of bondage." Above all else, Still wants his readers to understand that *The Underground Railroad* is the story of those individuals, and his book is an effort to ensure that those individuals were not forgotten. More than this, Still is clear that these hundreds of individuals, who had risked so much for their own liberty, were remarkable. "It scarcely needs be stated," he writes in the preface, "that, as a general rule the passengers of the U. G. R. R. were physically and intellectually above the average order of slaves. They were determined to have liberty even at the cost of life." Still was sometimes criticized as an elitist, an advocate for the "respectable" class of Black people, not for the

Black masses. Still's book shows that his vision of a Black elite was never the one his critics envisioned; it was an elite of character, of perseverance, of will.[40]

Still also makes it clear that his story of Black struggle against slavery is an argument for full Black citizenship rights. As an early review noted, "it will be an unanswerable witness against those who would deny to the colored man his rights or deny his claim to the capabilities and aspirations of highest manhood." A persistent theme of the book is the "intelligence" demonstrated by these fugitives from slavery. White authors sympathetic to the enslaved might at times have depicted Black people as intellectually inferior but spiritually superior (and therefore exemplars of a particular vision of Christian spirituality), but Still makes sure to emphasize the "native intelligence" of so many of these men, women, and children despite the barriers that had been placed in the way of their cultivation. "In order to succeed," Still wrote, "it required more than ordinary intelligence and courage, shrewdness and determination, and at the same time, a very ardent appreciation of liberty, without which there could be no success." These fugitive slaves, Still argued, were more than suited for the American citizenship they had been so long denied.[41]

Notably, what is most absent from Still's book is Still himself. In contrast to the allegations of Still's critics, who depicted him as a man desperate to claim credit for the work of others, in *The Underground Railroad* Still keeps himself in the background, as he had generally done in telling the story of his work aiding fugitives from slavery. The book opens with a story about Still's brother, but it largely focuses on Seth Conklin's fatal effort to rescue Peter Still's family. Still is most often present in the book in the form of the letters that are scattered throughout the text. Most of the accounts of individuals or of groups of fugitives, even those where Still and the Vigilance Committee clearly had an active hand in their flight, devote most of the attention to the life of bondage that preceded that flight, and to the actions of the fugitives in question. Here again, downplaying his own role in the flight of fugitive slaves is a part of his larger effort to emphasize the central role of enslaved people in their own emancipation. This is not the story of an Underground Railroad that frees enslaved people; it is rather a story of how the Underground Railroad provides an avenue for enslaved people to free themselves.

Still was a first-time author (if we exclude the pamphlet published a few years earlier in which he defended his actions in the effort to desegregate the streetcars), but he was not ignorant of the challenges of publishing. He knew that if the book was to reach the audience that he hoped it would, it would require a strenuous effort on his part. Surely, he had had conversations with friends and confidants like William Wells Brown and Frances Ellen Watkins Harper, about their efforts to promote their own work. Now that it was his turn, he was confident that he could apply all that he had learned, whether as a part of the abolitionist movement, as an advocate for Black citizenship, or as a businessman, to the selling of his book.

One of the most important forums in which Still advertised his book was the *Christian Recorder*, the Philadelphia-published newspaper of the AME Church. The *Recorder* was one of the most widely read Black publications of the nineteenth century, with a readership that spanned the United States. As befitting its affiliation with the AME Church, quite a bit of its content was related to Black Methodism, but it also covered a range of topics relevant to its Black readership. It had provided extensive coverage of Black service in the Civil War. Its pages featured Black literary works and debates among some of the leading figures of the day on the issues facing the nation. Still had a long association with the *Recorder* and saw it as the perfect venue in which to advertise his book; its readers were just the sort of respectable, politically engaged African Americans that Still expected to be interested in his history of the Underground Railroad.[42]

Still would produce a series of advertisements that ran in the *Christian Recorder*, each highlighting a different episode in the narrative. The first depicted the "resurrection" of Henry "Box" Brown in the Anti-Slavery Society office in Philadelphia, perhaps the most famous fugitive escape Still had been involved with. A second advertisement depicted the mayor of Norfolk, axe in hand, "searching Captain Fountain's Vessel for Runaways." Another depicted the heartrending death of Romulus Hall, with Still kneeling next to him, asking if freedom was worth this cost. A fourth advertisement depicted a dramatic scene of fugitives, both men and women, brandishing weapons to drive off slave catchers, depicting one of the central themes of the book: fugitives' role in their own escapes. A final advertisement featured an entire family of fugitives, accompanied by the text "The father died in the poor-house, a raving maniac, caused by the sale of two of his children. The heroic mother, with the balance, sought flight on the Underground Rail-Road." This advertisement celebrated another primary theme of Still's book, the threat that slavery posed to the Black family, and the resilience of Black families in the face of that threat. These advertisements occupied a full quarter of a page in the newspaper, and in addition to the specific images included selective endorsements from respected figures and glowing reviews from newspapers. Such advertisements were not cheap—in most issues of the *Christian Recorder*, these were the only advertisements with images—but clearly Still was convinced that such dramatic measures would build interest in the book.[43]

He did not, however, rely on this print advertising campaign as the only means to promote *The Underground Railroad*. Still also built a network of agents who traveled the country and sold the book directly to customers. As early as July 1872, his son-in-law, Edward Wiley, was in Cape May, on the Jersey Shore, selling the book, though he seemed to be less successful than he had hoped due the partisan leanings of the area. "One has a very good opportunity," Wiley wrote to his wife, Caroline, "to learn about people & what they think about the Colored man and especially the Democrats." Eventually Still would employ an army of agents, as many as a hundred at one point, ranging across the country as far as California, Texas, and Georgia. Still employed both men and women, white and Black agents, and he had strict standards for those he entrusted with this responsibility. All of his agents needed to be college educated. Still offered them 40 percent of each sale, a rate that he later would raise to 50 percent, so there was a strong financial incentive to maximize sales. He also kept strict tabs on his agents, making sure that they adhered to his standards. Still's network of agents seems to have been quite successful. One historian has estimated that by the late 1870s, Still had sold between five and ten thousand copies of the book.[44]

Sales of *The Underground Railroad* made Still quite a bit of money, especially after he acquired sole rights to the book from Porter & Coates in the summer of 1873, but for Still the book was never simply about making money. It was Still's way to continue the struggle that he had begun before he ever went to work at the Vigilance Committee, his way to fight for the rights of Black people everywhere. *The Underground Railroad* helped to ensure that fugitive slaves, and the people who helped them, would not be forgotten, and it helped depict those fugitive slaves as representatives of a different sort of Black elite, an elite who had been denied the fruits of their talents and labors by the lash, by the auction block, but who were now ready to assume the full rights of American citizenship. As one reviewer noted, there had been many books about heroic fugitive slaves, but they had always been about single heroic individuals. "The work of Mr. Still," he noted, "takes a broader scope. It is the study of scores of heroes." The book was, noted the reviewer, "a monument to Negro love of liberty, its pages tell us what he braved to be free."[45]

CHAPTER TWELVE

LOOKING FORWARD, LOOKING BACKWARD

On a Monday evening in October 1873, Still was invited by the Young People's Association of the Central Presbyterian Church to deliver a lecture. Still's daughter Caroline was a prominent member of the organization, and Still himself had become increasingly active in the church in recent years; in 1871 the church had appointed him one of the commissioners to the Presbytery, the church's regional organization. The evening began with a prayer, offered by a deacon of the church, then a hymn and a psalm reading. The members present discussed some business, which included a lament over the finances of the organization and a call for greater effort to ensure that members paid their dues. Finally, Still was called to speak.[1]

He chose as his subject the theme "Reforms and Reformers." Still had long sought every opportunity to impart what he saw as his hard-earned wisdom to young people. His children could expect a short lecture on prudence and good spending habits whenever they asked him for money. Still's sometimes severe moral posture could at times alienate the objects of such lectures. On this night, though, he was pleased to have a captive audience of young people with whom to share his advice; after all, this was an organization that he deemed particularly open to his vision of philanthropic labor and self-discipline as an avenue for benefiting the race. He

Portrait of William Still

planned to draw on the experiences of his generation of reformers in order to inspire this younger generation. "Contemplating as I do," he began, "the nature of the work that this association has undertaken to accomplish, it seems obvious to my mind that just in proportion as you may be fully convinced of the results following the labor of earnest self-sacrificing workers in the cause of humanity . . . will you be all the more willing to follow in their footsteps to battle for the same noble ends."[2]

Still implored his audience to lead the way in saving their generation of Black men and women from the temptations of the flesh. "None can deny," he told his audience, "that the fields all around us need many faithful intelligent and devoted workers to save hundreds and thousands of our youth from tippling shops and drinking houses; from gambling halls and brothels; from making shipwrecks of hope and character before reaching maturity." He called on his listeners to set an example of clean, disciplined living for their peers. "Spend no hard earnings for vain amusement," he warned, "or with the sporting thoughtless crew in society." This was, to Still, an essential step on the road to securing true and lasting progress for the Black race. None of this was new, of course. For decades Black reformers had been preaching the gospel of personal responsibility to Black audiences, even as they fought the legal and political barriers that Black people faced across the country. Still saw the recent success of the political struggle for Black rights both as a reason for celebration and as a moment for rededication to the principle of self-elevation. "The Fifteenth Amendment and Civil Rights Bills bring us suffrage and hope for other privileges," he noted, but he also warned that there were limits to what Black people could expect whites to do for them. "Nor are we likely to share in the future as much general sympathy as we did in the past when our race was under oppression," he predicted. "If we would see our race rising, we must work hard to effect the glorious object."[3]

Perhaps some in his audience felt that such work was pointless. After all, was reform of the sort that Still was advocating realistic? Here Still drew on the lessons of the previous generation, his generation, to remind his listeners that radical change was possible. "The day was very dark," he reminded them, when "the old hero John Brown, as he attested his love of freedom by stooping down and kissing a poor little colored child on the morning he was being led to the scaffold, hand cuffed and manacled. Who dreamed that in less than three short years the name of John Brown would be an inspiration to tens of thousands of soldiers and citizens all over this continent?" Similarly, he spoke of the violent resistance that William Lloyd Garrison had faced in the early days of his abolitionist struggle, but much had changed. "Garrison who had been hitherto so universally abused for nearly forty years," Still pointed out, "is now honored by millions of his Countrymen as a true and faithful philanthropist. As the Pioneer of the Anti-Slavery Cause." He urged his listeners to believe that such change could happen, and to personally commit themselves to making it happen. "I consider the time has come," he said in closing, "when we must personally put our shoulders to the wheel."[4]

Still was never known as a great speaker. He could never capture an audience the way that contemporaries like Frederick Douglass or William Wells Brown could. Still's oratory, like his prose, was workmanlike, but he clearly labored over it, and by the early 1870s he had become quite effective. "Of course Wm. Still does not profess to be an orator," remarked one observer, "but when it comes to down right sensible talk, and honest work, he is a very chief." Whether or not Still floored his audience, the address on "reforms and reformers" captured the essence of Still's vision for Black activism and the direction he hoped to take in the coming years. Still had long worked side by side with white activists, but he was increasingly skeptical that African Americans could rely on the goodwill of their white neighbors or allies in the Republican Party. If they were to continue their progress, Black people would need to look out for themselves.

Still had never been a partisan. Certainly he supported the Republican Party, and applauded its success over the years as it showed itself to be a tool in the war against slavery and for the advance of Black rights, but he had never placed his entire faith in the party itself. To an extent this was a position shared by many abolitionists, Black and white. Like many abolitionists, in the years after the great triumphs of emancipation and the passage of the Reconstruction Amendments, Still grew increasingly disillusioned with party politics. In this regard, he was at odds with the majority of African Americans, who continued to see the Republican Party, as Douglass famously put it in 1872, as "the deck of the ship, and all the other parties are the outside, in the sea." Still instead put his faith not in parties, but rather in the cluster of ideas that came to be called American liberalism, which one historian has defined as "faith in popular government, a close identification with progress and justice, and a commitment to orderly change and cosmopolitan open-mindedness." Still's alliance with liberalism was nothing new for him; in fact he had been an early investor in the quintessential journal of liberal ideas, the *Nation*, and Still's main avenue of activism in the 1860s, the Social, Civil, and Statistical Association, was clearly built on a liberal faith in the power of ideas to attack white supremacy, but the 1870s saw a flowering of Still's embrace of liberalism as an alternative to party loyalty.[5] Still's version of liberalism, however, should be distinguished from the mainstream version by its effort to merge liberalism with a fierce race consciousness. Many liberals, of course, had seen racial caste as a corruption of the values they held dear, but Still, more than most white liberals, recognized the continuing need for Black solidarity as a tool in the fight against discrimination.

Many liberals had become increasingly disillusioned by what they saw as the corruption of the Republican Party. Liberals had supported government intervention in the South as a necessary means of protecting Black Southerners from the violent white backlash to Reconstruction, and they recognized that it was only such intervention that made possible the expansion of Black rights, including suffrage, which liberals wholeheartedly supported. In general, though, many liberals accepted this intervention as a necessary evil, and continued to fear that this government intervention risked unleashing a host of unintended consequences. In comparison to more orthodox Republicans, then, liberals' embrace of robust government intervention in the South had been ambivalent. Many, therefore, were more sensitive to the accusations of corruption that plagued the Republican governments of the reconstructed Southern states, even if such accusations were clearly rooted in racist perceptions of Black unsuitability for self-government.[6]

These fears of corruption had helped fuel the Liberal Republican revolt of 1872. Liberal Republicans increasingly felt that the Grant administration had unleashed a torrent of corruption, in particular in the South, but also across the country, whereby the opportunities created by Civil War–era expansions of government had led to a scramble for individual wealth, whereby the "system, order, and rationality" that liberals valued in government was increasingly replaced by crass self-interest. Many liberals split from the Republican Party and nominated reformer, and former abolitionist, Horace Greeley for president. Greeley's support was not entirely liberal in allegiance; his candidacy became a kind of catch-all for anti-Grant sentiment, but indisputably by the early 1870s white liberals had grown uncomfortable in the Republican

Party, and increasing numbers of them were willing to, like Greeley, reconcile with white Southerners in order to address what they saw as the more pressing issues facing the nation.[7]

William Still demonstrated little sympathy for this sort of liberal critique of the Grant administration, and he generally remained supportive of the Republican Party's Reconstruction policies in the South. There were, however, developments closer to home that exacerbated his skepticism of the party. Following the setbacks suffered in 1868 in Philadelphia, the state Republican party, which still controlled the state legislature, pushed through the controversial Registry Act. Republicans had been convinced that Democratic success in Philadelphia had been a result of outof-town visitors and "repeaters," fraudulent voters who supposedly had gone to the polls multiple times in order to inflate the Democratic vote. The Registry Act was designed to curb this alleged voter fraud, but it functioned by placing the control of the registration of voters entirely in the hands of the Republican Party. The law had the desired effect and Republicans were able to once again seize control of the government of Philadelphia, but even some Republicans began to worry that the remedy for supposed voter fraud had gone too far.[8]

Even more than this, the renewed dominance of Philadelphia Republicans, and in particular their control of the city's election boards via the Registry Act, enabled the rise of a political machine under the control of "King" James McManes, the city's political boss. McManes had assumed this role by virtue of his control of the Philadelphia Gas Works, a private company that had been acquired by the city in 1841 and was thereafter administered by a twelve-member board. McManes was appointed to the board in 1865, by which time the Gas Works employed nearly two thousand Philadelphians and received about $2 million a year in city contracts. This flow of public money, which could be distributed as spoils, and the control of an army of city workers, loyal to McManes and spread throughout the city, enabled the boss to exert influence across Philadelphia.[9]

McManes's main rival for control of the Republican organization in Philadelphia was William S. Stokley, a longtime political boss who by the 1860s had ascended to leadership of the city's

Select Council. From this office Stokley would seize control of the city's Public Buildings Commission. Just as the gas trust would be a source of spoils for McManes, so too the Buildings Commission would provide Stokley with a way to line the pockets of political supporters. Stokley was able to parlay this financial clout and political patronage into a successful bid for mayor in 1871. From this position, Stokley was able to solidify his control over much of the city's political machinery, sometimes working in concert with McManes. This was a particularly lucrative period for men in such positions, as the city engaged in an extensive program of public construction, especially Philadelphia's massive new city hall, begun in 1872.[10]

Some historians have questioned the amount of influence that such "bosses" actually exerted over the city's politics, but what is clear is that contemporaries perceived men like McManes and Stokley as a threat to good government. By the time Stokley ran for re-election in 1874, many Philadelphians, including those Republicans who saw themselves as liberals, had grown critical of the culture of graft that the Republican Party had created. Some Philadelphians were especially concerned that the corrupt Stokley administration was a black eye on the city as it geared up to host the nation's centennial celebration in 1876. A group of reformist Republicans, in combination with Philadelphia Democrats, responded to these concerns by nominating Alexander McClure, a liberal Republican state senator who had supported Greeley in 1872, as candidate for what they called the "Citizens' Centennial Constitution Party." McClure reluctantly accepted the nomination. His supporters cast him as a sort of anti-politician. "There [is] no political issue involved in the present municipal contest," claimed one advocate. "It is solely a battle waged by the friends of a wise equitable and economical administration of the government of the city against a pack of political beagles who have fed and fattened upon the spoils." McClure managed to attract a decent coalition of reformist Republicans and Democrats, but he was soundly defeated by the incumbent mayor.[11]

At some point during the heated campaign, William Still let it slip that he supported McClure's candidacy. Unsurprisingly, given Still's prominence and the overwhelming support of Black Philadelphians for the Republican Party, news of Still's apostasy created a stir. No doubt the still-fresh memories of Octavius Catto's murder by a Democratic Party thug only sharpened the outrage that many Black Philadelphians, many of them Still allies, felt upon hearing this news. On February 19, the generally Still-friendly *Christian Recorder* reported that "we hear it hinted on the winds that Wm. Still Esq. is going to write a Political pamphlet. Hope the report is true." On March 2, a group of prominent Black leaders, many of them pastors, sent Still a formal request. "In view of the conflicting rumors relative to your vote for Col. A. K. McClure," they asked that he deliver a public address in order to respond to "the charges preferred against you," and to clarify his position. Still agreed to their request.[12]

He arranged to make his case before the public on the evening of March 10, in the Concert Hall. Though Still was a man of great confidence, and he surely was convinced of the correctness of his position, he was also eager to cloak himself in the approval of his most influential and respected friends, as well as to remind the audience of his long history of service to the Black community of Philadelphia. Seated on the platform were some of Still's oldest allies: Robert Purvis, Bishop Campbell of the AME Church, and his allies from the Vigilance Committee, Passmore Williamson and Charles Wise. When Still finally rose to speak, he was greeted by "an outburst of applause" by the audience of hundreds that filled the hall.[13]

Still denied that he had "deserted [his] principles," as his critics alleged, and he distanced himself from the world of partisan politics. "Politics for me have had no charms," he insisted. Politicians, he argued, were not what Black Philadelphians needed. "Of convincing or satisfying mere partisans or politicians," he said "I have no hope." But it was not such partisans, he argued, who would improve the lives of Black people. Still distinguished the corrupt Republican politicians of Philadelphia with those Republicans who were promoting Black education across the South, building schools like "Wilberforce University, Lincoln University, Howard University, Hampton Normal and Agricultural Institute, Berea College, and scores of others," which were now educating men who just a decade ago were enslaved. The Republican "Ring" of

Philadelphia had done nothing to contribute to these admirable institutions, nor had it meaningfully contributed to other efforts to promote Black progress in the South, and yet these Philadelphia politicians insisted they deserved the "gratitude" of Black voters.

"I will venture to add," continued Still, "that these benefits will not soon come to us through simply voting the Republican ticket as a matter of 'gratitude,' nor by waiting for offices from the Republican party—never. To my mind the work of our elevation, after all, must come mainly through our own exertions and self-reliance." What was needed, according to Still, were Black businessmen. Until more Black men owned their own businesses, they would be dependent on white bosses for their wages. Just as many Black Southerners saw land ownership as the key to Black progress in the South, so did Still see Black ownership of businesses as essential in the North. Until Black Philadelphians did away with this "lack of enterprise," they would remain subservient to their white bosses. "Landless and without capital," warned Still, "even with the Civil Rights' Bill secured by the Congress of the Nation, the condition of the colored man would still be pitiable, unless he is wise."

Still then went on to address the specifics of this election and his decision to vote for McClure, who, Still reminded his audience, was and had been a Republican. "For some time before the election I had made up my mind that I could not consistently with my sense of duty, vote for the 'Ring.' The numerous election frauds, high taxes, &c." convinced him that "provided that a Republican" should run against the incumbent then he would be willing to support him. Nor was he unique in this regard. Still noted that many of his old allies, leading abolitionists who had supported the Republican Party for years, were willing to support an independent Republican in order to bring down the corruption of Philadelphia's political machine.

Still was careful to insist that he was no Democrat. "With regard to the Democratic party, I will here take occasion to say, I have never joined it, have never sought to do so, nor have I ever been solicited to do so." He was, however, critical of the knee-jerk resistance to those who considered supporting the Democratic Party. Many Republican leaders, he reminded his readers, had begun their political careers in the Democratic Party. Black voters, insisted Still, would be best served not by blind loyalty to the Republican Party, an "extreme view held by some colored Republicans in Philadelphia," but by pushing both parties to compete for Black votes. This was especially true, Still argued, because many of the most pressing issues facing the country did not align neatly with "the slavery issues on which the two parties have so long been contending." Black voters needed to remain open to Democratic overtures if they were to hope that the party would continue to appeal to the interests of Black people. Still published the transcript of his speech in pamphlet form, just as he had several years earlier in the controversy over the streetcar fight. Once again, he hoped to counter those who felt he had betrayed the Black community.[14]

Still's willingness to break with the Republican Party, the party of Lincoln and the party of the Union, seems somewhat perplexing, as it did to many of his contemporaries. Nevertheless, a fair number of prominent Black leaders (many of them close allies) praised Still's position. Frances Ellen Watkins Harper wrote Still a personal letter expressing her support. "Well, I know nothing of the merits or demerits of the parties," she wrote, "but if you have a corrupt and thieving ring in Phil. whether it calls itself Republican or Democratic, it ought to be broken; and if you have acted on the side of political reform, permit me to thank you, not in the name of the political parties, but in the name of our common humanity." Still shared the letter with the *Christian Recorder*, which published portions of it. Redmon Fauset, a prominent preacher in the AME Church, wrote directly to the *Recorder*, to state his approval of Still's actions. "There need be great fear," he wrote, "that our people are too much concerned about voting for candidates set up by a particular political party, and not enough about how to prepare themselves for the ordinary and yet important affairs of life."[15]

Most Black Philadelphians, however, remained unconvinced by Still's argument. Even though the *Christian Recorder* had published letters supporting Still, the editor expressed his disagreement with Still's position on voting. "Troops of our friends say that the vote of the colored people ought to be divided," wrote the paper. "Many among ourselves feel the same way—feel that it is not exactly the thing for us to go, en masse for any one party. But how can we do otherwise?" The *Recorder* noted its respect for the men who had expressed their openness to voting for Democratic candidates, but it could not support this position. "There stand George Downing, Robert Purvis, Chas. B. Ray, William Still, who in the words of the poet, are all 'honorable men,'" but they challenged the call of these men to abandon the Republican Party. "We ask some of our friends—please tell us how it is possible for a negro to vote the Democratic ticket—those friends who say, we must." The writer admitted that some local and state Democrats had shown some promise, "but alas! the recent action of the party in Congress" had shown that Democrats could not be trusted. "Unless the negro is prepared to vote to his own hurt and to his country's distraction," wrote the editor, "there is nothing left for him to do but vote the Republican ticket."[16]

Much of the private correspondence Still received on this matter was less respectful. One was particularly ominous.

> Mr n___er which i cant cal such a man as you ar for you
> hante as good as one for he noes what to do and that is
> more than you do such a man as that ought to bee put
> back in slavery and never loud to look up a mienet in a
> day and i coud drive such a n___er as that from morining
> till nigh and i could stand and se your place burn down
> before you ar aware of it for i dont think you disserve
> such a place good by mr n___er. [racial slur edited from
> the original]

The letter is unsigned, so it is uncertain who actually wrote it, but there is reason to believe that it is some sort of performance. It is written on high-quality stationery, with a raised seal on it, and despite vulgar and ungrammatical language, the handwriting is smooth and practiced. The letter's mistakes, including an entire lack of capital letters, seems almost like an educated person's idea of what an uneducated person would write like. In any case, the letter sought to put Still in his place with a threat of violence.[17]

Still's actions seem to have alienated even some of his admirers, though there was some evidence that his "Address on Voting" would ultimately persuade some of them. "I never was more surprised," wrote Elizabeth Williams of Chatham, Canada, that Still had "turned tail to your Republican friends and voted with the Dimocrats. You are the last man I would of thought would of done such a thing . . . What will become of your Uncle Toms Cabin now? Who will bye Book now that you have distroid public confidence in your principles, none I am sorry for you but you have done the deed your self." Still had won great respect and admiration among the Black communities of towns like Chatham, where so many fugitive slaves had settled in the 1850s during the years of Still's work on the Underground Railroad. In one moment, the woman suggested, Still had squandered this goodwill. And yet less than a week later, the same woman wrote to Still again, this time apologizing for her earlier letter. She had read a copy of Still's pamphlet, explaining his position, and had been convinced. She praised his words, and expressed her hope that "the information it contains and the directions it gives may take root and spread amongst our People." This dramatic change was surely reassuring to Still, giving him hope that even those who were outraged by his decision to abandon the Republican Party might eventually be persuaded to see things his way.[18]

Notably, Still's rejection of the Republican Party was really a rejection of local Republicans, who he felt were corrupt and had demonstrated little interest in actually promoting the interests of Black people. He continued to support the Republican Party on a national level and in particular to support the Black Republicans who had been elected in the reconstructed states of the South. In September 1874, Still wrote to his daughter Caroline that the "Leit. Gov. of La.," presumably P. B. S. Pinchback, who had served in that office briefly before being elected to Congress (though Democrats blocked him from being seated), had been in the city and that "I had the pleasure of introducing him to a small company of invited guests at our neighbor Jones' the other evening." In March 1875, Still hosted a dinner in honor of Congressman John Lynch of Mississippi, who was then visiting Philadelphia. In Still's mind there was a vast difference between the Black Republicans working to transform the South and the corrupt white spoilsmen of Philadelphia who demanded Black loyalty.[19]

. . .

The controversy over his mayoral vote had briefly thrust Still into the partisan fray, but he continued to see sales of his book as his most important way of promoting Black progress. Still may have seen possibility in the openness of Black voters to abandoning the Republican Party, but he also realized that white Americans, North and South, continued to view African Americans as inferior to their white countrymen. His book challenged this notion, providing his readers, as one review noted, with "an illustration of the character of a peculiar race." It was his mission to spread this message.[20]

While Still continued his advertising campaign, the most important tool for spreading the word about his book was the growing network of agents who traveled the country. Still's son-in-law, Edward Wiley, was one of the most successful of these, though the work put severe strains on his health and his family. Still preferred that his agents focus intensively in one particular area, selling as many books as possible before moving on. In May of 1873, Wiley was working in western Pennsylvania, and he had looked into bringing his wife and newborn child, Willie, out to live with him in Pittsburgh, but nothing seems to have come of these plans. By the summer he had moved on and was working from Newport, Rhode Island. There were, it seems, at least two reasons for the move. On one hand he was selling the book among the affluent residents of the seaside town. On the other, Wiley was there to promote his own health. Shortly after arriving, he wrote to Caroline that "I have been in bathing twice since I came and feel that I am being benefited a great deal by it." His letters to his wife in this period include increasing references to only vaguely specified health troubles. Despite these troubles, Wiley continued his aggressive sales of Still's book, keeping in regular touch with both his concerned wife and his demanding father-in-law.[21]

Wiley's health continued to deteriorate. Caroline wrote to him, asking him to come back to Philadelphia to spend the winter with his family, though they both seemed to worry about what her father would think. In February 1874, as his father-in-law became embroiled in controversy over his mayoral vote, the *Christian*

Recorder reported simply that "Mr. Wiley, son in law of Mr. William Still, continues sick." Wiley did return home to his wife and child in Philadelphia. On March 3, he signed a will naming his wife and father-in-law as executors, and a few weeks later, on March 22, Edward A. Wiley died. He was not yet thirty years old.[22]

Later that year, Caroline and her young son left Philadelphia. For a short time, she moved to Oberlin with her sister, Frances Ellen, "Ella," who matriculated at the college in the fall. It is unclear why Caroline went with her sister. Perhaps she just needed a change of scenery. It seems that the return to her alma mater lifted her spirits. "I never enjoyed Oberlin half so much as I do now," she wrote her mother. Ella also seemed to adjust nicely to her new home and to her studies. "Well," she wrote her mother, "I like Oberlin very much indeed, and am beginning to get used to it." Their father resumed his correspondence with Caroline, offering his usual fatherly advice, but also sending along money specifically to pay for sweets for his beloved grandson, Willie.[23]

Later that fall, Caroline and Willie moved back to Philadelphia, but the following year, Caroline moved to Washington, D.C., this time leaving her son in Philadelphia in her parents' care. Caroline had entertained offers to teach in the South, but she ultimately decided to enroll at Howard University in order to study medicine. It seems that for some time Caroline had been considering medicine as a career, though it was never her sole interest. Perhaps she was influenced by her uncle, James Still, who had long practiced medicine in New Jersey. She may have also been influenced by her relationship with her cousin, James's son, James Thomas Still, to whom Caroline was close. The younger James Still graduated with honors from Harvard Medical School in 1871, after which he remained in Boston to practice medicine.[24]

Still had long been close to his eldest daughter, and no doubt he was proud of her academic progress. At times he even complained to Caroline about how her brother and sister, Ella and William Wilberforce, did not share her drive. Caroline was a prime example of the sort of Black person Still had spent his career celebrating. Intelligent, hardworking, and disciplined, Caroline was an example to the world of what Black people were able to accomplish if only they were given the opportunity. Still continued to subsidize his daughter's education, but the ever-diligent Caroline also taught elocution and drawing in order to support herself.[25]

No doubt the decision to leave Willie with his grandparents was driven by the realization that her studies would make it impossible for Caroline to care for her young son, but Still seems to have genuinely enjoyed having his grandson in Philadelphia with him. "Willie Wiley is O.K," Still wrote to his daughter in October 1875. "He visited The Home with me last Sabbath and had a good time as usual. He is not seeing one bit of trouble over his mother's absence but is perfectly happy."[26]

All was not well, however. Willie seems to have been a sickly child. On March 6, 1876, Still wrote to Caroline that "our little Willie is not very well," noting that "we have had a great deal of sickness in the city." Two weeks later, his condition seems to have gotten worse. Willie had "but little appetite," and Still wrote ominously that "I am not sure but our Heavenly Father means to take him under his own immediate supervision ere long. Of course we love to have our children stay with us in this unfriendly and wretched world, although I have long since been persuaded that He who created us knows far better than we." On April 13, Willie died at the home of his grandparents. It is unclear if his mother had been able to return home to Philadelphia in time to be with her only child before the end.[27]

With the publication of his book on the Underground Railroad, William Still had committed himself to the effort to use the past in order to push for Black progress in the present. Memories of the antislavery struggle became weapons in the fight for Black rights. While he continued to aggressively market his book across the country, Still also took a leading role in other sorts of commemorations of the movement to which he had dedicated himself. On March 11, 1874, Senator Charles Sumner, longtime champion of Black rights, died at his home in Washington, D.C. A few days later, Still organized a memorial meeting for the senator at Bethel AME Church, celebrating Sumner's service to the abolitionist cause and to the fight for Black equality. "The church was crowded," reported the *Inquirer*, "the audience being almost entirely composed of colored people." Still seems to have avoided a meeting held a few days earlier and organized mostly by staunch Black Republicans, but this meeting, befitting Still's influence, included mostly Black preachers and veteran abolitionists, though Isaiah Wears, one of the most vocal defenders of the Republican Party, did participate.[28]

When it came time for Still to speak, he praised Sumner and invoked his personal connection to the departed champion of civil rights. According to Still, he had been moved to speak by the fact that some newspapers had suggested that African Americans were insufficiently appreciative of the man. "Suffice it to say," Still told the audience, "that for more than twenty-five years I have known Mr. Sumner personally, and have watched closely his public labors for freedom, only to love and admire his unconquerable devotion to liberty; his wise and brave stand for equal rights." He praised Sumner's character, his sincerity, and his devotion to "the advocacy of our rights" throughout his long and distinguished career.

This much—the praise for Sumner and the celebration of his service to the cause of abolition and Black equality—was unsurprising; it echoed much of what had been said before. Next, though, Still made a more pointed assertion. "While it is doubtless true," admitted Still, "that some men identified with our race have unguardedly or wantonly aspersed his noble record, I think I may safely say that the hearts of the masses of the people, as far as they have been capable of judging, have been true to Mr. Sumner." Why had some Black men turned their backs on Sumner? Still did not say, but his audience surely knew. Sumner had supported Greeley and the Liberal Republicans against Grant in 1872. This had diminished Sumner's status among committed Republicans, though less so among African Americans, who continued to admire his support for Black civil rights. Still saw his eulogy as an opportunity to hold Sumner up as an example of high-minded statesmanship. Sumner was the sort of politician Still admired, the sort who was driven not by partisanship but by the desire to promote justice and good government, even if that meant opposing the Republican Party. "The majority of our people," Still insisted, as demonstrated by "the interest here manifested," agreed with him. It was only the partisan class, the Black leaders who mindlessly supported the Republican Party out of hope for personal gain, who cast aspersions on men like Sumner. Still's eulogy was both a celebration of a particular political ideal and a defense of his own personal conduct.[29]

In the years after his book was published, Still took an increasingly prominent role in public commemoration of the abolitionist movement, both as an organizer and as a participant. The year after he delivered his eulogy for Charles Sumner, Still served as the chair of the committee of arrangements for the centennial celebration of the Pennsylvania Abolition Society (PAS). This was the "old" abolition society, rather than the Pennsylvania Anti-Slavery Society (which had employed Still during his years with the Vigilance Committee), but in recent years Still had become active in the PAS as well. Still organized an afternoon meeting at the Concert Hall, which was followed by an evening session at Bethel AME. He helped ensure that the commemoration drew some of the most distinguished figures in the fight against slavery, not just those who had been directly involved with the PAS but also those who merely wished to honor its influential work. The vice president of the United States, Henry Wilson, presided over the meeting, and when he rose to open the occasion, he was accompanied to the stage by a trio of distinguished Black leaders: Still, Frederick Douglass, and Robert Purvis. Douglass would go on to deliver the lengthiest speech of the event, reminding his listeners of the distinguished history of the organization they were celebrating, but also noting that there was much work to be done. "The negro has freedom," Douglass noted, "but with conditions that make the continuation of the work of the society a necessity." This was the theme of the whole occasion, drawing on the memory of the antislavery struggle of the past in order to energize the fight for Black people and their rights in the present.[30]

This engagement with the past would only grow in the ensuing years. The following year, Still was one of many who sought to make sure that the grand celebration of the nation's centennial, hosted by Philadelphia, would give proper attention to the contributions of African Americans; incidentally he also used this as an opportunity to sell copies of his book. In the coming years Still would preside over a memorial for abolitionist William Lloyd

Garrison, and he helped plan the celebration of the bicentennial of William Penn's arrival in Pennsylvania. In 1883, Still joined with many of his longtime allies to celebrate the fiftieth anniversary of the founding of the Pennsylvania Anti-Slavery Society. Robert Purvis, one of the organization's founders, presided, and Still's work on the Underground Railroad was a particular focus of attention. Still himself spoke and exhibited several relics of his work, including a box that had been used to transport an enslaved girl named Lear Green from Baltimore to Philadelphia.[31]

While Still continued his work ensuring that the abolitionist past would be remembered, he also continued the fight to keep what he saw as the spirit of that struggle alive. Still's philanthropy in this period increasingly demonstrated a coherent philosophy, a clear sense of what was most important to him. On one hand, he embraced the idea that African Americans, Black men in particular, could, if given the right opportunities, lift themselves up into the Black middle class. On the other hand, Still also continued to fund charities that cared for the most vulnerable Black citizens, in particular the elderly. The Home for Aged and Infirm Colored Persons remained the most prominent recipient of Still's philanthropic efforts. He was a tireless fundraiser for the home and a longtime officer of the organization that managed it. Still also supported charity for impoverished Black Philadelphians, on one occasion supervising the distribution of eight hundred loaves of bread, and on another organizing a free excursion for poor Black children to Mount Pleasant in Philadelphia's Fairmount Park.[32]

In a sense, Still understood his own successful business as his most important contribution to the Black community. He saw himself as a model to be emulated, as an example for Black people everywhere. In his public addresses he constantly encouraged his Black listeners to go into business for themselves. Still increasingly played up his own personal story, emphasizing his rise from humble beginnings to wealth and respectability. His lectures on the Underground Railroad included increasing material about his own story, and he often began by noting that he arrived in Philadelphia, decades ago, "with a capital of $3.00 and wardrobe even less in value," and then went on to recount his various, unsuccessful efforts at starting a business before finally getting to his antislavery exploits. When Still published a revised edition of *The Underground Railroad* in 1883, it included an extensive biography, which included many of these stories and depicted Still as a sort of Black Horatio Alger character, pulling himself up by his bootstraps. In the preface to this revised edition, Still lamented the failure of "political struggles" to improve the position of African Americans, and argued that only with "the acquisition of knowledge and the exhibition of high moral character, in examples of economy and a disposition to encourage industrial enterprises conducted by men of their own rank, will it be possible to make political progress in the face of the present public sentiment."[33]

As a benefit to the Black community, Still's business success was more than an example to emulate, however. Still also understood that Black workers continued to experience discrimination in the job market. Despite the end of slavery and despite the decline of many forms of de jure racism, African Americans still found themselves largely confined to the lowest-paying, most menial sorts of work. Still and other prominent Black businessmen saw it as their responsibility to employ Black workers. "Refused then by white employers," observed the *Christian Recorder*, "is it not high time that our men of means, undertake to do for the colored poor, what white men of means do for the white poor?" They applauded the Black businessmen who did so, "for instance our townsman Wm. Still the coal merchant, or, young Mr. Boling, the flour merchant. These gentlemen in their businesses, employ possibly a dozen men each." As the *Christian Recorder* would note of Still, "We regard him as the leading colored man in the country. His strongest part is his disposition to cling more closely and work more earnestly for his race as his wealth and influence increases, and makes social recognition an easy possibility in other directions."[34]

Nor did Still's advocacy for Black workingmen end there. While he sometimes spoke the language of late-nineteenth century capitalists, Still coupled this with a strong sense of racial responsibility. In 1878 he was a member of the board of directors which organized a "Workingmen's Club," on Rodman Street. The organization collected dues each month, which provided aid to members who fell ill. The dues also supported a night school, a reading room, and a program of lectures. Members were also able to purchase coal "at a reduced price," presumably from Still's coal yard. He also supported the establishment of an "Industrial School for Colored Youth" as a means of preparing children for a trade.[35]

Still had always been supportive of Black education, perhaps acutely aware of the opportunities that had been denied to him. In 1879, he was chosen as a delegate to the National Convention of Colored People held in Nashville, where he particularly advocated for the expansion of educational opportunities for Black students. He delivered a lengthy address on the "Opportunities and Capabilities of Educated Negroes," in which he laid out his case. He implored his listeners, "For every one of us to renew our efforts to advance education and true and undefiled religion; to promote more economy, more union, more regard for morality, more willingness to seek out and extend a helping hand to the 'million' who are of the most lowly and degraded." Education was critical if the Black people of the South were to ever be able to reach their potential as workers and as citizens. Still praised the work that was already being done across the South to educate freedmen and -women, reeling off statistics about the number of students being educated in various Southern schools and colleges, but he reminded his audience that there was still much to be done. As usual, Still was sure to include calls for Black Southerners to take responsibility for themselves. "Being far behind in the race," he admitted, "our people must not deem it too great a requirement to be obliged to put forth double exertions to catch up," but Still also knew that these men and women needed help from their more advantaged brethren in the North.[36]

Still needed only to look at his own family as evidence of how African Americans could prosper when given the necessary opportunities. He was accompanied to Nashville by his daughter Caroline, who was also chosen as a delegate. Though Caroline seems not to have been an active participant in the convention, at least according to the recorded proceedings, she was an excellent example of Black education. After a year studying medicine in Washington, Caroline had returned to Philadelphia to continue her studies at the Philadelphia Female Medical College, where she received her degree in the spring of 1878. She spent a year as an intern at the New England Hospital for Women and Children in Boston, after which she returned to Philadelphia and entered into private practice. William Wilberforce Still had graduated with honors from Lincoln University in 1874, where he was asked to deliver the mathematics oration at commencement, and three years later he received his master's degree from the same school. After this he went into business for himself. It seems that his father hoped that he might work for him as a sales agent for his book, but the younger William Still showed little interest in working for his father. Frances Ellen Still graduated from Oberlin, like her older sister, after which she returned to Philadelphia where she worked as a kindergarten teacher. The Stills' youngest child, Robert, would follow in his brother's footsteps, graduating from Lincoln University in 1883.[37]

Shortly after returning to Philadelphia, Caroline remarried. Her second husband was Matthew Anderson, newly installed pastor of the Berean Presbyterian Church in the Fairmount neighborhood of Philadelphia. Frances Ellen Still also married a pastor, J. Richmond Harris, of Atlanta. The two were married in a lavish ceremony at her parents' home at 244 South Twelfth Street, on December 31, 1884. "The groom bore on his arm Mrs. Still, the bride's mother," reported the *Christian Recorder*, "and the bride was leaning on the arm of her father." Among the guests were old allies from their abolitionist days, including Passmore Williamson, Mary Grew, and Robert Purvis, as well as more recent colleagues of Still's, such as the Rev. Dr. I. N. Randall, president of Lincoln University; the Rev. Benjamin Tucker Tanner, editor of the *Christian Recorder*; and the influential Black activist and editor T. Thomas Fortune. Shortly after the wedding, the newly married couple left for Atlanta, where the groom served as pastor.[38]

The marriage of his youngest daughter was an opportunity for Still to reflect on his long career. His business had prospered and he had continued the philanthropic work to which he had devoted much of his life. His children had all graduated from college, and though his only grandchild, the beloved Willie, had died as a young child, William and Letitia Still looked forward to the many grandchildren they hoped would follow. Still could be forgiven for being optimistic about the future and proud of how far he had come.

. . .

As much as Still liked to portray himself as a businessman, above the fray of politics, he also continued to find himself drawn into the debate over Black partisanship. Still's vote in the mayoral election of 1874, and his subsequent defense of that vote, had laid out a philosophical case for breaking with the Republican Party, at least in state and local elections, but in subsequent years Still would become involved more directly in an effort to use Black independence as a means of forcing both political parties to make concessions to the demands of the Black community.

Despite the backlash to Still's statement of political independence in 1874, increasing numbers of Black Philadelphians began to question the wisdom of their fierce loyalty to the Republican Party. In an 1877 meeting at Liberty Hall, a "convention of colored voters" decried the lack of Black political appointees in the city, despite the unfailing support of Black voters for the Republican machine. "There should be," insisted the meeting, "at least one hundred patrolmen, and [black Philadelphians] should be represented in the gas, water, highway and all other city departments." It does not seem that Still himself participated in this convention, but he was surely sympathetic, and it is significant that they chose to meet at Liberty Hall, a building managed by Still.[39]

Political independence did not mean that Still had entirely turned his back on the Republican Party. When it lived up to its heritage as the party of Lincoln, he was an enthusiastic supporter. In 1880, Still was among a number of leading Black Philadelphians who formed a "Garfield Club," in order to support the election of the Republican James A. Garfield and to "rally their forces to the support of the Republican ticket." Garfield, in his time as a Radical Republican congressman from Ohio, had proven himself a reliable advocate for the rights of African Americans. As candidate for president, he had continued this support. "We have seen white men betray the flag and kill the Union," Garfield told a New York audience in 1880, "but in all that long, dreary war we never saw a traitor in black skin . . . And now that we have made them free, so long as we live we will stand by these black allies." Especially when it came to national politics, where Republicans still had the power, and sometimes the will, to fight for Black people in the states of the former Confederacy, Still was an enthusiastic supporter. He was just not willing to extend that support to local Republicans who had turned their backs on their Black allies.[40]

Locally, though, the sort of independent Black politics that Still had championed for years had begun to bear fruit. In the mayoral election of 1881, many Republicans had broken with the party to support Democrat Samuel King as a reform candidate who promised to reform the city's politics. Among those who had embraced King's candidacy were a significant number of Black voters, who saw King as a new sort of Democrat, a man who had rejected the white supremacist politics of his party. They recalled that he was the only Democrat to attend the funeral of Octavius Catto in 1871. King had also promised that as mayor he would hire Black police officers, something his opponent, the incumbent Republican mayor Stokley, had failed to do in almost a decade in office. Due to the defections of Republican voters, King won a surprise victory.[41]

When he took office, King followed through in his promise and quickly appointed the city's first Black police officers. Still took this as validation of his political strategy and organized a meeting, held at Liberty Hall, to celebrate both the act itself and its political implications. Still presided as president of the meeting, but the four Black police officers, Davis, Draper, Caldwell, and Carroll, were given the place of honor on the stage. Robert Purvis spoke first, somewhat hyperbolically comparing the men's appointments to Lincoln's Emancipation Proclamation and to Grant's endorsement of the right of Black men to vote. Purvis's presence was unsurprising, given that he had long sympathized with Still's call for political independence. Somewhat more surprising was the presence of Isaiah Wears, a staunch Republican who had criticized Still's willingness to support Democrats. Even Wears had to admit, however, that the political independence advocated by Black men like Still had born some fruit. "The white man needs to be taught liberty and human rights," announced Wears, "and the colored man has been teaching him." Wears might have had personal disagreements with Still in recent years, but he begrudgingly admitted that his old ally's strategy had forced Democrats to offer to Black Philadelphians what Republicans had not.[42]

Still would continue his push for Black independence in the coming years. In 1882, he joined Robert Purvis and other "colored Independent Republicans" in supporting the gubernatorial candidacy of John Stewart, who ran against the regular Republican, James Beaver. Once again, their critique focused on the corruption of the regular Republican Party and its abandonment of its past support for the rights of Black people. Because Republican voters split their votes between two candidates, Democrats were able to elect their man, Robert Pattison. Still's independence was praised by T. Thomas Fortune's *New York Globe*, which celebrated "such able men of the race as Mr. William Still" who "oppose such corruption and mismanagement of the party." Closer to home, though, Still was criticized by the normally sympathetic *Christian Recorder*, which defended its support of the regular Republican Party. "We grant that there is a measure, and possibly a very large measure, of rascality in the Republican Party," admitted the *Recorder*, "but pray tell us, how is it with the Democratic Party? One would think it all saintliness to hear these colored Independents talk; but both we and the country and the world know to the contrary." Like many Black leaders, they felt that for all its failings the Republican Party was still the party that offered Black voters the greatest protection, and a vote for an "independent" candidate was essentially a vote for the hated Democrats.[43]

Still hoped that his political independence would give him more leverage in pushing government officials to support Black rights. The following year, the Rev. Jabez P. Campbell, bishop of the AME Church and an ally of Still's, was forcibly removed from a first-class rail car while traveling through Georgia on church business. Still organized a public meeting to express outrage at Campbell's treatment, but he also pressed the Chester Arthur administration in Washington to take action in the case. He received responses both from the president's office and from the Department of Justice, indicating that they would look into the matter. It is unclear what, if anything, came of this effort (since evidently the conductor involved in the incident had been fired shortly thereafter), but nevertheless it shows that Still continued to involve himself in political affairs and that political independence did not mean removing himself from political matters altogether.[44]

In 1884, reports emerged that Still had gone one step further and supported the Democratic candidate for president, Grover Cleveland. It was one thing to support local Democrats, as Still continued to do, joining Purvis in a delegation of Black supporters honoring Samuel King, the Democratic mayor of Philadelphia, that same year. It was another to support a Democratic presidential candidate, even if he was running against the notoriously corrupt James G. Blaine. In the midst of the heated presidential campaign, the Democratic Harrisburg *Patriot* printed a lengthy profile of Still under the headline "A Negro Opponent of Blaine: An Old Philadelphia Ally of Garrison and Phillips Will Vote for Cleveland." According to the article, Still defended his vote largely on the grounds that Cleveland and the Democrats could be trusted with "purifying the administration from corruption, but he also defended the Democratic Party against charges that it was the enemy of Black people. "You don't share, then," the paper asked, "with your race their general distrust of the democratic party?" "Not the least," replied Still. "Why it's all foolishness to suppose that the democrats would antagonize the colored people. Revolutions never go backward, and parties out of power never degenerate—they grow. And besides, the democratic party of today is not what it was twenty years ago, nor is the republican party the same either."

The problem was, Still never gave this interview. Shortly after the publication of this "interview," Still denied that it had ever taken place. The entire thing, he said, was "a gross fabrication from beginning to end," a political ploy. Nevertheless, it was surely plausible that Still was willing to vote for Cleveland, even if he would not publicly admit to doing so. The Democratic Party was in the midst of a campaign to convince independent Republicans, men like Still, that it was safe to vote for Cleveland, and even if this published interview was a fabrication, it is suggestive of Still's general political status at the time, of the fact that he was representative of the sort of Republican voters who were willing to swing to the other side and who would, in fact, lead to Cleveland's victory in 1884.[45]

After the election, Still wrote a lengthy letter for the *Christian Recorder*, in which he reflected on Cleveland's victory. If he had not actually supported the Democrats, Still nevertheless saw great promise in the Democratic ascendency. According to Still, "the wise counsel of the large body of Independent Republicans" had helped to change the Democratic Party, leading the one-time party of slavery "to conciliate the colored people." He pointed especially to positive developments among Democrats in his own city and state, but he also saw reason for hope in the South. "I can't think," wrote Still, "that the Democratic party is going to butt her head against a stone wall in seeking to review old slavery prejudices and usages, to the detriment of the colored man." Overall, Still painted an optimistic picture of the progress that Black people had made, and were continuing to make, across the country. In hindsight, Still's optimism seems terribly naive, and certainly it seemed that way to many of his contemporaries. Nevertheless, it was reflective of both his liberal confidence in progress and his staunch religious faith. He closed by reminding his readers to place their faith in "the Great Captain of their salvation."[46]

Yet if Still sought to reassure his readers about the consequences of a Democratic victory, he again insisted that he himself was no Democrat. In fact, he admitted, he had supported neither major party in 1884, but had cast his vote for John St. John, the Prohibition Party candidate. Still had long been an advocate for temperance causes, but increasingly he would devote his time to the growing movement to elect candidates specifically pledged to the prohibition of alcohol. The Prohibition Party had been founded in 1869, and it increased its supporters in the ensuing years. Many party supporters saw their movement as an heir to abolitionism and consciously emulated the efforts of an earlier generation of reformers who used antislavery third parties to reorient the entire political system. In January 1885, the Prohibition Party put forward Still's name as candidate for magistrate in the Eighth Ward of Philadelphia. The following year Still appeared onstage at a mass meeting, held at the Academy of Music, supporting the gubernatorial bid of Prohibition candidate Charles S. Wolfe. In neither case was the Prohibition candidate elected, but neverthe-less, Still remained committed to the movement.[47]

In a certain sense, Still's support for the Prohibition Party seems an inevitable culmination of his political and reform career. Still had always coupled a belief in the power of reformers to bring about dramatic transformations in society with an equally firm belief in the importance of personal responsibility as the key to Black prog-ress. "Whoever may be in the Presidential chair at Washington," Still had written after the election of 1884, "there is for the race no permanent security and advancement to the degree desired without much self-denial, hard study, practical economy, patient endurance in well doing, by the seekers after a higher elevation ere the great boon can be fully attained." In this spirit, Still would also become increasingly involved in the movement to establish Black branches of the YMCA, an organization that sought to provide a "Christian" environment for young Black men who might otherwise be drawn to other, less wholesome diversions of urban life.[48]

Still had great hopes that such reforms could change the world, but he continued to draw on the past as a way of fueling the strug-gle for a more just future. In 1889, Still organized yet another commemoration of the abolitionist struggle, this time to celebrate "the first quarter century since the emancipation of negroes in this country." The meeting, hosted by the Pennsylvania Abolition Society, brought together a broad cross-section of the abolition movement and of the subsequent movement for Black progress. Old Still allies, both Black and white, were there, including Robert Purvis, Frances Ellen Watkins Harper, and William Furness, but there were younger activists there as well. There were religious and political leaders. There were representatives from the South, including General Samuel C. Armstrong of the Hampton Insti-tute, who spoke of the great progress being made in educating Black Southerners. A young Black educator from Alabama named Booker T. Washington had originally agreed to attend, but he had to back out at the last minute due to his wife's health problems.[49]

Indisputably, though, the star of the occasion was a giant of an earlier generation, Frederick Douglass. Still had invited Douglass, paying his expenses and even meeting him at the Broad Street train station, because he knew that the presence of the famed orator would energize the occasion like no other speaker could. As it so happened, Douglass was nursing a cold as he rose to speak, but if his illness meant he was not at his best, the audience seems not to have noticed. Douglass used his speech as an opportunity to reframe the struggle for Black progress. "I object at the outset, to calling the Southern question the negro problem. It is misleading," insisted Douglass. "It is illogical. It takes the burden from the great nation and places it on the shoulders of the negro." It was the nation, Douglass insisted, that needed to face the problem of how it treated its Black citizens, not those Black citizens alone.[50]

We can imagine Still nodding along with this sentiment, along with much of the audience. Then, however, Douglass shifted his focus, onto the proposed solutions to this problem. "Someone said recently," Douglass noted, "that the way to settle the Southern problem was to have a large portion of the negroes to go into the Democratic Party. Why, I would as soon go to a dram shop to promote temperance or to hell to get the good will of the devil." Perhaps Douglass looked over at the man who had invited him and who presided over the occasion. Perhaps not. In any case, it is hard to imagine that Still saw this as anything but a personal jab, even if a slight one. He and Douglass had enjoyed a mixed relationship over the years, but now, perhaps more than ever, Still felt the great shadow that Douglass cast.[51]

Whatever Still's reaction to this dig in the moment, their correspondence in the aftermath of the meeting suggests no ill will between the two men. Perhaps at this point Still had made peace with his place in the abolitionist firmament. He might not be Frederick Douglass, but Still was confident in the contributions he had made and which he continued to make to the struggle for Black progress. For forty years Still had been one of the most important Black activists in the struggle against slavery and in support of Black equality. That activism had for a time taken place behind the scenes, but for decades now Still had been recognized as one of the most important leaders not just in his adopted city of Philadelphia, but across the country. Still's status as a towering figure of his age was secure.[52]

THE DEATH OF WILLIAM STILL

On December 3, 1900, the *Philadelphia Inquirer* reported that William Still was sick, that he "has been confined to his home, 244 South Twelfth street for some time." Still had just passed his seventy-ninth birthday, and those years had caught up with him. Friends and family hoped that he would regain the "wonderful vitality" that had "borne him through several critical periods," but there were signs that Still's health was in steep decline.[1] About four years earlier, Still had been diagnosed with Bright's disease, what at the time was a catch-all term applied to kidney disease. Its defining feature was an excessive level of albumin in the urine, but it is not entirely clear what symptoms Still manifested. Typically, patients who were diagnosed with this ailment suffered from headaches, nausea, and vomiting, as well as from swelling of the face and of the extremities, first the feet and then later the hands. Function of the lungs and the heart were also often affected. In Still's case, there may also have been an alteration of his mental status.[2]

Physicians recommended that sufferers avoid dramatic variations of temperature, and in general that they avoid the cold if possible. If that was not possible, patients were encouraged to dress so as to protect from the cold, "woolen underclothing should be regularly used," recommended one expert, along with "light warm wraps." Physicians also saw diet as a critical means of managing

Bright's disease; consumption of milk was especially encouraged, and excessive consumption of alcohol was discouraged (not a problem for Still). Patients were advised to rest in bed, and sometimes physicians employed "kneading or rubbing" of swollen extremities to provide some relief. Unsurprisingly, treatment for Bright's disease was largely ineffective.[3]

This seems to have been true in Still's case. In April 1901, Still stepped down as president of the Pennsylvania Abolition Society. Upon the election of its new officers, the venerable institution offered a "minute of appreciation of the services of William Still, for many years president of the organization." They noted with regret "his extended condition of disability," which had made it impossible for him to continue to lead the organization. Still had given a substantial portion of his life to the fight against slavery and racial discrimination. That fight would continue, but Still's part in it was at an end.[4]

William Still died at the home where he and Letitia had moved in the past year, at 726 South Nineteenth Street, on July 14, 1902, due to heart trouble, presumably caused by his Bright's disease. "It was not unexpected," wrote one friend in a letter of condolence to Letitia, "and perhaps to him it was a relief." Memorial services were held at Central Presbyterian Church, where he had served as an elder for years. "I remember him," recalled another friend, as "a representative man of the most unblemished character, with a devotion to his home, to thee, to all, and most of all to God and the wide world of humanity and human rights."[5]

Still had continued to work up until the point when his illness made it impossible for him to do so. He had always been remarkably active, and while his pace slowed somewhat as he entered his seventies, Still remained a prominent presence in the activist and philanthropic circles of Philadelphia. He continued to serve as president of the Home for Aged and Infirm Colored Persons as late as 1900, though by the late 1890s it is not clear that Still was as active as he once had been. Nevertheless, he served as long as he could, and also lent his aid to other charitable endeavors that served Black Philadelphians. He helped to champion the new

Black YMCA, he was a member of the advisory board of the new Frederick Douglass Memorial Hospital and Training School, and he served as an elder of the Central Presbyterian Church. He continued to share his substantial wealth, and while he was less active in politics than he once had been, he would occasionally resurface, penning an article on "The Colored Man in Politics" in 1894, and joining in the fight to ensure the hiring of Black trolley workers in 1897.[6]

From time to time Still was called upon to share stories of the Underground Railroad, and in so doing to keep the abolitionist flame alive, but he was no longer the driving force in such meetings. He was instead an elder statesman, a connection to the past, called upon to say a few words. He was, as one account put it, among the "grey-bearded, earnest men, with silvery locks and narrowed countenances" who gathered to remember the old days. As others took responsibility for the continuing struggle for "the betterment of the condition of the race," Still helped remind them of the movement's glorious past, and in so doing helped inspire them to continue this work.[7]

Still's children also carried on his legacy, no doubt to their father's great pride. Caroline continued to practice medicine, but she also joined in many of her father's charitable causes. She was, for example, a member of the board of managers of the Home for Aged and Infirm Colored Persons. Her husband, the Rev. Matthew Anderson, also worked with his father-in-law, in particular in their joint effort to promote Black home ownership through the Berean Building and Loan Association, the largest such Black organization in Philadelphia. William Wilberforce Still, after a time serving as a lawyer and a teacher in South Carolina, returned to Philadelphia and entered the real estate business. Francis Ellen Still also returned to Philadelphia, where she resumed her work as a schoolteacher. Still's youngest surviving child, Robert, after graduating from Lincoln University, joined in his father's effort to challenge the allegiance of Black voters to the Republican Party, serving on the executive committee of the Colored Democratic League of Pennsylvania before his untimely death in 1896 at the age of thirty-one.[8]

Still may have remained physically active until 1900, but his illness seems to have affected his mind for some years before that. A letter of condolence to his daughter Frances Ellen noted that her father was "without mind for 6 years prior to his death, yet the body (without its usual exercise) lived beyond the allotted time." Perhaps his declining mental status was the result of a stroke, which would have been unsurprising due to his other diagnosed health issues. Eventually he could no longer continue his coal business, and in 1898 Still's coal yard no longer appeared in Boyd's Philadelphia business directory. The following year, Still sold the yard itself.[9]

Letitia Still would outlive her husband by more than five years. An account of her eighty-sixth birthday celebration in 1907 reported that she was "wonderfully preserved mentally and physically," but the following year, she passed away at the same Nineteenth Street home where her husband had died five years earlier, a home that would then pass on to their daughter Francis Ellen Still. Her eldest child, Caroline, signed her mother's death certificate, and then Letitia was laid to rest at Eden Cemetery, next to her husband.[10]

William Still died a respected man, treasured by friends and allies both in Philadelphia and around the country, and widely honored among both Black and white Americans as a hero of the struggle against slavery. Friends commissioned a bust of Still, to be displayed at the Home for Aged and Infirm Colored People, an institution to which he had devoted so many years of his life. Befitting Still's commitment to promoting Black artists, these friends secured the services of a young Philadelphia-born Black woman named Meta Vaux Warrick (later Fuller), who had studied in Paris at the Ecole des Beaux-Arts, and who would later go on to be an important figure in the Harlem Renaissance. The bust was displayed for the first time several months after his death, at a dedication ceremony; friends and colleagues gathered to remember Still and celebrate his legacy.[11]

While Philadelphians felt Still's death most acutely, newspapers across the country noted his passing, many praising him as "the Father of the Underground Railroad" (though this was a title Still had never claimed for himself) and celebrating him as "one of

the best-educated members of the negro race." Nearly all of the
obituaries noted that "he was for many years one of the most successful Afro-American businessmen in this country," though the
worth of the fortune he left behind was estimated at anywhere from
$100,000 to $1 million. More than a few mistakenly noted that he
had been born a slave and that he had helped his own mother "by
a most romantic escape from a slave dealer." Many of the obituaries recounted his first meeting with his brother Peter, which had
become not only the most famous incident in Still's life, but also a
distillation of the damage that slavery had done to Black families
and a demonstration of the ultimate resilience of those families.[12]

How did Still see his own legacy? What did he hope to have
left behind? As he grew older, Still increasingly sought to portray
his life as a rags-to-riches story. He especially liked to tell of how
he had arrived in Philadelphia nearly penniless, "with a capital of
$3.00 and a wardrobe even less in value." In this he was a clas-
sic exemplar of that nineteenth-century American ideal, the self-
made man. In this ideal, humble origins, even impoverished ones,
could be a blessing, serving as a training ground for men of skill
and discipline, preparing them for the struggles ahead. Ultimately,
a man succeeded or failed based on his own character, his own
willingness to work hard. Americans had long celebrated this ideal
as one of the defining characteristics of their nation, as one of the
things that set them apart from class-hardened European societies, and while wealthy businessmen were obviously the most vocal
champions of this ideal, they were hardly the only ones.[13]

For Still, while this celebration of his rise from poverty to
wealth might have echoed a largely white tradition, it was in fundamental ways distinct from it. For Black men like Still, the story
of individual progress always had a connection to the struggle to
promote the progress of the race. As historian John Stauffer has
noted of Frederick Douglass, another Black "self-made man," the
ability of a Black man to rise to wealth and prominence in the
United States was a blow to racist ideas that held that Black men
were incapable of doing so. Black men could do so through hard
work and self-improvement, but, as Stauffer has argued, to Douglass (and we might add, to Still) "the ultimate goal of such transformation was to improve society rather than to get rich." While

skeptical white observers might dismiss such men as exceptional, as unrepresentative of the Black masses, for exceptional Black men like Still and Douglass, their individual achievements were always about something larger than themselves. In a country where Black men had to be better, had to work harder, had to be smarter than their white countrymen in order to achieve the same success, each case of individual success was a blow to the system that made it difficult for Black men to prosper.[14]

As an abolitionist, however, Still's enduring legacy was less as a towering, heroic individual than as a connector, as someone who empowered ordinary Black people to find their own paths to freedom. Still's rivals might have sometimes dismissed him as an elitist, as a man only concerned with the Black upper class to which by the end of his life he had ascended, but his life's work showed otherwise. His friend William Wells Brown recalled that when traveling through the communities of Black refugees in Canada, as soon as it became known that he had come from the U.S., talk turned to William Still. "Did you know Mr. Still?" asked one woman. When Brown responded that he did, the woman exclaimed, "God love your heart!" Everywhere he went, Brown recalled, "as soon as it was known that I was well acquainted with William Still, the conversation turned entirely upon him." These fugitive slaves, then, these men and women he had helped to escape from bondage, would be Still's ultimate legacy. They would never forget the role he had played in their flight to freedom. Nor should we.[15]

ACKNOWLEDGMENTS

I have been working on this book for a long time, since before I even knew I was working on it. When I was researching my dissertation, which would become my first book, I kept uncovering material on William Still, an individual I knew a little about, but who kept turning up in unexpected places. I had far more Still material than I could possibly use for that book, so I filed it away, and when it came time to think about a second book project, I returned to it in earnest. I am glad I did.

This book could not have been written without the work of librarians and archivists who make it possible for writers to do the work we do. I would especially like to thank the staff at the following institutions: the Historical Society of Pennsylvania; the Library Company of Philadelphia; the Blockson Collection, Temple University; Friends Historical Library of Swarthmore College; Quaker and Special Collections, Haverford College; New York Public Library Special Collections; and the Presbyterian Historical Society. This book has also made me acutely aware of the fact that much of the material historians draw upon ends up in archives and historical societies only if it is first preserved and then donated to those institutions. The Still family, starting with William Still himself (who was, among other things, an archivist of the abolitionist movement) and continuing down to the present day, has been a custodian of the legacy of William Still's story. I hope that my book does justice to their generations of work.

Friends and colleagues have been more than generous with their time. Four individuals deserve special mention; each read the entire manuscript and each helped to make it a better book. Liz Varon has been an invaluable mentor. She was supportive when I doubted my ability to write this book, and she helped guide me as I took my first hesitant steps into the world of trade publishing. Her comments on the manuscript were characteristically incisive. Richard Blackett has been an enthusiastic supporter of this project since we first chatted about it in a conference hotel lobby. His careful reading of the manuscript saved me from some embarrassing blunders, and his vast knowledge of and insight into the abolitionist movement were invaluable to me. I had a pivotal conversation with Rich Newman early in the process of researching this book that helped me think about what sort of book I wanted to write. Later he read a version of the full manuscript and helped me to focus on the big questions I wanted the book to address. Finally, I was thrilled that Samuel C. Still, III, agreed to read the manuscript. I am a relative newcomer to the history of William Still, but Sam, who is the direct descendent of William's elder brother, James Still, has been sharing stories of the Still family for his whole life. He, too, caught a few errors that had slipped through, but more importantly, my conversations with him about the book and about William Still have immeasurably deepened my understanding of the history I have tried to write.

Others have read smaller portions of the book but their contributions have also made the book far better than it would have otherwise been. Martha Jones read several chapters and offered crucial advice. Many others read either full chapters or commented on my work in some other form, including Cory Brooks, Tom Cutterham, Catherine Denial, Nicole Dombrowski-Risser, Craig Thompson Friend, Kelly Gray, Christian Koot, John Larson, Brian Luskey, Jeffery Malanson, Mike Masatsugu, Caleb McDaniel, Margaret Newall, Tunde Oduntan, David Waldstreicher, and Nic Wood. I would like to especially thank Donna Rilling for sharing with me her research on Octavius Catto, research that helped me to rethink my understanding of Catto and Still's relationship.

Also, thanks to Jim Duffin for help navigating nineteenth-century Philadelphia property deeds.

While I was writing this book, I profited from the rich, scholarly home that is the History Department of Towson University. I am especially grateful for the support of two different chairs, Ronn Pineo and Christian Koot, plus an interim chair, Alhena Gadotti, and two different deans, Terry Cooney and Chris Chulos; this support included a sabbatical over the academic year 2017–2018, which enabled me to complete the bulk of the research for this book. I have also benefitted from my students more than they realize. Teaching makes us better historians, and I have especially learned from the students in my writing seminar on African American biography. Over the course of several semesters, this has been an opportunity to deepen my own connection with the long tradition of chronicling Black lives and to share that tradition with students.

Writing a book is a difficult thing, but publishing one is something else altogether. Thank you to Anthony Arnove at Roam Agency for seeing promise in this book and in helping me convince others to see that promise as well. It has been an honor to publish this book at Knopf, which has always been my dream press. I was doubly honored to work with Andrew Miller as my editor, and with his team, especially Maris Dyer and Tiara Sharma. A long time ago, Andrew told me that if I ever needed any advice, I should get in touch with him. It took me far too long to take him up on that offer, but I am glad that I finally did.

Above all else, I am grateful to my family for all of their support over the years I have spent working on this book. They have heard me talk endlessly about William Still, so I hope they have come to share a little bit of my passion for his story. My wife, Gretchen, is a true partner in life. I cannot imagine how this book would have happened without her. Our daughters, Katherine and Anna, have kept me grounded. Perhaps had I not spent all those afternoons coaching softball, or taking them to soccer practices or piano lessons, I might have finished this book sooner, but I do not regret that delay in the least. Lastly, my son, Marcus, will be off at college by the time this is in print. I miss the boy you were when I started writing this book, but I am proud of the young man you have become. I look forward to what is next. And so, this book is for you.

NOTES

ABBREVIATIONS USED IN NOTES

BAP—Black Abolitionists Papers, 1830–1865, https://proquest.com/bap
HSP—Historical Society of Pennsylvania
SCSA—Social, Civil, and Statistical Association of the Colored People
of Pennsylvania
UGRR—William Still, *Still's Underground Rail Road Records, with a Life
of the Author*, rev. ed. (Philadelphia: Published by the Author, 1883)
WSB—William Still Collection, Charles L. Blockson Afro-American
Collection, Temple University

INTRODUCTION

1. The opening scene is reconstructed from two sources, a letter written by William Still less than a week after the incident and a narrative written in 1856 by Kate Pickard from "the most authentic sources." The dialogue comes from Pickard's narrative, though I have only included such dialogue as corresponds to Still's presumably more reliable depiction. William Still to J. Miller McKim, Aug. 8, 1850, *Pennsylvania Freeman*, Aug. 22, 1850; Kate E. R. Pickard, *The Kidnapped and the Ransomed. Being the Personal Recollections of Peter Still and his wife "Vina" after Forty Years of Slavery* (Syracuse, NY: William T. Hamilton, 1856), 243–50.

2. This description is based on both William Wells Brown's 1862 written description and on the c. 1850s daguerreotype of Still in the collective portrait of the Philadelphia Vigilance Committee. William Wells Brown, *The Black Man, His Antecedents, His Genius, and His Achievements* (New York: Thomas Hamilton, 1863), 211–14; "Philadelphia Vigilance Committee, 1850–1859," daguerreotype, Boston Public Library, Print Department Collection.

3. James J. Gigantino II, *The Ragged Road to Abolition: Slavery and Freedom in New Jersey, 1775–1865* (Philadelphia: University of Pennsylvania Press, 2015); Richard Bell, *Stolen: Five Free Boys Kid-*

napped into *Slavery and Their Astonishing Odyssey Home* (New York: 37 INK, 2019); Gary B. Nash, *Forging Freedom: The Formation of Philadelphia's Black Community, 1720–1840* (Cambridge, MA: Harvard University Press, 1988); Carol Wilson, *Freedom at Risk: The Kidnapping of Free Blacks in America, 1780–1865* (Lexington: University Press of Kentucky, 1994). The phrase "in the shadow of slavery" is borrowed from Leslie Harris's fantastic study of African Americans in New York City, *In the Shadow of Slavery: African Americans in New York City, 1626–1863* (Chicago: University of Chicago Press, 2003).

4. On Douglass, see David W. Blight, *Frederick Douglass: Prophet of Freedom* (New York: Simon & Schuster, 2018). On Tubman, see Kate Clifford Larson, *Bound for the Promised Land: Harriet Tubman, Portrait of an American Hero* (New York: Ballantine, 2004), and Catherine Clinton, *Harriet Tubman: The Road to Freedom* (Boston: Little, Brown, 2004).

5. Scholarship on the Underground Railroad is voluminous, but for recent work, see Eric Foner, *Gateway to Freedom: The Hidden History of the Underground Railroad* (New York: W. W. Norton, 2015); R. J. M. Blackett, *The Captive's Quest for Freedom: Fugitive Slaves, the 1850 Fugitive Slave Law, and the Politics of Slavery* (New York: Cambridge University Press, 2018); Fergus M. Bordewich, *Bound for Canaan: The Underground Railroad and the War for the Soul of America* (New York: Amistad, 2005); Cheryl Janifer LaRoche, *Free Black Communities and the Underground Railroad: The Geography of Resistance* (Urbana: University of Illinois Press, 2013); David W. Blight, *Passages to Freedom: The Underground Railroad in History and Memory* (Washington, DC: Smithsonian Books in association with the National Underground Railroad Freedom Center, Cincinnati, Ohio, 2004); Damian Alan Pargas, ed., *Fugitive Slaves and Spaces of Freedom in North America* (Gainesville: University of Florida Press, 2018); Alice L. Baumgartner, *South to Freedom: Runaway Slaves to Mexico and the Road to the Civil War* (New York: Basic Books, 2020).

6. Still has been featured in innumerable works on abolition and the Underground Railroad, but overviews of Still's life can be found in Larry Gara, "William Still and the Underground Railroad," *Pennsylvania History* 28, no. 1 (January 1961): 33–44; Lurie Kahn, *William Still and the Underground Railroad: Fugitive Slaves and Family Ties* (Bloomington, IN: iUniverse, 2010); William Kashatus, *William Still: The Underground Railroad and the Angel at Philadelphia* (Notre Dame, IN: University of Notre Dame Press, 2021).

7. William Wells Brown, *The Black Man, His Antecedents, His Genius, and His Achievements* (New York: Thomas Hamilton, 1863), 211.

8. "William Still Dead," *Chronicle* (Augusta, GA), July 15, 1902; "Father of the Underground," *Boston Herald*, July 15, 1902; "In the Death of William Still," *Appeal* [Saint Paul, MN], July 19, 1902.

CHAPTER ONE

1. UGRR, vi; James Still, *Early Recollections and Life of Dr. James Still* (Philadelphia: J. B. Lippincott & Co., 1877), 17; E. M. Woodward and John F. Hageman, *History of Burlington and Mercer Counties, New Jersey* (Philadelphia: Everts. & Peck, 1883), 413; *Census for 1820. Published by Authority of an Act of Congress Under the Direction of the Secretary of State* (Washington, DC: Gales & Seaton, 1821), 69. In a biographical essay published in the 1883 edition of Still's Underground Railroad book, Still is identified as the youngest of eighteen children, though historians and genealogists have not identified all of these Still children. It is likely that at least some died in their infancy or were stillborn.

2. James P. Boyd, *William Still: His Life and Work to This Time*, foreword by Samuel C. Still (Galloway, NJ: South Jersey Culture and History Center, 2017), x–xi; *Return of the Whole Number of Persons within the Several Districts of the United States . . .* (Washington, DC: Department of State, 1801), 50. The foreword to this edition of Boyd's book, written by Samuel Still, a direct descendant of James Still, is invaluable for its insight into the Still family's time in bondage.

3. Ira Berlin, *Generations of Captivity: A History of African American Slaves* (Cambridge, MA: Harvard University Press, 2003), 111–14.

4. Berlin, *Generations of Captivity*, 209–30; T. Stephen Whitman, *The Price of Freedom: Slavery and Manumission in Baltimore and Early National Maryland* (Lexington: University Press of Kentucky, 1997), 8–25.

5. Whitman, *Price of Freedom*, 93–139; UGRR, iv, 37; Boyd, *William Still*, xi; Caroline County Court land records, 1797–1799 F., p. 370. Many thanks to Samuel Still III for sharing with me a copy of this manumission record.

6. Neither William's nor Peter Still's account is explicit about the year of this flight. However, William's account indicates that Peter was six at the time, and the Census of 1860 and family records indicate that Peter was born in 1801. These sources also suggest that

Samuel Still, the first Still child born in New Jersey, was born in 1807. "Catalogue of Children of Leven Still and Charity his wife," n.d., Peter Still papers, 1850–1875, Rutgers University, Special Collections, https://doi.org/doi:10.7282/T3H41RK7.

7. UGRR, iv–v; Thomas Cushing and Charles Sheppard, *History of the Counties of Gloucester, Salem, and Cumberland New Jersey* (Philadelphia: Everts & Peck, 1883), 681; Christopher P. Barton, "Antebellum African-American Settlements in Southern New Jersey," *African Diaspora Archaeology Newsletter* 12, no. 4 (Dec. 2009): 1–14; Boyd, *William Still*, xii.

8. UGRR, 37; 1800 U.S. Federal Census, Caroline County, Maryland, digital image s.v. "Alexander Griffith," Ancestry.com.

9. UGRR, v.

10. UGRR, 37; Kate Pickard, *The Kidnapped and Ransomed: Being the Personal Recollections of Peter Still and his wife "Vina," After Forty Years of Slavery* (Syracuse, NY: William T. Hamilton, 1856), 28.

11. Woodward and Hageman, *History of Burlington and Mercer Counties*, 413–15; UGRR, 38.

12. UGRR, v; John McPhee, *The Pine Barrens* (New York: Farrar, Straus, and Giroux, 1968), 16–17, 24, 43–44.

13. UGRR, v–vii; J. Still, *Early Recollections*, 13–14; McPhee, *Pine Barrens*, 25.

14. "Catalogue of Children of Leven Still and Charity his wife"; J. Still, *Early Recollections*, 16–18; UGRR, v–vi. Three more Still children would be born before William: John in 1815, Charles in 1817, and Joseph in 1819.

15. UGRR, vi; J. Still, *Early Recollections*, 18.

16. J. Still, *Early Recollections*, 19; UGRR, viii.

17. UGRR, viii–ix; J. Still, *Early Recollections*, 19; *The Young Man's Own Book* (Philadelphia: Key and Biddle, 1832).

18. Elizabeth R. Varon, *Disunion! The Coming of the Civil War, 1789–1859* (Chapel Hill: University of North Carolina Press, 2008), 39–49; John Craig Hammond, *Slavery, Freedom, and Expansion in the Early American West* (Charlottesville: University of Virginia Press, 2007), 150–68.

19. James Gigantino, "'The Whole North Is Not Abolitionized': Slavery's Slow Death in New Jersey, 1830–1860," *Journal of the Early Republic* 34, no. 3 (Fall 2014): 411–37; Hartog, *The Trouble with Minna: A Case of Slavery and Emancipation in the Antebellum North* (Chapel Hill: University of North Carolina Press, 2018), 118.

20. James J. Gigantino, *The Ragged Road to Abolition: Slavery and Freedom in New Jersey, 1775–1865* (Philadelphia: University of Pennsylvania Press, 2015), 215–20.

21. UGRR, vii–viii; Still's account does not tell us what year this event took place, but Gabriel, also known as "Able," had married Mahala Still in 1826. New Jersey, U.S., Marriage Records, 1670–1965, s.v. "Able Thompson," Ancestry.com.

22. Paul J. Polgar, *Standard Bearers of Equality: America's First Abolitionist Movement* (Chapel Hill: Published for the Omohundro Institute of Early American History and Culture, Williamsburg, Virginia, by the University of North Carolina Press, 2019); Nicholas P. Wood, "A 'Class of Citizens': The Earliest Black Petitioners to Congress and Their Quaker Allies," *William & Mary Quarterly* 74, no. 1 (Jan. 2017): 109–44; Richard S. Newman, *The Transformation of American Abolitionism: Fighting Slavery in the Early Republic* (Chapel Hill: University of North Carolina Press, 2002), 131–51; David Walker, *Walker's Appeal to the Coloured Citizens of the World . . .*, 3rd ed. (Boston, 1830), 86; Manisha Sinha, *The Slave's Cause: A History of Abolition* (New Haven, CT: Yale University Press, 2016), 229–39, 250–53.

23. UGRR, ix; Sinha, *The Slave's Cause*, 304–5.

24. *Colored American*, March 4, 1837; UGRR, ix–x.

25. "Responsibility of Colored People in the Free States," *Colored American*, March 3, 1837.

26. UGRR, x; U.S. Quaker Meeting Records, 1688–1935, Births and Deaths, Philadelphia Yearly Meeting Minutes, Haverford College, s.v. "Joshua Borton," Ancestry.com.

27. UGRR, x–xi; J. Still, *Early Recollections*, 19; New Jersey, Surrogate Court (Burlington County), digital image, s.v. "Levin Still" (1844), Ancestry.com.

28. UGRR, xl; Daniel Walker Howe, *What Hath God Wrought: The Transformation of America, 1815–1848* (New York: Oxford University Press, 2007), 289–91; "Wm. Miller's Address," *The Midnight Cry*, Nov. 18, 1842.

29. UGRR, xi; Jonathan Butler, "From Millerism to Seventh-day Adventism: 'Boundlessness to Consolidation,'" *Church History* 55, no. 1 (March 1986): 50–64.

30. David Walker, *Appeal*, 79; Noyes quoted in Henry Mayer, *All on Fire: William Lloyd Garrison and the Abolition of Slavery* (New York: W. W. Norton & Co., 1998), 225.

CHAPTER TWO

1. UGRR, xi–xii; James Still, *Early Recollections and Life of Dr. James Still* (Philadelphia, 1877), 42, 69. James Still recalled visiting his sister, Kitturah, in Philadelphia when he was a boy. He also mentions calling for "sisters" to come from Philadelphia when their father died in December 1842, though only Mary is mentioned by name. This minor inconsistency in the documentary record illustrates one of the difficulties in uncovering this period in Still's life. In contrast to his later years, for which historians have a substantial and varied base of documentation, for Still's early years we are reliant on just a few major sources. Perhaps most important of all is an account of Still's life, written in 1883 by James Boyd and published at the beginning of a later edition of *Still's Underground Rail Road Records*. Even though this sketch was not written by Still himself, we have reason to take it seriously as a reflection of his own memories. Boyd clearly interviewed Still for the project and includes extensive direct quotations from Still himself. Beyond this, Still took a hands-on approach to all aspects of his book, from its composition to its marketing and distribution. It is hard to imagine that he did not pay careful attention to the content of this biographical sketch. At the same time, this sketch was written almost forty years after Still moved to Philadelphia; it stands to reason that some details are slightly mistaken (the spelling of names for example). It is sometimes possible to confirm details of Boyd's sketch with other independent evidence, but in many cases, this is simply not possible. In those cases, I have tried to be clear about my sources and my reasons for trusting or doubting them.

2. UGRR, xii; "Tremendous Excitement in Philadelphia," *Liberator*, May 25, 1838; Samuel Otter, *Philadelphia Stories: America's Literature of Race and Freedom* (New York: Oxford University Press, 2010), 157–65; Donna J. Rilling, *Making Houses, Crafting Capitalism: Builders in Philadelphia, 1790–1850* (Philadelphia: University of Pennsylvania Press, 2001), 10–13; U.S. Census Bureau, "Population of the 100 Largest Cities and Other Urban Places in the United States: 1790 to 1990," https://www.census.gov/library/working-papers/1998/demo/POP-twps0027.html.

3. Gary B. Nash, *Forging Freedom: The Formation of Philadelphia's Black Community, 1720–1840* (Cambridge, MA: Harvard University Press, 1988), 158–71; Nicholas Wood, "'A Sacrifice on the Altar of Slavery': Doughface Politics and Black Disenfranchise-

ment in Pennsylvania, 1837–1838," *Journal of the Early Republic* 31, no. 1 (Spring 2011): 75–106. As Van Gosse has shown, Black Pennsylvanians outside Philadelphia had been voters prior to 1838, though he is somewhat more dismissive of the non-electoral political engagement of Black Philadelphians than I am. *The First Reconstruction: Black Politics in America from the Revolution to the Civil War* (Chapel Hill: University of North Carolina Press, 2021), 94–141.

4. Nash, *Forging Freedom*, 158–71.

5. Harry Kyriakodis, *Northern Liberties: The Story of a Philadelphia River Ward* (Charleston, SC: The History Press, 2012), 69–79; U.S. Census, "Historical Census Statistics by Race, 1790–1990, and Hispanic Origin, 1970–1990, for Large Cities and Other Urban Places in the United States," https://www.census.gov/library /working-papers/2005/demo/POP-twps0076.html; Hexamer & Locher, *Maps of the City of Philadelphia*, 1858–1860, Map Collection, Free Library of Philadelphia, Greater Philadelphia Geo-History Network, http://www.philageohistory.org/rdic-images /view-image.cfm/HXL1860-Super-Index (accessed May 31, 2018); Census of 1847 via Theodore Hershberg. Philadelphia Social History Project: Pennsylvania Abolition Society and Society of Friends Manuscript Census Schedules, 1838, 1847, 1856 (Ann Arbor, MI: Inter-university Consortium for Political and Social Research [distributor], 2009-02-26), https://doi.org/10.3886/ICPSR03805.v1. The manuscript of the 1847 "Statistical Inquirery into the Condition of the People of Color of the City and Districts of Philadelphia," conducted by the Philadelphia Yearly Meeting of the Society of Friends, is held by the Friends Historical Library at Swarthmore College.

6. UGRR, xii; Hexamer & Locher, *Maps*.

7. UGRR, xii; Michael Feldberg, *The Philadelphia Riots of 1844: A Study in Ethnic Conflict* (Westport, CT: Greenwood Press, 1975), 111–13.

8. Emma Jones Lapsansky, "'Since They Got Those Separate Churches,": Afro-Americans and Racism in Jacksonian Philadelphia," *American Quarterly* 32, no. 1 (Spring 1980): 54–78; Andrew K. Diemer, *The Politics of Black Citizenship: Free African Americans in the Mid-Atlantic Borderland, 1817–1863* (Athens: University of Georgia Press, 2016), 126–27.

9. Nash, *Forging Freedom*, 246–53; Theodore Hershberg, "Free Blacks in Antebellum Philadelphia: A Study of Ex-Slaves, Free-

born, and Socioeconomic Decline," in *Philadelphia: Work, Space, Family, and Group Experience in the 19th Century*, ed. Theodore Hershberg (New York: Oxford University Press, 1981), 368–91.

10. Census of 1847; Nash, *Forging Freedom*, 253; UGRR, xiii; "Importance of the Mechanic Arts to Colored Youth," *Colored American*, Dec. 22, 1838.

11. UGRR, xiii; Census of 1847; Rilling, *Making Houses*, 103–11.

12. Rilling, *Making Houses*, 105; UGRR, xiii.

13. Nash, *Forging Freedom*, 253; Walter Licht, *Getting Work: Philadelphia, 1840–1950* (Cambridge, MA: Harvard University Press, 1993), 133; Jacqueline Jones, *American Work: Four Centuries of Black and White Labor* (New York: W. W. Norton), 256.

14. UGRR, xiii; Theodore Hershberg et. al.,"The 'Journey to Work': An Empirical Investigation of Work, Residence and Transportation, Philadelphia, 1850 and 1880," in Hershberg, *Philadelphia*, 128–73.

15. Census of 1847. His name is spelled "Shankland" in the 1845 Philadelphia directory, and his occupation is listed as "carter." There are three other Shanklands listed, but none of them seem likely to be the man that Still describes. *McElroy's Philadelphia City Directory* (Philadelphia: Edward C. & John Biddle, 1845), 319.

16. UGRR, xiv; Census of 1847.

17. UGRR, xiv; Nash, *Forging Freedom*, 251–52; W. E. B. Du Bois, *The Philadelphia Negro: A Social Study, with a New Introduction by Elijah Anderson* (1899; Philadelphia: University of Pennsylvania Press, 1996), 33.

18. UGRR, xiv; John Fanning Watson, *Annals of Philadelphia and Pennsylvania . . .* , vol. 1 (Philadelphia: A. Hart, 1850), 240; Nash, *Forging Freedom*, 215. Watson comments that early oyster cellars "were entirely managed by blacks."

19. George Lippard, *The Quaker City: or, The Monks of Monk Hall . . .* (Philadelphia: Published by the Author, 1847), 9.

20. UGRR, xiv; Kyriakodis, *Philadelphia's Lost Waterfront*, 44–45.

21. UGRR, xiv.

22. Ibid.; Watson, *Annals*, vol. 1, 240; Juliet E. K. Walker, *The History of Black Business in America: Capitalism, Race, and Entrepreneurship* (Chapel Hill: University of North Carolina Press, 2009), 141–44; Census of 1847.

23. UGRR, xv; Rilling, *Making Houses*, 174–75.

24. UGRR, xv; "Notices," Philadelphia *Public Ledger*, Jan. 12, 1846; Licht, *Getting Work*, 132; Watson, *Annals*, vol. 1, 240.

25. UGRR, xv–xvi; *O'Brien's Wholesale Business Directory* (Philadelphia: King & Baird, 1844), 208; Hexamer & Locher, *Maps.*

26. UGRR, xvi; *McElroy's City Directory*, 1845, 105; Elwyn Family Papers [Finding Aid], Portsmouth Athenaeum, Portsmouth, NH, https://portsmouthathenaeum.org/langdon-whipple-elwyn-50/ (retrieved July 13, 2021).

27. UGRR, xvi.

28. "An Afternoon Walk," *The Friend: A Religious and Literary Journal*, Dec. 2, 1847, 12; Martin R. Delany to Frederick Douglass, *The North Star*, March 3, 1849; April R. Haynes, *Riotous Flesh: Women, Physiology, and the Solitary Vice in Nineteenth-Century America* (Chicago: University of Chicago Press, 2015), 98–99.

29. "An Afternoon Walk"; "Letter from Philadelphia," *Antislavery Standard*, March 18, 1847; Committee for the Improvement of Colored People, Minute Book, Dec. 24, 1845, Pennsylvania Abolition Society Papers (HSP).

30. Philadelphia Saving Fund Society Records: Names and Addresses of Depositors, 1836–1845 (HSP), p. 1828. Microform.

31. David L. Mason, "Savings Societies," in *Encyclopedia of Greater Philadelphia*, http://philadelphiaencyclopedia.org/archive/savings -societies/ (accessed June 11, 2018); James M. Willcox, *A History of the Philadelphia Saving Fund Society* (Philadelphia: J. B. Lippincott, 1916), 141–42.

32. 1900 United States Federal Census, Ward 8, Philadelphia, Pennsylvania, digital image, s.v. "Letitia George," Ancestry.com.

33. Census of 1847.

34. Philadelphia Saving Fund Society Records (HSP), p. 1828; *McElroy's Philadelphia City Directory* (Philadelphia: Edward C. & John Biddle, 1841), 244.

35. George Green Shackelford, *Jefferson's Adoptive Son: The Life of William Short, 1759–1849* (Lexington: University Press of Kentucky, 1993); William Short to Thomas Jefferson, Feb. 27, 1798, https://founders.archives.gov/documents/Jefferson/01-30-02-0098; "American Colonization Society," Philadelphia *North American*, Feb. 21, 1846; "Local Items," Philadelphia *Inquirer*, Nov. 1, 1847.

36. Haynes, *Riotous Flesh*, 99; Joseph Boromé, "The Vigilant Committee of Philadelphia," *Pennsylvania Magazine of History and Biography* 92, no. 3 (July 1968): 320–51; "At a Meeting of the Vigilant Association," *National Reformer* 1, no. 8 (April 1839): 119.

37. Carol Wilson, *Freedom at Risk: The Kidnapping of Free Blacks in America, 1780–1865* (Lexington: University Press of Kentucky,

1994), 9–39. For a closer look at kidnapping and slave-catching in Philadelphia, see Elliot Drago, "Neither Northern nor Southern: The Politics of Slavery and Freedom in Philadelphia, 1820–1847" (PhD diss., Temple University, 2017).

38. UGRR, vii.

39. Sean Patrick Adams, *Home Fires: How Americans Kept Warm in the 19th Century* (Baltimore: Johns Hopkins University Press, 2014), 60.

40. UGRR, xvii; *African Repository and Colonial Journal* 20 (Dec. 1844): 382. The U.S. Census records Wurts's son as "William W." but later sources indicate that the W stood for "Wilberforce." 1850 United States Federal Census, Trenton West Ward, Mercer County, New Jersey, digital image, s.v. "William Wurtz," Ancestry.com.

41. Thomas Young to William Wurts, March 15, 1847; June 3, 1847, Wurts Family Papers (HSP).

42. UGRR, xviii.

43. UGRR, xviii; Committee for the Improvement of Colored People, Minute Book, Jan. 2, 1846, Pennsylvania Abolition Society Papers (HSP).

44. Ira V. Brown, "Miller McKim and Pennsylvania Abolition," *Pennsylvania History* 30, no. 1 (Winter 1963): 56–72.

45. Boromé, "The Vigilant Committee," 323, 336–51.

46. UGRR, xvii; "Mr. Humphries and Mr. Lester," *Pennsylvania Freeman*, Jan. 8, 1846; Boromé, "The Vigilant Committee," 351.

47. UGRR, xviii; Census of 1847.

48. Brian P. Luskey, *On the Make: Clerks and the Quest for Capital in Nineteenth-Century America* (New York: New York University Press, 2010); Michael Zakim, *Accounting for Capitalism: The World the Clerk Made* (Chicago: University of Chicago Press, 2018), 3.

49. UGRR, xvii; Boromé, "The Vigilant Committee," 328.

50. UGRR, xviii–xix; Census of 1847; *McElroy's City Directory* (1849), 361. Today this street is named Rodman Street and stretches the length of the city, but in the nineteenth century, it had a different name on each block. See Hexamer & Locher, *Maps*.

51. UGRR, xix; Minute Books of the Board of Managers, Dec. 22, 1847, Jan. 6, 1848, Apprentices Library Company of Philadelphia Records (HSP).

52. UGRR, xix.

53. Margaret Hope Bacon, *But One Race: The Life of Robert Purvis* (Albany: State University of New York Press, 2010); Boromé, "The Vigilant Committee," 324. On the concept of practical abolition,

see Graham Russell Hodges, *David Ruggles: A Radical Black Abolitionist and the Underground Railroad in New York City* (Chapel Hill: University of North Carolina Press, 2010), xxx.

54. This is the argument made by Boromé.

55. In addition to the gap in the extant records of the Philadelphia Vigilance Committee, there is almost no mention of the Vigilance Committee in the *Pennsylvania Freeman* for these years, in contrast with the sporadic mention between 1837 and 1842.

56. Richard Bell, "Making Tracks: Naming and Framing the Underground Railroad," paper presented at Black Lives and Freedom Journeys: The Legacies of the Still Family of Philadelphia, McNeil Center, Philadelphia, Oct. 7–8, 2021; 1850 United States Federal Census, Moyamensing Ward 2, Philadelphia, Pennsylvania, digital image, s.v. "William Steel," Ancestry.com; Erica Ball, *To Live an Antislavery Life: Personal Politics and the Antebellum Black Middle Class* (Athens: University of Georgia Press, 2012).

CHAPTER THREE

1. Numbering of streets would eventually change, so that earlier it was recorded as 31 North Fifth Street, but at this point it was 107.

2. Ira V. Brown, "Miller McKim and Pennsylvania Abolition," *Pennsylvania History* 30, no. 1 (Winter 1963): 56–59.

3. Ibid., 60–61.

4. UGRR, 659.

5. Brown, "Miller McKim," 72.

6. "The Free Produce Store," *Pennsylvania Freeman*, Sept. 23, 1847, 4; "Green Corn in All Seasons," *Pennsylvania Freeman*, Feb. 21, 1850.

7. UGRR, xviii–xix.

8. See, for example, "Slavery the Destroyer," *Pennsylvania Freeman*, Oct. 14, 1847.

9. "A Brisk Business," *Pennsylvania Freeman*, Oct. 7, 1847; UGRR, 42, 46.

10. William Still, *Journal C of the Underground Railroad, 1852–1857*, HSP.

11. Manisha Sinha, *The Slave's Cause: A History of Abolition* (New Haven, CT: Yale University Press, 2016), 256–65.

12. Brown, "Miller McKim," 64–65, quote on 65; Carol Faulkner, *Lucretia Mott's Heresy: Abolition and Women's Rights in Nineteenth-Century America* (Philadelphia: University of Pennsylvania Press),

82–83; Margaret Hope Bacon, *But One Race: The Life of Robert Purvis* (Albany: State University of New York Press, 2010), 114; "Annual Report of the Executive Committee," Eighth Annual Meeting, Pennsylvania Anti-Slavery Society, Records, 1837–1854, HSP.

13. Lucretia Mott to George Combe and Cecelia Combe, March 3, 1846, *Selected Letters of Lucretia Coffin Mott,* ed. Beverly Wilson Palmer et al. (Urbana: University of Illinois Press, 2002), 137–38; "Annual Report of the Executive Committee," Ninth Annual Meeting, Pennsylvania Anti-Slavery Society, Records, 1837–1854, HSP; Andrew K. Diemer, *The Politics of Black Citizenship: Free African Americans in the Mid-Atlantic Borderland, 1817–1863* (Athens: University of Georgia Press, 2016), 138–39.

14. "From Harrisburg," Philadelphia *Public Ledger,* Feb. 8, 1847; "Anti-Kidnapping Law of Pennsylvania," *Signal of Liberty* (Ann Arbor, MI), June 5, 1847.

15. Elizabeth R. Varon, *Disunion! The Coming of the Civil War, 1789–1859* (Chapel Hill: University of North Carolina Press, 2008), 186–94.

16. Stanley Harrold, *Border War: Fighting over Slavery Before the Civil War* (Chapel Hill: University of North Carolina Press, 2010), 116–27; Thomas D. Morris, *Free Men All: The Personal Liberty Laws of the North, 1780–1861* (Baltimore: Johns Hopkins University Press, 1974).

17. "Local Affairs," Philadelphia *Public Ledger,* May 4, 1847, 2; *Case of the Slave Isaac Brown: an Outrage Exposed* (Philadelphia, 1847), 2.

18. "Local Affairs," Philadelphia *Public Ledger,* May 5, 1847, 2.

19. *Case of the Slave Isaac Brown,* 1–3.

20. Ibid., 4–5, italics in original.

21. "Gov. Pratt's Message," *Baltimore Sun,* Dec. 29, 1847.

22. Lucretia Mott to George Combe, April 26, 1847, *Letters of Lucretia Mott,* 148–51.

23. "A Brisk Business," *Pennsylvania Freeman,* Oct. 7, 1847.

24. Seventh Annual Meeting, Pennsylvania Anti-Slavery Society, Report of Executive Committee, Records, 1837–1854, HSP.

25. UGRR, 649.

26. On Mott's attitude toward the Vigilance Committee in the 1840s, see Faulkner, *Lucretia Mott's Heresy,* 113–14.

27. William Craft and Ellen Craft, *Running a Thousand Miles for Freedom; or, the Escape of William and Ellen Craft from Slavery* (London: William Tweedie, 1860), 2; R. J. M. Blackett, *Beating Against the*

Barriers: The Lives of Six Nineteenth-Century Afro-Americans (Ithaca, NY: Cornell University Press, 1986), 87–89.

28. Craft and Craft, *Running a Thousand Miles*, 42–77, quote on 77.

29. Ibid., 81–82; UGRR, 370.

30. Henry Brown, *Narrative of the Life of Henry Box Brown, Written by Himself* (Manchester, UK: Lee and Glynn, 1851), 1–47; Jeffrey Ruggles, *The Unboxing of Henry Brown* (Richmond: Library of Virginia, 2003), 15, 20–21.

31. Lucretia Mott places Miller McKim and Cyrus Burleigh in the office at the time of Smith's visit. She makes no mention of Still, though he was almost certainly there as well. Lucretia Mott to Joseph and Ruth Dugdale, March 28, 1849, *Mott Letters*, 178–80.

32. Ruggles, *Unboxing*, 30–31; UGRR, 82.

33. UGRR, 83–84; Brown, *Life of Henry Box Brown*, 57.

34. Charles Rosenberg, "Bustill, Joseph Cassey," Oxford African American Studies Center, https://doi-org.proxy-tu.researchport.umd.edu/10.1093/acref/9780195301731.013.38846.

35. UGRR, 688–89.

36. James A. McGowen, *Station Master on the Underground Railroad: The Life and Letters of Thomas Garrett* (Jefferson, NC: McFarland, 2005), quote on 209; "Barbarous," *National Era*, July 13, 1848; UGRR, 630–31.

37. Sarah H. Bradford, *Scenes in the Life of Harriet Tubman* (Auburn, NY: W. J. Moses, 1869), 19–20; Kate Clifford Larson, *Bound for the Promised Land: Harriet Tubman, Portrait of an American Hero* (New York: Ballantine, 2004), 16–21, 62, 76–96.

38. Oscar Beisert et al., Nomination for the Philadelphia Register of Historic Places, William & Letitia Still House, Underground Railroad Way Station, 625 S. Delhi Street, Philadelphia, Pennsylvania, 2017.

39. "Postscript: Dreadful Riot," *Philadelphia Inquirer*, Oct. 10, 1849; George Lippard, *The Killers: A Narrative of Real Life in Philadelphia*, ed. Matt Cohen and Edlie L. Wong (Philadelphia: University of Pennsylvania Press, 2014), 15–18; "A Bloody Riot in Philadelphia," *National Era*, Oct. 18, 1849.

40. Emma Jones Lapsansky, "'Since They Got Those Separate Churches': Afro-Americans and Racism in Jacksonian Philadelphia," *American Quarterly* 32, no. 1 (Jan. 1980): 54–78.

41. "At a Large and Respectable Meeting . . . ," Philadelphia *Public Ledger*, May 1, 1850; Sinha, *Slave's Cause*, 160–71; Richard S. Newman, *The Transformation of American Abolitionism: Fighting Slavery*

in the Early Republic (Chapel Hill: University of North Carolina Press, 2003), 96–100.

42. William Still to [?], Aug. 7, 1850, Still Papers, Rutgers University, BAP; UGRR, xxxii–xxxiv.

43. *McElroy's Philadelphia City Directory* (Philadelphia: Edward C. & John Biddle, 1850), 400.

44. Kate E. R. Pickard, *The Kidnapped and the Ransomed* (Syracuse, NY: William T. Hamilton, 1856), 252.

45. Pickard, *Kidnapped and the Ransomed*, 260; William Still to J. Miller McKim, Aug. 8, 1850, *Pennsylvania Freeman*, Aug. 22, 1850.

CHAPTER FOUR

1. Henry Brown, *Narrative of the Life of Henry Box Brown, Written by Himself* (Manchester, UK: Lee and Glynn, 1851), 59; Jeffrey Ruggles, *The Unboxing of Henry Brown* (Richmond: Library of Virginia, 2003), 38.

2. Ruggles, *Unboxing*, 38–43; Baltimore *Sun*, June 5, 1849.

3. Ruggles, *Unboxing*, 47–59.

4. Campbell, *The Slave Catchers: Enforcement of the Fugitive Slave Law, 1850–1860* (Chapel Hill: University of North Carolina Press, 1970), 1–25; R. J. M. Blackett, *The Captive's Quest for Freedom: Fugitive Slaves, the 1850 Fugitive Slave Law, and the Politics of Slavery* (New York: Cambridge University Press, 2018), 3–7.

5. Blackett, *Captive's Quest*, 6–7; *Congressional Globe*, 31st Congress, 1st Session, Appendix, 1586–88.

6. Campbell, *Slave Catchers*, 23–25; Blackett, *Captive's Quest*, 7.

7. Elizabeth R. Varon, *Disunion! The Coming of the Civil War, 1789–1859* (Chapel Hill: University of North Carolina Press, 2008), 210–23; Manisha Sinha, *The Slave's Cause: A History of Abolition* (New Haven, CT: Yale University Press, 2016), 490–91; Blackett, *Captive's Quest*, 13–14; Campbell, *Slave Catchers*, 23.

8. "Fugitive Slave Case," Philadelphia *North American*, Oct. 19, 1850; Deposition of Thomas P. Jones in the Matter of Henry Garnet, Fugitive Slave, Oct. 17, 1850, Records of District Courts of the United States, 1685–2009, National Archives (Philadelphia).

9. "Fugitive Slave Case," Philadelphia *North American*, Oct. 19, 1850; Order Releasing Henry Garnett, Oct. 18, 1850, Fugitive Slave

Case #4 Garnett, Fugitive Slave Case Files, 1850–1860, Records of the District Courts of the United States, 1685–2009, National Archives (Philadelphia); Blackett, *Captive's Quest*, 65–66.

10. Blackett, *Captive's Quest*, 15–22.

11. "Visit to Philadelphia," *North Star*, Oct. 13, 1848.

12. "Meeting of Colored Citizens," *Liberator*, Nov. 8, 1850.

13. Ibid.

14. Kellie Carter Jackson, *Force and Freedom: Black Abolitionists and the Politics of Violence* (Philadelphia: University of Pennsylvania Press, 2019), 15–47; "For the Pennsylvania Freeman," *Pennsylvania Freeman*, Jan. 23, 1851.

15. "Kidnapping in Philadelphia," *National Era*, Jan. 2, 1851; Samuel May, *The Fugitive Slave Law and Its Victims* (New York: American Anti-Slavery Society, 1856), 12; Blackett, *Captive's Quest*, 54–56.

16. "The Fugitive Slave Case," Philadelphia *Public Ledger*, Feb. 10, 1851; "The Case of Mahala Purnell," *Philadelphia Inquirer*, Feb. 10, 1851; Blackett, *Captive's Quest*, 61–62.

17. Pickard, *Kidnapped and Ransomed*, 272.

18. William Still to J. Miller McKim, Aug. 8, 1850, *Pennsylvania Freeman*, Aug. 22, 1850.

19. Pickard, *Kidnapped and Ransomed*, 279.

20. 1850 U.S. Federal Census, South Ward, Philadelphia, PA, digital image, s.v. "Seth Conklin," Ancestry.com; Pickard, *Kidnapped and Ransomed*, 282–83; 377–99.

21. Pickard, *Kidnapped and Ransomed*, 284–85; UGRR, 26.

22. Seth Conklin to William Still, Feb. 3, 1851, in UGRR, 27–28.

23. Seth Conklin to William Still, Feb. 18, 1851, in UGRR, 28–29.

24. UGRR, 29.

25. N. R. Johnston to William Still, March 31, 1851, in UGRR, 30–31; Levi Coffin to William Still, April 10, 1851; UGRR, 33; UGRR, 30–31; Pickard, *Kidnapped and Ransomed*, 409. In Pickard's account, it seems possible that Conklin drowned trying to escape, though the exact cause of his death is ambiguous. Coffin's letter to Still suggests instead that he was murdered.

26. B. McKiernon to William Still, Aug. 6, 1851, UGRR, 34–35.

27. William Still to B. McKiernon, Aug. 16, 1851, UGRR, 35–36.

28. "Colored Mechanics Institute," Windsor (Ontario) *Voice of the Fugitive*, May 21, 1851.

29. UGRR, xxi; Matthew J. Grow, *"Liberty to the Downtrodden": Thomas L. Kane, Romantic Reformer* (New Haven, CT: Yale Uni-

versity Press, 2009), 114–20. Grow's biography of Thomas Kane does not mention that he was the source, but Still's account of the Christiana events does.

30. Still, UGRR (1883), xxi; William Parker, "The Freedman's Story," *Atlantic Monthly* 17 (1866), 282–83.

31. Thomas P. Slaughter, *Bloody Dawn: The Christiana Riot and Racial Violence in the Antebellum North* (New York: Oxford University Press, 1991), 43–58, Blackett, *Captive's Quest*, 294.

32. Parker, "Freedman's Story," 283–84; Slaughter, *Bloody Dawn*, 59–62.

33. UGRR, 350–51; Slaughter, *Bloody Dawn*, 62–70.

34. "The Slave Hunting Tragedy in Lancaster County," *Pennsylvania Freeman*, Sept. 18, 1851.

35. Andrew K. Diemer, *The Politics of Black Citizenship: Free African Americans in the Mid-Atlantic Borderland, 1817–1863* (Athens: University of Georgia Press, 2016), 148–51.

36. W. U. Hensel, *The Christiana Riot and the Treason Trials of 1851: An Historical Sketch* (Lancaster, PA: Press of the New Era Printing Co., 1911), 44–45; "The New Law of Treason," *Pennsylvania Freeman*, Oct. 9, 1851; Slaughter, *Bloody Dawn*, 89–93; Indictment for Treason for the Christiana Riot Participants, Nov. 13, 1851, *United States v. Castner Hanaway* et al., #1 October Session 1851, Criminal Case Files, 1791–1883, Records of the District Courts of the United States, 1685–2009, National Archives (Philadelphia).

37. "County Convention of Colored People," *Pennsylvania Freeman*, Nov. 6, 1851.

38. "An Appeal," *Frederick Douglass' Paper*, Nov. 13, 1851; "Aid for the Prisoners," *Pennsylvania Freeman*, Nov. 20, 1851.

39. "William Still's Offence," *Weekly Anglo-African*, June 2, 1860.

40. UGRR, xxii.

41. UGRR, 357.

42. Hensel, *Christiana Riot*, 83–84.

43. Maryland Attorney General's Office, *Report of Attorney General Robert Brent to His Excellency, Gov. Lowe, in Relation to the Christiana Treason Trials in the Circuit Court of the United States, Held in Philadelphia* (Annapolis, MD: Martin, 1852); Slaughter, *Bloody Dawn*, 135–38.

44. "Letter from William Still," Windsor (Ontario) *Voice of the Fugitive*, Jan. 1, 1852.

45. "Philadelphia Correspondence," *Frederick Douglass' Paper*, Feb. 19, 1852.

46. "From Harrisburg," *Philadelphia Inquirer,* Feb. 26, 1852; Diemer, *Politics of Black Citizenship,* 159.

47. "The Fugitive Slave Case," *Philadelphia Inquirer,* Nov. 8, 1852; "Outrageous Attack," *Philadelphia Inquirer,* Nov. 9, 1852; Richard Bell, "Counterfeit Kin: Kidnappers of Color, the Reverse Underground Railroad, and the Origins of Practical Abolition," *Journal of the Early Republic* 38, no. 2 (Summer 2018): 199–230.

48. William Still to Peter Still, Oct. 12, Dec. 18, 1852, Still Papers, Rutgers University, BAP; Samuel J. May to Peter Still, Still Papers, Rutgers University, BAP; Pickard, *Kidnapped and Ransomed,* 319–38, 371–72.

49. William Still to Peter Still, Dec. 18, 1852, Still Papers, Rutgers University, BAP; *McElroy's Philadelphia City Directory* (Philadelphia: Edward C. & John Biddle, 1852), 424.

50. "A Paper Published . . . ," *Philadelphia Inquirer,* June 29, 1852; "Refugees and Colored Settlements," *Frederick Douglass' Paper,* June 17, 1852.

51. UGRR, 612; Joseph A. Boromé, "The Vigilant Committee of Philadelphia," *Pennsylvania Magazine of History and Biography* 92, no. 3 (July 1968): 327–28, 348–49.

52. "William Still's Offence," *Weekly Anglo-African,* June 2, 1860.

53. "Meeting to Form a Vigilance Committee," *Pennsylvania Freeman,* Dec. 9, 1852, also reprinted in UGRR, 611–12.

54. Ibid.

55. William Still, *Journal C of the Underground Railroad, 1852–1857,* Dec. 25, 1852, HSP. It is possible, maybe even likely, that there are other records that Still kept that have not survived.

56. On Paxson, see Robert Clemons Smedley, *History of the Underground Railroad in Chester and the Neighboring Counties* (Lancaster, PA: Office of the Journal, 1883), 222–26.

CHAPTER FIVE

1. UGRR, 61–63; William Still, *Journal C of the Underground Railroad, 1852–1857,* Nov. 3, 1854, HSP.

2. Tommy L. Bogger, *Free Blacks in Norfolk, Virginia, 1790–1860: The Darker Side of Freedom* (Charlottesville: University Press of Virginia, 1997); Cassandra L. Newby-Alexander, *Virginia Waterways and the Underground Railroad* (Charleston, SC: The History Press, 2017), 52–93.

3. UGRR, 61–63; Still, *Journal C,* Nov. 3, 1854.

4. As John Hope Franklin and Loren Schweninger demonstrate, most fugitives never traveled far from their enslaver. Franklin and Schweninger, *Runaway Slaves: Rebels on the Plantation* (New York: Oxford University Press, 1999), 95–123.

5. George Rogers Taylor, *The Transportation Revolution, 1815–1860* (New York: Rinehart, 1951), 116–17.

6. UGRR, 152.

7. Still, *Journal C*, Sept. 23, 1853.

8. Still, *Journal C*, Oct. 25, 1853.

9. Isaac Forman to William Still, Feb. 20, 1854, in UGRR, 65; Still, *Journal C*, Dec. 13, 1853. On Bagnell, see Newby-Alexander, *Virginia Waterways*, 52, 114.

10. William Still, *Account Book of the Vigilance Committee of Philadelphia, 1854–1857*, Nov. 1, 1854, HSP.

11. UGRR, 54–58.

12. "J. Miller McKim," *Pennsylvania Freeman*, May 5, 1853; R. J. M. Blackett, *Building an Antislavery Wall: Black Americans in the Abolitionist Movement, 1830–1860* (Baton Rouge: LSU Press, 1983); Manisha Sinha, *The Slave's Cause: A History of Abolition* (New Haven, CT: Yale University Press, 2016), 340–47; Henry Mayer, *All on Fire: William Lloyd Garrison and the Abolition of Slavery* (New York: W. W. Norton, 1998), 152–65.

13. "Whereas James Miller McKim . . . ," April 27, 1853, Maloney Collection, Rare Books and Manuscripts Division, New York Public Library.

14. Minutes, Executive Committee, April 26, 1853; May 24, 1853; and July 5, 1853, Pennsylvania Anti-Slavery Society, Records, HSP.

15. "Great Anti-Colonization Meeting," *Liberator*, Oct. 7, 1853.

16. On connections between Black conventions and the Underground Railroad, see Cheryl Janifer LaRoche, "Secrets Well Kept: Colored Conventions and Underground Railroad Activism," in *The Colored Convention Movement: Black Organizing in the Nineteenth Century*, ed. P. Gabrielle Forman, Jim Casey, and Sarah Lynn Patterson (Chapel Hill: University of North Carolina Press, 2021), 246–60.

17. Jane Rhodes, *Mary Ann Shadd Cary: The Black Press and Protest in the Nineteenth Century* (Bloomington: Indiana University Press, 1998), 1–50.

18. William Still to Mary A. Shadd, Jan. 8, 1854, Mary A. Shadd Papers, Ontario Archives, BAP.

19. William Still to Mary A. Shadd, Feb. 1, 1854, Mary A. Shadd Papers, Ontario Archives, BAP.

20. Melba Joyce Boyd, *Discarded Legacy: Politics and Poetics in the Life of Frances E. W. Harper, 1825–1911* (Detroit, Mich.: Wayne State University Press, 1994), 33–48, 58–60.

21. William Still to Mary Ann Shadd, July 1854, in *Provincial Freeman*, Sept. 2, 1854; "Died of Starvation," *Provincial Freeman*, Sept. 2, 1854.

22. Minutes, Executive Committee, Nov. 5, 1850, Pennsylvania Anti-Slavery Society, Records, HSP; UGRR, xix. On women in the anti-slavery movement, see Julie Roy Jeffrey, *The Great Silent Army of Abolitionism: Ordinary Women in the Antislavery Movement* (Chapel Hill: University of North Carolina Press, 1998); Mayer, *All on Fire*, 133–34.

23. See chapter 2.

24. "Fashionable Dress Making," *Pennsylvania Freeman*, April 24, 1851.

25. UGRR, xlvi; Philadelphia Deed Book, G.W.C., no. 49, p. 525, Familysearch.org. Thanks to Jim Duffin for his help in locating these records.

26. "Coal," *Pennsylvania Freeman*, Dec. 22, 1853.

27. 1860 U.S. Federal Census, Philadelphia Ward 4 West Division, Philadelphia, Pennsylvania; digital image, s.v. "William Still," Ancestry.com; Pew Rent Ledger, First African Presbyterian Church Records, 1841–1990, Presbyterian Historical Society.

28. UGRR, xxiv. For a Black Bostonian family that is comparable to the Stills, Lewis and Harriet Hayden, see Stephen Kantrowitz, *More Than Freedom: Fighting for Black Citizenship in a White Republic, 1829–1889* (New York: Penguin Books, 2013), 187–89.

29. UGRR, 66; Daina Ramey Berry, *The Price for their Pound of Flesh: The Value of the Enslaved, from Womb to Grave, in the Building of a Nation* (Boston: Beacon Press, 2017), 48–49; Walter Johnson, *Soul by Soul: Life Inside the Antebellum Slave Market* (Cambridge, MA: Harvard University Press, 1999), 19–44.

30. William Donar to William Still, Nov. 3, 1859, in UGRR, 275.

31. Ellen Saunders to William Still, Oct. 16, 1854, in UGRR, 276.

32. Harriet Eglin to William Still, June 1856, in UGRR, 221.

33. UGRR, 65.

34. UGRR, xxxiii.

35. UGRR, 229; Still, *Journal C*, April 12, 1854.

36. Solomon Brown to William Still, Feb. 20, 1854, in UGRR, 163. For another example of Still helping a fugitive recover his clothes, see John Atkins to William Still, Oct. 5, 1854, in UGRR, 300.

37. Johnson, *Soul by Soul*, 23; UGRR, 246–47; Still, *Journal C*, Aug. 28, 1854.

38. Kate Clifford Larson, *Bound for the Promised Land: Harriet Tubman, Portrait of an American Hero* (New York: Ballantine, 2004), 89–96.

39. Still, *Journal C*, July 29, 1854; Larson, *Bound for the Promised Land*, 106; *McElroy's Philadelphia City Directory* (Philadelphia: Edward C. & John Biddle, 1854), 195.

40. In his published version, Still suggests that Tubman merely inspired Kinnard's flight, but in his records, he indicates that she had left him instructions. Still, *Journal C*, Aug. 28, 1854; UGRR, 246–47.

41. Thomas Garrett to J. Miller McKim, Dec. 29, 1854, in UGRR, 296; Still, *Journal C*, Dec. 29, 1854; Still, Account Book, Vigilance Committee, Dec. 31, 1854. James McGowan argues that the tone of Garrett's letter suggests he was already familiar with Tubman, but nevertheless there is no evidence that the two had met or worked together prior to this. McGowan, *Station Master on the Underground Railroad: The Life and Letters of Thomas Garrett*, rev. ed. (Jefferson, NC: McFarland, 2009), 98.

42. Still, *Journal C*, Sept. 14; Oct. 7, 1854; Oct. 9; Oct. 21; Nov. 3, 1854; Still, Account Book, Vigilance Committee, Nov. 1, 1854.

43. Still, *Journal C*, Oct. 1; Oct. 2, 1854; William Lloyd Garrison to Helen E. Garrison, Oct. 19, 1854, *The Letters of William Lloyd Garrison*, ed. Louis Ruchames, vol. 4, *From Disunionism to the Brink of War* (Cambridge, MA: Harvard University Press, 1975), 321–24; "Vigilance Committee Meeting," *National Anti-Slavery Standard*, Oct. 14, 1854; "Meetings in Philadelphia," *National Anti-Slavery Standard*, Nov. 4, 1854. Ezra Greenspan, *William Wells Brown: An African American Life* (New York: W. W. Norton, 2014), 183. Brown was featured in the advertisements for the meeting. It is possible that Garrison was a late addition, since he was already in Philadelphia to attend a women's rights convention.

44. "Self Emancipation," Windsor (Ontario) *Voice of the Fugitive*, reprinted in *Pennsylvania Freeman*, Dec. 15, 1853.

45. "Help the Fugitives," *Provincial Freeman*, July 8, 1854; "Pennsylvania Vigilance Committee," *National Anti-Slavery Standard*, Nov. 25, 1854.

46. "Imposters," *Pennsylvania Freeman*, Sept. 22, 1853; "An Imposter

Checked," *Pennsylvania Freeman*, Dec. 22, 1843; Still, *Journal C*, Dec. 21, 1854.

47. William Still to Mary Ann Shadd, Jan. 8, 1854, Mary A. Shadd Papers, Ontario Archives, BAP.

48. "For the Provincial Freeman," *Provincial Freeman*, April 29, 1854.

49. UGRR, 172–76; Still, *Journal C*, May 24, 1854; "The Late Fugitive Case," *Frederick Douglass' Paper*, June 9, 1854; Eric Foner, *Gateway to Freedom: The Hidden History of the Underground Railroad* (New York: W. W. Norton, 2015), 169–70; R. J. M. Blackett, *Beating Against the Barriers: The Lives of Six Nineteenth-Century Afro-Americans* (Ithaca, NY: Cornell University Press, 1986), 58.

50. UGRR, 176; Foner, *Gateway to Freedom*, 170.

51. "The Rev. Dr. Pennington's Brother . . . ," *Provincial Freeman*, June 10, 1854.

52. Ibid.; Zachary J. Lechner, "'Are We Ready for the Conflict?' Black Abolitionist Response to the Kansas Crisis, 1854–1856," *Kansas History* 31, no. 1 (Spring 2008): 20.

53. "Our Philadelphia Correspondence," *National Anti-Slavery Standard*, Feb. 3, 1855. Elizabeth Varon, "Beautiful Providences," in *Antislavery and Abolition in Philadelphia: Emancipation and the Long Struggle for Justice in the City of Brotherly Love*, ed. Richard Newman and James Mueller (Baton Rouge: LSU Press, 2011), 229–45.

54. "From Our Philadelphia Correspondent," *Provincial Freeman*, May 12, 1855.

55. Varon, "Beautiful Providences," 237; "From Our Philadelphia Correspondent," *Provincial Freeman*, June 23, 1855; "Underground Railroad News," *National Antislavery Standard*, Feb. 2, 1856.

56. Stanley Harrold, *Border War: Fighting over Slavery Before the Civil War* (Chapel Hill: University of North Carolina Press, 2010); "The Kansas Outrages—Slave Piracy, &c.," *Provincial Freeman*, May 19, 1855.

CHAPTER SIX

1. "The Thermometer at noon in the shade yesterday, stood at 94 degrees": *Philadelphia Inquirer*, July 19, 1855.

2. "The Philadelphia Slave Case," *Liberator*, Aug. 10, 1855.

3. The following scene is related in the "Statement by Passmore Williamson's Father," *National Anti-Slavery Standard*, Sept. 29, 1855.

4. Still's account of the arrival at the hotel is a little confusing. He

states that he encountered Williamson at the wharf, but also states that Williamson advised him that he should ask for the description, which means that Williamson was there with him at Bloodgood's Hotel before he got to the wharf. UGRR, 88.

5. The scene on board the steamship is constructed from a combination of Still's account, written for the *New York Tribune* and later published in his UGRR book, and the testimony from the Williamson trial. Williamson's testimony largely has him doing the talking, though it is possible that he was trying to spare Still any legal liability. Still's account often uses the passive voice, so unless Still specifically indicates that he is the one talking I have assumed Williamson to have been testifying truthfully. UGRR, 88–90; *Case of Passmore Williamson, Report of the Proceedings . . .* (Philadelphia: Uriah Hunt & Son, 1856), 9–10.

6. UGRR, 90–91.

7. "A Champion of Liberty, *Times* (Philadelphia), Feb. 23, 1892, 4; John H. Wheeler, *Reminiscences and Memoirs of North Carolina and Eminent North Carolinians* (Columbus, OH: Columbus Printing Works, 1884), iv; UGRR, 88. Wheeler was, in fact, recovering from a case of "Panama fever," probably cholera, which he had contracted in Nicaragua. Nat Brandt with Yanna Kroyt Brandt, *In the Shadow of the Civil War: Passmore Williamson and the Rescue of Jane Johnson* (Columbia: University of South Carolina Press, 2007), 57–58.

8. At Williamson's trial, he would testify that he had merely offered her his hand, while Wheeler insisted that he had forcibly seized her. *Case of Passmore Williamson*, 7, 9–10.

9. UGRR, 89; "Legal Intelligence," *Philadelphia Inquirer*, Aug. 30, 1855. Still's account notes simply that Jane and her boys "were assisted." Other reports held that a Black man carried the younger child, and one of the witnesses at the Aug. 29 trial identified this man as Still. Another witness, however, identified the man carrying the Johnson boy as James Martin.

10. *Case of Passmore Williamson*, 7–8.

11. UGRR, 90; *Case of Passmore Williamson*, 7; Hexamer & Locher, *Maps of the City of Philadelphia, 1858–1860*, Map Collection, Free Library of Philadelphia Greater Philadelphia GeoHistory Network, http://www.philageohistory.org/rdic-images/view-image.cfm /HXL1860-Super-Index (accessed July 19, 2021); "Legal Intelligence," *Philadelphia Inquirer*, Aug. 31, 1855.

12. *Case of Passmore Williamson*, 7.

13. Leonard Richards, *The Slave Power: The Free North and Southern Domination, 1780–1860* (Baton Rouge: LSU Press: 2000).

14. Brandt, *In the Shadow*, 54–55.

15. Brandt, *In the Shadow*, 56; Matthew Karp, *This Vast Southern Empire: Slaveholders at the Helm of American Foreign Policy* (Cambridge, MA: Harvard University Press, 2016), 183–84; Robert E. May, *Manifest Destiny's Underworld: Filibustering in Antebellum America* (Chapel Hill: University of North Carolina Press, 2002).

16. Brandt, *In the Shadow*, 56–58.

17. Brandt, *In the Shadow*, 37–38; UGRR, 90; William Still, *Account Book of the Vigilance Committee of Philadelphia, 1854–1857*, July 18, 1855, HSP. Still made no record of Jane Johnson in his Vigilance Committee journal, but he did record the expenses for the carriage and the two men.

18. Brandt, *In the Shadow*, 29–31; UGRR, 94; *Case of Passmore Williamson*, 164.

19. Paul Finkelman, *An Imperfect Union: Slavery, Federalism, and Comity* (Chapel Hill: University of North Carolina Press, 1981) 46–69, 137.

20. UGRR, 94.

21. *Narrative of Facts in the Case of Passmore Williamson* (Philadelphia: Pennsylvania Anti-Slavery Society, 1855), 3; UGRR, 91, 94.

22. UGRR, 92.

23. "Statement by Passmore Williamson's Father," *National Anti-Slavery Standard*, Sept. 29, 1855.

24. "Statement by Passmore Williamson's Father," *National Anti-Slavery Standard*, Sept. 29, 1855; *Case of Passmore Williamson*, 3–4; Brandt, *In the Shadow*, 75–76.

25. "Statement by Passmore Williamson's Father," *National Anti-Slavery Standard*, Sept. 29, 1855; UGRR, 92. It would have made sense for Williamson to stop in at the Anti-Slavery Society office on the way to Hopper's office, since it was on the way. On the other hand, it is also on the way from Hopper's office to the courthouse, so it is possible that he did so on the way to court.

26. "The Fugitive Slave Law—Important Opinion of Judge Kane," *Philadelphia Inquirer*, Nov. 19, 1850; Brandt, *In the Shadow*, 61–67. For an example of Kane's previous interactions with Williamson, see "Another Important Slave Case," *Pennsylvania Freeman*, Feb. 13, 1851.

27. Brandt, *In the Shadow*, 60–61; *Case of Passmore Williamson*, 14; *Narrative of Facts*, 8.

28. *Narrative of Facts*, 12; "The Philadelphia Slave Case," *National Anti-Slavery Standard*, July 26, 1855; "Legal Intelligence," *Philadelphia Inquirer*, July 20, 1855.

29. *Case of Passmore Williamson*, 4–5.

30. *Case of Passmore Williamson*, 6–11.

31. Sydney Howard Gay, *Record of Fugitives*, July 31, 1855, 9. https://exhibitions.library.columbia.edu/exhibits/show/fugitives/record_fugitives.

32. *Case of Passmore Williamson*, 6–15.

33. Andrew K. Diemer, *Politics of Black Citizenship: Free African Americans in the Mid-Atlantic Borderland, 1817–1863* (Athens: University of Georgia Press, 2016); Nicholas Wood, "'A Sacrifice on the Altar of Slavery': Doughface Politics and Black Disfranchisement in Pennsylvania, 1837–1838," *Journal of the Early Republic* 31, no. 1 (Spring 2011): 75–106.

34. *Narrative of Facts*, 13; "Legal Intelligence," *Philadelphia Inquirer*, July 30, 1855; "The Alleged Abduction Case," Philadelphia *Public Ledger*, July 30, 1855. Another witness claimed it was in fact Ballard who made this threat. See "Legal Intelligence," *Philadelphia Inquirer*, Aug. 30, 1855. On Kelley, see Ira V. Brown, "William D. Kelley and Radical Reconstruction," *Pennsylvania Magazine of History and Biography* 85, no. 3 (July 1961), 316–29.

35. *Narrative of Facts*, 13; "Quarter Sessions," Philadelphia *Public Ledger*, Aug. 10, 1855.

36. "The Wheeler Slave Case," New York *Daily Tribune*, Aug. 1, 1855; "The Wheeler Slave Case," Philadelphia *North American*, Aug. 2, 1855.

37. "Quarter Sessions," Philadelphia *Public Ledger*, Aug. 9, 1855.

38. "The Real Criminal in Peril," *National Anti-Slavery Standard*, Aug. 18, 1855; Brandt, *In the Shadow*, 118. According to a report in the Democratic newspaper *The Pennsylvanian*, Still later found a "Know Nothing and Abolition officer" who was willing to serve the warrant, though nothing seems to have come of this either. This report from the *Pennsylvanian* was excerpted in "The Wheeler Slave Case," *Weekly North Carolina Standard*, Aug. 22, 1855.

39. William Still, *Journal C of the Underground Railroad, 1852–1857*, Sept. 7–Dec. 11, 1855, HSP; William Still, *Account Book of the Vigilance Committee of Philadelphia, 1854–1857*, July 18–Aug. 17, HSP; UGRR, 259. Still lists "Crummell" in his journal and "Cromwell" in the published version of the *Underground Railroad*.

40. "From Philadelphia," New York *Daily Tribune*, Aug. 1, 1855.

41. "Letter of Sympathy," *Frederick Douglass' Paper*, Aug. 24, 1855. It is possible that Still remained wary of sending fugitives his way, but it had been more than a year since the recapture of Pennington's brother.

42. "The Wheeler Slave Case," Philadelphia *Sunday Dispatch*, Aug. 5, 1855.

43. "Our Philadelphia Correspondence," *National Anti-Slavery Standard*, Aug. 25, 1855.

44. "The Wheeler Slave Case," Philadelphia *Public Ledger*, Aug. 31, 1855.

45. "Trial of the Emancipators of Wheeler's Chattels," *National Anti-Slavery Standard*, Sept. 8, 1855; *Narrative of Facts*, 15; Lucretia Mott to Martha Coffin Wright, Sept. 4, 1855, Mott Manuscripts, Friends Historical Library, Swarthmore College, https://digital collections.tricolib.brynmawr.edu/object/sc158951.

46. "Trial of the Emancipators of Wheeler's Chattels," *National Anti-Slavery Standard*, Sept. 8, 1855.

47. "Legal Intelligence," *Philadelphia Inquirer*, Aug. 31, 1855; *Narrative of Facts*, 14–15.

48. "Trial of the Emancipators of Wheeler's Chattels," *National Anti-Slavery Standard*, Sept. 8, 1855; *Narrative of Facts*, 15; Margaret Bacon, *Valiant Friend: The Life of Lucretia Mott* (New York: Walker & Co., 1980), 151.

49. "Local Items," *Philadelphia Inquirer*, Sept. 3, 1855; "Legal Intelligence," *Philadelphia Inquirer*, Sept. 4, 1855; *Narrative of Facts*, 16.

50. A facsimile of the prison's visitor log book is available at https://passmorewilliamson.omeka.net/items/show/7.

51. "The Republican Convention," Philadelphia *Public Ledger*, Sept. 8, 1855; Brandt, *In the Shadow*, 107.

52. "From Philadelphia," New York *Daily Tribune*, Aug. 1, 1855.

53. "Passmore Williamson in Jail," New York *Evening Post*, Aug. 6, 1855; "The Wheeler Slave Case," New York *Herald*, Aug. 5, 1855; "The Slave Outrage in Philadelphia," Raleigh *North Carolina Standard*, Aug. 1, 1855.

54. UGRR, 93.

CHAPTER SEVEN

1. John Henry Hill to William Still, Oct. 30, 1853, in UGRR, 193.

2. "Fugitive Slave Colony in Canada," New York *Herald*, Oct. 1, 1854.

3. "Prejudice Against Color in Canada," *Frederick Douglass' Paper*, Aug. 25, 1854.

4. "Dr. Litch's Restorative," *Christian Recorder*, Oct. 20, 1855.

5. Henry Grew, letter of introduction, Sept. 10, 1855, William Still Letters, Leon Gardiner Collection of American Negro Historical Society Records, Series I, Box 9G, HSP.

6. Samuel Rhoads, letter of introduction, Sept. 4, 1855, William Still Letters.

7. Dillwyn Parrish, letter of introduction, Sept. 8, 1855, William Still Letters. For additional letters of introduction, see UGRR, xxv.

8. James Still, *Early Recollections and Life of Dr. James Still* (Philadelphia: J. B. Lippincott & Co., 1877), 90.

9. Jane Rhodes, *Mary Ann Shadd Cary: The Black Press and Protest in the Nineteenth Century* (Bloomington: Indiana University Press, 1998), 29–31; Robin W. Winks, *The Blacks in Canada: A History*, 2nd ed. (Montreal: McGill–Queen's University Press, 1997), 142–55.

10. Rhodes, *Mary Ann Shadd Cary*, 29.

11. "Important Railroad Convention," New York *Herald*, April 13, 1855. Emma Brown had written to Still about crossing the bridge earlier that year. Emma Brown to William Still, March 14, 1855, in UGRR, 76.

12. Benjamin Drew, *The Refugee; or a Northside View of Slavery* (Boston: John P. Jewett and Company, 1856), 17–18.

13. UGRR, xxv; "The Colored Population in Canada," Philadelphia *Public Ledger*, Jan. 21, 1860.

14. UGRR, xxvi; "For the North American and U.S. Gazette," Philadelphia *North American*, Feb. 1, 1860; James Still, *Recollections*, 90.

15. "To the Editor," *Provincial Freeman*, Oct. 6, 1855; UGRR, xxvi; James Still, *Recollections*, 90.

16. "For the North American and U.S. Gazette," Philadelphia *North American*, Feb. 1, 1860; Mary Ann Shadd, *A Plea for Emigration, or, Notes of Canada West* . . . (Detroit, MI: George W. Pattison, 1852).

17. David Walker, *Walker's Appeal to the Coloured Citizens of the World* . . . , 3rd ed. (Boston, 1830), quote on 47.

18. UGRR, 295–96; William Still, *Journal C of the Underground Railroad, 1852–1857*, Oct. 7, 1855, HSP.

19. On Black abolitionists and their embrace of violence as a political necessity, see Kellie Carter Jackson, *Force and Freedom: Black Abolitionists and the Politics of Violence* (Philadelphia: University of Pennsylvania Press, 2019). On Garrison's own ambivalence about the tension between nonresistance and the defense of fugitive slaves,

see Henry Mayer, *All on Fire: William Lloyd Garrison and the Abolition of Slavery* (New York: W. W. Norton, 1998), 410.

20. "For the Provincial Freeman," *Provincial Freeman*, Nov. 3, 1855; *Proceedings of the Colored National Convention, held in Franklin Hall, Sixth Street, Below Arch, Philadelphia, October 16th, 17th and 18th, 1855* (Salem, NJ: National Standard Office, 1856), https://omeka .coloredconventions.org/items/show/281; "From Our Brooklyn Correspondent," *Frederick Douglass' Paper*, Nov. 9, 1855; Rhodes, *Mary Ann Shadd Cary*, 108–10.

21. "For the Provincial Freeman," *Provincial Freeman*, Dec. 22, 1855; "From Our Philadelphia Correspondent," *Provincial Freeman*, Dec. 1, 1855.

22. "New Boarding House," *National Anti-Slavery Standard*, Nov. 24, 1855; 1860 U.S. Federal Census, Philadelphia Ward 4 West Division, Philadelphia, Pennsylvania, digital image, s.v. "Wm Still," Ancestry.com (accessed June 22, 2020).

23. "From the Liberator," *Provincial Freeman*, July 19, 1856.

24. Wendy Gamber, *The Boardinghouse in Nineteenth-Century America* (Baltimore: Johns Hopkins University Press, 2007), 1–10.

25. "From the Liberator," *Provincial Freeman*, July 19, 1856; Gamber, *Boardinghouse*, 56–57.

26. Minutes, Executive Committee, Oct. 23, 1855, Pennsylvania Anti-Slavery Society Records, HSP.

27. UGRR, 177–87; Still, *Journal C*, Nov. 22, 1855; Stanley Harrold, "Freeing the Weems Family: A New Look at the Underground Railroad," *Civil War History* 42, no. 4 (December 1996): 289–306.

28. J. Bigelow to William Still, June 27, 1854, in UGRR, 177.

29. Still noted only that Dr. H was his family's doctor and also that he worked at a college. UGRR, 179–82; *McElroy's Philadelphia City Directory* (Philadelphia: Edward C. & John Biddle, 1855), 251.

30. UGRR, 179–82; Harrold, "Freeing the Weems Family," 301.

31. Eric Foner, *Gateway to Freedom: The Hidden History of the Underground Railroad* (New York: W. W. Norton, 2015), 165–67.

32. Sydney Howard Gay to William Still, Aug. 17, 1855, in UGRR, 40–41; Foner, *Gateway to Freedom*, 172–74.

33. Sydney Howard Gay, *Record of Fugitives*, Aug. 17, 1855, https:// exhibitions.library.columbia.edu/exhibits/show/fugitives/record _fugitives; Still, *Journal C*, Aug. 16, 1855; Foner, *Gateway to Freedom*, 177.

34. William Still to Elijah F. Pennypacker, Nov. 24, 1855, Pennypacker Papers, Friends Historical Library, Swarthmore College, BAP;

Elijah F. Pennypacker to William Still, Nov. 29, 1855, in UGRR, 339.

35. Joseph C. Bustill to William Still, March 24, 1856, in UGRR, 43.

36. Thomas Garrett to William Still, Dec. 19, 1855, in UGRR, 131.

37. UGRR, 165–66.

38. UGRR, 165–68; Still, *Journal C*, Nov. 29, 1855; Thomas Garrett to Eliza Wigham, Dec. 16, 1855, in James A. McGowen, *Station Master on the Underground Railroad: The Life and Letters of Thomas Garrett* (Jefferson, NC: McFarland & Co., 2005), 166–68.

39. UGRR, 150–52. Years later, Galloway would return to his native North Carolina and serve in the state senate.

40. Kate E. R. Pickard, *The Kidnapped and the Ransomed. Being the Personal Recollections of Peter Still and his wife "Vina" after Forty Years of Slavery* (Syracuse, NY: William T. Hamilton, 1856); "Underground Railroad News," *National Anti-Slavery Standard*, Feb. 2, 1856.

41. "Underground Railroad News," *National Anti-Slavery Standard*, Feb. 2, 1856.

42. On the influence of *Uncle Tom's Cabin*, see John L. Brooke, *There Is a North: Fugitive Slaves, Political Crisis, and Cultural Transformation in the Coming of the Civil War* (Amherst: University of Massachusetts Press, 2019), 159–201

43. UGRR, 329–30.

44. "From Our Philadelphia Correspondent," *Provincial Freeman*, Feb. 9, 1856.

45. David M. Potter, *The Impending Crisis: America Before the Civil War, 1848–1861*, completed and edited by Don Fehrenbacher (New York: Harper & Row, 1976), 246–48.

46. "For the Provincial Freeman," *Provincial Freeman*, March 15, 1856; Henry Mayer, *All on Fire: William Lloyd Garrison and the Abolition of Slavery* (New York: W. W. Norton, 1998), 454–56.

47. "The National Republican Convention," *Provincial Freeman*, June 28, 1856.

48. UGRR, 320–24.

49. R. J. M. Blackett, *The Captive's Quest for Freedom: Fugitive Slaves, the 1850 Fugitive Slave Law, and the Politics of Slavery* (New York: Cambridge University Press, 2018), 275.

50. *A Review of the Trial, Conviction, and Sentence of George F. Alberti, for Kidnapping* ([Philadelphia?], 1851); "The Mitchell Case Sentences on the Charge of Kidnapping," *National Era*, March 27, 1851.

51. Richard R. John, *Network Nation: Inventing American Telecommunications* (Cambridge, MA: Harvard University Press, 2010), 24–64.

52. UGRR, 218–19.

53. "Meeting of Coloured Citizens of Philadelphia," *National Anti-Slavery Standard*, July 26, 1856; UGRR, 84–86.

54. Kate Clifford Larson, *Bound for the Promised Land: Harriet Tubman, Portrait of an American Hero* (New York: Ballantine, 2004), 121–26; Thomas Garrett to Eliza Wigham, Dec. 16, 1855, in McGowen, *Station Master*, 166–68; Still, *Journal C*, Dec. 25, 1855.

55. Larson, *Bound for the Promised Land*, 126; Thomas Garrett to William Still, May 11, 1856, in UGRR, 387; Still, *Journal C*, May 13, 1856.

56. Elizabeth R. Varon, *Disunion! The Coming of the Civil War, 1789–1859* (Chapel Hill: University of North Carolina Press, 2008), 274; Potter, *Impending Crisis*, 256–65; William Dusinberre, *Civil War Issues in Philadelphia, 1856–1865* (Philadelphia: University of Pennsylvania Press, 1965), 41–43; "Pennsylvania Elections—Official," *Philadelphia Inquirer*, Nov. 15, 1856.

57. N. R. Johnston to William Still, in UGRR, 587–88; "Our Philadelphia Correspondence," *National Anti-Slavery Standard*, Nov. 15, 1856.

58. "The Election," *National Anti-Slavery Standard*, Nov. 8, 1856; "Our Philadelphia Correspondence," *National Anti-Slavery Standard*, Nov. 15, 1856.

59. Potter, *Impending Crisis*, 267–68; Don E. Fehrenbacher, *The Dred Scott Case: Its Significance in American Law and Politics* (New York: Oxford University Press, 2001), 335–88; Lea VanderVelde, *Mrs. Dred Scott: A Life on Slavery's Frontier* (New York: Oxford University Press, 2009), 233–319.

60. Potter, *Impending Crisis*, 268–76; Varon, *Disunion!*, 295–98.

61. "From our Philadelphia Correspondent," *Provincial Freeman*, March 28, 1857; Andrew K. Diemer, *Politics of Black Citizenship: Free African Americans in the Mid-Atlantic Borderland, 1817–1863* (Athens: University of Georgia Press, 2016), 170–74.

62. "The Voice of the Colored People of Philadelphia," *Anti-Slavery Bugle* (New Lisbon, OH), April 11, 1857.

63. "Meetings at Philadelphia," *Provincial Freeman*, April 18, 1857; Rhodes, *Mary Ann Shadd Cary*, 112.

CHAPTER EIGHT

1. *Call for a National Convention on Disunion* (Philadelphia, 1857), Miscellaneous Anti-Slavery Collection, American Antiquarian Society, BAP; Henry Mayer, *All on Fire: William Lloyd Garrison and the Abolition of Slavery* (New York: W. W. Norton, 1998), 313–29; Elizabeth R. Varon, *Disunion! The Coming of the Civil War, 1789–1859* (Chapel Hill: University of North Carolina Press, 2008), 301–3.

2. Leonard L. Richards, *The Slave Power: The Free North and Southern Domination, 1780–1860* (Baton Rouge: LSU Press, 2000), 190–215; Robert E. May, *Manifest Destiny's Underworld: Filibustering in Antebellum America* (Chapel Hill: University of North Carolina Press, 2002), 183–216; David M. Potter, *The Impending Crisis: America Before the Civil War, 1848–1861*, completed and edited by Don Fehrenbacher (New York: Harper & Row, 1976), 267–96.

3. Petition of William H. Gatchell in the Fugitive Slave Petition Book, Jan. 13, 1857, Records of the District Courts of the United States, National Archives (Philadelphia), https://catalog.archives.gov/id/278903; "Fugitive Slave Case," Philadelphia *Public Ledger*, Jan. 17, 1857; "Arrest of a Fugitive Slave from Baltimore," Baltimore *Sun*, Jan. 17, 1857; William Still, "Slave Case" [undated], Mary A. Shadd Papers, Ontario Archives, BAP; Eric H. Walther, *The Shattering of the Union: America in the 1850s* (Wilmington, DE: Scholarly Resources, 2004), 115.

4. Still, "Slave Case"; "The Fugitive Slave Case," Philadelphia *Public Ledger*, Jan. 19, 1857.

5. "Mass Meeting of Coloured Citizens in Philadelphia," *National Anti-Slavery Standard*, Feb. 14, 1857.

6. UGRR, 51–54.

7. Ibid., 73–74.

8. Thomas Garrett to Samuel Rhodes, March 13, 1857, in UGRR, 73–74.

9. UGRR, 404–6; "Another Slave Hunt in Philadelphia," *National Anti-Slavery Standard*, Aug. 1, 1857.

10. UGRR, 534–36.

11. Oscar Ball to William Still, Oct. 25, 1857, in UGRR, 400; John Delaney [Oscar Ball] to William Still, Nov. 21, 1857, in UGRR, 400.

12. Earro Weems to William Still, Sept. 19, 1857, in UGRR, 186; Stanley Harrold, "Freeing the Weems Family: A New Look at the

Underground Railroad," *Civil War History* 42, no. 4 (December 1996): 289–306.

13. John B. Woods to William Still, Aug. 15, 1858, in UGRR, 402; UGRR, 401–2.

14. UGRR, 452–54.

15. "At a meeting of the Committee of the Library," *National Anti-Slavery Standard*, Feb. 7, 1857; "From Our Philadelphia Correspondent," *Provincial Freeman*, March 28, 1857; Melba Joyce Boyd, *Discarded Legacy: Politics and Poetics in the Life of Frances Watkins Harper* (Detroit, MI: Wayne State University Press, 1994), 57–58; Ezra Greenspan, *William Wells Brown: An African American Life* (New York: W. W. Norton, 2014), 183–84.

16. Ezra Greenspan, *William Wells Brown*, 386–89; William Wells Brown, *The Black Man, His Antecedents, His Genius, and His Achievements* (New York: Thomas Hamilton, 1863), 211–14.

17. "Meetings in Philadelphia," *Liberator*, Oct. 22, 1858; "The Anti-Slavery Convention," *Philadelphia Inquirer*, Dec. 17, 1858; "Pennsylvania A.S. Convention," *Liberator*, Dec. 31, 1858; *William Wells Brown: A Reader*, ed. Ezra Greenspan (Athens: University of Georgia Press, 2008), 102–6.

18. "Underground Railroad Report," *New York Tribune*, Dec. 16, 1857.

19. Richard Josiah Hinton, *John Brown and His Men; With Some Account of the Roads They Travelled to Reach Harper's Ferry* (New York: Funk & Wagnalls Co., 1894), 169; *The Life and Letters of John Brown, Liberator of Kansas and Martyr of Virginia*, ed. Franklin Benjamin Sanborn (Boston: Roberts Brothers, 1891), 451; Oswald Garrison Villard, *John Brown, 1800–1859, A Biography Fifty Years After* (New York: Houghton Mifflin Co., 1910), 323; *McElroy's Philadelphia City Directory* (Philadelphia: Edward C. & John Biddle, 1859), 664.

20. David Reynolds, *John Brown, Abolitionist: The Man Who Killed Slavery, Sparked the Civil War and Seeded Civil Rights* (New York: Alfred A. Knopf, 2005), 1–94, quote on 65.

21. Ibid., 138–78.

22. "Minutes of the Convention," in Osborne P. Anderson, *Voice from Harpers Ferry: A Narrative of Events at Harpers Ferry* (Boston, 1861), 10–13; Reynolds, *John Brown*, 239–67; Kate Clifford Larson, *Bound for the Promised Land: Harriet Tubman, Portrait of an American Hero* (New York: Ballantine, 2004), 157–60; David W. Blight, *Frederick Douglass: Prophet of Freedom* (New York: Simon & Schuster, 2018), 298.

23. Hinton, *John Brown*, 169; UGRR, xxii.

24. [J. Miller McKim?], *Arrest, Trial, and Release of Daniel Webster, a Fugitive Slave* (Philadelphia: Pennsylvania Anti-Slavery Society, 1859), 3; R. J. M. Blackett, *The Captive's Quest for Freedom: Fugitive Slaves, the 1850 Fugitive Slave Law, and the Politics of Slavery* (New York: Cambridge University Press, 2018), 347–49.

25. *Arrest, Trial, and Release of Daniel Webster,* 4.

26. *Arrest, Trial, and Release of Daniel Webster,* 7–8; Blackett, *Captive's Quest,* 348–49.

27. "The Fugitive Slave Case," Philadelphia *Public Ledger,* April 6, 1859; "The Fugitive Slave Case," Philadelphia *Press,* April 7, 1859; Fugitive Slave Excitement at Harrisburg," *National Era,* April 7, 1859; *Arrest, Trial, and Release of Daniel Webster,* 8–16.

28. *The Journal of Charlotte Forten: A Free Negro in the Slave Era,* ed. Ray Allen Billington (New York: Dryden Press, 1953; New York: W. W. Norton, 1981), 127; *Arrest, Trial, and Release of Daniel Webster,* 27; "How the Alleged Fugitive Was Treated," *Philadelphia Inquirer,* April 8, 1859; "Our Philadelphia Correspondence," *National Anti-Slavery Standard,* April 23, 1859; Daniel Webster to J. Miller McKim, May 1, 1859, Anti-Slavery Collection, Olin Library, Cornell University, BAP.

29. "A Call for a Convention of the Colored Citizens of New England," *Liberator,* July 29, 1859; "New England Colored Citizens' Convention, August 1, 1859," Colored Conventions Project Digital Records, https://omeka.coloredconventions.org/items /show/269 (accessed July 8, 2020).

30. "New England Colored Citizens' Convention."

31. "The Recent Conventions of Colored Men," Boston *Daily Advertiser,* Aug. 3, 1859, from Colored Conventions Project Digital Records, https://omeka.coloredconventions.org/items/show/1709 (accessed July 8, 2020).

32. "New England Colored Citizens' Convention."

33. "Meetings in Boston," *Liberator,* Aug. 26, 1859; "Fugitive Slaves in Boston and New Bedford," *National Anti-Slavery Standard,* Sept. 3, 1859.

34. Frances E. Still Death Certificate, Death certificates, 1906–1963. Records of the Pennsylvania Department of Health, Record Group 11. Pennsylvania Historical and Museum Commission, Harrisburg, Pennsylvania, digital image, s.v. "Frances E. Still," Ancestry .com (accessed July 8, 2020).

35. UGRR, xxii.

36. "The Harper's Ferry Insurrection," Philadelphia *Press,* Oct. 19,

1859; UGRR, xxii; Sanborn, *Life and Letters*, 540; Reynolds, *John Brown*, 306–13.

37. Reynolds, *John Brown*, 320–27.

38. "The Negro Insurrection," *Philadelphia Inquirer*, Oct. 20, 1859; "The Harper's Ferry Insurrection," Philadelphia *Press*, Oct. 19, 1859.

39. "The Harper's Ferry Insurrection. Highly Important Details," Philadelphia *Public Ledger*, Oct. 21, 1859; "Brown Invasion Further Particulars," *National Anti-Slavery Standard*, Oct. 29, 1859; Alberta S. Norwood, "Negro Welfare Work in Philadelphia" (master's thesis, University of Pennsylvania, 1931), 42; William Still to Amy Post, Oct. 21, 1859, Post Papers, University of Rochester, BAP; Blight, *Frederick Douglass*, 306; William S. McFeely, *Frederick Douglass* (New York: W. W. Norton, 1991), 199. McFeely suggests that Douglass's flight to Canada was a direct response to Still's message, but it is possible that Douglass left before Still's message arrived. Blight makes no mention of Still's message.

40. "The Insurrection at Harper's Ferry," Philadelphia *Public Ledger*, Oct. 19, 1859; "The Harper's Ferry Insurrection," Baltimore *Sun*, Oct. 19, 1859; William Dusinberre, *Civil War Issues in Philadelphia, 1856–1865* (Philadelphia: University of Pennsylvania Press, 1965), 83–85; *A Philadelphia Perspective: The Diary of Sidney George Fisher Covering the Years 1834–1871*, ed. Nicholas Wainwright (Philadelphia: Historical Society of Pennsylvania, 1967), 334; "Our Philadelphia Letter," *Weekly Anglo-African*, Oct. 29, 1859.

41. UGRR, xxiii; Reynolds, *John Brown*, 270–72.

42. Anderson, *A Voice from Harper's Ferry*, 51–55; UGRR, xxiii; Reynolds, *John Brown*, 271.

43. UGRR, xxiii; Annie Brown to William Still, Dec. 20, 1859, William Still Letters, Leon Gardiner Collection of American Negro Historical Society Records, Series I, Box 9G, HSP; William Still to Soloman Brown, Oct. [day unclear], 1859, Miscellaneous Manuscripts, Henry E. Huntington Library, BAP.

44. "Our Philadelphia Letter," *Weekly Anglo-African*, Dec. 17, 1859; "Prayers for John Brown," Philadelphia *Press*, Dec. 1, 1859; "Local Intelligence," *Philadelphia Inquirer*, Dec. 2, 1859.

45. Varon, *Disunion!*, 329–35; Reynolds, *John Brown*, 402–37; Potter, *Impending Crisis*, 379.

46. Andrew K. Diemer, *Politics of Black Citizenship: Free African Americans in the Mid-Atlantic Borderland, 1817–1863* (Athens: University of Georgia Press, 2016), 175–77; Reynolds, *John Brown*, 418–19.

47. "Beware of an Imposter," *Liberator*, Sept. 23, 1859.

48. "The Underground Railroad Co.," *Weekly Anglo-African*, Oct. 15, 1859.

49. "The Underground R. R. Co.," *Weekly Anglo-African*, Oct. 29, 1859.

50. *Narrative of Dimmock Charlton, A British Subject* . . . , ed. Mary L. and Susan Cox (Philadelphia, 1859); "Dimmock Charlton and His Grandchild," *National Anti-Slavery Standard*, Aug. 29, 1857.

51. *Narrative of Dimmock Charlton*; "Caution," *National Anti-Slavery Standard*, Nov. 27, 1858; "Dimmock Charlton," *Douglass' Monthly*, August 1859; "Dimmock Charlton—Letter from William Still," *Frederick Douglass' Paper*, Aug. 19, 1859; "The Case of Dimmock Charlton," *Frederick Douglass' Paper*, Oct. 14, 1859.

52. "Our Philadelphia Letter," *Weekly Anglo-African*, Oct. 22, 1859; "The Underground R. R. Co.," *Weekly Anglo-African*, Oct. 29, 1859; "Our Philadelphia Letter," *Weekly Anglo-African*, Nov. 5, 1859; "Our Philadelphia Letter," *Weekly Anglo-African*, Nov. 12, 1859.

53. "Defense of William Still," *Frederick Douglass' Paper*, Nov. 4, 1859.

54. "Quarter Sessions," Philadelphia *Public Ledger*, March 15, 1860; "Letter from William Still," *National Anti-Slavery Standard*, May 5, 1860; "The Late Philadelphia Libel Suit," *Weekly Anglo-African*, May 19, 1860.

55. "Our Philadelphia Letter," *Weekly Anglo-African*, Dec. 24, 1859; "Quarter Sessions," Philadelphia *Public Ledger*, March 15, 1860; William Still to Samuel May, Jr., March 7, 1860, Anti-Slavery Collections, Boston Public Library, BAP; City of Philadelphia Department of Records, City Archives, RG 21, Quarter Sessions Court, Docket 68, p. 323.

56. "The Late Philadelphia Libel Suit," *Weekly Anglo-African*, May 19, 1860; William Still to Samuel May, March 2, 16, 1860, Anti-Slavery Collections, Boston Public Library, BAP.

57. "The Late Philadelphia Libel Suit," *Weekly Anglo-African*, May 19, 1860.

58. Ibid.; "Quarter Sessions," Philadelphia *Public Ledger*, March 15, 1860.

59. "The Late Philadelphia Libel Suit," *Weekly Anglo-African*, May 19, 1860; City of Philadelphia Department of Records, City Archives, RG 21, Quarter Sessions Court, Docket, Vol. 68, p. 323.

60. "Letter from William Still," *National Anti-Slavery Standard*, May 5,

1860; "Quarter Sessions," Philadelphia *Public Ledger*, April 23, 1860.

61. "Tribute to William Still," *National Anti-Slavery Standard*, May 19, 1860; 1860 U.S. Federal Census, Philadelphia Ward 4 West Division, Philadelphia, Pennsylvania, digital image, s.v. "Wm Still," Ancestry.com; Harry C. Silcox, "The Black "Better Class" Political Dilemma: Philadelphia Prototype Isaiah C. Wears," *Pennsylvania Magazine of History and Biography* 113, no. 1 (January 1989): 45–66.

62. "Our Philadelphia Letter," *Weekly Anglo-African*, May 12, 1860; Brown, *Black Man*, 271–72; "The Late Philadelphia Libel Suit," *Weekly Anglo-African*, May 19, 1860; "The Still Sympathy Meeting," *Weekly Anglo-African*, May 26, 1860.

63. "Fugitive Slave Case," Philadelphia *Public Ledger*, March 27, 1860; "Fugitive Slave Case," Philadelphia *Public Ledger*, March 28, 1860; "Fugitive Slave Case," Philadelphia *Public Ledger*, March 29, 1860; Blackett, *Captive's Quest*, 351–52.

64. "Wm. Still's Offence—Libels, &c.," *Weekly Anglo-African*, June 2, 1860.

65. William Still to Mary Ann Shadd, Jan. 8, 1854, Ontario Archives, BAP; William Still to Mary Ann Shadd, Jan. 30, 1858, Mary A. Shadd Papers, Ontario Archives, BAP; "Wm. Still's Offence—Libels, &c.," *Weekly Anglo-African*, June 2, 1860.

66. "William Still," *National Anti-Slavery Standard*, April 28, 1860; Minutes, Executive Committee, March 28, 1860, Pennsylvania Anti-Slavery Society, Pennsylvania Abolition Society Papers, HSP.

CHAPTER NINE

1. Ham & Eggs to William Still, Oct. 17, 1860, in UGRR, 41–42.

2. Jon Grinspan, "'Young Men for War': The Wide Awakes and Lincoln's 1860 Presidential Campaign," *Journal of American History* 96, no. 2 (Sept. 2009): 357–378.

3. Steven Hahn, *A Nation Under Our Feet: Black Political Struggles in the Rural South, from Slavery to the Great Migration* (Cambridge, MA: Harvard University Press, 2003), 13–16; Stephanie McCurry, *Confederate Reckoning: Power and Politics in the Civil War South* (Cambridge, MA: Harvard University Press, 2010), 229.

4. David M. Potter, *The Impending Crisis: America Before the Civil War, 1848–1861* (New York: Harper & Row, 1977), 405–47.

5. "Our Philadelphia Letter," *Weekly Anglo-African*, Dec. 22, 1860.

6. Ibid.; William Still to Charles Sumner, June 12, 1860, Sumner Papers, Harvard University, BAP; Charles Sumner, *The Barbarism of Slavery* (New York: Young Men's Republican Union, 1860).

7. UGRR, xxviii, 530–31. Still's book is an imperfect measure in this regard, in part due to his admitted lack of record-keeping after Harpers Ferry, but of those mentioned in the book only 26 fugitives escaped in 1860, as compared to a high of 155 in 1857. The author is grateful for the work of James McGowan in tabulating these numbers. For a closer look at McGowan's database of Still's fugitives, see William C. Kashatus, *William Still: The Underground Railroad and the Angel at Philadelphia* (Notre Dame, IN: University of Notre Dame Press, 2021).

8. Frederick W. Speirs, "The Street Railway System of Philadelphia, Its History and Present Condition," *Johns Hopkins University Studies in Historical and Political Science*, 15th ser. (Baltimore: Johns Hopkins University, 1897), quote on 23; John Hepp, "Streetcars," *The Encyclopedia of Greater Philadelphia*, https://philadelphiaencyclopedia.org/archive/streetcars/.

9. "Colored People and the Cars," Philadelphia *North American*, Aug. 31, 1859; Kate Masur, *Until Justice Be Done: America's First Civil Rights Movement, from the Revolution to Reconstruction* (New York: W. W. Norton, 2021), 212; R. J. M. Blackett, *Beating Against the Barriers: The Lives of Six Nineteenth-Century Afro-Americans* (Ithaca, NY: Cornell University Press, 1986), 59–62.

10. "Colored People and the Cars," Philadelphia *North American*, Aug. 31, 1859.

11. J. Thomas Sharf and Thompson Westcott, *History of Philadelphia, 1609–1884*, 3 vols. (Philadelphia: L. H. Everts & Co., 1884), 3:1970–73; William Dusinberre, *Civil War Issues in Philadelphia, 1856–1865* (Philadelphia: University of Pennsylvania Press, 1965), 35.

12. This has led some historians to criticize free Black leaders for their supposed naivete and disconnect from the Black masses. As I argue here, and have argued more explicitly elsewhere, this misses the context of such language, which tended to be a part of a broader abolitionist and reformist program, as evidenced by people like Still. For a classic statement of this critique, see Frederick Cooper, "Elevating the Race: The Social Thought of Black Leaders, 1827–1850," *American Quarterly* 24, no. 5 (December 1972), 604–25; or more recently, see Van Gosse, *The First Reconstruction:*

Black Politics in America from the Revolution to the Civil War (Chapel Hill: University of North Carolina Press, 2021), 61–93.

13. Howard H. Bell, "The American Moral Reform Society," *Journal of Negro Education* 27 (Winter 1958): 34–40; Julie Winch, *Philadelphia's Black Elite: Activism, Accommodation, and the Struggle for Autonomy, 1797–1848* (Philadelphia: Temple University Press, 1988), 108–29.

14. "Self-Improvement," *Weekly Anglo-African*, March 17, 1860.

15. "Speech of William Still," *National Anti-Slavery Standard*, Aug. 18, 1860.

16. 1860 U.S. Federal Census, Philadelphia Ward 4 West Division, Philadelphia, Pennsylvania, digital image, s.v. "Wm Still," Ancestry .com. The census lists Letitia's age as "1/12" and the census taker lists the date as July 13, 1860.

17. Minutes, Records of the Social, Civil, and Statistical Association of the Colored People of Pennsylvania (SCSA), 51–52, Leon Gardiner Collection of American Negro Historical Society Records, Series IX, Box 1G, HSP.

18. Minutes, Records of the SCSA, 1–19, 53.

19. Dusinberre, *Civil War Issues*, 100–101; Michael Burlingame, *Abraham Lincoln: A Life*, 2 vols. (Baltimore: Johns Hopkins University Press, 2008), 1:635–37; "Political," *Philadelphia Inquirer*, Oct. 24, 1860; "Local Intelligence—The People's Barbecue," *Philadelphia Inquirer*, Oct. 29, 1860; "What Is the Duty of Radical Abolitionists in the Present Campaign," *Douglass' Monthly*, October 1860; "Our Philadelphia Letter," *Weekly Anglo-African*, Dec. 22, 1860.

20. "Declaration of Immediate Causes Which Induce and Justify the Secession of South Carolina from the Federal Union," https:// avalon.law.yale.edu/19th_century/csa_scarsec.asp.

21. Sharf and Westcott, *History of Philadelphia*, 1:740; Dusinberre, *Civil War Issues*, 102–3; "A Union Meeting and a Stormy Time," Philadelphia *North American*, Jan. 7, 1861; Joseph George, Jr., "Philadelphians Greet Their President-Elect," *Pennsylvania History* 29, no. 4 (Oct. 1962): 381–90.

22. UGRR, 530–31.

23. J. W. Dungy to William Still, Jan. 11, 1861, in UGRR, 545–46.

24. "Legal Intelligence," *Philadelphia Inquirer*, Jan. 22, 1861; "The Rights of the Colored People," *Christian Recorder*, Jan. 26, 1861.

25. "The Rights of the Colored People," *Christian Recorder*, Jan. 26, 1861.

26. Abraham Lincoln, *Collected Works*, 8 vols., ed. Roy P. Basler (New Brunswick, N.J.: Rutgers University Press, 1953), 2:492, https://quod.lib.umich.edu/l/lincoln/.

27. Lincoln, *Collected Works*, 4:261–71.

28. Ibid.

29. Richard Blackett, "Lincoln and Colonization," *OAH Magazine of History* 21, no. 4 (October 2007): 19–22; Eric Foner, "Lincoln and Colonization," in *Our Lincoln: New Perspectives on Lincoln and His World*, ed. Eric Foner (New York, W. W. Norton, 2008), 135–66.

30. Potter, *Impending Crisis*, 570–83; James Oakes, *Freedom National: The Destruction of Slavery in the United States, 1861–1865* (New York: W. W. Norton, 2013), 79; Lincoln, *Collected Works*, 4:331–32.

31. Oakes, *Freedom National*, 90; Ira Berlin, *Generations of Captivity: A History of African American Slaves* (Cambridge, MA: Harvard University Press, 2003), 249–51.

32. "The Inaugural Address," *Douglass' Monthly*, April 1861; "Our Philadelphia Correspondence," *National Anti-Slavery Standard*, April 20, 1861; "Proclamation Calling Militia and Convening Congress, April 15, 1861," in Lincoln, *Collected Works*, 4:332–33.

33. Oakes, *Freedom National*, 95–97.

34. Oakes, *Freedom National*, 98–100; *The War of the Rebellion: A Compilation of the Official Records of the Union and Confederate Armies* (Washington DC: Government Printing Office, 1880–1901), ser. II, vol. 1, 754–55.

35. "Fugitive Slaves at Fortress Monroe," Philadelphia *Press*, June 4, 1861; UGRR, xviii–xxix; "Removal," *National Anti-Slavery Standard*, July 6, 1861.

36. UGRR, xxviii–xxx; "It will be seen . . . ," *National Anti-Slavery Standard*, July 6, 1861; Minutes, Executive Committee, May 29, 1861, Pennsylvania Anti-Slavery Society Records, HSP.

37. "New Stove Store," *Christian Recorder*, Oct. 19, 1861; Sean Patrick Adams, *Home Fires: How Americans Kept Warm in the 19th Century* (Baltimore: Johns Hopkins University Press, 2014), 23–38.

38. "New Stove Store," *Christian Recorder*, Oct. 19, 1861.

39. "Coal, Stoves, Etc, Etc.," *National Anti-Slavery Standard*, July 20, 1861.

40. "Pennsylvania, Philadelphia City Death Certificates, 1803–1915," [database online], s.v. "Letitia Still," Ancestry.com; Jane Eva Baxter, "How to Die a Good Death: Teaching Young Children About Mortality in Nineteenth Century America," *Childhood in the Past* 12, no. 1 (2019): 35–49; David S. Reynolds, *Mightier Than the*

Sword: Uncle Tom's Cabin and the Battle for America (New York: W. W. Norton, 2011), 25–26.

41. Still, *Underground Railroad*, xlvii–xlviii; Adams, *Home Fires*, 105.

42. Elizabeth R. Varon, *Armies of Deliverance: A New History of the Civil War* (New York: Oxford University Press, 2019), 24–27; "The Rebellion," *Philadelphia Inquirer*, July 25, 1861.

43. Oakes, *Freedom National*, 106–44; "Gen. Butler's Contraband of War," *Liberator*, Sept. 6, 1861.

44. "Colored Philadelphians Forming Regiments," *Weekly Anglo-African*, May 4, 1861; Brian Taylor, *Fighting for Citizenship: Black Northerners and the Debate over Military Service in the Civil War* (Chapel Hill: University of North Carolina Press, 2020), 39–68.

45. Varon, *Armies of Deliverance*, 190–91; Willie Lee Rose, *Rehearsal for Reconstruction: The Port Royal Experiment* (New York: Oxford University Press, 1964).

46. *Philadelphia Freedmen's Relief Association* ([Philadelphia?], 1864), 1; "Local Intelligence," *Philadelphia Inquirer*, March 4, 1862; Executive Committee Minutes, SCSA, March 12, 1862; "Notice," *Christian Recorder*, April 5, 1862.

47. William Still to Dillwyn Parrish, March 11, 1862; William Still to Joseph Truman, March 13, 1862, Pennsylvania Abolition Society Papers, BAP.

48. William Still to Joseph Truman, May 8, 1862; William Still to Educational Committee of the Abolition Society, May 8, 1862, Pennsylvania Abolition Society Papers, BAP; "Contrabands in Philadelphia," Philadelphia *Press*, April 7, 1862.

49. "The Second Confiscation Act," http://www.freedmen.umd.edu/conact2.htm; Oakes, *Freedom National*, 224–55, 301–39.

50. "The President's Proclamation," *National Anti-Slavery Standard*, Dec. 20, 1862.

51. Oakes, *Freedom National*, 341; Frank H. Taylor, *Philadelphia in the Civil War, 1861–1865* ([Philadelphia] The City: 1913), 187; "Meeting in Favor of the Formation of the Massachusetts (Colored) Brigade," *Philadelphia Inquirer*, March 31, 1863.

52. "Colored Enlistments," *Philadelphia Inquirer*, June 26, 1863; "Colored Troops to Be Raised in Pennsylvania," *Philadelphia Inquirer*, June 15, 1863.

53. Taylor, *Philadelphia in the Civil War*, 187; "Colored Troops from Philadelphia," Philadelphia *North American*, June 19, 1863; "Encampment for Colored Troops," *Philadelphia Inquirer*, June 25, 1865; *Addresses of the Hon. W. D. Kelley, Miss Anna E. Dickinson, and*

Mr. Frederick Douglass, at a Mass Meeting . . . (Philadelphia, 1863). Examples of the handbills can be found at the Library Company of Philadelphia, and online at http://librarycompany.org/mcallister exhibition/section3.htm.

54. George E. Stephens to William Still, Sept. 19, 1863, Leon Gardiner Collection of American Negro Historical Society Records, Series I, Box 9G, HSP; Thomas Garrett to William Still, Jan. 23, 1864, in UGRR, 641; "United States Colored Troops" Philadelphia *Press*, Feb. 4, 1864; Eugene C. Murdock, "New York City's Bounty Brokers," *Journal of American History* 53, no. 2 (September 1966): 259–78.

55. "Pennsylvania, Philadelphia City Death Certificates, 1803–1915," database, s.v. "William Still" (father), Ancestry.com.

56. William Wells Brown to William Still, July 13, 1863, Leon Gardiner Collection of American Negro Historical Society Records, Series I, Box 9G, HSP; William Wells Brown, *The Black Man, His Antecedents, His Genius, and His Achievements* (New York: Thomas Hamilton, 1863), 211–14.

57. Brown, *The Black Man*, 211–14.

58. "Letter from William Wells Brown," *Weekly Anglo-African*, Aug. 8, 1863, reprinted in Dorothy Sterling, *Speak Out in Thunder Tones: Letters and Other Writings by Black Northerners, 1787–1865* (New York: Doubleday, 1973), 233.

59. Jeffry D. Wert, "Camp William Penn and the Black Soldier," *Pennsylvania History* 46, no. 4 (October 1979): 335–46; Donald Scott, Sr., *Camp William Penn, 1863–1865: America's First Federal African American Soldiers' Fight for Freedom* (Atglen, PA: Shiffer Military History, 2012), 78; John E. Tobey and Nicolas H. Ellis, *U.S. Army Sutler, 1861–1865* (Wellsboro, PA: Milatus Publications, 2012), 49–89.

60. Tobey and Ellis, *Sutler*, 103–6; Scott, *Camp William Penn*, 19.

61. Louis Wagner to C. W. Foster, Aug. 8, 1863, Record Group 110, National Archives (Philadelphia); James N. Hardie to William Still, Feb. 4, 1864, Leon Gardiner Collection of American Negro Historical Society Records, Series I, Box 9G, HSP; UGRR, xlix; Scott, *Camp William Penn*, 90–91.

62. James Elton Johnson, "A History of Camp William Penn and Its Black Troops in the Civil War, 1863–1865" (PhD diss., University of Pennsylvania, 1999), 99; UGRR, xlix–l.

63. "From Camp Shelton Hill, Pa.," *Christian Recorder*, March 26, 1864; "Legal Intelligence," *Philadelphia Inquirer*, May 25, 1864;

"The Courts," Philadelphia *Daily Age*, May 25, 1864; "Legal Intelligence," *Philadelphia Inquirer*, May 26, 1864.

64. "Card to the Public," *Philadelphia Inquirer*, May 27, 1864; UGRR, l.

65. "Assault on Sergeant-Major Green (Colored)," *Christian Recorder*, Oct. 1, 1864; Scott, *Camp William Penn*, 284–302; UGRR, xlviii.

66. Scott, *Camp William Penn*, 132–39, 141–43, 162–65, 212–16; "Camp William Penn," *Christian Recorder*, April 29, 1865; Assistant Adjutant General Schultz to Lieutenant Colonel Louis Wagner, April 15, 1865, Record Group 110, National Archives (Philadelphia); "Obsequies of the Late President, Abraham Lincoln," Philadelphia *Press*, April 24, 1865.

CHAPTER TEN

1. "The Passenger Cars of Philadelphia," Philadelphia *Press*, reprinted in *Christian Recorder*, Dec. 26, 1863.

2. Minutes of the Executive Committee, Records of the SCSA, Nov. 25, 1861, Leon Gardiner Collection of American Negro Historical Society Records, Series IX, Box 1G, HSP; William Still, *A Brief Narrative of the Struggle for the Rights of the Colored People of Philadelphia in the City Railway Cars . . .* (Philadelphia: Merrihew & Sons, 1867), 4–5.

3. Still, *A Brief Narrative*, 10–11; "The Colored People and the City Cars," Philadelphia *Press*, reprinted in *National Anti-Slavery Standard*, Dec. 17, 1864.

4. Minutes of the Executive Committee, SCSA Records, Dec. 19, 1864; Still, *A Brief Narrative*, 11.

5. Still, *A Brief Narrative*, 11–12; "The Passenger Cars and Our Colored Population," Philadelphia *Press*, Jan. 14, 1865; Philip S. Foner, "The Battle to End Discrimination Against Negroes on Philadelphia Streetcars: (Part 1) Background and Beginning of the Battle," *Pennsylvania History* 40, no. 3 (Summer 1973): 287.

6. "The Passenger Cars and Our Colored Population," Philadelphia *Press*, Jan. 14, 1865.

7. "Shall the People Ride in the City Passenger Cars?," *Philadelphia Inquirer*, Jan. 31, 1865; "Voting in the Cars," Philadelphia *Press*, Jan. 31, 1865; "Colored Persons in Passenger Cars," Philadelphia *Public Ledger*, Jan. 31, 1865; Benjamin Peter Hunt, *Why Colored People in Philadelphia Are Excluded from the Street Cars* (Philadelphia: Merrihew & Son, 1866).

8. Minutes of the Executive Committee, SCSA Records, May 29, 1865.

9. "The Speech of Hon. Morrow B. Lowry," *Liberator,* Feb. 3, 1865; Hunt, *Why Colored People in Philadelphia Are Excluded,* 4.

10. "Interesting Lectures," *Christian Recorder,* Jan. 7, 1865.

11. Minutes, SCSA Records, Sept. 5, 1860; Minutes of the Executive Committee, SCSA Records, July 10, 1865; "The Right of Suffrage," *Christian Recorder,* July 22, 1865.

12. "The Right of Suffrage," *Christian Recorder,* July 22, 1865; Minutes of the Executive Committee, SCSA Records, Sept. 4; *Proceedings of the State Equal Rights' Convention, of the Colored People of Pennsylvania, held in the city of Harrisburg February 8th, 9th, and 10th, 1865* (Philadelphia, 1865), https://omeka.coloredconventions.org/items/show/242; Hugh Davis, "The Pennsylvania State Equal Rights League and the Northern Black Struggle for Legal Equality, 1864–1877," *Pennsylvania Magazine of History and Biography* 126, no. 4 (October 2002): 611–34.

13. Minutes of the Executive Committee, SCSA Records; "Interesting Lectures," *Christian Recorder,* Jan. 7, 1865.

14. Minutes of the Executive Committee, SCSA Records, July, 25, 1864; Edward M. Davis to [?], Aug. 8, 1865, and Samuel Rhodes to Col. O. Brown, Aug. 8, 1865, Leon Gardiner Collection of American Negro Historical Society Records, Series I, Box 9G, HSP.

15. Geraldine Rhoades Beckford, "Anderson, Caroline Virginia Still Wiley," Oxford African American Studies Center, May 31, 2013, https://oxfordaasc-com.proxy-tu.researchport.umd.edu/view/10.1093/acref/9780195301731.001.0001/acref-9780195301731-e-36070 (accessed Oct. 22, 2020); UGRR, lxiv; "Annual Report of the Managers of the Institute for Colored Youth," *Christian Recorder,* Oct. 8, 1864; J. Brent Morris, *Oberlin, Hotbed of Abolition: College, Community and the Fight for Freedom and Equality in Antebellum America* (Chapel Hill: University of North Carolina Press, 2014), 12–35, 72–77.

16. "Oberlin Commencement," *Christian Recorder,* Sept. 15, 1865.

17. William Still to Caroline Still, Aug. 15, 1866, Caroline Still to William Still, June 1, 1866, WSB.

18. Caroline Still to Edward Wiley, Jan. 16, 1866; William Still to Caroline Still, April 30, 1866; WSB.

19. "Wanted," *Christian Recorder,* Sept. 9, 1865; "Lights and Shadows: Colored Gentlemen of Philadelphia," Philadelphia *Saturday Night,* reprinted in *Colored American,* Nov. 4, 1865.

20. "Stoves, Heaters, Ranges, &c.," Philadelphia *Press*, Feb. 6, 1866; UGRR, lxi–lxii; G. M. Hopkins, *City Atlas of Philadelphia*, vol. 6, *Wards 2 through 20, 29 and 31* (1875), http://www.philageohistory .org/tiles/viewer/?SelectedLayers=Overlay,GMH1875v6.

21. UGRR, lxii; *McElroy's Philadelphia City Directory* (Philadelphia: Edward C. & John Biddle, 1866), 781; Philadelphia Deed Book, L.R.B., no. 181, p. 386, Familysearch.org. Thanks to Jim Duffin for his help in locating these records.

22. "Coal Yard," *Christian Recorder*, July 7, 1866; "The Subscriber Having Opened a Coal Yard," Philadelphia *Press*, March 23, 1867; UGRR, lxii; "Mr. Editor," *Christian Recorder*, Oct. 20, 1866.

23. William Still to Caroline Still, April 30, 1866, WSB; *McElroy's Philadelphia City Directory* (Philadelphia: Edward C. & John Biddle, 1867), 873.

24. Pew Rent Ledger, First African Presbyterian Church Records, 1841–1990, Presbyterian Historical Society; William T. Catto, *A Semi-Centennial Discourse Delivered in the First African Presbyterian Church, Philadelphia . . .* (Philadelphia: Joseph M. Wilson, 1857), 101; Jacob C. White, Jr., to Board of Trustees, First African Presbyterian Church, Dec. 4, 1865, Leon Gardiner Collection of American Negro Historical Society Records, HSP.

25. Hunt, *Why Colored People in Philadelphia Are Excluded*, 4.

26. "Colored Passengers in Streetcars," *Liberator*, March 24, 1865.

27. Philip S. Foner, "The Battle to End Discrimination Against Negroes on Philadelphia Streetcars: (Part 2) The Victory," *Pennsylvania History* 40, no. 4 (Fall 1973): 359–60.

28. Minutes, SCSA Records, Feb. 2, 1866; "The Colored People and the Cars," *Philadelphia Inquirer*, March 21, 1866; Hunt, *Why Colored People in Philadelphia Are Excluded*, 5.

29. "The Colored People and the Cars," *Philadelphia Inquirer*, March 21, 1866; "Local Affairs," Philadelphia *Public Ledger*, March 21, 1866.

30. Douglas R. Egerton, *The Wars of Reconstruction: The Brief Violent History of America's Most Progressive Era* (New York: Bloomsbury, 2014), 172–74.

31. Eric Foner, *The Second Founding: How the Civil War and Reconstruction Remade the Constitution* (New York: W. W. Norton, 2019), 46–49; Egerton, *Wars of Reconstruction*, 178–79.

32. "Our Charleston Letter," *Christian Recorder*, Sept. 30, 1865; "Legislative Acts," Harrisburg (PA) *Patriot*, Jan. 31, 1866.

33. Foner, *Second Founding*, 63–64; *An Act to Protect All Persons in the United States in Their Civil Rights, and Furnish the Means of Their*

Vindication, https://www.loc.gov/item/llsl-v14/; "Civil Rights of Freedmen," Philadelphia *North American,* Jan. 9, 1866. For a deeper history of the Black struggle for birthright citizenship, see Martha S. Jones, *Birthright Citizens: A History of Race and Rights in Antebellum America* (New York: Cambridge University Press, 2018), esp. 16–34.

34. Foner, *Second Founding,* 65–66.

35. "Veto of the Civil Rights Bill," Philadelphia *Age,* March 28, 1866; Mark Wahlgren Summers, *The Ordeal of the Reunion: A New History of Reconstruction* (Chapel Hill: University of North Carolina Press, 2014), 87–90.

36. Summers, *Ordeal of the Reunion,* 97–98; David Montgomery, "Radical Republicanism in Pennsylvania, 1866–1873," *Pennsylvania Magazine of History and Biography* (October 1961): 439–57; "Reconstruction," Philadelphia *Age,* May 1, 1866; *The Freedman's Bureau! An agency to keep the Negro in idleness at the expense of the white man,* photograph, Pennsylvania 1866, https://www.loc.gov/item/2008661698/; *The Two Platforms,* photograph, Pennsylvania 1866, https://www.loc.gov/item/2008661700/.

37. "The Campaign," Philadelphia *Press,* Aug. 31, 1866; "Johnson-ism," Philadelphia *Press,* July 19, 1866; "Negro Suffrage a Home Issue," Philadelphia *Age,* May 9, 1866.

38. "An Address by Hon. Wm. D. Kelley," *Liberator,* March 31, 1865; "Colored Men Distributing Loyal Publications," *Christian Recorder,* April 21, 1866; Executive Committee Minutes, SCSA Records, Feb. 26, April 30, 1866; Ira V. Brown, "William D. Kelley and Radical Reconstruction," *Pennsylvania Magazine of History and Biography* (July 1961): 316–29.

39. Summers, *Ordeal of the Reunion,* 98–99; Executive Committee Minutes, SCSA Records, June 4, 1866; "The Flag Presentation," Philadelphia *Press,* July 3, 1866; "Freedmen's Aid Fair," Philadelphia *Public Ledger,* July 4, 1866, "Freedmen's Fair," *Christian Recorder,* June 30, 1866.

40. "Colored Soldiers and Sailors Convention," *Christian Recorder,* Jan. 12, 1867.

41. Still, *A Brief Narrative,* 16.

42. "Equal Rights Association," Philadelphia *Evening Telegraph,* Jan. 18, 1867; "Equal Rights," Philadelphia *North American,* Jan. 18, 1867.

43. Minutes, PA State Equal Rights League, Feb. 19, 1867, Leon Gardiner Collection of American Negro Historical Society Records, Series IX, Vol. 1, HSP; "Pennsylvania Legislature," Harrisburg

Patriot, Feb. 1, 1867; Daniel R. Biddle and Murry Dubin, *Tasting Freedom: Octavius Catto and the Battle for Equality in Civil War America* (Philadelphia: Temple University Press, 2010), 351; Still, *A Brief Narrative*, 17–19.

44. "Pennsylvania Legislature," Philadelphia *Press*, Feb. 1, 1867; "Pennsylvania Legislature," Philadelphia *Press*, March 19, 1867; "General Intelligence," Philadelphia *National Baptist*, March 28, 1867; *Laws of the General Assembly of the Commonwealth of Pennsylvania passed at the session* (Harrisburg, PA: Singerly & Myers, 1867), 38–39.

45. "Colored People in the Cars," Philadelphia *Press*, March 27, 1867; "Testing the New Railroad Law," Philadelphia *Evening Telegraph*, March 27, 1867; "Colored People in the Cars," Philadelphia *Press*, March 28, 1867; Biddle and Dubin, *Tasting Freedom*, 352.

46. "The Colored People and the Cars—The Grand Result," Philadelphia *Press*, March 28, 1867; "Interesting Occasion," Philadelphia *Press*, Nov. 12, 1866; Philadelphia Deed Book, J.T.O., no. 81, pp. 419–21, Familysearch.org. Thanks to Jim Duffin for his help in locating these records.

47. Still, *A Brief Narrative*, 1–2.

48. Still, *A Brief Narrative*, 16–17; Minutes, SCSA Records, Dec. 17, 1866; Feb. 18, 1867; Octavius Catto and Rebecca Underwood, 1861–62, Philadelphia, Pennsylvania, Death Certificates Index, 1803–1915. I am indebted to Donna Rilling for sharing with me this information about Catto's child and relationship with Underwood, which she uncovered in the course of her own research.

49. "Colored People and the Cars," Philadelphia *North American*, Aug. 31, 1859.

50. Alberta S. Norwood, "Negro Welfare Work in Philadelphia" (master's thesis, University of Pennsylvania, 1931), 63; Still, *A Brief Narrative*.

51. Still, *A Brief Narrative*.

CHAPTER ELEVEN

1. Robert Jones, *Fifty Years in the Lombard Street Central Presbyterian Church* (Philadelphia: Edward Stern & Co., 1894), 82; William Still to Caroline Still, Aug. 13, 1867, WSB.

2. William Still to Caroline Still, Aug. 13, 1867, WSB.

3. Andrew Hook, "Macaulay and America," *Journal of American Studies* 9, no. 3 (December 1975): 335–46.

4. Ibid, 343–44.

5. William Still, *A Brief Narrative of the Struggle for the Rights of the Colored People of Philadelphia in the City Railway Cars . . .* (Philadelphia: Merrihew & Sons, 1867), 23. On the memory of the Civil War and its relationship to the struggle for Black rights, see Caroline Janney, *Remembering the Civil War: Reunion and the Limits of Reconciliation* (Chapel Hill: University of North Carolina Press, 2013); David W. Blight, *Race and Reunion: The Civil War in American Memory* (Cambridge, MA: Harvard University Press, 2001).

6. "The Freedmen's Monument to Lincoln," *San Francisco Bulletin*, May 10, 1867; Kirk Savage, *Standing Soldiers, Kneeling Slaves: Race, War, and Monument in Nineteenth-Century America* (Princeton, NJ: Princeton University Press, 1997), 100.

7. William Still to Caroline Still, Aug. 13, 1867, WSB; "A Model Coal Yard," *Christian Recorder*, July 13, 1867.

8. "Prices Reduced," Philadelphia *Press*, Jan. 1, 1870; Sean Patrick Adams, *Home Fires: How Americans Kept Warm in the 19th Century* (Baltimore: Johns Hopkins University Press, 2014), 107–10; William Still to Caroline Still, March 5, 1868, WSB.

9. "PA Equal Rights League," *Philadelphia Inquirer*, Aug. 15, 1867; Andrew Diemer, "Reconstructing Philadelphia: African Americans and Politics in the Post-Civil War North," *Pennsylvania Magazine of History and Biography* 133, no. 1 (January 2009): 44; "The Election," Philadelphia *Press*, Oct. 7, 1867.

10. Diemer, "Reconstructing Philadelphia," 44.

11. "The Election," Philadelphia *North American*, Oct. 10, 1867; *A Philadelphia Perspective: The Diary of Sidney George Fisher covering the years 1834–1871*, ed. Nicholas Wainwright (Philadelphia: Historical Society of Pennsylvania, 1967), 533; James Buchanan to Augustus Schell, Nov. 9, 1867, in *The Works of James Buchanan, Comprising His Speeches, State Papers, and Private Correspondence*, ed. John Bassett Moore (Philadelphia: J. B. Lippincott, 1908–11), 11:455; "The Salt River Gazette—Extra. Wednesday, Oct. 9, 1867," political cartoon, 1867, Library Company of Philadelphia.

12. William Still to Caroline Still, Nov. 19, 1867; Letitia Still to Caroline Still, March 5, 1868, WSB.

13. "Oberlin Commencement," *Boston Recorder*, Aug. 13, 1868; "Oberlin College," Philadelphia *Messenger*, Aug. 26, 1868; "A Wedding," *Christian Recorder*, Jan. 8, 1870; Caroline Still to Edward Wiley, Feb. 17, 1869, WSB.

14. "Our Colored Soldiers' Orphans," Philadelphia *Press*, March 26, 1868; "Meeting of the Colored Soldiers' and Sailors' Orphans' Home Association," Philadelphia *Press*, May 7, 1868; Constitution, By-Laws and Rules of the Home for Aged and Infirm Colored Persons (Philadelphia: Merrihew & Son, 1865), 2; Tenth Annual Report of the Board of Managers of the Home for Aged and Infirm Colored Persons (Philadelphia: Merrihew & Son, 1874), 3; Leslie J. Pollard, "Black Beneficial Societies and the Home for Aged and Infirm Colored People," *Phylon* 4, no. 3 (3rd Quarter 1980): 230–34.

15. Roger Lane, *William Dorsey's Philadelphia and Ours: On the Past and Future of the Black City in America* (New York: Oxford University Press, 1991), 289; David Lawrence Mason, *From Buildings and Loans to Bail-Outs: A History of the American Savings and Loan Industry, 1831–1995* (Cambridge: Cambridge University Press, 2004), 12–26.

16. "Parlor Reading," *Christian Recorder*, July 11, 1868; Melba Joyce Boyd, *Discarded Legacy: Politics and Poetics in the Life of Frances E. W. Harper, 1825–1911* (Detroit, MI: Wayne State University Press, 1994), 92–109.

17. "Mrs. F.E.W. Harper," *Christian Recorder*, Oct. 3, 1868; Boyd, *Discarded Legacy*, 33–78.

18. Caroline Still to Edward Wiley, Feb. 17, 1869, WSB; "A Wedding," *Christian Recorder*, Jan. 8, 1870.

19. "A Wedding," *Christian Recorder*, Jan. 8, 1870.

20. Diemer, "Reconstructing Philadelphia," 45–46; David Montgomery, *Beyond Equality: Labor and the Radical Republicans, 1862–1872* (New York: Alfred A. Knopf, 1967), 450–51.

21. "Speech of Hon. Richmond L. Jones," Harrisburg *Patriot*, March 4, 1868; Diemer, "Reconstructing Philadelphia," 46–47.

22. "Address of the Republican State Central Committee," Philadelphia *Evening Telegraph*, Oct. 15, 1868; "The Official Count," *Philadelphia Inquirer*, Oct. 17, 1868; J. Thomas Sharf and Thompson Westcott, *History of Philadelphia, 1609–1884*, 3 vols. (Philadelphia L. H. Everts & Co., 1884), 1:835; Diemer, "Reconstructing Philadelphia," 48–49; "Salt River Express. Wednesday, October 14, 1868," political cartoon, 1868, Library Company of Philadelphia.

23. "The Pennsylvania State Equal Rights League," Philadelphia *Press*, Aug. 13, 1968.

24. Eric Foner, *The Second Founding: How the Civil War and Reconstruction Remade the Constitution* (New York: W. W. Norton, 2019), xvii,

102–8; Ira V. Brown, "Pennsylvania and the Rights of the Negro, 1865–1887," *Pennsylvania History* 28, no. 1 (January 1861): 52.

25. "Ratified," Philadelphia *Press*, Feb. 5, 1870; "Colored Union League," Philadelphia *Press*, Feb. 9, 1870; "Jubilanto," Philadelphia *Evening Telegraph*, April 26, 1870.

26. "Jubilanto," Philadelphia *Evening Telegraph*, April 26, 1870; "The Fifteenth Amendment," Philadelphia *Press*, April 26, 1870.

27. Foner, *The Second Founding*, 105–8.

28. "The Pennsylvania Anti-Slavery Society a Thing of the Past," Philadelphia *Press*, May 6, 1870; Kate E. R. Pickard, *The Kidnapped and the Ransomed* (Syracuse, NY: William T. Hamilton, 1856), 25–27.

29. "The Pennsylvania Anti-Slavery Society a Thing of the Past," Philadelphia *Press*, May 6, 1870.

30. "Pennsylvania Anti-Slavery Society," *Philadelphia Inquirer*, May 6, 1870.

31. "The Moyamensing Hose Company," Philadelphia *Press*, April 18, 1870; Harry C. Silcox, "William McMullen, Nineteenth-Century Political Boss," *Pennsylvania Magazine of History and Biography* 110, no. 3 (July 1986): 389–412.

32. "Election Day," Philadelphia *Evening Telegraph*, Oct. 11, 1870.

33. "Local Affairs," Philadelphia *Public Ledger*, Oct. 12, 1870; "The Election," Philadelphia *Evening Telegraph*, Oct. 12, 1870; Diemer, "Reconstructing Philadelphia," 53; Foner, *The Second Founding*, 118.

34. "The Election," Philadelphia *Evening Telegraph*, Oct. 12, 1870; "Governor's Message," Philadelphia *North American*, Jan. 5, 1871; Diemer, "Reconstructing Philadelphia," 53–54.

35. Harry C. Silcox, "Nineteenth Century Black Militant: Octavius Catto (1839–1871)," *Pennsylvania History* 44, no. 1 (Winter 1977): 73; "The Assassination of Catto," *Philadelphia Inquirer*, Oct. 13, 1871; Daniel R. Biddle and Murray Dubin, *Tasting Freedom: Octavius Catto and the Battle for Equality in Civil War America* (Philadelphia: Temple University Press, 2010), 421–30.

36. UGRR, xxxv; "The Coal Strike," Philadelphia *Public Ledger*, May 25, 1871; William Still to J. Miller McKim, Nov. 10, 1871, James Miller McKim Papers, New York Public Library.

37. Stephen G. Hall, "To Render the Private Public: William Still and the Selling of 'The Underground Railroad,'" *Pennsylvania Magazine of History and Biography* 127, no. 1 (January 2003): 47; UGRR, xxxv; William Still, *The Underground Railroad: A Record of*

Facts, Authentic Narratives, Letters, &c . . . (Philadelphia: Porter & Coates, 1872), 1.

38. UGRR, xxxv–xxxvi.
39. Still, *Underground Railroad* (1872), 2–4, 8.
40. Still, *Underground Railroad* (1872), 2.
41. "The Underground Railroad," Philadelphia *National Baptist*, April 4, 1872. For just a small sample of such depictions, see UGRR, 173, 194, 241, 267, quote on 267. On white antislavery depictions of "childlike" slaves, in this case Harriet Beecher Stowe, see Ibram X. Kendi, *Stamped from the Beginning: The Definitive History of Racist Ideas in America* (New York: Nation Books, 2016), 193–95.
42. Hall, "To Render the Public Private," 47–48; Eric Gardner, *Black Print Unbound: The Christian Recorder, African American Literature, and Periodical Culture* (New York: Oxford University Press, 2015), 10–11.
43. Hall, "To Render the Public Private," 47–50. For an example of the Henry "Box" Brown advertisement, see "Underground Railroad," *Christian Recorder*, April 24, 1873.
44. Hall, "To Render the Public Private," 50–55.
45. "Literary Notes," *Lutheran Observer* (Philadelphia), July 11, 1873; "The Underground Railroad," *Christian Recorder*, April 27, 1872.

CHAPTER TWELVE

1. "Wm. Still, Esq.," *Christian Recorder*, Nov. 6, 1873; Robert Jones, *Fifty Years at Lombard Central Presbyterian Church* (Philadelphia: Edward Stern & Co., 1894), 85.
2. "Reforms and Reformers," *Christian Recorder*, Nov. 27, 1873.
3. "Reforms and Reformers," *Christian Recorder*, Nov. 27, 1873; "Reforms and Reformers (Concluded)," *Christian Recorder*, Dec. 4, 1873.
4. "Reforms and Reformers (Concluded)," *Christian Recorder*, Dec. 4, 1873.
5. "National Convention at New Orleans, LA," Colored Conventions Project Digital Records, https://omeka.coloredconventions .org/items/show/544 (accessed January 29, 2021); Leslie Butler, *Critical Americans: Victorian Intellectuals and Transatlantic Liberal Reform* (Chapel Hill: University of North Carolina Press, 2007), quote on 10; UGRR, xxxi.
6. David Montgomery, *Beyond Equality: Labor and the Radical Repub-*

licans, 1862–1872 (New York: Alfred A. Knopf, 1967), 379–86; Andrew Slap, *The Doom of Reconstruction: The Liberal Republicans in the Civil War Era* (New York: Fordham University Press, 2006), 73–89; Mark Wahlgren Summers, *The Ordeal of the Reunion: A New History of Reconstruction* (Chapel Hill: University of North Carolina Press, 2014), 285–86.

7. Summers, *Ordeal of the Reunion*, 303–21, quote on 304.

8. Frank B. Evans, *Pennsylvania Politics, 1872–1877: A Study in Political Leadership* (Harrisburg: Commonwealth of Pennsylvania, Pennsylvania Historical and Museum Commission, 1966), 15; Alexander McClure, *Old Time Notes of Pennsylvania*, 2 vols. (Philadelphia: John C. Winston Co., 1905), 2:237.

9. Peter McCaffery, *When Bosses Ruled Philadelphia: The Emergence of the Republican Machine, 1867–1933* (University Park: Pennsylvania State University Press, 1993), 17–22.

10. Evans, *Pennsylvania Politics*, 28–30; McCaffery, *When Bosses Ruled Philadelphia*, 22–27.

11. Evans, *Pennsylvania Politics*, 95–98; "The Centennial Mayoralty," *Philadelphia Inquirer*, Jan. 28, 1874; "McClure Meeting at Spring Garden Hall," *Philadelphia Inquirer*, Feb. 11, 1874.

12. "We Hear It Hinted," *Christian Recorder*, Feb. 19, 1874; William Still, *An Address on Voting and Laboring, Delivered at Concert Hall* (Philadelphia: Jas. B. Rodgers Co., 1874), 1.

13. "Philadelphia Items," *Christian Recorder*, March 12, 1874; Still, *Address on Voting*, 3.

14. Still, *Address on Voting*.

15. "We have been permitted to copy . . . ," *Christian Recorder*, April 9, 1874; "Wm. Still's Address," *Christian Recorder*, April 16, 1874; Francis Grimké to William Still, March 18, 1874, Leon Gardiner Collection of American Negro Historical Society Records, Series I, Box 9G, HSP. On debates over Black partisanship in Boston, see Millington W. Bergeson-Lockwood, *Race over Party: Black Politics and Partisanship in Late Nineteenth-Century Boston* (Chapel Hill: University of North Carolina Press, 2018).

16. "How?" *Christian Recorder*, Feb. 18, 1875.

17. Anonymous to William Still, March 14, 1874, Leon Gardiner Collection of American Negro Historical Society Records, Series I, Box 9G, HSP.

18. Elizabeth Williams to William Still, March 24, March 29, 1874, Leon Gardiner Collection of American Negro Historical Society Records, Series I, Box 9G, HSP.

19. William Still to Caroline Still Wiley, Sept. 7, 1874, WSB.

20. "Endorsements and Opinions," *Christian Recorder*, May 21, 1874.

21. Edward Wiley to Caroline Still Wiley, May 6, Aug. 6, 1873, William Still to Edward Wiley, May 22, 1873, WSB; Stephen G. Hall, "To Render the Private Public: William Still and the Selling of 'The Underground Railroad,'" *Pennsylvania Magazine of History and Biography* 127, no. 1 (January 2003): 51.

22. Caroline Still Wiley to Edward Wiley, Aug. 22, 1873, WSB; "Mr. Wiley," *Christian Recorder*, Feb. 19, 1874; Will of Edward A. Wiley, Pennsylvania, U.S., Wills and Probate Records, 1683–1993; Pennsylvania, Philadelphia City Death Certificates, 1803–1915, digital image, s.v. "Edward A. Wiley," Ancestry.com.

23. Frances Ellen Still to Letitia Still, Sept. 7, 1874; William Still to Caroline Still Wiley, Sept. 7, 1874; Caroline Wiley Still to Letitia Still, Sept. 9, 1874, WSB.

24. James Rhoads to Caroline Still Wiley, Sept. 22, 1875; William Still to Caroline Still Wiley, Oct. 12, 1875; James Still to Caroline Still, Sept. 3, 1867, WSB; Charles Fred. White, *Who's Who in Philadelphia: A Collection of Thirty Biographical Sketches of Philadelphia Colored People* (Philadelphia: A.M.E. Book Concern, 1912), 18–19; Nora N. Nercessian, "Nineteenth-Century Black Graduates of Harvard Medical School," *Journal of Blacks in Higher Education*, no. 47 (Spring 2005): 88–92.

25. White, *Who's Who*, 18; William Still to Caroline Still Wiley, Oct. 12, 1875, and Feb. 1, 1876, WSB.

26. William Still to Caroline Still Wiley, Oct. 12, 1875, WSB.

27. William Still to Caroline Wiley Still, March 6, March 23, 1876, WSB; Philadelphia, Pennsylvania, U.S., Death Certificates Index, 1803–1915, digital image, s.v. "William A. Wiley," Ancestry.com.

28. Francis Grimké to William Still, March 18, 1874, Leon Gardiner Collection of American Negro Historical Society Records, Series I, Box 9G, HSP; "Hon. Charles Sumner," *Philadelphia Inquirer*, March 17, 1874; "The Lamented Senator," *Philadelphia Inquirer*, March 20, 1874.

29. "The Lamented Senator," *Philadelphia Inquirer*, March 20, 1874; Mark Wahlgren Summers, *The Ordeal of the Reunion: A New History of Reconstruction* (Chapel Hill: University of North Carolina Press, 2014), 307–9, 316.

30. "Anti-Slavery," *Philadelphia Inquirer*, April 15, 1875; "The Pennsylvania Anti-Slavery Society," *Christian Recorder*, April 22, 1875. Note that contemporary accounts and even some of the partic-

ipants referred to the organization they were celebrating as the Pennsylvania Anti-Slavery Society even though that was technically the name of a different organization.

31. UGRR, lxiii; "William Lloyd Garrison Memorial Meeting," *Philadelphia Inquirer*, June 13, 1879; "William Still, Esq.," *Christian Recorder*, Dec. 8, 1881; "Abolitionists' Reunion," *Christian Recorder*, Dec. 13, 1883.

32. *Sixteenth Annual Report of the Board of Managers of the Home for Aged and Infirm Colored Persons* (Philadelphia: Castle & Heilman, Steam-Power Printers, 1880); "Brief Notes of Minor Occurrences," *Philadelphia Inquirer*, Feb. 13, 1874; "Our Colored Poor," *Philadelphia Inquirer*, Aug. 11, 1876.

33. "Local News," *Christian Recorder*, April 14, 1881; UGRR, i–lxiv.

34. "Cooperative Associations," *Christian Recorder*, April 12, 1877; "Editor Marshall W. Taylor in Philadelphia," *Christian Recorder*, June 26, 1884.

35. "A Workingmen's Club," *Christian Recorder*, Nov. 7, 1878; "Industrial School for Colored Youth," *Christian Recorder*, July 5, 1883.

36. "We Give Place to a Letter," Philadelphia *North American*, April 28, 1879; *Proceedings of the National Conference of Colored Men of the United States, Held in the State Capitol at Nashville Tennessee, May 6, 7, 8 and 9, 1879* (Washington, DC: Rufus H. Darby, Steam Power Printer, 1879), 56–65.

37. "The Loudest and Longest Applause," *Christian Recorder*, March 21, 1878; White, *Who's Who*, 18; *Catalogue of the Officers and Students of Lincoln University, 1873–74* (Oxford, PA: Republican Steam Power Print, 1874), 9; Still, i, lxiv; William Still to Caroline Still Wiley, Sept. 7, 1874, WSB.

38. "News from the Churches," Richmond (VA) *Central Presbyterian*, July 28, 1880; White, *Who's Who*, 18; "A Grand Wedding," *Christian Recorder*, Jan. 8, 1885; "Matrimony Notice," *Philadelphia Inquirer*, Jan. 1, 1885.

39. "Want Political Recognition," Philadelphia *North American*, Feb. 2, 1877; "A Third Party," *Philadelphia Inquirer*, Feb. 2, 1877.

40. "Rallying Round the Flag," *Philadelphia Inquirer*, July 3, 1880; Elvena S. Bage, *Negro History Bulletin* 14, no. 9 (June 1951): 195–97, 206, 214; *Speech of Gen. Jas. A. Garfield, Delivered to the "Boys in Blue" New York, August 6, 1880* (New York, 1880), https://www.loc.gov/resource/rbpe.12900200/?sp=1.

41. "Philadelphia Politics," Lancaster (PA) *Intelligencer Journal*, Jan. 29,

1881; "Broken Party Ties," *Philadelphia Inquirer*, Jan. 29, 1881; Harry C. Silcox, "The Black 'Better Class' Political Dilemma: Philadelphia Prototype Isaiah Wears," *Pennsylvania Magazine of History and Biography* 113, no. 1 (January 1989): 57–58.

42. "The Entering Wedge," *Philadelphia Inquirer*, Aug. 23, 1881; Silcox, "Isaiah Wears," 60.

43. "The Colored Vote," *Philadelphia Inquirer*, Sept. 19, 1882; "Why Are We Republican?" *Christian Recorder*, Oct. 26, 1882.

44. "Another Assault," *Christian Recorder*, March 15, 1883; "The Bishop Campbell Outrage," *Christian Recorder*, March 22, 1883; "The Treatment of Bishop Campbell," *Philadelphia Inquirer*, April 18, 1883; "The Outrage Recently Perpetrated," *Christian Recorder*, April 26, 1883.

45. "A Negro Opponent of Blaine," Harrisburg *Patriot*, Aug. 9, 1884; August Meier, "The Negro and the Democratic Party, 1875–1915," *Phylon* 17, no. 2 (2nd Quarter 1956): 173–91; Richard White, *The Republic for Which It Stands: The United States During Reconstruction and the Gilded Age, 1865–1896* (New York: Oxford University Press, 2017), 469–75; "The Post, of Their City," *Christian Recorder*, Aug. 21, 1884.

46. "The Political Situation," *Christian Recorder*, Nov. 20, 1884.

47. "Prohibition Party," *Philadelphia Inquirer*, Jan. 24, 1885; "Prohibition's Strength," *Philadelphia Inquirer*, Oct. 4, 1886; Lisa M. F. Andersen, *The Politics of Prohibition: American Governance and the Prohibition Party, 1869–1933* (New York: Cambridge University Press, 2013), 9–24.

48. "The Political Situation," *Christian Recorder*, Nov. 20, 1884; "A Colored YMCA," *Philadelphia Inquirer*, July 3, 1889; Nina Mjagkij, *Light in the Darkness: African Americans and the YMCA, 1852–1946* (Lexington: University Press of Kentucky, 1994).

49. "A Day of Deliverance," *Philadelphia Inquirer*, Jan. 3, 1889; "The Emancipation Celebration," *Christian Recorder*, Jan. 10, 1889; Booker T. Washington to William Still, Nov. 18, 1888, Dec. 30, 1888, Leon Gardiner Collection of American Negro Historical Society Records, Series I, Box 9G, HSP.

50. "A Day of Deliverance," *Philadelphia Inquirer*, Jan. 3, 1889; "The Emancipation Celebration," *Christian Recorder*, Jan. 10, 1889; Frederick Douglass to William Still, Nov. 30, 1888, Dec. 28, 1888, Leon Gardiner Collection of American Negro Historical Society Records, Series I, Box 9G, HSP.

51. "A Day of Deliverance," *Philadelphia Inquirer*, Jan. 3, 1889.

52. Frederick Douglass to William Still, Jan. 4, 1889, Leon Gardiner Collection of American Negro Historical Society Records, Series I, Box 9G, HSP.

EPILOGUE

1. "William Still's Illness," *Philadelphia Inquirer*, Dec. 3, 1900.

2. Seth Pancoast, *What Is Bright's Disease? Its Curability* (Philadelphia: Published by the Author, 1882), 116–18; "Death of a Noted Colored Abolitionist," Washington, DC, *Evening Times*, July 15, 1902.

3. T. Grainger Stewart, "On the Treatment of Chronic Bright's Disease," *British Medical Journal* 2, no. 1546 (Aug. 16, 1890): 389–92; "Treatment of Bright's Disease," *Scientific American* 56, no. 11 (March 12, 1887): 161.

4. "Abolition Society Elects Officers," *Philadelphia Inquirer*, April 28, 1901; Alberta S. Norwood, "Negro Welfare Work in Philadelphia" (master's thesis, University of Pennsylvania, 1931), 103.

5. "Death of a Noted Colored Abolitionist," Washington, DC *Evening Times*, July 15, 1902; William Ashman to Letitia Still, July 15, 1902; Alfred Love to Letitia Still, July 15, 1902, Leon Gardiner Collection of American Negro Historical Society Records, Series I, Box 9G, HSP. The Stills seem to have moved to this home in the last year of William Still's life. After Letitia died it would pass to their daughter, Ella.

6. *Thirty-Sixth Annual Report of the Board of Managers of the Home for Aged and Infirm Colored Persons* (Philadelphia: Press of the Leeds & Biddle Co., 1900), 5; "Semi-Centennial Celebration," *Christian Recorder*, Sept. 27, 1894; "New Hospital," *Philadelphia Inquirer*, Sept. 2, 1895; "The Letter of Mr. William Still," *Christian Recorder*, Oct. 18, 1894; "The Color Line," *Philadelphia Inquirer*, Feb. 12, 1897.

7. "Old Time Friends of the Colored Race," *Philadelphia Inquirer*, Jan. 4, 1893.

8. "Noted Colored Women," Harrisburg *Patriot*, Jan. 20, 1888; *Thirty-Sixth Annual Report of the Board of Managers of the Home for Aged and Infirm Colored Persons*, 5; Roger Lane, *William Dorsey's Philadelphia and Ours: On the Past and Future of the Black City in America* (New York: Oxford University Press, 1991), 250; "Teacher Arrested," *Philadelphia Inquirer*, Aug. 24, 1887; "A Brown Beast in Beufort," Newberry (SC) *Herald and News*, Aug. 25, 1887; *Boyd's*

Co-Partnership and Residence Business Directory of Philadelphia City (Philadelphia, 1899), 694; 1920 U.S. Federal Census, Philadelphia Ward 30, Philadelphia, Pennsylvania, digital image, s.v. "Frances E. Still," Ancestry.com; "Colored Democratic League," *Philadelphia Inquirer,* Sept. 14, 1889; "Mr. Robert G. Still," *Christian Recorder,* Jan. 9, 1896.

9. *Boyd's Co-Partnership and Residence Business Directory of Philadelphia City* (Philadelphia: Boyd's Directory Office, 1898); "Real Estate Transfers," *Philadelphia Inquirer,* Jan. 24, 1899. Thank you to Dr. Gretchen Diemer for her thoughts on kidney disease and its implications for William Still.

10. "Paragraphic News," Washington (DC) *Bee,* Jan. 19, 1907; "Mortuary Notice," *Philadelphia Inquirer,* Jan. 16, 1908; Pennsylvania (State) Death Certificates, 1906–1968; Certificate Number: 8148, Ancestry.com.

11. "To Unveil Bust of William Still," *Philadelphia Inquirer,* April 26, 1903; "On Friday Evening," *Philadelphia Inquirer,* May 3, 1903; Margaret Barlow, "Fuller [née Warrick], Meta Vaux," Grove Art Online, 2003, https://www-oxfordartonline-com.proxy-tu.research port.umd.edu/groveart/view/10.1093/gao/9781884446054 .001.0001/oao-9781884446054-e-7000030178 (accessed July 7, 2021).

12. "Father of the Underground," Boston *Herald,* July 15, 1902; "William Still Dead," Augusta *Chronicle,* July 15, 1902; "Mortuary Notice," Philadelphia *Inquirer,* July 16, 1902; "The Father of the Underground Railroad," Savannah (GA) *Tribune,* July 19, 1902; "William Still," Chicago *Broad Ax,* July 26, 1902.

13. "The Regular Meeting of Bethel Literary," *Christian Recorder,* April 14, 1881; Irvin G. Wyllie, *The Self-Made Man in America: The Myth of Rags to Riches* (New Brunswick, NJ: Rutgers University Press, 1954), 8–24.

14. John Stauffer, *Giants: The Parallel Lives of Frederick Douglass & Abraham Lincoln* (New York: Twelve, 2008), xii–xiii.

15. William Wells Brown, *The Black Man, His Antecedents, His Genius, and His Achievements* (New York: Thomas Hamilton, 1863), 211–12.

BIBLIOGRAPHY

ARCHIVAL PRIMARY SOURCES

Charles L. Blockson Afro-American Collection, Temple University
William Still Collection
City of Philadelphia Department of Records, City Archives
Quarter Sessions Court, Docket
Friends Historical Library, Swarthmore
Elijah F. Pennypacker Antislavery Correspondence
Mott Manuscripts
National Archives, Philadelphia
Records of the District Courts of the United States, 1685–2009
Records of the Provost Marshal General's Bureau (Civil War), 1861–
    1907
Pennsylvania Historical Society
Apprentices Library Company of Philadelphia Records, 1820–1948
Leon Gardiner Collection of American Negro Historical Society
    Records, 1715–1962
Pennsylvania Abolition Society Papers, 1751–1992
Pennsylvania Anti-Slavery Society Records, 1837–1856
Philadelphia Saving Fund Society Records, 1836–1845
William Still, *Journal C of the Underground Railroad in Philadelphia . . .* ,
    1852–1857
Wurts Family Papers, 1796–1884
Presbyterian Historical Society
First African Presbyterian Church Records, 1841–1990
Rare Books and Manuscripts Division, New York Public Library
James Miller McKim Papers, Maloney Collection
Special Collections, Rutgers University
Peter Still papers, 1850–1875

ONLINE DATABASES

Ancestry.com, http://ancestry.com
Black Abolitionist Papers, 1830–1865, https://proquest.com/bap
Familysearch.com, http://familysearch.com
Sydney Howard Gay, Record of Fugitives, Columbia University Libraries, https://exhibitions.library.columbia.edu/exhibits/show/fugitives/record_fugitives

NEWSPAPERS

African Repository and Colonial Journal
Anti-Slavery Bugle (New Lisbon, OH)
Appeal (Saint Paul, MN)
Atlantic Monthly
Augusta (GA) *Chronicle*
Baltimore Sun
Boston Daily Advertiser
Boston Herald
Boston Recorder
Chicago Broad Ax
Christian Recorder
Colored American
Douglass' Monthly
Frederick Douglass' Paper
The Friend: A Religious and Literary Journal
Harrisburg (PA) *Patriot*
Lancaster (PA) *Intelligencer Journal*
Liberator
Lutheran Observer (Philadelphia)
The Midnight Cry
National Anti-Slavery Standard
National Era
National Reformer
New York Daily Tribune
New York Evening Post
The New York Herald
Newberry (SC) *Herald and News*
The North Star
Pennsylvania Freeman
Philadelphia Daily Age

Philadelphia Evening Telegraph
Philadelphia Inquirer
Philadelphia Messenger
Philadelphia National Baptist
Philadelphia North American
Philadelphia Press
Philadelphia Public Ledger
Philadelphia Sunday Dispatch
Provincial Freeman
Raleigh (NC) *Standard*
Richmond (VA) *Central Presbyterian*
San Francisco Bulletin
Savannah (GA) *Tribune*
The Times (Philadelphia)
Voice of the Fugitive (Windsor, Ontario)
Washington Bee
Washington Evening Times
Weekly Anglo-African
Weekly (NC) *Standard*

PRINTED PRIMARY SOURCES

A Review of the Trial, Conviction, and Sentence of George F. Alberti, for Kidnapping. [Philadelphia?], 1851.

Addresses of the Hon. W. D. Kelley, Miss Anna E. Dickinson, and Mr. Frederick Douglass, at a Mass Meeting . . . Philadelphia, 1863.

An Act to Protect all Persons in the United States in their Civil Rights, and Furnish the Means of their Vindication, https://www.loc.gov/law/help/statutes-at-large/39th-congress/session-1/c39s1ch31.pdf.

Anderson, Osborne P. *Voice from Harpers Ferry: A Narrative of Events at Harpers Ferry.* Boston, 1861.

Billington, Ray Allen, ed. *The Journal of Charlotte Forten: A Free Negro in the Slave Era.* New York: Dryden Press, 1953; New York: W. W. Norton & Co., 1981.

Boyd, James P. *William Still: His Life and Work to This Time.* Foreword by Samuel C. Still. Galloway, NJ: South Jersey Culture and History Center, 2017.

Boyd's Co-Partnership and Residence Business Directory of Philadelphia City. Philadelphia: Boyd's Directory Office, 1898.

Brown, Henry. *Narrative of the Life of Henry Box Brown, Written by Himself.* Manchester, UK: Lee and Glynn, 1851.

Brown, William Wells. *The Black Man, His Antecedents, His Genius, and His Achievements.* New York: Thomas Hamilton, 1863.

Case of Passmore Williamson, Report of the Proceedings... Philadelphia: Uriah Hunt & Son, 1856.

Catalogue of the Officers and Students of Lincoln University, 1873–74. Oxford, PA: Republican Steam Power Print, 1874.

Catto, William T. *A Semi-Centennial Discourse Delivered in the First African Presbyterian Church, Philadelphia*... Philadelphia: Joseph M. Wilson, 1857.

Constitution, By-Laws and Rules of the Home for Aged and Infirm Colored Persons. Philadelphia: Merrihew & Son, 1865.

Craft, William, and Ellen Craft. *Running a Thousand Miles for Freedom; or, the Escape of William and Ellen Craft from Slavery.* London: William Tweedie, 1860.

"Declaration of Immediate Causes Which Induce and Justify the Secession of South Carolina from the Federal Union," https://avalon.law.yale.edu/19th_century/csa_scarsec.asp.

Drew, Benjamin. *The Refugee; or a Northside View of Slavery.* Boston: John P. Jewett and Company, 1856.

Elwyn Family Papers [Finding Aid], Portsmouth Athenaeum, Portsmouth, NH. Retrieved 7/13/2021 [https://portsmouthathenaeum.org/langdon-whipple-elwyn-50/].

The Freedman's Bureau! An agency to keep the Negro in idleness at the expense of the white man. Pennsylvania, 1866. Photograph. https://www.loc.gov/item/2008661698/.

Garrison, William Lloyd. *The Letters of William Lloyd Garrison.* Vol. 4, *From Disunionism to the Brink of War,* edited by Louis Ruchames. Cambridge, MA: Harvard University Press, 1975.

Greenspan, Ezra, ed. *William Wells Brown: A Reader.* Athens: University of Georgia Press, 2008.

Hexamer & Locher, *Maps of the City of Philadelphia, 1858–1860.* Map Collection, Free Library of Philadelphia, Greater Philadelphia GeoHistory Network. http://www.philageohistory.org/rdic-images/view-image.cfm/HXL1860-Super-Index.

Hopkins, G. M. *City Atlas of Philadelphia.* Vol. 6, *Wards 2 through 20, 29 and 31* (1875). http://www.philageohistory.org/tiles/viewer/?Selected Layers=Overlay,GMH1875v6.

Hunt, Benjamin Peter. *Why Colored People in Philadelphia Are Excluded from the Street Cars.* Philadelphia: Merrihew & Son, 1866.

Jones, Robert. *Fifty Years at Lombard Central Presbyterian Church.* Philadelphia: Edward Stern & Co., 1894.

Laws of the General Assembly of the Commonwealth of Pennsylvania passed at the session. Harrisburg, PA: Singerly & Myers, 1867.

Lincoln, Abraham. *Collected Works.* Edited by Roy P. Basler. 8 vols. New Brunswick, NJ: Rutgers University Press, 1953. https://quod.lib .umich.edu/l/lincoln/.

Lippard, George. *The Killers: A Narrative of Real Life in Philadelphia.* Edited by Matt Cohen and Edlie L. Wong. Philadelphia: University of Pennsylvania Press, 2014.

Lippard, George. *The Quaker City: or, The Monks of Monk Hall . . .* Philadelphia: Published by the Author, 1847.

Maryland Attorney General's Office. *Report of Attorney General Robert Brent to His Excellency, Gov. Lowe, in Relation to the Christiana Treason Trials in the Circuit Court of the United States, Held in Philadelphia.* Annapolis: Martin, 1852.

May, Samuel. *The Fugitive Slave Law and Its Victims.* New York: American Anti-Slavery Society, 1856.

McElroy's Philadelphia City Directory. Philadelphia: Edward C. & John Biddle, 1841.

McElroy's Philadelphia City Directory. Philadelphia: Edward C. & John Biddle, 1845.

McElroy's Philadelphia City Directory. Philadelphia: Edward C. & John Biddle, 1849.

McElroy's Philadelphia City Directory. Philadelphia: Edward C. & John Biddle, 1850.

McElroy's Philadelphia City Directory. Philadelphia: Edward C. & John Biddle, 1852.

McElroy's Philadelphia City Directory. Philadelphia: Edward C. & John Biddle, 1854.

McElroy's Philadelphia City Directory. Philadelphia: Edward C. & John Biddle, 1855.

McElroy's Philadelphia City Directory. Philadelphia: Edward C. & John Biddle, 1859.

McElroy's Philadelphia City Directory. Philadelphia: Edward C. & John Biddle, 1866.

McElroy's Philadelphia City Directory. Philadelphia: Edward C. & John Biddle, 1867.

McGowen, James A. *Station Master on the Underground Railroad: The Life and Letters of Thomas Garrett.* Jefferson, NC: McFarland & Co., 2005.

[McKim, J. Miller?]. *Arrest, Trial, and Release of Daniel Webster, a Fugitive Slave.* Philadelphia: Pennsylvania Anti-Slavery Society, 1859.

Narrative of Dimmock Charlton, A British Subject . . . Edited by Mary L. and Susan Cox. Philadelphia, 1859.

Narrative of Facts in the Case of Passmore Williamson. Philadelphia: Pennsylvania Anti-Slavery Society, 1855.

"National Convention at New Orleans, LA." Colored Conventions Project Digital Records, https://omeka.coloredconventions.org/items /show/544. Accessed January 29, 2021.

"New England Colored Citizens' Convention, August 1, 1859." Colored Conventions Project Digital Records, https://omeka.colored conventions.org/items/show/269. Accessed July 8, 2020.

O'Brien's Wholesale Business Directory. Philadelphia: King & Baird, 1844.

Pancoast, Seth. *What Is Bright's Disease? Its Curability.* Philadelphia: Published by the Author, 1882.

Philadelphia Freedmen's Relief Association. [Philadelphia?], 1864.

"Philadelphia Vigilance Committee, 1850–1859." Daguerreotype. Boston Public Library, Print Department Collection.

Pickard, Kate E. R. *The Kidnapped and the Ransomed. Being the Personal Recollections of Peter Still and his wife "Vina" after Forty Years of Slavery.* Syracuse, NY: William T. Hamilton, 1856.

Proceedings of the Colored National Convention, held in Franklin Hall, Sixth Street, Below Arch, Philadelphia, October 16th, 17th and 18th, 1855. Salem, NJ: National Standard Office, 1856.

Proceedings of the National Conference of Colored Men of the United States, Held in the State Capitol at Nashville Tennessee, May 6, 7, 8 and 9, 1879. Washington, DC: Rufus H. Darby, Steam Power Printer, 1879.

Proceedings of the State Equal Rights' Convention, of the Colored People of Pennsylvania, held in the city of Harrisburg February 8th, 9th, and 10th, 1865. Philadelphia, 1865.

Return of the Whole Number of Persons within the Several Districts of the United States . . . Washington, DC: Department of State, 1801.

"The Salt River Gazette—Extra. Wednesday, Oct. 9, 1867." Political cartoon, 1867. Library Company of Philadelphia.

Sanborn, Franklin Benjamin, ed. *The Life and Letters of John Brown, Liberator of Kansas and Martyr of Virginia.* Boston: Roberts Brothers, 1891.

"The Second Confiscation Act." http://www.freedmen.umd.edu/conact2 .htm.

Shadd, Mary Ann. *A Plea for Emigration, or, Notes of Canada West* . . . Detroit, MI: George W. Pattison, 1852.

Speech of Gen. Jas. A. Garfield, Delivered to the "Boys in Blue." New York, August 6, 1880. New York, 1880. https://www.loc.gov/resource/rbpe .12900200/?sp=1.

Sterling, Dorothy. *Speak Out in Thunder Tones: Letters and Other Writings by Black Northerners, 1787–1865*. New York: Doubleday, 1973.

Sixteenth Annual Report of the Board of Managers of the Home for Aged and Infirm Colored Persons. Philadelphia: Castle & Heilman, Steam-Power Printers, 1880.

Stewart, T. Grainger. "On the Treatment of Chronic Bright's Disease." *The British Medical Journal* 2, no. 1546 (Aug. 16, 1890): 389–92.

Still, James. *Early Recollections and Life of Dr. James Still*. Philadelphia: J. B. Lippincott & Co., 1877.

Still, William. *A Brief Narrative of the Struggle for the Rights of the Colored People of Philadelphia in the City Railway Cars . . .* Philadelphia: Merrihew & Sons, 1867.

Still, William. *An Address on Voting and Laboring, Delivered at Concert Hall*. Philadelphia: Jas. B. Rodgers Co., 1874.

Still, William. *Still's Underground Rail Road Records, with a Life of the Author*. Rev. ed. Philadelphia: Published by the Author, 1883.

Still, William. *The Underground Railroad: A Record of Facts, Authentic Narratives, Letters, &c . . .* Philadelphia: Porter & Coates, 1872.

Sumner, Charles. *The Barbarism of Slavery*. New York: Young Men's Republican Union, 1860.

Tenth Annual Report of the Board of Managers of the Home for Aged and Infirm Colored Persons. Philadelphia: Merrihew & Son, 1874.

Thirty-Sixth Annual Report of the Board of Managers of the Home for Aged and Infirm Colored Persons. Philadelphia: Press of the Leeds & Biddle Co., 1900.

"Treatment of Bright's Disease." *Scientific American* 56, no. 11 (March 12, 1887).

The Two Platforms. Pennsylvania, 1866. Photograph. https://www.loc.gov/item/2008661700/.

United States Census Bureau. "Historical Census Statistics by Race, 1790–1990, and Hispanic Origin, 1970–1990, for Large Cities and Other Urban Places in the United States." https://www.census.gov/library/working-papers/2005/demo/POP-twps0076.html.

United States Census Bureau. "Population of the 100 Largest Cities and Other Urban Places in the United States: 1790 to 1990." https://www.census.gov/library/working-papers/1998/demo/POP-twps0027.html.

United States Congress. *Congressional Globe*. Washington, DC: Blair & Rives, 1834–1873.

Wainwright, Nicholas, ed. *A Philadelphia Perspective: The Diary of Sidney George Fisher covering the years 1834–1871*. Philadelphia: Historical Society of Pennsylvania, 1967.

Walker, David. *Walker's Appeal to the Coloured Citizens of the World* . . . 3rd ed. Boston, 1830.

The War of the Rebellion: A Compilation of the Official Records of the Union and Confederate Armies. Washington, DC: Government Printing Office, 1880–1901.

Wheeler, John H. *Reminiscences and Memoirs of North Carolina and Eminent North Carolinians.* Columbus, OH: Columbus Printing Works, 1884.

Works of James Buchanan, Comprising his Speeches, State Papers, and Private Correspondence. Edited by John Bassett Moore. Philadelphia: J. B. Lippincott, 1908–11.

The Young Man's Own Book. Philadelphia: Key and Biddle, 1832.

SECONDARY SOURCES

Adams, Sean Patrick. *Home Fires: How Americans Kept Warm in the 19th Century.* Baltimore: Johns Hopkins University Press, 2014.

Andersen, Lisa M. F. *The Politics of Prohibition: American Governance and the Prohibition Party, 1869–1933.* New York: Cambridge University Press, 2013.

Bacon, Margaret Hope. *But One Race: The Life of Robert Purvis.* Albany: State University of New York Press, 2010.

Bacon, Margaret Hope. *Valiant Friend: The Life of Lucretia Mott.* New York: Walker & Co., 1980.

Bage, Elvena S. "President Garfield's Forgotten Pronouncement." *Negro History Bulletin* 14, no. 9 (June 1951): 195–214.

Ball, Erica. *To Live an Antislavery Life: Personal Politics and the Antebellum Black Middle Class.* Athens: University of Georgia Press, 2012.

Barlow, Margaret. "Fuller [née Warrick], Meta Vaux." *Grove Art Online.* 2003. Accessed July 7, 2021. https://www-oxfordartonline-com.proxy -tu.researchport.umd.edu/groveart/view/10.1093/gao/978188444 6054.001.0001/oao-9781884446054-e-7000030178.

Barton, Christopher P. "Antebellum African-American Settlements in Southern New Jersey." *African Diaspora Archaeology Newsletter* 12, no. 4 (Dec. 2009): 1–14.

Baumgartner, Alice L. *South to Freedom: Runaway Slaves to Mexico and the Road to the Civil War.* New York: Basic Books, 2020.

Baxter, Jane Eva. "How to Die a Good Death: Teaching Young Children About Mortality in Nineteenth Century America." *Childhood in the Past* 12, no. 1 (2019): 35–49.

Beckford, Geraldine Rhoades. "Anderson, Caroline Virginia Still Wiley."

Oxford African American Studies Center. May 31, 2013. Accessed Oct. 22, 2020. https://oxfordaasc-com.proxy-tu.researchport.umd .edu/view/10.1093/acref/9780195301731.001.0001/acref-978019 5301731-e-36070.

Beisert, Oscar, et al. *Nomination for the Philadelphia Register of Historic Places, William & Letitia Still House, Underground Railroad Way Station, 625 S. Delhi Street, Philadelphia, Pennsylvania, 2017.* https://www .phila.gov/media/20190401092648/625-S-Delhi-St-nomination.pdf.

Bell, Howard H. "The American Moral Reform Society." *Journal of Negro Education* 27 (Winter 1958): 34–40.

Bell, Richard. "Counterfeit Kin: Kidnappers of Color, the Reverse Underground Railroad, and the Origins of Practical Abolition." *Journal of the Early Republic* 38, no. 2 (Summer 2018): 199–230.

Bell, Richard. *Stolen: Five Free Boys Kidnapped into Slavery and Their Astonishing Odyssey Home.* New York: 37 INK, an imprint of Simon & Schuster, 2019.

Bell, Richard. "Making Tracks: Naming and Framing the Underground Railroad." Paper presented at Black Lives and Freedom Journeys: The Legacies of the Still Family of Philadelphia, McNeil Center, Philadelphia, October 7–8, 2021.

Bergeson-Lockwood, Millington W. *Race over Party: Black Politics and Partisanship in Late Nineteenth-Century Boston.* Chapel Hill: University of North Carolina Press, 2018.

Berlin, Ira. *Generations of Captivity: A History of African American Slaves.* Cambridge, MA: Harvard University Press, 2003.

Berry, Daina Ramey. *The Price for Their Pound of Flesh: The Value of the Enslaved, from Womb to Grave, in the Building of a Nation.* Boston: Beacon Press, 2017.

Biddle, Daniel R., and Murry Dubin. *Tasting Freedom: Octavius Catto and the Battle for Equality in Civil War America.* Philadelphia: Temple University Press, 2010.

Blackett, R. J. M. *Beating Against the Barriers: The Lives of Six Nineteenth-Century Afro-Americans.* Ithaca, NY: Cornell University Press, 1986.

Blackett, R. J. M. *Building an Antislavery Wall: Black Americans in the Abolitionist Movement, 1830–1860.* Baton Rouge: Louisiana State University Press, 1983.

Blackett, R. J. M. *The Captive's Quest for Freedom: Fugitive Slaves, the 1850 Fugitive Slave Law, and the Politics of Slavery.* New York: Cambridge University Press, 2018.

Blackett, Richard. "Lincoln and Colonization." *OAH Magazine of History* 21, no. 4 (Oct. 2007): 19–22.

Blight, David W. *Frederick Douglass: Prophet of Freedom.* New York: Simon & Schuster, 2018.

Blight, David W., ed. *Passages to Freedom: The Underground Railroad in History and Memory.* Washington, DC: Smithsonian Books in association with the National Underground Railroad Freedom Center, 2004.

Blight, David W. *Race and Reunion: The Civil War in American Memory.* Cambridge, MA: Harvard University Press, 2001.

Bogger, Tommy L. *Free Blacks in Norfolk, Virginia, 1790–1860: The Darker Side of Freedom.* Charlottesville: University Press of Virginia, 1997.

Bordewich, Fergus M. *Bound for Canaan: The Underground Railroad and the War for the Soul of America.* New York: Amistad, 2005.

Boromé, Joseph. "The Vigilant Committee of Philadelphia." *Pennsylvania Magazine of History and Biography* 92, no. 3 (July 1968): 320–51.

Boyd, Melba Joyce. *Discarded Legacy: Politics and Poetics in the Life of Frances E. W. Harper, 1825–1911.* Detroit, MI: Wayne State University Press, 1994.

Bradford, Sarah H. *Scenes in the Life of Harriet Tubman.* Auburn, NY: W. J. Moses, 1869.

Brandt, Nat, with Yanna Kroyt Brandt. *In the Shadow of the Civil War: Passmore Williamson and the Rescue of Jane Johnson.* Columbia: University of South Carolina Press, 2007.

Brooke, John L. *There Is a North: Fugitive Slaves, Political Crisis, and Cultural Transformation in the Coming of the Civil War.* Amherst: University of Massachusetts Press, 2019.

Brown, Ira V. "Miller McKim and Pennsylvania Abolition." *Pennsylvania History* 30, no. 1 (Winter 1963): 56–72.

Brown, Ira V. "Pennsylvania and the Rights of the Negro, 1865–1887." *Pennsylvania History* 28, no. 1 (Jan. 1861): 45–57.

Brown, Ira V. "William D. Kelley and Radical Reconstruction." *Pennsylvania Magazine of History and Biography* 85, no. 3 (July 1961): 316–29.

Butler, Jonathan. "From Millerism to Seventh-day Adventism: 'Boundlessness to Consolidation.'" *Church History* 55, no. 1 (March 1986): 50–64.

Butler, Leslie. *Critical Americans: Victorian Intellectuals and Transatlantic Liberal Reform.* Chapel Hill: University of North Carolina Press, 2007.

Clinton, Catherine. *Harriet Tubman: The Road to Freedom.* Boston: Little, Brown, 2004.

Cooper, Frederick. "Elevating the Race: The Social Thought of Black

Leaders, 1827–1850." *American Quarterly* 24, no. 5 (Dec. 1972): 604–25.

Cushing, Thomas, and Charles Sheppard. *History of the Counties of Gloucester, Salem, and Cumberland New Jersey.* Philadelphia: Everts & Peck, 1883.

Davis, Hugh. "The Pennsylvania State Equal Rights League and the Northern Black Struggle for Legal Equality, 1864–1877." *Pennsylvania Magazine of History and Biography* 126, no. 4 (Oct. 2002): 611–34.

Diemer, Andrew K. "Reconstructing Philadelphia: African Americans and Politics in the Post–Civil War North." *Pennsylvania Magazine of History and Biography* 133, no. 1 (Jan. 2009): 29–58.

Diemer, Andrew K. *The Politics of Black Citizenship: Free African Americans in the Mid-Atlantic Borderland, 1817–1863.* Athens: University of Georgia Press, 2016.

Drago, Elliot. "Neither Northern nor Southern: The Politics of Slavery and Freedom in Philadelphia, 1820–1847." PhD diss., Temple University, 2017.

DuBois, W. E. B. *The Philadelphia Negro: A Social Study.* With a new introduction by Elijah Anderson. Philadelphia: University of Pennsylvania Press, 1996. Originally published in 1899.

Dusinberre, William. *Civil War Issues in Philadelphia, 1856–1865.* Philadelphia: University of Pennsylvania Press, 1965.

Egerton, Douglas R. *The Wars of Reconstruction: The Brief Violent History of America's Most Progressive Era.* New York: Bloomsbury, 2014.

Evans, Frank B. *Pennsylvania Politics, 1872–1877: A Study in Political Leadership.* Harrisburg: Commonwealth of Pennsylvania, Pennsylvania Historical and Museum Commission, 1966.

Faulkner, Carol. *Lucretia Mott's Heresy: Abolition and Women's Rights in Nineteenth-Century America.* Philadelphia: University of Pennsylvania Press, 2011.

Fehrenbacher, Don E. *The Dred Scott Case: Its Significance in American Law and Politics.* New York: Oxford University Press, 2001.

Feldberg, Michael. *The Philadelphia Riots of 1844: A Study in Ethnic Conflict.* Westport, CT: Greenwood Press, 1975.

Finkelman, Paul. *An Imperfect Union: Slavery, Federalism, and Comity.* Chapel Hill: University of North Carolina Press, 1981.

Foner, Eric. *Gateway to Freedom: The Hidden History of the Underground Railroad.* New York: W. W. Norton, 2015.

Foner, Eric. "Lincoln and Colonization." In *Our Lincoln: New Perspectives on Lincoln and His World,* edited by Eric Foner, 135–66. New York: W. W. Norton, 2008.

Foner, Eric. *The Second Founding: How the Civil War and Reconstruction Remade the Constitution*. New York: W. W. Norton, 2019.

Foner, Philip S. "The Battle to End Discrimination Against Negroes on Philadelphia Streetcars: (Part I) Background and Beginning of the Battle." *Pennsylvania History* 40, no. 3 (Summer 1973): 260–90.

Foner, Philip S. "The Battle to End Discrimination Against Negroes on Philadelphia Streetcars: (Part II) The Victory." *Pennsylvania History* 40, no. 4 (Fall 1973): 355–79.

Franklin, John Hope, and Loren Schweninger. *Runaway Slaves: Rebels on the Plantation*. New York: Oxford University Press, 1999.

Gamber, Wendy. *The Boardinghouse in Nineteenth-Century America*. Baltimore: Johns Hopkins University Press, 2007.

Gara, Larry. "William Still and the Underground Railroad." *Pennsylvania History* 28, no. 1 (January 1961): 33–44.

Gardner, Eric. *Black Print Unbound: The Christian Recorder, African American Literature, and Periodical Culture*. New York: Oxford University Press, 2015.

George, Joseph, Jr. "Philadelphians Greet Their President-Elect." *Pennsylvania History* 29, no. 4 (Oct. 1962): 381–90.

Gigantino, James J., II. *The Ragged Road to Abolition: Slavery and Freedom in New Jersey, 1775–1865*. Philadelphia: University of Pennsylvania Press, 2015.

Gigantino, James. "'The Whole North Is Not Abolitionized': Slavery's Slow Death in New Jersey, 1830–1860." *Journal of the Early Republic* 34, no. 3 (Fall 2014): 411–37.

Gosse, Van. *The First Reconstruction: Black Politics in America from the Revolution to the Civil War*. Chapel Hill: University of North Carolina Press, 2021.

Greenspan, Ezra. *William Wells Brown: An African American Life*. New York: W. W. Norton, 2014.

Grinspan, Jon. "'Young Men for War': The Wide Awakes and Lincoln's 1860 Presidential Campaign." *Journal of American History* 96, no. 2 (Sept. 2009): 357–78.

Grow, Matthew J. *"Liberty to the Downtrodden": Thomas L. Kane, Romantic Reformer*. New Haven, CT: Yale University Press, 2009.

Hahn, Steven. *A Nation Under Our Feet: Black Political Struggles in the Rural South, from Slavery to the Great Migration*. Cambridge, MA: Harvard University Press, 2003.

Hall, Stephen G. "To Render the Private Public: William Still and the Selling of 'The Underground Railroad.'" *Pennsylvania Magazine of History and Biography* 127, no. 1 (Jan. 2003): 35–55.

Hammond, John Craig. *Slavery, Freedom, and Expansion in the Early American West*. Charlottesville: University of Virginia Press, 2007.

Harris, Leslie. *In the Shadow of Slavery: African Americans in New York City, 1626–1863*. Chicago: University of Chicago Press, 2003.

Harrold, Stanley. *Border War: Fighting over Slavery Before the Civil War*. Chapel Hill: University of North Carolina Press, 2010.

Harrold, Stanley. "Freeing the Weems Family: A New Look at the Underground Railroad." *Civil War History* 42, no. 4 (Dec. 1996): 289–306.

Hartog, Hendrik. *The Trouble with Minna: A Case of Slavery and Emancipation in the Antebellum North*. Chapel Hill: University of North Carolina Press, 2018.

Haynes, April R. *Riotous Flesh: Women, Physiology, and the Solitary Vice in Nineteenth-Century America*. Chicago: University of Chicago Press, 2015.

Hensel, W. U. *The Christiana Riot and the Treason Trials of 1851: An Historical Sketch*. Lancaster, PA: Press of the New Era Printing Co., 1911.

Hepp, John. "Streetcars." In *The Encyclopedia of Greater Philadelphia*. https://philadelphiaencyclopedia.org/archive/streetcars/.

Hershberg, Theodore. "Free Blacks in Antebellum Philadelphia: A Study of Ex-Slaves, Freeborn, and Socioeconomic Decline." In *Philadelphia: Work, Space, Family, and Group Experience in the 19th Century*, edited by Theodore Hershberg, 368–91. New York: Oxford University Press, 1981.

Hinton, Richard Josiah. *John Brown and His Men; With Some Account of the Roads They Traveled to Reach Harper's Ferry*. New York: Funk & Wagnalls, 1894.

Hodges, Graham Russell. *David Ruggles: A Radical Black Abolitionist and the Underground Railroad in New York City*. Chapel Hill: University of North Carolina Press, 2010.

Hook, Andrew. "Macaulay and America." *Journal of American Studies* 9, no. 3 (Dec. 1975): 335–46.

Howe, Daniel Walker. *What Hath God Wrought: The Transformation of America, 1815–1848*. New York: Oxford University Press, 2007.

Jackson, Kellie Carter. *Force and Freedom: Black Abolitionists and the Politics of Violence*. Philadelphia: University of Pennsylvania Press, 2019.

Janney, Caroline. *Remembering the Civil War: Reunion and the Limits of Reconciliation*. Chapel Hill: University of North Carolina Press, 2013.

Jeffrey, Julie Roy. *The Great Silent Army of Abolitionism: Ordinary Women in the Antislavery Movement*. Chapel Hill: University of North Carolina Press, 1998.

John, Richard R. *Network Nation: Inventing American Telecommunications*. Cambridge, MA: Harvard University Press, 2010.

Johnson, James Elton. "A History of Camp William Penn and Its Black Troops in the Civil War, 1863–1865." PhD diss., University of Pennsylvania, 1999.

Johnson, Walter. *Soul by Soul: Life Inside the Antebellum Slave Market*. Cambridge, MA: Harvard University Press, 1999.

Jones, Jacqueline. *American Work: Four Centuries of Black and White Labor*. New York: W. W. Norton, 1998.

Jones, Martha S. *Birthright Citizens: A History of Race and Rights in Antebellum America*. New York: Cambridge University Press, 2018.

Jones, Robert. *Fifty Years in the Lombard Street Central Presbyterian Church*. Philadelphia: Edward Stern & Co., 1894.

Kahn, Lurie. *William Still and the Underground Railroad: Fugitive Slaves and Family Ties*. Bloomington, IN: iUniverse, 2010.

Kantrowitz, Stephen. *More Than Freedom: Fighting for Black Citizenship in a White Republic, 1829–1889*. New York: Penguin Books, 2013.

Karp, Matthew. *This Vast Southern Empire: Slaveholders at the Helm of American Foreign Policy*. Cambridge, MA: Harvard University Press, 2016.

Kashatus, William. *William Still: The Underground Railroad and the Angel at Philadelphia*. Notre Dame, IN: University of Notre Dame Press, 2021.

Kendi, Ibram X. *Stamped from the Beginning: The Definitive History of Racist Ideas in America*. New York: Nation Books, 2016.

Kyriakodis, Harry. *Northern Liberties: The Story of a Philadelphia River Ward*. Charleston, SC: The History Press, 2012.

Lane, Roger. *William Dorsey's Philadelphia and Ours: On the Past and Future of the Black City in America*. New York: Oxford University Press, 1991.

Lapsansky, Emma Jones. "'Since They Got Those Separate Churches': Afro-Americans and Racism in Jacksonian Philadelphia." *American Quarterly* 32, no. 1 (Spring 1980): 54–78.

LaRoche, Cheryl Janifer. *Free Black Communities and the Underground Railroad: The Geography of Resistance*. Urbana: University of Illinois Press, 2013.

LaRoche, Cheryl Janifer. "Secrets Well Kept: Colored Conventions and Underground Railroad Activism." In *The Colored Convention Movement: Black Organizing in the Nineteenth Century*, edited by P. Gabrielle Forman, Jim Casey, and Sarah Lynn Patterson, 246–60. Chapel Hill: University of North Carolina Press, 2021.

Larson, Kate Clifford. *Bound for the Promised Land: Harriet Tubman, Portrait of an American Hero*. New York: Ballantine, 2004.

Lechner, Zachary J. "'Are We Ready for the Conflict?': Black Abolitionist Response to the Kansas Crisis, 1854–1856." *Kansas History* 31, no. 1 (Spring 2008): 14–31.

Licht, Walter. *Getting Work: Philadelphia, 1840–1950*. Cambridge, MA: Harvard University Press, 1993.

Luskey, Brian P. *On the Make: Clerks and the Quest for Capital in Nineteenth-Century America*. New York: New York University Press, 2010.

McPhee, John. *The Pine Barrens*. New York: Farrar, Straus, and Giroux, 1968.

Mason, David L. *From Buildings and Loans to Bail-Outs: A History of the American Savings and Loan Industry, 1831–1995*. Cambridge: Cambridge University Press, 2004.

Mason, David L. "Saving Societies." In *The Encyclopedia of Greater Philadelphia*. http://philadelphiaencyclopedia.org/archive/savings-societies/.

Masur, Kate. *Until Justice Be Done: America's First Civil Rights Movement, from the Revolution to Reconstruction*. New York: W. W. Norton, 2021.

May, Robert E. *Manifest Destiny's Underworld: Filibustering in Antebellum America*. Chapel Hill: University of North Carolina Press, 2002.

Mayer, Henry. *All on Fire: William Lloyd Garrison and the Abolition of Slavery*. New York: W. W. Norton, 1998.

McCaffery, Peter. *When Bosses Ruled Philadelphia: The Emergence of the Republican Machine, 1867–1933*. University Park: Pennsylvania State University Press, 1993.

McClure, Alexander. *Old Time Notes of Pennsylvania*. 2 vols. Philadelphia: John C. Winston Co., 1905.

McCurry, Stephanie. *Confederate Reckoning: Power and Politics in the Civil War South*. Cambridge, MA: Harvard University Press, 2010.

McFeely, William S. *Frederick Douglass*. New York: W. W. Norton, 1991.

Meier, August. "The Negro and the Democratic Party, 1875–1915." *Phylon* 17, no. 2 (2nd Quarter, 1956): 173–91.

Mjagkij, Nina. *Light in the Darkness: African Americans and the YMCA, 1852–1946*. Lexington: University Press of Kentucky, 1994.

Montgomery, David. *Beyond Equality: Labor and the Radical Republicans, 1862–1872*. New York: Alfred A. Knopf, 1967.

Montgomery, David. "Radical Republicanism in Pennsylvania, 1866–1873." *Pennsylvania Magazine of History and Biography* (Oct. 1961) 439–57.

Morris, J. Brent. *Oberlin, Hotbed of Abolition: College, Community and the Fight for Freedom and Equality in Antebellum America*. Chapel Hill: University of North Carolina Press, 2014.

Murdock, Eugene C. "New York City's Bounty Brokers." *Journal of American History* 53, no. 2 (Sept. 1966): 259–78.

Nash, Gary B. *Forging Freedom: The Formation of Philadelphia's Black Community, 1720–1840*. Cambridge, MA: Harvard University Press, 1988.

Nercessian, Nora N. "Nineteenth-Century Black Graduates of Harvard Medical School." *Journal of Blacks in Higher Education*, no. 47 (Spring 2005): 88–92.

Newby-Alexander, Cassandra L. *Virginia Waterways and the Underground Railroad*. Charleston, SC: The History Press, 2017.

Newman, Richard S. *The Transformation of American Abolitionism: Fighting Slavery in the Early Republic*. Chapel Hill: University of North Carolina Press, 2002.

Norwood, Alberta S. "Negro Welfare Work in Philadelphia." MA thesis, University of Pennsylvania, 1931.

Oakes, James. *Freedom National: The Destruction of Slavery in the United States, 1861–1865*. New York: W. W. Norton, 2013.

Otter, Samuel. *Philadelphia Stories: America's Literature of Race and Freedom*. New York: Oxford University Press, 2010.

Pargas, Damian Alan, ed. *Fugitive Slaves and Spaces of Freedom in North America*. Gainesville: University of Florida Press, 2018.

Polgar, Paul J. *Standard Bearers of Equality: America's First Abolitionist Movement*. Chapel Hill: Published for the Omohundro Institute of Early American History and Culture, Williamsburg, Virginia, by the University of North Carolina Press, 2019.

Pollard, Leslie J. "Black Beneficial Societies and the Home for Aged and Infirm Colored People." *Phylon* 4, no. 3 (3rd Quarter, 1980): 230–34.

Potter, David M. *The Impending Crisis: America Before the Civil War, 1848–1861*. Completed and edited by Don Fehrenbacher. New York: Harper & Row, 1976.

Reynolds, David S. *John Brown, Abolitionist: The Man Who Killed Slavery, Sparked the Civil War and Seeded Civil Rights*. New York: Alfred A. Knopf, 2005.

Reynolds, David S. *Mightier Than the Sword: Uncle Tom's Cabin and the Battle for America*. New York: W. W. Norton, 2011.

Rhodes, Jane. *Mary Ann Shadd Cary: The Black Press and Protest in the Nineteenth Century*. Bloomington: Indiana University Press, 1998.

Richards, Leonard. *The Slave Power: The Free North and Southern Domination, 1780–1860.* Baton Rouge: Louisiana State University Press, 2000.

Rilling, Donna J. *Making Houses, Crafting Capitalism: Builders in Philadelphia, 1790–1850.* Philadelphia: University of Pennsylvania Press, 2001.

Rose, Willie Lee. *Rehearsal for Reconstruction: The Port Royal Experiment.* New York: Oxford University Press, 1964.

Rosenberg, Charles. "Bustill, Joseph Cassey." Oxford African American Studies Center, 2013. https://doi-org.proxy-tu.researchport.umd .edu/10.1093/acref/9780195301731.013.38846.

Ruggles, Jeffrey. *The Unboxing of Henry Brown.* Richmond: The Library of Virginia, 2003.

Savage, Kirk. *Standing Soldiers, Kneeling Slaves: Race, War, and Monument in Nineteenth-Century America.* Princeton, NJ: Princeton University Press, 1997.

Scott, Donald, Sr. *Camp William Penn, 1863–1865: America's First Federal African American Soldiers' Fight for Freedom.* Atglen, PA: Shiffer Military History, 2012.

Shackelford, George Green. *Jefferson's Adoptive Son: The Life of William Short, 1759–1849.* Lexington, KY: University Press of Kentucky, 1993.

Sharf, J. Thomas, and Thompson Westcott. *History of Philadelphia, 1609–1884.* 3 vols. Philadelphia: L. H. Everts & Co., 1884.

Silcox, Harry C. "The Black 'Better Class' Political Dilemma: Philadelphia Prototype Isaiah Wears." *Pennsylvania Magazine of History and Biography* 113, no. 1 (Jan. 1989): 45–66.

Silcox, Harry C. "Nineteenth Century Black Militant: Octavius Catto (1839–1871)." *Pennsylvania History* 44, no. 1 (Winter 1977): 52–76.

Silcox, Harry C. "William McMullen, Nineteenth-Century Political Boss." *Pennsylvania Magazine of History and Biography* 110, no. 3 (July 1986): 389–412.

Sinha, Manisha. *The Slave's Cause: A History of Abolition.* New Haven, CT: Yale University Press, 2016.

Slap, Andrew. *The Doom of Reconstruction: The Liberal Republicans in the Civil War Era.* New York: Fordham University Press, 2006.

Slaughter, Thomas P. *Bloody Dawn: The Christiana Riot and Racial Violence in the Antebellum North.* New York: Oxford University Press, 1991.

Smedley, Robert Clemons. *History of the Underground Railroad in Chester and the Neighboring Counties.* Lancaster, PA: Office of the Journal, 1883.

Speirs, Frederick W. "The Street Railway System of Philadelphia, Its History and Present Condition." *Johns Hopkins University Studies in Historical and Political Science*, 15th ser. Baltimore: Johns Hopkins University, 1897.

Stauffer, John. *Giants: The Parallel Lives of Frederick Douglass & Abraham Lincoln.* New York: Twelve, 2008.

Summers, Mark Wahlgren. *The Ordeal of the Reunion: A New History of Reconstruction.* Chapel Hill: University of North Carolina Press, 2014.

Taylor, Brian. *Fighting for Citizenship: Black Northerners and the Debate over Military Service in the Civil War.* Chapel Hill: University of North Carolina Press, 2020.

Taylor, Frank H. *Philadelphia in the Civil War, 1861–1865.* [Philadelphia] The City, 1913.

Taylor, George Rogers. *The Transportation Revolution, 1815–1860.* New York: Rinehart, 1951.

Tobey, John E., and Nicolas H. Ellis. *U.S. Army Sutler, 1861–1865.* Wellsboro, PA: Milatus Publications, 2012.

VanderVelde, Lea. *Mrs. Dred Scott: A Life on Slavery's Frontier.* New York: Oxford University Press, 2009.

Varon, Elizabeth R. *Armies of Deliverance: A New History of the Civil War.* New York: Oxford University Press, 2019.

Varon, Elizabeth R. "Beautiful Providences." In *Antislavery and Abolition in Philadelphia: Emancipation and the Long Struggle for Justice in the City of Brotherly Love*, edited by Richard Newman and James Mueller, 229–45. Baton Rouge: Louisiana State University Press, 2011.

Varon, Elizabeth R. *Disunion! The Coming of the Civil War, 1789–1859.* Chapel Hill: University of North Carolina Press, 2008.

Villard, Oswald Garrison. *John Brown, 1800–1859, A Biography Fifty Years After.* New York: Houghton Mifflin, 1910.

Walker, Juliet E. K. *The History of Black Business in America: Capitalism, Race, and Entrepreneurship.* Chapel Hill: University of North Carolina Press, 2009.

Walther, Eric H. *The Shattering of the Union: America in the 1850s.* Wilmington, DE: Scholarly Resources, 2004.

Watson, John Fanning. *Annals of Philadelphia and Pennsylvania . . .* Philadelphia: A. Hart, 1850.

Wert, Jeffry D. "Camp William Penn and the Black Soldier." *Pennsylvania History* 46, no. 4 (Oct. 1979): 335–46.

White, Charles Fred. *Who's Who in Philadelphia: A Collection of Thirty Bio-*

graphical Sketches of Philadelphia Colored People. Philadelphia: A.M.E. Book Concern, 1912.

White, Richard. *The Republic for Which It Stands: The United States During Reconstruction and the Gilded Age, 1865–1896.* New York: Oxford University Press, 2017.

Whitman, T. Stephen. *The Price of Freedom: Slavery and Manumission in Baltimore and Early National Maryland.* Lexington: University Press of Kentucky, 1997.

Willcox, James M. *A History of the Philadelphia Saving Fund Society.* Philadelphia: J. B. Lippincott, 1916.

Wilson, Carol. *Freedom at Risk: The Kidnapping of Free Blacks in America, 1780–1865.* Lexington: University Press of Kentucky, 1994.

Winch, Julie. *Philadelphia's Black Elite: Activism, Accommodation, and the Struggle for Autonomy, 1797–1848.* Philadelphia: Temple University Press, 1988.

Winks, Robin W. *The Blacks in Canada: A History.* 2nd ed. Montreal: McGill–Queen's University Press, 1997.

Wood, Nicholas P. "A 'Class of Citizens': The Earliest Black Petitioners to Congress and Their Quaker Allies." *William & Mary Quarterly* 74, no. 1 (Jan. 2017): 109–44.

Wood, Nicholas P. "'A Sacrifice on the Altar of Slavery': Doughface Politics and Black Disenfranchisement in Pennsylvania, 1837–1838." *Journal of the Early Republic* 31, no. 1 (Spring 2011): 75–106.

Woodward, E. M., and John F. Hageman. *History of Burlington and Mercer Counties, New Jersey.* Philadelphia: Everts. & Peck, 1883.

Wyllie, Irvin G. *The Self-Made Man in America: The Myth of Rags to Riches.* New Brunswick, NJ: Rutgers University Press, 1954.

Zakim, Michael. *Accounting for Capitalism: The World the Clerk Made.* Chicago: University of Chicago Press, 2018.

INDEX

Page numbers in *italics* refer to photograph captions.

ILLUSTRATION CREDITS

A NOTE ABOUT THE AUTHOR

Andrew Diemer is an associate professor of history and the director of Metropolitan Studies at Towson University in Maryland. He received his PhD from Temple University. He is the author of *The Politics of Black Citizenship: Free African Americans in the Mid-Atlantic Borderland, 1817–1863* (University of Georgia Press, 2016). He lives in Philadelphia with his wife, Gretchen, and their three children.

A NOTE ON THE TYPE

This book was set in Janson, a typeface long thought to have been made by the Dutchman Anton Janson, who was a practicing type-founder in Leipzig during the years 1668–1687. However, it has been conclusively demonstrated that these types are actually the work of Nicholas Kis (1650–1702), a Hungarian, who most probably learned his trade from the master Dutch typefounder Dirk Voskens. The type is an excellent example of the influential and sturdy Dutch types that prevailed in England up to the time William Caslon (1692–1766) developed his own incomparable designs from them.

Composed by North Market Street Graphics,
Lancaster, Pennsylvania

Printed and bound by Lakeside Book Company,
Harrisonburg, Virginia

Designed by Soonyoung Kwon